SLAVERY, ISLAM AND DIASPORA

AFRICA WORLD PRESS

Publications in Association with

The Harriet Tubman Institute for Research on the Global Migrations of African Peoples

Toyin Falola and Paul E. Lovejoy, eds., *Pawnship, Slavery and Colonialism in Africa*, 2003

Donald G. Simpson, *Under the North Star: Black Communities in Upper Canada before Confederation (1867)*, 2005

Paul E. Lovejoy, *Slavery, Commerce and Production in West Africa: Slave Society in the Sokoto Caliphate*, 2005

Paul E. Lovejoy, *Ecology and Ethnography of Muslim Trade in West Africa*, 2005

Naana Opoku-Agyemang, Paul E. Lovejoy and David Trotman, eds., *Africa and Trans-Atlantic Memories: Literary and Aesthetic Manifestations of Diaspora and History*, 2008

Boubacar Barry, Livio Sansone, and Elisée Soumonni, eds., *Africa, Brazil, and the Construction of Trans-Atlantic Black Identities*, 2008

Carolyn Brown and Paul E. Lovejoy, eds., *Repercussions of the Atlantic Slave Trade: The Interior of the Bight of Biafra and the African Diaspora*, 2009

Behnaz Asl Mirzai, Ismael Musah Montana, and Paul E. Lovejoy, eds., *Slavery, Islam and Diaspora*, 2009

Ana Lucia Araujo, Mariana Pinho Cândido and Paul E. Lovejoy, eds., *Crossing Memories: Slavery and African Diaspora*, 2009

SLAVERY, ISLAM AND DIASPORA

Behnaz A. Mirzai,
Ismael Musah Montana
and Paul E. Lovejoy

Africa World Press, Inc.

P.O. Box 1892
Trenton, NJ 08607

P.O. Box 48
Asmara, ERITREA

Africa World Press, Inc.

P.O. Box 1892
Trenton, NJ 08607

P.O. Box 48
Asmara, ERITREA

First Printing 2009

Book design: Saverance Publishing Services

Cover design: Ashraful Haque

Cover artwork: "North African man in travelling costume", ca. 1900-1910, William Wiehe Collins (1862-1951) - Courtesy of the Victoria and Albert Museum, London

Library of Congress Cataloging-in-Publication Data

Slavery, Islam and diaspora / edited by Behnaz A. Mirzai, Ismael Musah Montana, and Paul E. Lovejoy.

p. cm.

Contains papers originally presented at the conference on Slavery, Islam and Diaspora, sponsored by the Harriet Tubman Resource Centre on the African Diaspora, York University, Ontario, 24-26 Oct. 2003.

Includes bibliographical references and index.

ISBN 1-59221-704-4 (hardcover) -- ISBN 1-59221-705-2 (pbk.) 1. Slavery and Islam--History. 2. Slavery--Islamic countries--History. 3. African diaspora. I. Mirzai, Behnaz A. II. Montana, Ismael Musah. III. Lovejoy, Paul E. IV. Harriet Tubman Resource Centre on the African Diaspora.

HT919.S56 2009
306.3'62091767--dc22

2009017754

Published in Association with...

The Harriet Tubman Institute for Research on the Global Migrations of African Peoples

Dedicated to

Nehemia Levtzion

&

John Hunwick

TABLE OF CONTENTS

LIST OF MAPS

PREFACE

The papers in this volume were originally presented at the conference on Slavery, Islam and Diaspora, sponsored by the Harriet Tubman Resource Centre on the African Diaspora, York University, on 24-26 October 2003. The conference was funded in part by a grant from the Social Sciences and Humanities Research Council of Canada and by the Canada Research Chair in African Diaspora History. The editors wish to thank LaRay Denzer for her assistance in preparing the manuscript for publication. The editors also wish to thank Northern Illinois University for its support.

The volume is dedicated to Nehemia Levtzion, who was scheduled to attend the conference but died unexpectedly, and to John Hunwick, who participated in the conference, despite failing health. Both scholars have made major contributions to the study of Islam and slavery.

The cover image is based on a watercolor by William Weile Collins (1862-1951), entitled "North African man in travelling costume," drawn sometime in 1900-1910. The original is in the Victoria and Albert Museum, SD. 240, and is reproduced here courtesy of the Museum.

Chapter 1

INTRODUCTION: SLAVERY, ISLAM AND DIASPORA

Behnaz Asl Mirzai, Ismael Musah Montana, and Paul E. Lovejoy

This volume explores the relationship between slavery and Islam in the context of diaspora.[1] Inevitably, slavery involved the movement of individuals from their places of origin to various parts of the Muslim world.[2] To some extent, the enslaved population was able to establish a sense of identity in diaspora that was based on social status and the common experience of enforced migration. Despite the diversity of the Islamic world and different interpretations of Islamic law, it is clear that slavery was widespread and that we need to know more about how individuals responded to enslavement under Islam.[3] Certainly, this book does not aim to examine Islam as a religion, but attempts to promote discussion on how various communities and societies used Islam to justify enslavement, liberate slaves, and defend or maintain their communities and indeed their individual identities. The volume reflects on how various societies understood slavery and how these views influenced local perceptions of Islam.

Research on the relationship between slavery and Islam has been difficult, partly because of language barriers that scholars encounter. The languages of Muslim societies included not just Arabic but also Turkish, Persian, Swahili, Hausa, Malinke, and so on. Access to extensive and widely dispersed documentation is also a problem, and the representation of slavery under Islam in European languages requires special care.[4] As Brower and Mirzai discuss in this volume, the misrepresentation of Muslims as "others" is reflected in colonial sources and is particularly apparent in discussions of slavery. These limitations have to be overcome in understanding the legacy of slavery in Muslim societies and the contributions that enslaved Muslims made in non-Muslim countries.

Besides, scholars examining the African diaspora have focused their attention on the well-researched Atlantic slave trade to the Americas, but enslaved Africans also crossed the Sahara, the Red Sea and the Indian Ocean to various parts of the Islamic world.[5] Most of the enslaved Africans taken along these routes, as well as a significant number of those who remained in Africa and indeed crossed the Atlantic, were from Muslim communities.[6] Thanks to recent research in the Islamic factor as it pertains to slavery, we now know that the period of the Atlantic slave trade was also an era during which slavery was also a powerful force in *Dar al-Islam* (the world of Islam), especially in West Africa and inland from the "Slave Coast" of the Atlantic.[7]

In this volume, the contributors attempt to redress the imbalance in the study of slavery with respect to the Islamic factor by examining the history of enslavement, the development of the African diaspora and the responses of enslaved Muslims. The chapters examine the African diaspora in the Indian Ocean, slavery in North Africa, slavery beyond the Mediterranean, and African Muslims in the Americas. Our contributors focus on the abolition of slavery under Islam and the interconnection of slavery and race as a means of highlighting the significance of studying the relationship between Islamic law, culture and slavery.The essays demonstrate that religious identity was an important factor in the resistance of enslaved Muslims to the institution of slavery in the trans-Atlantic context and that laws pertaining to slavery, the treatment of slaves and paths to emancipation in Muslim society also differed. Although the examples cover various geographical areas from Africa and the Middle East to the Caribbean and South America, they share a common goal in attempting to explain the essence of Islam in relation to slavery and displacement that characterized the movement of Muslims into diaspora. In spite of thematic and geographical diversity of the contributions, the authors show that slave-master relations were built on social and economic exploitation, but nonetheless, the enslaved were successful in spreading an Islamic sub-culture that had an impact on identity, resistance, language, and culture.

The essays originate in an international conference entitled "Islam, Slavery and Diaspora" held at York University from October 24-26, 2003 under the auspices of the Harriet Tubman Resource Centre on the African Diaspora, now the Harriet Tubman Institute for Research on the Global Migrations of African Peoples. The conference built on earlier conferences with similar objectives and thematic focus, including "Slavery and Religion in the Modern World," Essaouira (Morocco), June 15-17, 2001, and "Liberty, Integration and Slavery in the Muslim World," Université al-Akhwayn, Morocco, June 29-30, 2000, both co-sponsored by the York/UNESCO Nigerian Hinterland Project. There was also an earlier workshop, "Slavery and the African Diaspora in the Lands of Islam," held at the Program of African Studies, Northwestern University, Evanston, USA, April 30-May 2, 1999. The York conference extended these previous conferences and workshops in terms of scope and participation by looking more broadly into the relationship between slavery, diaspora and the Islamic factor and providing a unique opportunity for scholars from various parts of the world to discuss their findings.[8]

Among other objectives, the conference provided graduate students and post-doctoral fellows from different disciplines and cultural and geographical backgrounds the opportunity to discuss their work in a context in which conceptual, theoretical, and methodological issues related to slavery, diaspora and the Islamic factor were debated. Being inter-disciplinary in framework, the conference did not compartmentalize themes in isolation, but rather attempted to transcend the regional focus of many studies of slavery and Islam.

Toledano's chapter is concerned with the absence of voices of slaves in the Middle Eastern and Ottoman societies. He examines several cases concerning the lives of former African slaves who occupied the lower and uneducated rung of Ottoman society. As he strives to overcome the methodological impediments that conceal the voices of the enslaved in these societies, he argues that despite the absence of first-person slave narratives, it is possible to recover their experiences and interpret them within a satisfactory socio-cultural and political framework. For Toledano, reconstructing the experiences of the enslaved and interpreting their stories must take into consideration not just a close reading of their accounts filtered through travelers' narratives, court records and consular reports, but more importantly the "actions" and "intentions" of the enslaved must be treated with reasonable amount of attention.

Kravets shares Toledano's commitment to recovering the voices of enslaved Africans in the Ottoman domains. Using Crimean, Ottoman and Muscovite sources, she sheds light on the less known impact of black slave eunuchs who were re-exported from the Ottoman Empire further north across the Black Sea and employed in the royal court of the Crimean Khanate. Kravets shows how an elite corps of enslaved Africans sustained the ruling family structure and Crimean culture. Focusing on female slaves and eunuchs in the Qajar's court in the Persian Gulf, Mirzai argues that they have been misrepresented in Persian and European literature. She discusses slaves and eunuchs as real individuals with their own voices and as active participants in the daily life of the court, "without whom the political system could not have functioned." Her study is thus a departure from the scholarship that reinforces "orientalist" misconceptions and stereotypical perceptions of the harem by viewing its subjects as voiceless and helpless victims.

Ghazal is concerned with the Arab Middle East. She argues that the Muslim polemical debate over abolition caused by European criticism of Muslim attitudes towards slavery, as well as political and socioeconomic transformations at the turn of the twentieth century, produced two opposing intellectual camps. Relying on *al-Manar* and *al-Haqa`iq,* she documents the views of reformists and conservative perspectives in the debate. One of the main points of her essay is that while the two intellectual camps shared a common response to European criticism of slavery in Islam, their approaches to slavery and abolition were very different.

Three contributions in this volume deal with the Sokoto Caliphate and the *jihad* in the central Sudan that resulted in its establishment and expansion in the nineteenth century. To begin with, Salau makes an interesting connection between Islam and expansion of slavery in Kano. He argues that while Islam and slavery coexisted before the caliphate, the latter expanded after the *jihad.* Salau examines the scale, conditions and the methods that were used to regulate slavery both before and after the *jihad.* Ojo's argument that "the expansion of Muslim slave exports [from the caliphate] had far reaching implications at home and abroad" builds on the same premise as Salau's thesis. Ojo, however, looks at the impact of the Sokoto *jihad* on the process of ethnic categorization of Hausa slaves labelled as Gambari in Yorubaland. Lofkrantz's essay deals with ransoming in the nineteenth century. In her analysis, ransoming was an important feature of slavery in the caliphate. It was used as a safety net and while not promoted from the initial phase of the *jihad*, even though it was sanctioned and regulated by the Shari'a, it was later practiced as a means of securing the freedom of Muslim prisoners.

Hall's chapter, "Slave Banditry and Crime in Colonial Mali," discusses colonial ambivalence towards slavery in the desert-edge. He untangles the dynamism between the French colonial state, Tuareg and Arab pastoralists who owned slaves, and former slaves as well. His contribution lies in his examination of how Tuareg and Arab slave-holders responded to French policy on abolition by racial strategies to control former slaves. Following Eric Hobsbawn, Hall shows how slaves undermined their masters by resorting to crime and banditry not as criminals in a rebellious sense, but as individuals determined to pursue a strategy based on their masters' cultural practices to resist and attain their freedom.

Brower's contribution complements Hall's essay quite neatly in that he reiterates French ambivalence towards slavery in the Algerian oases. Here, the slave-holding notables, as was also the case with the slave-owning elite of the desert-edge nomadic pastoralists in Mali, tried to devise strategies to maintain their status derived from slave-holding. The original contribution of his essay lies in his critical assessments of French sources as a means of reflecting their attitudes towards slavery in Algeria.

Montana's study documents the *bori* network of communal and religious households in Tunis and the social organization of their inhabitants, the "Sudan-Tunis," in the nineteenth century. He attempts to situate these households within the context of the history of the Husaynid dynasty of Tunisia, founded in 1705. Accordingly, he argues against generalizations that homogenize black populations in North Africa. He uses the history of *bori* households to establish cultural and social distinctions that separated *abid* (slaves) labelled "Sudan-Tunis" and former freed slaves whose history predates the Husaynid dynasty.

Vernet's essay on the slave trade and slavery on the Swahili Coast reassesses previous assertions concerning the volume of slave exports before the nineteenth century. His essay not only revisits the historiographical debate about the slave trade but also re-examines the nature and scope of the slave trade organized by Swahili traders and their network from the coastal city states to the region of the wider Indian ocean. Thus the Swahili trade was already important before French and Omani demand led to its expansion in the nineteenth century.

Warner-Lewis and Dobronravin examine the cultural contributions of enslaved Muslim Africans in the Americas. As they both show, Muslim religious practices were introduced into the New World through Arabic scripts written and used by slaves from West Africa. Arabic was not only a language of communication and prayer, but also a source of resistance to subjugation by Muslims who found themselves isolated in a Christian environment. As Warner-Lewis demonstrates, the enslaved Muslim community did not remain intact so that shifting religious allegiances by converting to Christianity and dual religious affiliation were signs of mutual cultural and religious influence in nineteenth century Jamaica and Trinidad. The link to the source of power in the new environment was a strategy used by enslaved Africans for empowerment and survival. While Warner-Lewis also carefully traces the presence of African Muslims in the Americas, using Arabic, Ajami and Hausa texts, Dobronravin examines the processes of Islamic cultural transfer, production of knowledge and retention of customs in Trinidad and Brazil.

Notes

1. On Islam and slavery, see W. Arafat, "The Attitude of Islam to Slavery," *Islamic Quarterly* 10: 1-2 (1966); Hammouda Ghoraba, "Islam and Slavery," *Islamic Quarterly* 2 (1955): 153-59; Amar Samb, "L'Islam et l'esclavage," *Notes Africaines* 168 (1980): 93-97; and William Gervase Clarence-Smith, *Islam and the Abolition of Slavery* (Oxford, 2006). For Islam and slavery in the context of diaspora, see Alan D. Austin, *African Muslims in Antebellum America* (New York, 1997); Ronald Segal, *Islam's Black Slaves: The Other Black Diaspora* (New York, 2001), Michael A. Gomez, *Reversing Sail: A History of the African Diaspora* (Cambridge, 2005) and Gomez, *Black Cresent: The Experience and Legacy of African Muslims in the Americas* (Cambridge, 2005).
2. See Garrett E. DeJong, "Slavery in Arabia," *The Muslim World* 24 (1934): 126-44; John Hunwick and Eve Trout Powell, eds., *The African Diaspora in the Mediterranean Lands of Islam* (New Jersey, 2002); John Ralph Willis, ed., *Slaves and Slavery in Muslim Africa* (London, 1985); Jacques Heers, *Esclaves et domestiques au moyen âge dans le monde mediterranéen* (Paris, 1981); and Murray Gordon, *Slavery in the Arab World* (New York, 1989).
3. See Ehud R. Toledano, *As If Silent and Absent: Bonds of Enslavement in the Islamic Middle East* (New Haven, CN, 2007).
4. See for instance, Joseph Miller, "Muslim Slavery and Slaving, A Bibliography," in Elizabeth Savage, ed., *The Human Commodity: Perspectives on the Trans-Saharan Slave Trade* (London, 1992), 249-71; and Alan W. Fisher, "Studies in Ottoman Slavery and Slave Trade," *Journal of Turkish Studies* 4 (1980): 49-56.
5. Ralph A. Austen, "The Mediterranean Islamic Slave Trade out of Africa: A Tentative Census," in Elizabeth Savage, ed., *The Human Commodity: Perspectives on the Trans-Saharan Slave Trade* (London, 1992); Ehud R. Toledano, *Slavery and Abolition in the Ottoman Middle East* (Seattle, 1998); John Hunwick, "Black Africans in the Mediterranean World: Introduction to a Neglected Aspect of the African Diaspora," in Elizabeth Savage, ed., *The Human Commodity: Perspectives on the Trans-Saharan Slave Trade* (London, 1992), 5-38; and Gwyn Campbell, ed., *The Structure of Slavery in the Indian Africa and Asia* (London, 2004).
6. Paul E. Lovejoy, "Slavery, Bilad al-Sudan and the Frontiers of African Diaspora," in Paul E. Lovejoy, ed., *Slavery on the Frontiers of Islam* (Trenton NJ, 2004); and David V. Trotman and Paul E. Lovejoy, "Community of Believers: Trinidad Muslims and the Return to Africa, 1810-1850," in Lovejoy, *Slavery on the Frontiers of Islam*, 219-32.
7. Peter B. Clarke, *West Africa and Islam: A Study of Religious Development from the 8th to the 20th Century* (London, 1982).
8. The conference brought together over 70 scholars and students working on issues concerning Islam, slavery and related subjects in various parts of the world. We wish to thank the Social Sciences and Humanities Research Council of Canada, the Canada Research Chair in African Diaspora History, and York University for supporting the conference.

Chapter 2

BRINGING THE SLAVES BACK IN

Ehud R. Toledano

HISTORIOGRAPHY AND THE RESEARCH ENVIRONMENT

In the past twenty years, new studies on slavery and the slave trade have created the framework for interpreting the history of enslaved people in the Ottoman Empire.[1] We have covered the traffic from Africa and the Caucasus, described the main routes, determined the types of slaves, their prices, the customs duties levied on them, the jobs they performed, and the social roles they played. Scholars have explained the project of the Tanzimat reforms, the impact of foreign pressures, the mechanisms of homegrown manumission, the attitudes toward slavery, and the problems of suppression and abolition. Although some of us have brought out the stories of individual slaves, however, the absence of slave narratives has, to a large extent, silenced the voices of the enslaved, especially the Africans, who occupied the lower, uneducated rungs of Ottoman society. With the mounting interest in Ottoman slavery, combined with the first expressions of radical criticism from Africans toward the enslavers in Middle Eastern societies, the time has come to heed the call to recover the suppressed narratives of Ottoman-African slaves.

In this study, as I read with fresh eyes both new and familiar archival sources, it soon became evident that one could easily find those lost voices. Despite the absence of first-person slave narratives, it is possible to recover their experiences and interpret them within a satisfactory socio-cultural framework. Stories of individual slave experiences abound in the sources, though they are often obscured, covered with layers that need to be excavated. Consequently, this study became a book that deals with phenomena such as the absconding of enslaved persons, crimes committed by them, the interjection of the Tanzimat-state into the slaveholder-enslaved relationship, and what I call the "creolization" of African-Ottoman and Circassian-Ottoman cultures.[2] Since it will be quite impossible to cover all these effectively in this chapter, I propose to deal with just a few of the main methodological issues, and provide three examples to illustrate these points.

In May 1977 the following footnote appeared in the opening paragraph of a paper presented by Alan Fisher to a conference held at Princeton University: "To my knowledge, no book or article has appeared in any language which deals with the institution of chattel slavery in the Ottoman Empire." The conference, which was organized by John Willis to deal with the topic of slavery in Muslim societies, with special emphasis on Africa, was predicated on Willis' adaptation of H. J. Fisher's statement that "Islamic Slavery in Africa has been a fascinating subject to which many scholars have referred, but of which no detailed modern study has been made." Alan Fisher asserts that "it is doubly accurate for the Ottoman Empire," adding that "scholars have not only not studied chattel slavery there, they have not admitted its existence."[3] Exactly a quarter of a century later, Eve Troutt Powell, in an Istanbul conference, which took place in May 2002, spent an entire paper surveying and critiquing the literature on African slavery in the Islamic societies of the Middle East, most notably the Ottoman Empire.[4] Her paper not only shows the significant amount of work done to understand the history of slavery and the slave trade in Middle Eastern societies, but also demands a change of our research agenda. She calls for an effort to recover slave voices, and puts forth a partially new set of questions pertaining to the life the slaves made in these societies, their manumission, and the attitude of society toward freed slaves. This call for breaking the silence of slaves, to bring them back into history, is both timely and relevant. It is made possible by the achievements of three decades of scholarly work that has managed, in large measure, to lay the groundwork and provide the basic tools for the coming stage of research.

What may be called the research environment is also of vital importance for the development of any field of study. As I have previously argued, the study of slavery in the Ottoman Empire has suffered from the lack of an interested, engaged constituency, namely that there are no active, self-conscious descendent communities of enslaved Africans or Caucasians (coming from the Caucasus) in Turkey or the successor Arab states.[5] This absence meant that no group saw Ottoman slavery as its heritage or demanded to have that past properly investigated. This research environment seems to be changing now, in part attested to by Troutt Powell's demand to recover slave voices in past Middle Eastern societies, which might signal a willingness on the part of African Americans to stand for the absent communities of Africans in the former Ottoman Empire.

Perhaps as significant is the demand of an African group, gathered in a conference in Johannesburg on 22 February 2003, that Arab countries own up to what the group called "Arab-led slavery of Africans," apologize for it, and pay reparations. While certainly as controversial as the similar demand raised by African American leaders vis-à-vis the United States, this is a first step in developing another constituency in Africa itself that seeks to represent the absent voices of former African slaves in the Middle East. "We the people, Africans and African descendents, herein referred to as Africans, striving for the unity of the African Nation," the conference participants declared, "intend to *reclaim our voice*, and to speak for ourselves on the above and related issues, after centuries of silence and non-self-expression" (author's emphasis).[6] The declaration rightly links African inaction on this issue to the "collective amnesia about Arab enslavement of Africans," calling for "more research…on the Arab and Ottoman slave trade of Africans," and seeking "to establish relations between continental Africans and the African diaspora in the Arab world."

There is, as yet, no parallel development with regard to Caucasian slavery in the Ottoman Empire, and I doubt that a similar interest may soon—or ever—emerge. Unlike African Americans or Africans, Circassians (including Abkhazians) and Georgians, whether in the lands formerly governed by the Ottoman Empire or in various diasporas, including Georgia, have not been sensitized to their slave heritage. While theoretically this may still occur following nation building in Georgia and Abkhazia, the engine of consciousness-raising that drove abolition and emancipation in the Americas is not there to drive a significant protest movement against, in our case, Turkey. The existence of such a consciousness is a precondition for challenging the accepted view that white slaves from the Caucasus were happily integrated into elite and nonelite Ottoman families, erasing within one generation the "embarrassment of slavery," to borrow Michael Salman's phrase.[7] The harsher agricultural slavery endured by the Circassians after their forced migration into the Ottoman Empire in the 1860s was, in most aspects, akin to serfdom, its cognate institution in contemporary Eastern Europe and Russia. Descendents of those enslaved people probably still live in village communities across Turkey, the Balkans, and even the Middle East (for example, in Israel and Jordan) and one may doubt how aware they are of issues raised by their slave past.

Nevertheless, the changing research environment with regard to the enslavement of Africans in the Ottoman Empire, and the generally growing interest in the study of slavery in Middle Eastern and other Muslim societies have convinced me that a fresh examination of the available evidence, and the development of effective tools for such a reexamination, could yield a better account of the voice and experience of enslaved people in Ottoman societies than so far achieved. In this chapter, I shall go back to the evidence that has already been uncovered, briefly examine three of the many stories in the records, and offer a method of gleaning from them some insights into the lives of enslaved Africans and Caucasians in the empire.

A RENEWED AGENDA FOR THE STUDY OF SLAVERY IN ISLAMIC SOCIETIES

A straightforward approach to the available sources is likely to yield the following observation: slaves appear quite often in various kinds of state and court records, both Ottoman and European, and in travel accounts of similar types. Direct-speech accounts of slave experiences, or first-person slave narratives, however, are very rare in these sources. Even when such voices are present, they come to us through the handwritten texts of the court scribes, the narration of a traveler, or the report of a foreign consul, agent, missionary, or trader. All these are obviously both linguistically and culturally filtered. Such fragmented statements, as limited as they are, can form the basis of a viable and credible social reconstruction. I shall refer to this work alternately as "voice recovery" and "experience reconstruction." The historian's craft in this case means filling the holes by resorting to the knowable and verifiable sociocultural context, bridging the gaps by carefully allowing a measured use of the historian's educated imagination. For this to work, both the historian and the audience must be comfortable enough with a reasonable amount of speculation.

We first need to modify our sense of the term "voice." To create a working space for our project, we must extend the notion of voice beyond mere utterances, verbal statements, or speech. Given the paucity of direct speech, first-person accounts, or statements by Ottoman slaves, we shall try to recover voice from action. "Actions speak louder than words" will be an essential motto and concept in our working environment, since information about what the enslaved did and how they acted in various situations abounds. In our process of experience reconstruction, action and intention are almost inseparable. We shall first try to establish what enslaved individuals did, but immediately ask the questions: What did they intend by their actions? What did they want to achieve by their deeds? Since actions are not always intended, or intentions are not always followed by corresponding actions, we shall try to weigh all the options available to a specific person at the time of action, look at the choices made, and assess motivation. When "backing and filling," options will be assessed by plausibility, and their implications will be evaluated.

In our approach here, action will include both commission and omission. That is, not only what the enslaved did, but also what they did not do, either by choice or because of various constraints. Thus, we ask questions that enable us to map the range of expectations an enslaved person could have constructed in specific circumstances, trying to build a bank of options that were available to them, and assess of which options they could have been aware or unaware at the time of action or nonaction. To be able to offer credible scenarios—both on the basis of the available evidence and by filling the existing gaps—we need to reconstruct the social and cultural environment in which these life stories unfolded. Although in this area, quantitative and statistically acceptable studies are relatively rare, qualitative, in-depth, "thick description"-type work is fairly common. Hence, significant contributions by Ottomanists help most of us feel comfortable enough with the economic, social, and cultural space in which we work. We now possess excellent studies of the physical surrounding, material culture, social conditions, economic realities, and political environment that make it possible to embed most of the slave stories in their appropriate urban, rural, or pastoralist settings.

Thus, in cases of absconding we may ask: Why did an enslaved person decide to run away? What were the motivations involved? What were the risks taken? And does the action constitute a social statement about resistance or defiance? Crimes committed by enslaved people raise additional questions, such as why did the individual choose to commit arson, theft, or murder? Who were the intended, or unintended, victims of these crimes? Did the crime "make sense," that is, were cause and effect factored in, or was it a random act of whim, committed in uncontrolled anger, out of despair, or to make a statement rather than achieve a concrete goal? These and other considerations should then be woven into the story to fill the gaps in the records and enable us to assess how the enslaved in Ottoman society experienced their predicament and coped with it.

For this kind of puzzle work, social historians will always need to use their imagination, albeit with due circumspection, to travel the distance between the time and space in which they work, and those in which the subjects of their study lived—in our case, enslaved Africans and Caucasians in the Ottoman Empire. We need to move constantly between our careful reading of the texts, which we must do with wide-open, critical eyes, and imagining the actual lives of the men and women with whom we deal, for which we often need to close our eyes. Constructing the Other requires both of these actions simultaneously, especially when the Other is removed from our world in many respects: time, space (for those who do not live in the Middle East), class, culture, and ethnicity (for those not African or coming from the Caucasus), and often gender, too. But my feeling is that human empathy can cross all these boundaries, given the willingness to engage any Other and see him/her, first and foremost, as human, with all that this predicament entails emotionally, psychologically, and materially.

THE "GOOD-TREATMENT DEBATE" AND THE VALUE OF FREEDOM

The first obstacle on the way to an open and honest treatment of slavery in Ottoman and other Islamic societies is the "attitude hurdle." Writers about Islamic societies in general have been sensitive—some might argue, overly so—to any shred of criticism, be it hedged, balanced, or even implied. The Orientalist tradition in Middle Eastern studies has been seen—often with good reason—as judgmental, patronizing, moralistic, and deprecating toward Arabs and Muslims, their culture, their religion and belief systems, and their political and economic life. These have then been seen as reinforcing negative political attitudes toward their contemporary causes, ultimately marginalizing, or even excluding, them from what became known as the "international community." Too often, the debate over the history of slavery has fallen victim to the reluctance of Arab and Muslim writers to engage in an open discussion about human bondage with their foreign counterparts. Except for modern Turkish scholarship and a few contributions from scholars in Arab countries, the work produced has been apologetic or polemical, and so has taught us very little about the life of enslaved people in Islamic societies.[8] All the while, various aspects of slavery have been hotly debated and, consequently, thoroughly researched and analyzed in most non-Islamic societies. There are, however, indications that the defensive posture about Islamic slavery is gradually eroding.

Still, one can hardly fault writers who feel that their cultures and values are being constantly scrutinized, and who perceive their countries as being politically, economically, and at times militarily, under attack from stronger and richer countries. Threatened by the knowns and the unknowns of globalization, many find solace and a sense of security in local culture, Islamic tradition, and also, on the margins, in radical, violent activism. While these phenomena are relatively recent, the defensive attitude about Islamic slavery is at least a century-and-a-half old. It dates back to the early attempts by British abolitionists, through their powerful government representatives in Islamic countries, especially in the Ottoman Empire, to persuade local and imperial authorities to suppress the slave trade and abolish slavery.[9] Seen as interference targeting the foundations of Ottoman social order, because slavery was an integral part of family and culture, European criticism of Ottoman slavery elicited a defensive—though complex and differentiated—reaction from Ottoman officials, writers, and intellectuals.[10] Only in the last quarter of the nineteenth century do we see such attitudes explicitly articulated in published works, including a growing number of voices who criticized slavery on moral grounds.

For our purposes here, suffice it to mention briefly that the crux of the Ottoman argument was that slavery in the empire, as in other Muslim societies, was fundamentally different from slavery in the Americas. In the main, it was far milder because slaves were not employed on plantations, were well-treated, frequently manumitted, and could integrate into the slave-owning society. Islamic law, it was further maintained, encouraged owners to treat their slaves well, and manumission was considered a pious act, for which the believer could expect spiritual remuneration.[11] On the whole, scholars working on Islamic and non-Islamic slavery have tended to accept this view, arguing that Islamic societies were "societies with slaves" rather than "slave societies." Hence, they have maintained that Islamic slavery was milder, better integrated, more open to inclusion, and consequently, abolition came to them late, and was never a major political issue.

Perceptions, however, have been changing over the past two decades or so, overall becoming more critical, less accepting, perhaps less prepared to tolerate the broader implications of what I call "the good-treatment thesis." A word about attitude is in order here. It seems to me absolutely essential to reassure the readers that at least I—and arguably most scholars working in this field—view slavery as a universal phenomenon, neither peculiar to any culture, nor deriving from any specific set of shared social values. Human bondage in its various forms existed in almost all known historical societies and cultures, and no writer therefore may claim the moral high ground vis-à-vis any culture in this regard. Since Biblical times, all monotheistic religions sanctioned slavery, though they did try to mitigate its harsh realities, and other belief systems were not free from various forms of bondage either. Something in human nature made slavery possible everywhere, and it took major transformations in our thinking to get rid of it; and that, barely a century-and-a-half ago, an admittedly late stage in our history. Even today, at the beginning of the twenty-first century, various forms of slavery continue to be practiced across the globe, albeit under different names.

By thus leveling the moral playing field, we in no way wish to suspend judgment with regard to slavery as a phenomenon in human societies, nor do we advocate an abdication of responsibility. As we strive to understand the social, economic, political, and cultural circumstances in which slavery was made possible, widespread, and universally acceptable in many historic societies, we also do not shy from finding it reprehensible in any society that practiced it. Understanding why slavery was so natural in so many societies does not lead to condoning it. But I also wish to take this argument one step further. As we reconstruct the world in which the slaves lived, we need also to consider all the options available to owners, slaves, and other members of society, recognizing that such options did include at least three that could always be chosen: one could decide not to own slaves; slave owners could choose not to mistreat their slaves; and slave owners could manumit their slaves after a reasonable period of service—which in Ottoman social practice was between seven and ten years.

All these options, and others, were on the "menu" of free members in most societies, including the Ottoman and other Islamic ones. We are not talking about situations in which free labor was unavailable, not even about free labor being less efficient or less economically sensible to use. Hence, I argue, it was a matter of choice to own slaves, to treat them well or badly, and then either to manumit them in due course, to keep them longer, or even to resell them after many years of service. Obviously, when there is choice, there is also responsibility, but this was so in many societies throughout history, and no special blame is here being assigned to Ottoman, Arab, or Muslim slave owners in particular. As we dispose of that distressing obstacle to proper investigation of slave experiences in the Ottoman Middle East, we must also reexamine the argument that Islamic slavery was so much milder than its counterparts that it perhaps cannot be discussed in the same analytic framework.

TUTI'S STORY

In November 1866 a slave dealer named Ahmet transported three enslaved Circassian women on a boat that was carrying timber from Trabzon to Istanbul.[12] One of the three, Tuti, was on the deck when the captain told her to go down into the hold. When she refused, he started beating her, and consequently, she threw herself into the water in an angry tantrum. She was later rescued and put back on board. On arrival in Istanbul, the incident was reported to the police, and both the captain and Ahmet were taken into custody. Soon after the captain was released without being charged, but the slave dealer was accused of throwing Tuti into the water and sentenced to five years in prison. Ahmet refused to accept the verdict; he must have continued to complain about it to various people, stressing that his children were suffering from poverty as a result of his absence. His efforts were successful when after fifteen months in jail, the imam of the Fatime Sultan mosque—probably moved to act by intermediaries—petitioned the authorities to reconsider the case and do justice by Ahmet. A high court investigation found Ahmet's story to be true, meaning that he was not to blame for Tuti's jump into the sea in reaction to the captain's blows. The court recommended that he be released, with both the grand vizier and the sultan endorsing the decision.

Here we have a case of an enslaved woman, this time a Circassian, who was unwilling to put up with abuse, and reacting in an extreme manner that was potentially harmful to herself. To fill in the gaps of the story, we need to separate what the record tells us from what it does not, but may still be assumed, with varying degrees of confidence. The document describes the captain's actions: he ordered Tuti to go down to the hold, then he beat her. It also describes what Tuti did: she refused to go down, and when beaten, threw herself in the water. By adding the phrase that she did so "in anger," the record describes her mood, and indirectly, an impetus to her action. We should now try to fill in the gaps. First we may deal with her refusal to obey the captain's orders to go down to the hold, as we can only surmise a motive or a reason for it. Clearly her initial act of defiance may have been triggered by some immediate circumstance, such as a desire to breathe fresh air; or, having an argument with the other slaves downstairs, she may have wished not to return to their company. In any event, it is noteworthy that although both enslaved and a woman, Tuti did not find it unfathomable to disobey the free male in charge of the boat.

The next step is to understand her reaction when the captain tried to deal with her insubordination by beating her. Instead of accepting the realities of life and the situation, that is, to surrender to superior force, Tuti chose another way. By jumping into the water, and clearly putting herself in harm's way, she attempted to draw a certain line for the captain, and probably also for the slave dealer, and perhaps also to offer an example to the two other enslaved women, who were undoubtedly aware of what was happening on the deck and watching it curiously. In a way, she spoke to all these people: "That's it, no more beating, I won't take it anymore." Of course, this could have been only a moment of irrational behavior, an action taken in the height of emotion, under pain and humiliation, and desperately looking for a way out, which only the sea could offer.

İHSAN AĞA'S STORY

In March 1881, the British consul in Jidda reported to the ambassador in Istanbul about a fascinating case involving an Ethiopian eunuch who ran away from Mecca and sought refuge at the Jidda consulate.[13] The man İhsan Ağa had already been freed and asked to be sent to Egypt, where he could, as a free man, earn a livelihood. His story begins in his native land, when in 1872, nine years prior to his appearance at the consulate, his father had to flee because he could not pay the heavy taxes imposed by King Yohannes. The tax collectors seized İhsan and sold him into slavery. Those who purchased the boy, made him a eunuch,[14] and brought him to Jidda where he was purchased by Ömer Nasif Efendi, agent to the late sharif of Mecca, who sent him to the former Grand Vizier Ali Paşa in Istanbul. The latter gave him as a present to the Valide Sultan, who passed him on to Prince Murat, later Sultan Murat V, in whose service he remained until the sultan was deposed during the tumultuous events of 1876. At that point, İhsan and five other eunuchs were manumitted and sent to Mecca where imperial eunuchs normally retired, serving as a special corps at the grand mosque.

For about three years İhsan continued to receive a comfortable monthly pay of 450 piaster, but six months before seeking refuge at the Jidda consulate, he and two other eunuchs were sent to Medina, and their pay stopped. Apparently, this was quite common, as old eunuchs would be allocated the wages of young ones, in return for feeding and clothing them, until such point as the eunuch was senior enough to deserve a stipend of his own, which was then taken from a younger, incoming one. Having spent all his savings, İhsan made up his mind to escape. His plan was to ask for permission to make the pilgrimage to Mecca, and from there to head for Jidda, which was actually what he managed to do. Although technically a free man, the Ottoman authorities ordered İhsan to return to Mecca, so that matters could be sorted out there, since the sultan manumitted his eunuchs on the condition that they serve at the Mecca holy site. Thus, for all intents and purposes, they were still treated as unfree. İhsan refused to do that, and threatened to take his own life if the consul turned him over to the Ottomans. He argued that once in their custody, he would be considered a traitor, and therefore tortured and ultimately killed. Following high-level contacts and pressures going all the way to the grand vizier and council of ministers in Istanbul, the British, nevertheless, stood their ground, refused to turn him in, and finally facilitated his passage to Egypt as he wished.

İhsan's story is about the refusal to settle for less and the determination to maximize options in a harsh environment. Notice the fact that, had he been willing to accept the dependent status of a junior eunuch in

Medina until he reached seniority in a number of years, he would not have been exposed to any threat that would have caused him to abscond. There was no imminent danger of abuse and life was probably fairly easy, quiet, and slow-moving for a eunuch in those circumstances. Nonetheless, he was confident enough of his ability to earn a better living and enjoy the benefits of a free person in Egypt, and was prepared to risk a great deal, perhaps including his life, to realize that option. This story brings out the remarkable strength in this young man, who must have been only in his late teens when he made those crucial decisions in life. In addition, it highlights İhsan's considerable capacity to gather information and plan the deceptive pilgrimage to Mecca that would enable him to get out of Medina and flee to Jidda. His suicide threat was also a clever move to get the consul's resistance to high-level Ottoman pressures under which he operated in this case. Although clearly an intelligent and ambitious young man, we must not forget that İhsan had also been exposed to life in the imperial harem, where he probably learned about the good life in Egypt. Elite life experience gave him a wider view of the world, and broadened the options he was willing to entertain for his future, an invaluable advantage that many non-kul/harem slaves did not have.

DILFERAH AND AHMET: A LOVE STORY

This was a love story gone very bad, which takes us to a major Ottoman port city on the Mediterranean, Salonika, in today's Greece.[15] The main character is Dilferah, a twenty-one-year-old enslaved African woman, who since 1857 had served in the household of Hatice Hanım and her husband Mehmet Ağa. Mehmet Ağa was the tobacco customhouse director in Salonika, a fairly senior figure in the provincial administration. Another important participant in the drama unfolding in the court records was Ahmet, a nineteen-year-old free servant in Hatice and Mehmet's household. By 1861 Ahmet and Dilferah had formed a relationship, and Ahmet promised Dilferah that he would marry her. To accomplish that, he intended either to purchase her freedom from the owners; that is, to do it the legal way, or to elope with her illegally. Dilferah, who seems to have been the more pragmatic and assertive of the two, and seemingly preferring the legal path, asked Ahmet how he planned to get the money to buy her from Hatice and Mehmet.

The record does not provide Ahmet's answer to that crucial question, but it may be inferred from the events that followed later on. We next read that the mansion of Hatice Hanım and Mehmet Ağa was set on fire, and was heavily damaged in consequence. Immediately afterward Dilferah and

Ahmet were nowhere to be found, but later the police seized Dilferah at a house in town. There was no mention of Ahmet being apprehended, just that he managed to escape through the Citadel gate. Following a search of the burnt house, it was discovered that money was missing from a drawer in the harem. The police then concluded that Dilferah was the arsonist, and charged that she conspired with Ahmet to steal the money, burn the house, and run away. It thus becomes clear that Ahmet had no legitimate way to come up with the money needed to purchase Dilferah, and that the two decided to steal it from Hatice and Mehmet, either for the purchase of Dilferah or to fund their escape. It is likely, however, that Dilferah did the actual stealing, since she had easy access to the harem where the money was kept, whereas Ahmet was barred from entering that part of the house. She also knew the household routine and had ample opportunity.

The case reached the high court in the capital, which sentenced Dilferah to death, while Ahmet—perhaps in absentia—received ten years imprisonment. The sultan confirmed the death penalty, and issued a ferman to the governor-general of Salonika, Hüsnü Paşa, to carry out the sentence. We do not know if Dilferah was ever executed, although this is more likely than not. The only way she could avoid death was for her mistress Hatice Hanım to forgive her and ask for the sentence to be commuted. If this happened, and it occasionally did in other cases, the notation of the procedure would normally be attached to the case file. It was not found here, yet we may find it some day in another box, in another file, in another register perhaps, and if we do, we shall be visibly relieved, for it is not hard to see that the sentence meted to this enslaved woman-in-love was cruel and unusual punishment.

For our purposes, it is worthwhile noting that we again come upon one of the most unprivileged persons in Ottoman society—an enslaved African woman—who simply refused to accept her predicament, but rather tried to do something to change it. Dilferah, which, ironically, means in Turkish "heart's joy", did not want to remain enslaved; she had other plans for her life that included marriage and family. She did, however, come against a wall that must have seemed insurmountable. After four years of service, she could look forward to manumission in no less than three years, perhaps six, and even that was not certain. At twenty-one, she was expected to have already borne children, either to her master, as his concubine, or, if liberated, to a man of her standing in society. Dilferah found someone she liked enough to want to marry and raise a family with, but circumstances prevented that option from being realized, although the man, Ahmet, was quite willing. These were the walls that she faced, surrounding her not only physically but also mentally, and she chose not to accept that reality, but rather to challenge it, cross the line, break the chains and the law, and steal the money needed to elope with her lover.

The burning of the house is, however, the hardest part to explain, as it does not make sense. The documents, alas, remain forever silent on this. Why, we may ask, did she torch the house? It was totally superfluous to the main purpose she and Ahmet had in mind, for they could take the money she stole from the harem drawer and simply run away immediately. In fact, burning the house was so counterproductive that it may have cost her life. Even if she did not imagine that the court would impose the death penalty for arson, she must have known it was a major offense, for which the punishment would be onerous. Of course, she did not expect to get caught, but somehow this is not enough. We need something else to complete the story, to explain Dilferah's behavior in this tragic fate.

The "something else" missing here must be speculative, perhaps too speculative, but it is worth at least a chance. It is called rage or uncontrollable anger. It could be a targeted anger at the masters of the house, who may have abused her in the past, who may have balked at her romance with Ahmet, if they knew about it; or laughed at her plan to marry him, if she divulged it to them. Or, it could be a more generalized anger at "the system"—the realities of slavery that brought her from her native land in Africa to a major Ottoman city and placed such overwhelming shackles over her freedom that rendered her almost powerless, dependent on her masters' will or whim. It could, of course, be both, but in any event, there can be little doubt that such tremendously destructive energies had to be motivated by a great rage, perhaps greater than she could contain, and most likely resistant to any rationalized process of weighing cost and effect, action and consequences. And, to complete the circle, somehow it seems almost befitting that these passions of love and rage be vented by setting fire to the house she was leaving to begin a new life—simply to expunge the old humiliation and powerlessness of servitude, and perhaps set the record clean.

Notes

1. For a survey of the literature, see the introduction in my book, *Slavery and Abolition in the Ottoman Middle East* (Seattle and London, 1998).
2. Ehud R. Toledano, *As if silent and absent: bonds of enslavement in the Islamic Middle East* (New Haven, 2007).
3. Alan Fisher, "Chattel Slavery in the Ottoman Empire: Some Preliminary Considerations," *Slavery and Abolition* 1 (1980), 1.

4. "Will That Subaltern Ever Speak? Finding African Slaves in the Historiography of the Middle East," paper presented at the conference on "Twentieth Century Historians and Historiography of the Middle East," Boğaziçi University, Istanbul, Turkey, 23–26 May 2002.
5. Toledano, *Slavery and Abolition*, 158.
6. Declaration of the Conference on Arab-led Slavery of Africans, Sunnyside Park Hotel, Johannesburg, 22 February 2003.
7. Michael Salman, *The Embarrassment of Slavery: Controversies over Bondage and Nationalism in the American Colonial Philippines* (Berkeley: University of California Press, 2001).
8. For a discussion of the discourses on slavery in Middle Eastern societies, see Toledano, *Slavery and Abolition*, chapter 5.
9. For a detailed discussion of these issues, see Ehud R. Toledano, *The Ottoman Slave Trade and Its Suppression, 1840–1890* (Princeton, 1982).
10. For an analysis of Ottoman attitudes, see Toledano, *Slavery and Abolition*, chapter 4.
11. Ibid., 15.
12. Petition of the imam of Fatime Sultan, 30 April 1867; report of the prison director, 10 July 1867; mazbata of the Meclis-i Vala, 11 December 1867; the grand vizier to the sultan, 12 January 1867; and the sultan's response, 13 January 1867, no. 26185, Meclis-i Vala, İrade.
13. Cons Zohrab (Jidda) to Amb Goschen (Istanbul), and enclosures, 22 December 1880–14 March 1881, FO 84/1596/63–83, National Archives of the United Kingdom, Kew.
14. For more on Ottoman imperial eunuchs, see Toledano, *Slavery and Abolition*, 41–53.
15. Investigation report by the Salonika court, 4 September 1861; mazbata of the Salonika court, 30 December 1861; mazbata of the Meclis-i Vala, 2 February 1862; the grand vizier to the sultan, 14 February 1862; and the sultan's response, 15 February 1862, no. 20803, Meclis-i Vala, İrade.

Chapter 3

BLACKS BEYOND THE BLACK SEA: EUNUCHS IN THE CRIMEAN KHANATE

Maryna Kravets

Eunuchs constituted the elite of the black slave population in the Islamic world.[1] Notwithstanding their initial mutilation and ensuing physical, psychological, and emotional trauma, they were the highest-priced black slave category, assured of employment in elite households or holy places, and capable at times of attaining great power and wealth of their own. In the medieval and early modern Muslim world, eunuchs were indispensable for the efficient functioning of a variety of institutions associated with sophisticated urban and court culture.[2] This chapter examines the role of eunuchs who were transplanted from such a cultural milieu to a society that experienced comparatively late Islamization, while at the same time preserving a strong pre-Islamic political and cultural ethos.

Research into the history of the black diaspora in the Islamic world has presented the Ottoman Empire as the northerly limit of the Muslim trade in black African slaves.[3] However, as I will demonstrate in this chapter, some black slaves imported into the region were trafficked further north, across the Black Sea, and ended up at the royal court of the Crimean Khanate. The involvement of the Crimean Khanate and its parental state, the Golden Horde, in the slave trade is well documented and has been the subject of scholarly inquiry since the nineteenth century. In the case of the Golden Horde, researchers have focused mainly on its role in supplying new recruits for the Mamlūk Sultanate of Egypt and

Syria and domestic slaves throughout the European Mediterranean.[4] In the case of the Crimean Khanate, its slave-raiding activities in Eastern Europe and the ensuing traffic in captives to the slave markets of the Ottoman Empire have received the most attention.[5] The presence of black slaves in the Crimea, however, is not widely known, and has not hitherto been the subject of a special study. The present discussion of the roles black African eunuchs played at the court of the Crimean khans will open this little known chapter in the African slave experience.

The Crimean Khanate was a successor state of the Golden Horde that arose on the eastern Eurasian steppes as a result of the thirteenth-century Mongol conquests.[6] It was created on the basis of an appanage allotted by Chinggis Khan to his eldest son, Jochi, and was ruled by a Chinggisid dynasty that traced its origin to the latter. By the early fourteenth century the ruling elite of the Golden Horde adopted Islam and subsequently so did the majority of the population, albeit somewhat superficially.[7] Having been formed by nomadic Mongol and Turkic tribes, the Golden Horde preserved its predominantly nomadic tribal character, although it was also receptive to influences of high Islamic civilization from Central Asia and the Mamlūk Sultanate.

The Crimean Khanate,[8] which had emerged by the mid-fifteenth century within the territory of the Golden Horde in the Crimean peninsula and adjacent steppes, and which was populated mainly by tribal Tatars and Nogays, inherited the lifestyle and institutions of its ancestral state. The subsequent history of the Crimea witnessed juxtaposition and adaptation between the indigenous practices and institutions of the khanate, on the one hand, and those of high Islamic civilization, on the other. Increasingly the influence of the latter reached the Crimean Khanate from the Ottoman Empire into whose orbit it was drawn in the second half of the fifteenth century, becoming an Ottoman vassal in 1475. Ottoman hegemony over the Crimea lasted almost to the end of the khanate's existence in 1783.

Among aspects of the Crimean society most affected by the cultural influences from the more established Muslim milieu were household organization, gender relations, and the position of women, especially among the upper strata. To illuminate their development, it is useful to recall the lifestyle of the Golden Horde's elite. In the 1330s the great Moroccan traveler Ibn Baṭṭūṭa passed through the region and in the northern Caucasus steppes visited the mobile summer camp (*urdū*) of the khan of the Golden Horde, Özbek (1313–1341), who is generally credited with making Islam his state's official religion. Ibn Baṭṭūṭa's report[9] confirms the freedom enjoyed by elite women in traditional nomadic tribal societies.[10] Coming from a more religiously influenced, urbanized Muslim environment

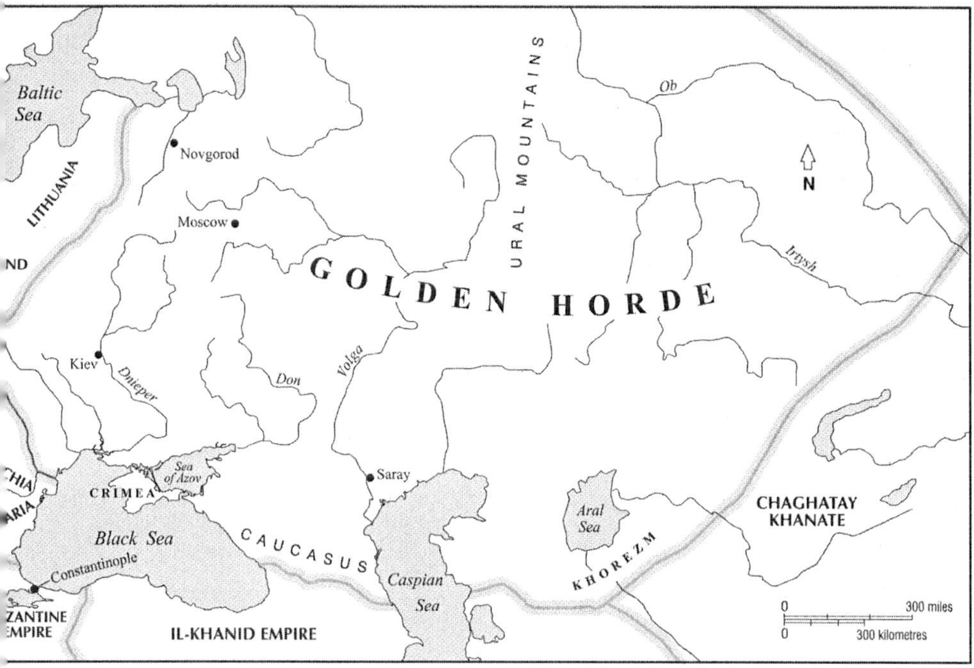

3.1 – The Golden Horde around 1300

characterized by strict seclusion of upper-strata women, the traveler was astonished by the high social status, prominent public position, respect, and freedom of movement enjoyed by female members of the ostensibly Muslim elite of the Golden Horde. In the royal camp Ibn Baṭṭūṭa observed that each of the four wives and the daughter of Özbek Khan had her own small camp, and one of the wives did not consider it objectionable to invite Ibn Baṭṭūṭa to set up his tent in the vicinity of her camp—an invitation he chose not to accept. Though waited upon by a numerous retinue of servants and slaves, none of the royal ladies had difficulty receiving unrelated male visitors in person, paying visits to other people, or attending public gatherings with their faces uncovered. Regrettably, Ibn Baṭṭūṭa left no testimony of the arrangements adhered to by the khan's womenfolk at the winter quarters in the city of Saray, the capital of the Golden Horde.[11]

Ibn Baṭṭūṭa reported that the royal women had Byzantine and Indian *fityān*[12] in their retinues.[13] Here the term *fityān*, which can mean both pages and eunuchs, ought to be understood as referring to eunuchs as demonstrated by the personal names of the *fityān* belonging to Özbek Khan's third wife, Bayalun,[14] whose retinue Ibn Baṭṭūṭa describes in great detail. She is said to have had ten Byzantine and ten Indian *fityān* in attendance. Ibn Baṭṭūṭa gives the name of the chief of her Indian *fityān* as Sunbul (Hyacinth) and that of the chief of the Byzantine ones as "Mīkhā'īl, called by the Tatars (*atrāk*) Lu'lu'[Pearl]."[15] Such personal names point to their bearers being eunuchs, for according to a long-standing practice in the Islamic world, eunuchs—unlike free men and non-emasculated slaves—were frequently named after beautiful, pleasant, or agreeable things, including flowers and gems.[16] Owing to the lack of further evidence, the issue of how common the employment of eunuchs was among royal women of the Golden Horde beyond the reign of Özbek Khan must remain open. The question also remains whether, and to what degree, the roles assigned to their eunuchs reflected some indigenous perceived protective, ceremonial, or symbolic need. From Ibn Baṭṭūṭa's account, their roles appear to be those of personal ceremonial guard and bodyguard: eunuchs are reported to accompany their lady in public, richly dressed and bearing gold or silver staffs, as well as on trips.[17] Coupled with the royal ladies' lifestyle, such use of eunuchs bears little resemblance to those practiced in the elite households of coeval sedentary Muslim societies. A century after Ibn Baṭṭūṭa's visit, when the Golden Horde was in the process of disintegrating, a reversion to a more simple lifestyle took place at the courts of its nascent successor states,[18] presumably caused by more limited local resources, and the use of eunuchs—if indeed it went beyond the episode discussed above—appears to have had been discontinued.[19]

Against this background the household of the Gereys, the Crimean ruling family of Chinggisid origin, evolved under the influence of the elite household pattern of sedentary, urbanized Islamic societies. As proposed by Marshall G. S. Hodgson,[20] this household pattern was based on the concept of masculine honor, characteristic for the geographical area he termed the Irano-Mediterranean zone. In this zone, masculine honor was traditionally understood as a man's ability to exercise control over his womenfolk, manifested in the seclusion of women, particularly in the upper strata. Hodgson argues that with the advent of Muslim society, which was characterized by greater social mingling and a more relaxed societal structure than that found in pre-Islamic Irano-Mediterranean societies, sensitivity about masculine honor was probably reinforced. The infusion of an Islamic cultural style into the traditional Middle Eastern household resulted in the creation of the slave household, or harem system. Ideally, this system presupposed segregation from outside male company of the household's inner part, populated by free wives and slave concubines of the master of the house and their children. In English usage, this inner part of the household is commonly known as the harem (after the Turkish form, originally from the Arabic *ḥaram* or *ḥarīm*, derived from the root *ḥ-r-m*, meaning "inviolable," "forbidden," or "sacred"). This inviolable enclave was served by female slaves and guarded and supervised by eunuchs, who mediated between the harem and the men's world outside of it. The marked preference for slaves in the Islamic household, both as sexual partners and servants, is explained by their complete dependence on their master, which was to guarantee their obedience, reliability, and confidential service. Eunuchs, owing to their greater social marginalization, were especially well-suited for serving such a household. Although the harem system achieved its full development only among the elite, the rest of the population emulated it to the degree allowed by its financial capacity. In the Crimea the slave household was most prominently adopted by the members of the ruling family. This resulted in the seclusion of the royal women and the use of eunuchs to guard and supervise them.

The fragmentary nature of sources of Crimean history does not allow for a comprehensive presentation of the early evolution of many of the khanate's institutions, including that of the royal harem. No written or archeological evidence has been recovered concerning the structure of the khans' earliest palaces known to us from the sources: in the fortress of Kırk Yer (later known as Çufut Kal'e) and in a nearby locale called Salacık in the southwest of the peninsula.[21] Since the Chinggisid Gerey khans retained for some time the seminomadic lifestyle of seasonal peregrination of their Golden Horde predecessors, the living arrangements of the khans' womenfolk were initially not unlike those witnessed by Ibn Baṭṭūṭa in Özbek Khan's camp.[22] The transition to a more sedentary—and for the khan's womenfolk, more secluded—lifestyle must have occurred gradually, as the khans' early palaces evolved from temporary dwellings occupied only for a short part of the year into more permanent residences. During the reign of Sahib Gerey I (1532–1551), most likely in the early 1530s,[23] this evolution culminated in the relocation of the khan's chief residence from Salacık to a locality in its close proximity, Bahçesaray, which remained the khanate's capital.

A harem compound must have been one of the original structures of the Bahçesaray palace: it is mentioned in the chronicle by Sahib Gerey's court astrologer Remmal Hoca who discusses the events of the 1530s–1540s.[24] In the next two centuries references to the khan's harem and its reclusive inhabitants—official wives (sing. *biyim*) and concubines (sing. *bikeç)*—become commonplace, although no description of the physical structure of the harem before the 1730s is known. The presently extant palace compound dates, with some modifications, from the mid-eighteenth century when the palace was rebuilt following its destruction in 1736, during the Russo-Turkish War of 1735–1739. The layout of the rebuilt palace appears to follow the three-courtyard plan of the Ottoman Topkapı Palace, and its harem exhibits the main features of the Ottoman imperial harem, being a walled compound relegated to the back of the palace and provided with its own garden and a pool.[25] A comparison of the palace's layout with the only known detailed description of the palace before its destruction[26] suggests a continuity between the pre- and post-1736 palaces, but the lack of further data precludes us from establishing definitively when these features of the Ottoman palatial architecture were first adopted in the Crimea.

Being connected with the evolution of the Crimean royal harem, the employment of eunuchs in the khan's palace must have also begun in the course of the sixteenth century. Muscovite diplomatic materials—the largest extant complex of sources for Crimean affairs from the late fifteenth and early sixteenth century—do not include a single reference to eunuchs in the khan's service, thus allowing us to assume that there were none as yet.[27] But in the earliest extant Crimean judicial records (*sicill*s), dating from the beginning of the seventeenth century, eunuchs (recognizable by the title *hadim*)[28] appear as a well-established institution. For example, in 1602 Hadim Ahmed Ağa is listed as a witness to the re-marriage of a woman likely connected with the royal household, whereas in 1610 a confirmation of the manumission of a harem eunuch, Hadim Mahmud Ağa, by his late master, Khan Selamet Gerey I (1608–1610), is recorded upon the request of the khan's successor.[29] Ottoman practices are known to have been introduced into the Crimea on a large scale during the reign of Sahib Gerey I, although this process had begun already under his predecessors in the early sixteenth century.[30] Hence it is possible that the use of eunuchs in the khan's household also dates from Sahib Gerey's time, even though no eunuchs are explicitly mentioned in Remmal Hoca's chronicle, completed following the khan's death in 1551.

Describing the state of the Crimean Khanate to his Swedish hosts in 1669, the Crimean envoy Mustafa Ağa stated that eunuchs were presented to the Crimean khans by their Ottoman suzerains as a "particular rarity."[31] How this supply was organized can at present only be conjectured. Since the new slave eunuchs often reached the Ottoman imperial harem as children—the castration survival rates being highest when the operation was performed before the age of puberty—they were commonly raised and trained there.[32] Such practices were consistent with the Ottoman imperial harem's function as a training institution for its personnel[33] and must also have been applied to the eunuchs destined for the Crimea. However, such training would also transform the eunuchs into proponents of the Ottoman imperial harem's practices in other places they happened subsequently to

Map 3.2 - The Crimean Khanate around 1600

serve. Considerable assimilation of the khan's harem to the Ottoman model by the mid-seventeenth century is suggested by Mustafa Ağa's testimony. As presented by him, the harem's routine (for example, eunuchs managing the matters pertaining to the khan's bedchamber and the ritual of selecting a new concubine for the khan by throwing a kerchief over her) is strikingly similar to corresponding practices in the Ottoman imperial harem as reported by locals and European visitors to Istanbul in the sixteenth and seventeenth centuries.[34] Although the veracity of such accounts by outsiders has been deservedly doubted,[35] no harem insider accounts are known to exist for comparison prior to the eighteenth century. Provided that Mustafa Ağa's account is entirely his own and reflects some common idea of the practices in the Crimean royal harem held by those with direct access to the palace, though not to the harem itself, his account may yet prove useful not only as evidence of Crimean practices and their likely Ottoman origin, but also as a corroboration of the outsider accounts about the practices in the Ottoman imperial harem itself. Ottoman cultural influences reached the Crimea in a variety of ways: through members of the Gerey house residing in the empire as exiles or hostages; through education received by children of the Crimean elite in Istanbul; through contacts with the Ottoman province (*sancak*, later *eyalet*) located on the southern shores of the Crimean peninsula; and other ways. Yet in establishing and regulating the intricacies of harem life, the role of competent eunuchs was essential. Therefore it is likely that the Ottoman-trained eunuchs influenced the evolution of the Crimean royal harem along Ottoman lines from the sixteenth to the eighteenth century.

The Crimean correspondence with Muscovy from the mid-1630s mentions four eunuchs employed in the khan's harem and one each in the harems of the *kalga* and *nureddin*, the first and second heirs to the Crimean throne.[36] In 1669 Mustafa Ağa reported the number of the khan's eunuchs as being "always twelve."[37] Louis Charles Peyssonnel, a French consul to the khanate in the 1750s, noted the presence of six, namely, two chief eunuchs (*Kislar-Aga*, i.e., *kızlar ağası*) and four ordinary ones.[38] Finally, an account by a Viennese businessman, Nikolaus Ernst Kleeman, shows that in the last year of Khan Kırım Gerey's second reign (1768–1769) the total number of eunuchs in his harem amounted to seven, one of whom was described as their chief.[39] The precise division of responsibilities between chief eunuchs and ordinary ones is not known, although it is possible that the hierarchy of the eunuch posts emulated to some degree that found in the Ottoman imperial harem.[40]

The early sources do not specify the race of the Crimean eunuchs, allowing for the possibility that either black or white eunuchs, or both, might have been employed. Not until the 1660s do sources clearly indicate the presence of black eunuchs in the khan's harem. During his 1665–1666 visit to the khanate, the famous Ottoman traveler Evliya Çelebi observed black eunuchs (*kara hâdim ağalar*) guarding the harem gates of the khan's palace.[41] In addition, Mustafa Ağa's 1669 account implies that the harem eunuchs were usually black.[42] Infrequent race-specific reports of Crimean eunuchs of the later period also portray those eunuchs as black. For example, Kleeman testifies to the African origin of the chief eunuch whom he observed in 1769 and whom he describes as "ein sehr dicker Mohr."[43] This preference for black eunuchs over white ones in the khanate was most certainly a consequence of a similar trend found in the Ottoman Empire. The conquest of Egypt in 1517, which brought the Ottoman domain closer to the source of black slaves and places of production of eunuchs, resulted in the growing preference for black eunuchs in the Ottoman imperial harem and other elite harems.[44] Hence it can be presumed that the Crimean eunuchs, who served during at least the last century and a half of the khanate's existence, and whose race was left unspecified in sources, were more likely to be black than white.

Although the presence of eunuchs in the harems of the Gerey family is beyond doubt, very few particulars about their lives are known. Sources consulted for the present study offer no information about their precise origin(s), age upon arrival in the khanate, duration of service, retirement options, final resting places,[45] and so on. The evidence amassed regarding the khans' eunuchs suggests that the royal harem was likely the only sphere of their activity: they are depicted guarding its gate, managing its day-to-day routine, accompanying its inmates on trips, witnessing court cases involving those in some way connected to it, and ultimately being manumitted after years of harem service.

Most probably eunuch involvement in the khanate's political affairs did not equal that of the eunuchs of the Ottoman imperial harem, who could exercise a great deal of influence, especially during the "sultanate of the women" (*kadınlar saltanatı*), which lasted from the mid-sixteenth to the mid-seventeenth century.[46] This difference resulted from the considerable power members of the Crimean Tatar tribal aristocracy retained in the khanate in accordance with the traditional Turko-Mongolian political culture.[47] Consequently, the khan could normally exercise only limited authority in the state, and the women and eunuchs of his harem were largely prevented from playing an active part in the khanate's political affairs. Also unlike the Ottoman Empire, where the sultan's eunuchs could occupy positions of authority outside the imperial harem, in the Ottoman military-administrative system,[48] in the khanate such positions were reserved for members of the Crimean tribal elite and thus unavailable to the khan's eunuchs.

Further research into Crimean, Ottoman, Muscovite, and other sources should yield additional information about the lives of Crimean eunuchs. On the basis of the above discussion it is possible to conclude that black

Africans constituted a great, if not predominant, component of the eunuchs employed by the Crimean ruling family. Although at any given time their number in the khanate amounted to only a few persons, their impact upon the functioning of the khan's harem must have been considerable. It seems very likely that, in the Crimean royal court, where the Turko-Mongolian nomadic tribal traditions were being gradually supplanted by those of the Ottoman civilization, the black slave eunuchs trained and supplied by the Ottomans, served as agents of cultural change, transplanting the rules and practices of the Ottoman imperial harem into the khanate.

The importation of black eunuchs into the Crimea is also noteworthy for other reasons. The khanate's location at the eastern European steppe frontier, which remained largely open well into the eighteenth century, coupled with the idea of the holy war on behalf of Islam and considerations of commercial profitability, turned the khanate into the main supplier of white slave manpower to the Ottoman Empire during the sixteenth and seventeenth centuries.[49] Although the exact numbers of Ukrainians, Russians, Poles, and other Eastern Europeans captured in Crimean slave raids will never be established, these captives likely numbered into the hundreds of thousands, if not millions.[50] To their numbers should be added slaves from the Caucasus, who had been captured through raids or had been presented to the khans as tribute by Circassian polities.[51] While some of the slaves thus obtained remained in the khanate, the majority of them were channeled to Istanbul, the hub of the Ottoman slave trade, as well as to other slave markets throughout the empire. In the eighteenth century, as the flow of Eastern European slaves was reduced to a trickle, a large proportion of slaves from the Caucasus still reached the Ottoman Empire via the Crimea.[52] Thus, insignificant as it may appear in contrast to the mass movement of slave manpower in the opposite direction, in terms of the overall slave trade in the Middle East, the import of black eunuchs into the khanate represented the main, if not the only, slave traffic from the Ottoman Empire to the Crimean Khanate.

Notes

1. The best general treatment of the history of black slavery in the Islamic world remains Bernard Lewis, *Race and Slavery in the Middle East: An Historical Enquiry* (New York and Oxford, 1990). I am grateful to Maria E. Subtelny and Victor Ostapchuk for commenting on earlier drafts of this paper; to Sebastian Günther for help with seventeenth-century German; and to Jane R. Davie of the Cartography Office, Department of Geography, University of Toronto, for drawing the maps.

2. For an innovative discussion of eunuchs in urban and court settings as well as in tending tombs and holy places, see Shaun Marmon, *Eunuchs and Sacred Boundaries in Islamic Societies* (New York, 1995).
3. John O. Hunwick, "Black Africans in the Islamic World: An Understudied Dimension of the Black Diaspora," *Tarikh* 5 (1978), 20–40, especially the map on 21; and Ronald Segal, *Islam's Black Slaves: The Other Black Diaspora* (New York, 2001), 103–17.
4. See, for example, Lajos Tardy, *Sklavenhandel in der Tartarei: Die Frage der Mandscharen,* trans. Mátyás Esterházy (Szeged, 1983); Charles Verlinden, *L'esclavage dans l'Europe médiévale*, 2v. (Brugge, 1955–1977), as well as an online bibliography of secondary studies concerning the Mamlūk Sultanate maintained by The Mamluk Bibliography Project, Middle East Documentation Center, University of Chicago, http://www.lib.uchicago.edu/e/su/mideast/mamluk/ [accessed 1 March 2004].
5. See M. N. Berezhkov, "Russkie plienniki i nevol'niki v Krymu," in *Trudy VI Arkheologicheskago s"iezda v Odessie, 1884 g.* (Odessa, 1886–1889), 2:342–72; A. A. Novosel'skii, *Bor'ba Moskovskogo gosudarstva s tatarami v pervoi polovine XVII veka* (Moscow and Leningrad, 1948); S. O. Shmidt, "Russkie polonianiki v Krymu i sistema ikh vykupa v seredine XVI v.," in N.V. Ustiugov et al., eds., *Voprosy sotsial'no-ėkonomicheskoi istorii i istochnikovedeniia perioda feodalizma v Rossii: Sbornik statei k 70-letiiu A. A. Novosel'skogo* (Moscow, 1961), 30–34; Maurycy Horn, "Chronologia i zasięg najazdów tatarskich na ziemie Rzechypospolitej polskiej w latach 1600–1647," *Studia i materialy do istorii wojskowości* 8 (1963), 3–71; Alan W. Fisher, "Muscovy and the Black Sea Slave Trade," *Canadian-American Slavic Review* 6 (1972), 575–94; V. Khenzel' [Hensel], "Problema iasyria v pol'sko-turetskikh otnosheniiakh XVI–XVII vv.," in B.A. Rybakov et al., eds., *Rossia, Pol'sha i Prichernomor'e v XV–XVIII vv.* (Moscow, 1979), 147–58; Ia. R. Dashkevych, "Iasyr z Ukraïny (XV–persha polovyna XVII st.) iak istoryko-demohrafichna problema," *Ukraïns'kyi arkheohrafichnyi shchorichnyk,* n.s. 2 (1993), 40–47.
6. For the history of the Golden Horde, see Joseph von Hammer-Purgstall, *Geschichte der Goldenen Horde in Kiptschak, das ist: Der Mongolen in Russland* (Amsterdam, [1840] 1979); Berthold Spuler, *Die Goldene Horde: Die Mongolen in Russland, 1223–1502*, 2nd ed. (Wiesbaden, 1965); and G. A. Fedorov-Davydov, *Obshchestvennyi stroi Zolotoi Ordy* (Moscow, 1973).
7. Concerning the spread of Islam in the Golden Horde, see Devin DeWeese, *Islamization and Native Religion in the Golden Horde: Baba Tükles and Conversion to Islam in Historical and Epic Tradition* (University Park, PA, 1994).
8. For a discussion of the history of the Crimean Khanate, see V. D. Smirnov, *Krymskoe khanstvo pod verkhovenstvom Otomanskoi Porty do nachala XVIII vieka* (St. Petersburg, 1887); idem, *Krymskoe khanstvo pod verkhovenstvom Otomanskoi Porty v XVIII stolietii* (Odessa, 1889); Alan W. Fisher, *The*

Crimean Tatars (Stanford, 1978), 1–69, and bibliography; Halil İnalcık, "Kırım," [2]: "Kırım hanlığı," in *Islâm ansiklopedisi* (Ankara, 1940–1988), 6:746–56; and B. Spuler, "Ḳırım," *The Encyclopaedia of Islam*, 2nd ed. [henceforth *EI-2*] (Leiden, 1960–2002), 5:136–43.

9. Ibn Baṭṭūṭa, *Voyages d'Ibn Batoutah: Text arabe, accompagné d'une traduction*, ed. and trans. C. Defrémery and B. R. Sanguinetti (Paris, 1874–1879), 2:377–98, 402–18, 444–50; and 3:1–20; V. Tizengauzen [Tiesenhausen], ed. and trans., *Sbornik materialov, otnosiashchikhsia k istorii Zolotoi Ordy*, v.1: *Izvlecheniia iz sochinenii arabskikh* (St. Petersburg, 1884), 288–302, 305–14; Ibn Baṭṭūṭa, *The Travels of Ibn Baṭṭūṭa, A.D. 1325–1354*, trans. H. A. R. Gibb (Cambridge, 1958–2000), 2:480–90, 492–500; and 3:539–49.
10. For discussion of the difference between the position of sedentary and nomadic women in the medieval and early modern Islamic world, see N. Tomiche, "Al-Mar'a," 1: "In the Arab World," *EI-2*, 6:466–72; A. K. S. Lambton, "Al-Mar'a," 3: "In Persia. a. Before 1900," *EI-2*, 6:481–85.
11. Ibn Baṭṭūṭa mentions Özbek Khan's palace (*qaṣr*) in Saray. See *Voyages*, 2:448. But the palace's location and structure still have not been verified. See G. A. Fedorov-Davydov, *Zolotoordynskie goroda Povolzh'ia* (Moscow, 1994), 20–77.
12. The term *fityān* (sg. *fatā*) was frequently used to denote eunuchs in the Muslim west (the Maghreb and Spain) and is used by the Moroccan-born traveler in this meaning on at least one other occasion. See David Ayalon, *Eunuchs, Caliphs and Sultans: A Study in Power Relationships* (Jerusalem, 1999), 284. It is not always easy to distinguish between the possible meanings of the term. Defrémery and Sanguinetti attempt to distinguish between eunuchs and pages in Ibn Baṭṭūṭa's narrative based on the context—see Ibn Baṭṭūṭa, *Voyages*, 2:388, 394 (eunuchs) vs. 381, 385, 413 (pages); whereas Tizengauzen and Gibb render this term as "pages" throughout their translations—see Tizengauzen, *Sbornik materialov*, 1:289, 291–92, 294, 302; and Ibn Baṭṭūṭa, *Travels*, 2:482, 484–86, 488, 498 (compare however 486 n.269, where a possibility of the alternative translation is acknowledged).
13. Ibn Baṭṭūṭa, *Voyages*, 2:388.
14. Ross E. Dunn, *The Adventures of Ibn Battuta: A Muslim Traveler of the 14th Century* (Berkeley, 1986), 171, 180, and bibliography. Bayalun was the daughter of the Byzantine Emperor Andronikos III Palaiologos (1328–1341). Her Greek name is unknown, Bayalun being the Mongol name she bore in her husband's milieu.
15. Ibn Baṭṭūṭa, *Voyages*, 2:413.
16. David Ayalon, "The Eunuchs in the Mamluk Sultanate," in Myriam Rosen-Ayalon, ed., *Studies in Memory of Gaston Wiet* (Jerusalem, 1977), 275–79. Therefore the translators are hardly justified in rendering Ibn Baṭṭūṭa's *fityān* on this occasion as "pages"—see Ibn Baṭṭūṭa, *Voyages*, 2:413; Tizengauzen,

Sbornik materialov, 1:302; Ibn Baṭṭūṭa, *Travels*, 2:498; and Dunn, *Adventures*, 170.

17. Ibn Baṭṭūṭa, *Voyages*, 2:388, 394, 413.
18. Muslim successor states of the Golden Horde included the khanates of Astrakhan, Kasimov, Kazan, Siberia, and the Crimea, as well as the Nogay Horde.
19. There has been no comprehensive study of slavery in the Muslim successor states of the Golden Horde with the exception of the Crimean Khanate—see n.5 above. General treatment of the other states makes no reference to eunuchs. See especially A. N. Kurat, *IV–XVIII yüzyıllarda Karadeniz kuzeyindeki Türk kavimleri ve devletleri* (Ankara, 1972); V. V. Vel'iaminov-Zernov, *Izsliedovanie o Kasimovskikh tsariakh i tsarevichakh*, 4v. (St. Petersburg, 1863–1887); Mikhail Khudiakov, *Ocherki po istorii Kazanskogo khanstva* (Kazan, [1923] 2004); Edward Louis Keenan, Jr., "Muscovy and Kazan', 1445–1552: A Study in Steppe Politics," Ph.D. dissertation, Harvard University, 1965; V. V. Trepavlov, *Istoriia Nogaiskoi Ordy* (Moscow, 2001); and I. V. Zaitsev, *Astrakhanskoe khanstvo* (Moscow, 2004).
20. Marshall G. S. Hodgson, *The Venture of Islam*, v.2: *The Expansion of Islam in the Middle Period* (Chicago, 1974), 140–45. The following discussion also draws on Marmon, *Eunuchs and Sacred Boundaries*.
21. Oleksa Haivorns'kyi, "Khanskii dvorets v Bakhchisarae: Vozniknovenie Krymskogo Khanstva...," http://www.hansaray.iatp.org.ua/r_ist_devlet.html [accessed 1 March 2004].
22. V.E. Syroechkovskii, "Mukhammed-Gerai i ego vassaly," *Uchenye zapiski Moskovskogo gosudarstvennogo universiteta*, vyp. 61, ser. Istoriia (1940), 4–5, 17.
23. Fisher, *The Crimean Tatars*, 44. The earliest dated structure of the palace compound believed to be constructed in Bahçesaray, as opposed to structures moved from Salacık—the Sarı Güzel bathhouse—bears the date of 939 A.H./1532–1533 C.E. in its commemorative inscription. See N. L. Ėrnst, "Bakhchisaraiskii Khanskii dvorets i arkhitektor vel. kn. Ivana III friazin Aleviz Novyi," *Izvestiia Tavricheskogo obshchestva istorii, arkheologii i ėtnografii* 2 (1928), 42; and A. L. Iakobson, *Srednevekovyi Krym: Ocherki istorii i istorii material'noi kul'tury* (Leningrad, 1964), 144, 146.
24. [Remmal Hoca], *Tāriẖ-i Ṣāḥib Giray H̱ān: Histoire de Sahib Giray, Khan de Crimée de 1532 à 1551* [with French translation by M. Le Roux], ed. Özalp Gökbilgin (Ankara, 1973), 36.
25. For one of the earliest detailed plans of the Bahçesaray palace dating from 1798, see Iakobson, *Srednevekovyi Krym*, 145. Concerning features of premodern Ottoman palatial architecture, see Gülru Necipoğlu, *Architecture, Ceremonial, and Power: The Topkapı Palace in the Fifteenth and Sixteenth Centuries* (New York, 1991).

26. [Cristof Hermann Manstein], *Zapiski Manshteina o Rossii, 1727–1744* (St. Petersburg, 1875), 350–53.
27. G. F. Karpov, ed., *Pamiatniki diplomaticheskikh snoshenii Moskovskago gosudarstva s Krymskoiu i Nagaiskoiu ordami i s Turtsiei*, v.1: *S 1474 po 1505 god, ėpokha sverzheniia mongol'skago iga v Rossii*, Sbornik Imperatorskago Russkago Istoricheskago Obshchestva, v.41 (St. Petersburg, 1884); and G. F. Karpov and G. F. Shtendman, eds., *Pamiatniki diplomaticheskikh snoshenii Moskovskago gosudarstva s Krymom, nagaiami i Turtsieiu*, v.2: *1508–1521*, Sbornik Imperatorskago Russkago Istoricheskago Obshchestva, v.95 (St. Petersburg, 1895).
28. The denomination *hadim* strongly suggests the bearer's identity as a eunuch. This euphemism (from Ar. *khādim*, pl. *khadam*, lit. servant) was applied almost exclusively to eunuchs in both Arabic and Ottoman usage. See David Ayalon, "On the Eunuchs in Islam," *Jerusalem Studies in Arabic and Islam* 1 (1979), 67–124, esp. 82–92; and Ayalon, *Eunuchs, Caliphs and Sultans*, 207–84.
29. Fond 917, no. 1, fols. 46a:i and 38a:ii, respectively, Division of Manuscripts, National Library of Russia, St. Petersburg.
30. Halil Inalcik, "The Khan and the Tribal Aristocracy: The Crimean Khanate under Sahib Giray I," *Harvard Ukrainian Studies* 3/4 (1979–1980), 445–46; Alexandre Bennigsen and Chantal Lemercier-Quelquejay, "Le khanat de Crimée au début du XVIe siècle de la tradition mongole a la suzeraineté ottomane d'après un document inédit des Archives ottomanes," *Cahiers du monde russe et soviétique* 13 (1972), 321–37; and Victor Ostapchuk, "The Publication of Documents on the Crimean Khanate in the Topkapı Sarayı: The Documentary Legacy of Crimean-Ottoman Relations," *Turcica* 19 (1987), 255.
31. J. Matuz, "Eine Beschreibung des Khanats der Krim aus dem Jahre 1669," *Acta Orientalia ediderunt Societates Orientales Danica, Norvegica, Svecica* 28 (1964–1965), 141.
32. Cengiz Orhonlu, "Khāṣī," iii: "In Turkey," *EI-2* 4:1093.
33. For a discussion of the Ottoman imperial harem as the training institution for its staff, see Leslie Peirce, *The Imperial Harem: Women and Sovereignty in the Ottoman Empire* (New York and Oxford, 1993), 139–43.
34. Matuz, "Eine Beschreibung," 139–40. For the kerchief story in the Ottoman context, see especially the following accounts which informed a number of later European descriptions of the imperial harem: [Domenico Hierosolimitano], *Domenico's Istanbul*, trans. with an introduction and commentary by Michael Austin, ed. Geoffrey Lewis (Warminster, Wiltshire, 2001), 32, 110, 149–152; Ottaviano Bon, *The Sultan's Seraglio: An Intimate Portrait of Life at the Ottoman Court (From the Seventeenth-Century Edition of John Withers)*, ed. Godfrey Goodwin (London, 1996), 48; and [Albertus Bobovius], "Topkapı Sarayı in the Mid-Seventeenth Century: Bobovi's Descrip-

tion," trans. C. G. Fisher and A. Fisher, *Archivum Ottomanicum* 10 (1985 [1987]), 67–68.

35. See, for example, Peirce, *Imperial Harem*, 113–118.
36. F. F. Lashkov, ed., *Pamiatniki diplomaticheskikh snoshenii Krymskago khanstva s Moskovskim gosudarstvom v XVI i XVII v.v., khraniashchiesia v Moskovskom Glavnom Arkhive Ministerstva Inostrannykh Diel* (Simferopol, 1891), 61, 66. The sources give names of the khan's eunuchs as Makbul, Gazanfer, Cihangir, and Diker Ağas—see Lashkov, *Pamiatniki*, 61. See also V. V. Vel'iaminov-Zernov [and Huseyn Feyzhanoğlı], eds., *Materialy dlia istorii Krymskago khanstva = Matériaux pour servir à l'histoire du khanat de Crimée = Qırım yurtına ve ol ṭaraflarġa dā'ir bolġan yarlıqlar ve ḫaṭṭlar* (St. Petersburg, 1864), 140, 147, 163, 178, 208, 218.
37. Matuz, "Eine Beschreibung," 142.
38. Louis Charles Peyssonel [Peyssonnel], *Traite sur le commerce de la Mer Noire* (Paris, 1787), 2:267.
39. [Nikolaus Ernst Kleeman], *Nikolaus Ernst Kleemans Reisen von Wien über Belgrad bis Kilianova, durch die Butschack Tartarey über Kavschan, Bender, durch die Nogew Tartarey in die Crimm…in den Jahren 1768, 1769 und 1770* (Vienna, 1771), 46.
40. For the eunuch hierarchy in the Ottoman imperial harem, see İsmail Hakkı Uzunçarşılı, *Osmanlı Devletinin saray teşkilâtı* (Ankara, 1945), 172–83; Orhonlu, "Khāṣī," 1092–93.
41. Evliyâ Çelebi b. Derviş Mehemmed Zıllî, *Evliyâ Çelebi Seyahatnâmesi* (Istanbul, 1996–2007), 7:228.
42. Matuz, "Eine Beschreibung," 140.
43. Kleeman, *Reisen*, 46.
44. Norman Penzer, *The Harem* (London, [1936] 1965), 161–67. For a discussion of the geographical location of emasculation of black slaves destined for the Islamic Mediterranean, see Jan S. Hogendorn, "The Location of the 'Manufacture' of Eunuchs," in Miura Toru and John Edward Philips, eds., *Slave Elites in the Middle East and Africa: A Comparative Study* (London and New York, 2000), 41–68.
45. Among the published tombstone inscriptions dating from the period of the Crimean Khanate none can be conclusively identified as belonging to a eunuch. See "Bakhchisaraiskiia arabskiia i turetskiia nadpisi," *Zapiski Imperatorskago Odesskago Obshchestva Istorii i Drevnostei* 2 (1850), section 2–3, 489–528.
46. About this phenomenon, see Peirce, *The Imperial Harem.*
47. Inalcik, "The Khan and the Tribal Aristocracy," and Beatrice Forbes Manz, "The Clans of the Crimean Khanate, 1466–1532," *Harvard Ukrainian Studies* 2 (1978), 282–309.
48. Orhonlu, "Khāṣī," 1093.

49. Fisher, "Muscovy and the Black Sea Slave Trade." Widely employed as domestic slaves in virtually every part of the Ottoman Empire, Eastern Europeans were especially prominent in the seventeenth-century Ottoman navy, where they constituted more than half of the slave oarsmen. Representatives from virtually all other European countries comprised the rest. See Michel Fontenay, "Chiourmes turques au XVIIe siècle," in Rosalba Ragosta, ed., *Le Genti del mare Mediterraneo* (Naples, 1981), 2:889–97, especially 889–90n.37.
50. A. A. Novosel'skii arrives at a minimum of 150,000 to 200,000 people captured in the first half of the seventeenth century on Muscovite territory alone, whereas Iaroslav Dashkevych estimates the loss of the Ukrainian population during the fifteenth to the middle of the seventeenth century at between 2 million and 2.5 million killed and captured. See Novosel'skii, *Bor'ba Moskovskogo gosudarstva*, 436; and Dashkevych, "Iasyr z Ukraïny," 45.
51. Hezarfen Hüseyin Efendi, *Telhîsü'l-beyan fî kavânîn-i Âl-i Osmân*, ed. Sevim İlgürel (Ankara, 1998), 172; and Halil Inalcik, "Čerkes," iii: "Ottoman period," *EI-2*, 2:24.
52. Frederick Calvert Baltimore, *A Tour to the East in the Years 1763 and 1764: With Remarks on the City of Constantinople and the Turks* (London, 1767), 72.

Chapter 4

SLAVE TRADE AND SLAVERY ON THE SWAHILI COAST, 1500–1750[1]

Thomas Vernet

A great deal of research has been carried out on the slave trade and slavery on the Swahili coast. John Middleton wrote, "Slavery has been perhaps the best-studied of all Swahili institutions."[2] The great majority of these works, however, deal only with the nineteenth century.[3] Contrary to the previous centuries, economic upheavals occurred in the region during this period, because from the 1810s onward a plantation economy flourished on the coast, which demanded plentiful servile manpower. The slave trade, centered on Zanzibar, developed on an unparalleled scale in Eastern Africa, and an actual slave mode of production became widespread on the coast.[4]

Conversely, very few publications have dealt with the slave trade for the period from the sixteenth to the eighteenth centuries. Almost all deal with the second part of the eighteenth century, mostly from the 1770s onward. During this time the French from the Mascarene Islands developed an intense slave trade with the Swahili coast, mostly from the port towns of Kilwa and Zanzibar, giving new momentum to the slave trade in East Africa. In the same period the Omani imposed their sovereignty on Zanzibar and progressively took over the entire coast. They controlled more and more of the trading networks and encouraged new trends to the slave trade. Historical documentation on the Swahili coast is a little more prevalent for the last third of the century, with an increasing number published in English.[5] The first half of the eighteenth century has received much less attention from the historians. Finally, the few existing studies of the slave trade before the nineteenth century have mainly focused on slave demand from the French or the Omani, but not the role the Swahili had in it.[6]

Debates have occurred concerning the number of slaves exported from the East African coast before the nineteenth century, but they were limited in scope and did not lead to deep historical investigation. Coupland's book is the only one to tackle the slave trade in detail over a long period of time. He claims that the East African slave trade had been continuous and massive since antiquity, led by the "Arabs" who according to him settled on the coast and began trading in the interior. A "prodigious" number of slaves were exported, contributing to the depopulation of East Africa, and exceeding the transatlantic slave trade.[7] Such allegations, which aimed to justify British colonization, have been seriously criticized for lack of evidence. Rejecting Coupland's thesis, some historians have minimized the slave trade and its economic impact before the eighteenth century.[8] Because of the lack of explicit evidence, some scholars even question the existence of the slave trade on the Swahili coast before the Omani settlement on the coast in the eighteenth century.[9] Other scholars contest the claims of Alpers and Freeman-Grenville and have asked for a revaluation of the slave trade.[10] Nevertheless, most of the historians of the Swahili world have generally adopted a prudent position, admitting the existence of the slave trade, but maintaining that before the end of the eighteenth century, it remained a minor part of the coastal trade compared to the trade in ivory or gold.[11]

The lack of interest in Swahili historiography on this issue can be explained by the proportionally small amount of research conducted on the sixteenth, seventeenth, and eighteenth centuries, which have not aroused as much debate as the origins of Swahili civilization or its evolution in the nineteenth century. Studies on ancient social and political organization are few, and are often too linked to nineteenth-century historiography and ethnography.[12] Moreover, works on this period so far undertaken have often neglected contemporary documentation, mostly Portuguese, although it can be a rich source of information. For the most part, historians have relied on a few useful, but incomplete, publications.[13] As such, it is revealing that historians who have recently rediscovered the Portuguese sources have all mentioned the existence and the importance of the slave trade or servile work.[14] Several studies dealing with Madagascar tackled the slave trade between Madagascar and the Comoro Islands and the Swahili coast,[15] but they have been neglected by Swahili historiography, which is too often separated from the Malagasy and Comorian historiography.

Since the 1970s the revival of Swahili historiography has often ignored these matters. For a long time a major goal of Swahili studies has been to demonstrate the sociocultural proximity of Swahili society with the African interior. Thus, studies of the East African slave trade and the use of slaves have emphasized Omani participation and influence as well as French demand. Moreover, the controversial status of Swahili populations in the modern states of East Africa, and more generally the issue of African involvement in the slave trade, remain sensitive issues, which have probably inhibited research on this matter. Last but not least, until recently the slave trade in the Muslim world was rarely investigated and often underestimated.[16] This study reconsiders the slave trade and slavery on the East African coast before the second half of the eighteenth century, mostly through Portuguese sources. It focuses on the region from Cape Delgado in the south to the Lamu archipelago in the north, because this area is the heart of cultural debates about Swahili civilization. Yet this does not mean that Swahili communities inhabiting other parts of the coast, in particular the Mozambique area or the Comoros, were not concerned with the slave trade.

Between the early sixteenth century and the first half of the eighteenth century the Swahili were widely involved in slave trading networks. Most captives came from northwestern Madagascar and were destined to fill demands for servile labor in Arabia, the Persian Gulf, and the Swahili city-states, and from the late seventeenth century, the Omani. This study primarily examines the nature of the slave trade organized by Swahili traders, especially its scale, its role in the development of prosperous new trading networks of some coastal city-states. In addition, it will shed light on the movements of some Swahili and Hadrami groups on the East African coast. Conclusions arising from these investigations largely question the earlier assumptions about and estimations of the East African slave trade.

So far historical sources are too few to estimate the scale of the Swahili coast slave trade before the sixteenth century. The famous Zanj rebellion in Iraq (869–883) is often cited to attest to the antiquity and importance of the slave trade at this time and its decline after the uprising. [17] A rarely cited study by G. H. Talhami, however, has shown that slaves imported from the Swahili coast formed a very small minority in these rebellious.[18] Moreover, most Africans involved came from other regions of Africa or were of free status. According to Talhami, Arab and Persian geographers did not mention slave trading between the East African coast and the Arabian peninsula before the tenth century. Buzurg ibn Shahriyar, who wrote around 950, is the first to state that Zanj slaves were caught or purchased in the area between Sofala and Zanzibar to be sold in Oman. Later in the mid-twelfth century al-Idrisi wrote that Arab traders captured Zanj to enslave them, but generally speaking, medieval geographers rarely mentioned the slave trade on the Swahili coast, although they often did so

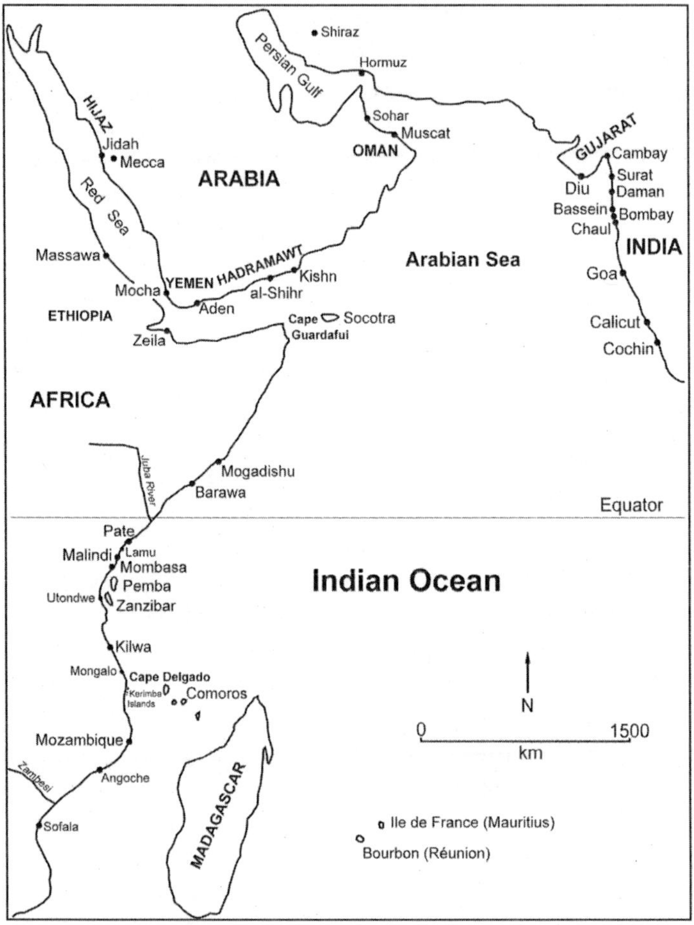

The Swahili Coast and the Indian Ocean, 1500 - 1750

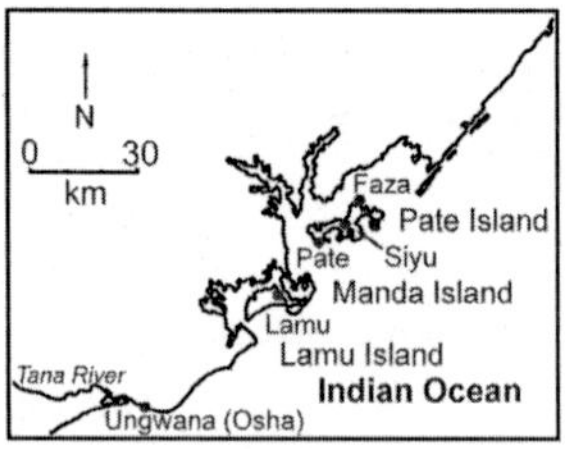

The Lamu Archipelago

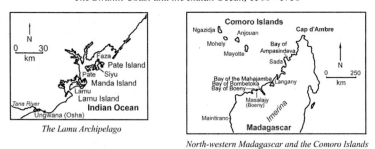

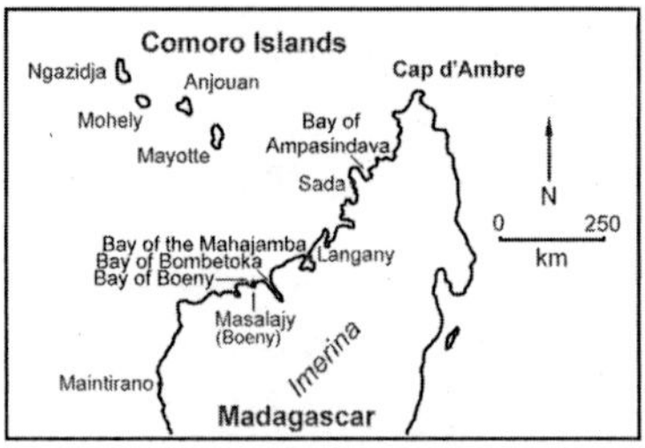

North-western Madagascar and the Comoro Islands

Map 4.1: The Swahili Coast and the Indian Ocean, 1500-1750

for other regions, particularly western Africa.[19] For instance, Ibn Battuta reported the existence of slaves in Kilwa in 1331, but not their trade.[20] Thus before the sixteenth century most of the slaves shipped by merchants to southern Arabia probably came from the Horn of Africa. A recent study based on the exceptional Rasulid administrative documentation has shown that the port town of Zayla, in present day Somaliland, was the coastal terminus of major slave routes from the Ethiopian highland. Slaves, including eunuchs, were then shipped to Aden on small ships. This maritime route between Zayla and Aden flourished between the thirteenth and the fifteenth centuries. Conversely the Rasulid documentation tells very few about Zanj slaves.[21]

Between the tenth and fifteenth centuries the presence of African slaves is documented in Arabia and the Persian Gulf, as well as in China and India in smaller numbers, although it is difficult to determine their origins, due to the ambiguity of the word Zanj.[22] Most of them seem to have come from the Horn of Africa or Nubia.[23] Thus, by the end of the fifteenth century the slave trade was already an established practice on the Swahili coast, probably continuous for around five centuries, but in relatively small proportions in comparison with other commodities or other parts of Africa.

THE SWAHILI SLAVE TRADE FROM MADAGASCAR TO ARABIA IN THE SIXTEENTH AND SEVENTEENTH CENTURIES

Portuguese accounts are our main sources for the sixteenth and seventeenth century period; yet they do not mention much about the slave trade since Portuguese merchants were not as involved in the trade in slaves as they were in other commodities like gold and ivory. This relative lack of evidence about the slave trade, and the fact that what trade did exist was centered on the Comoro Islands and Madagascar, has probably resulted in the underestimation of the Swahili slave trade during that era. Nevertheless, slave trading was noteworthy during the sixteenth and seventeenth centuries, mainly due to a steady demand for slaves in Arabia and the Persian Gulf. These slaves were Islamized and assigned various roles, such as servants, soldiers, guards, craftsmen, sailors, dock workers, or pearl divers in the Persian Gulf as well as concubines who seem to have been widespread.[24] Slaves were also employed for agricultural tasks, notably in the palm groves and in the maintenance of the irrigation systems. Before the expansion of Omani agriculture in the late seventeenth century, however, agricultural slavery seems to have been relatively limited.[25] Some Portuguese authors report that captives imported in Arabia, whether males or females, often children or adolescents, were trained in their masters' homes.[26] Emancipation was considered an act of piety, and slaves could also be redeemed, which explains the need for a continuous flow of slaves.[27] Important Swahili and Arab trade networks based in Malagasy as well as the Horn of Africa supplied these slaves.

The northwestern shore of Madagascar from Maintirano to the Cap d'Ambre was sporadically settled by Muslims population known by the Malagasy name "Antalaotra." The Antalaotra inhabited a few port towns, mostly situated in the region from the Bay of Boeny to the Bay of Ampasindava. Although the composition of this community was vague, it seems to have been influenced by Swahili civilization, sharing an adherence to Islam, the Swahili language, some Shirazi traditions, and a similar material culture. The trading ports of this mercantile society appeared around the eleventh century, expanded from the end of the fourteenth century and increased in the fifteenth century.[28] In the early sixteenth century the main Antalaotra town was Langany, located in the Bay of the Mahajamba, probably founded in the fifteenth century.[29] Around the 1580s Langany was supplanted by Boeny, another port city, founded at this time and located on the island of Antsoheribory in the Bay of Boeny. This town was often referred to as "Mazalagem Nova" by the Portuguese, or "New Masselage" by the English (from the Antalaotra name Masalajy), as opposed to Langany, which the Europeans began to call "Mazalagem Velha" or "Old Masselage."[30] Boeny was prosperous during the seventeenth century and attracted most of the maritime trade in the area. The Jesuit friar Luís Mariano, who had traveled several times to the town between 1613 and 1620, described it as a Muslim city with an estimated population of 6,000 to 7,000, which engaged in trade with Swahili and Arab ships. Townsmen spoke both the "*Buque*" language (that is Malagasy) and the tongue of "the Malindi coast," the Swahili language. [31] Other sources corroborate these details. The smaller Antalaotra port towns also engaged in the coastal trade, in particular Sada (Anorotsangana) and the region of the Bay of Ampasindava in the north.[32]

It seems that the prosperity of these towns was largely based on the slave trade. Some kingdoms situated in central Madagascar continuously waged war on each other. Capturing slaves was certainly one of the main purposes of these conflicts, because the numerous war prisoners were intended for sale to the "Moors" of Langany or Boeny.[33] Moreover, the aim of these sorties was "to capture rather than kill."[34] Most of the slaves seem to have been driven to the shore by inhabitants from the interior and the highlands named "Hova,"[35] who were certainly settled in the region later called Imerina.[36] An account dated 1640 states that every year the Hova came down the river Mahavavy, south of the Bay of Boeny, forming "caravans" of 10,000 head of cattle and 2,000–3,000 captives to be sold in Boeny.[37] The Antalaotra monopolized the trade with the island inhabitants like the Swahili did with the African mainland.[38] Thus, the intense slave trade in northwestern Madagascar in this period can be explained by this continuous supply of slaves from the center of the island. According to Philippe Beaujard fortified villages appeared in the highlands around the fifteenth century and the development of humid rice cultivation may have sustained a demographic growth and indirectly the slave trade.[39] Although this traffic may have originally been linked to a troubled political situation, it is beyond doubt that this trade was supported by conflicts that became razzias, if not actual enslaving wars, to supply the slave market controlled by the Antalaotra. They then sold the captives to Swahili and Arab traders in the port towns of Langany, and later Boeny, and sometimes in the region of Sada.[40]

The Comoro archipelago, particularly the islands of Anjouan and Mohely, was the second area frequented by Swahili or Arab slave traders because it acted as a platform for redistributing northwestern Madagascar slaves. That trade was one of the principal incomes of the archipelago, which enjoyed trading prosperity in the sixteenth and seventeenth centuries and stood apart from Portuguese claims.[41] As early as 1521 there are references that Comorian traders bought slaves in Madagascar, along with rice, meat and cattle, and then sold them to the ships reaching the archipelago.[42] It even seems, if we accept the claims of Turkish author Piri Reis, that slaves were not only stocked but also encouraged to breed before their export.[43] This raises the issue of whether slaves owned by Swahili or Comorian masters could be sold after they had spent some time as domestic or field slaves during which time they had undergone some acculturation. This problem, more broadly linked to the general issue of African slavery, needs further research.[44]

The Arab traders visiting Madagascar and the Comoro Islands during the sixteenth and seventeenth centuries mainly came from the Red Sea and the South Arabian coast. Yet most of the slave purchasers were Swahili from cities of the "Malindi coast," that is from Mombasa to Mogadishu. This trade is mentioned as early as 1506, and some seventeenth century sources specify that they went to Madagascar each year.[45] Other goods were bought by the Swahili traders in the northwestern part of the island: chiefly rice, cattle and meat, which were plentiful; however, the modes of transaction between the Swahili and the Antalaotra are not well known.

Slaves and other commodities might have been bartered for Indian cloth and metals.[46] There was also a permanent trade in agricultural goods or slaves between the Comoros and the Swahili coast.[47]

Among the Swahili merchants, traders from the Lamu archipelago apparently dominated the Malagasy slave traffic to the East African coast. The trade of the city of Pate with Madagascar is mentioned for the first time in 1589,[48] followed by more frequent references during the seventeenth century. Pate Island and the towns of Lamu and Faza are also cited.[49] Furthermore, when Dom Jerónimo Chingulia, the rebellious king of Mombasa, took refuge in Boeny in 1635, he was defended by numerous Swahili from Pate, Lamu, and Siyu.[50] More broadly, the accounts about Chingulia between 1633 and 1637 are explicit on the networks between Pate, northwestern Madagascar, the Comoros, and the Hadramawt, mostly operated by the political elites of the Swahili city-state.[51] According to Mariano in 1616 and 1619, and Buckeridge in 1663, Pate ships sailed almost every year to Boeny to load slaves.[52] According to Buckeridge, an estimated 2,000 slaves were shipped each year from Boeny and Sada by Pate island merchants, but a Portuguese report dated 1663 (cited by Axelson) gives a higher estimate of around 3,000–4,000.[53] Very likely traders from the Lamu archipelago formed a powerful and active community in Boeny. We do not know if they resided in large numbers in the town outside the winter period, but we know that they were an influential element in town politics. In 1619 they were blamed by the Portuguese for the troubles that arose between the Jesuit missionaries and the Antalaotra leaders.[54] Lamu merchants were also much involved in the Comoro Islands slave trade. In 1620 the French trader Beaulieu met two ships off Ngazidja (la Grande Comore) coming from Mayotte and heading for Lamu, their port of registry: they were loaded with a great quantity of rice, smoked meat, and "many slaves."[55]

The connections between Madagascar, the Comoros, and the Swahili coast, particularly the Lamu archipelago, may be explained by the trading networks established by Hadrami and Yemeni lineages during the sixteenth and seventeenth centuries. Probably from 1520–1540, many clans of sharifs and shaikhs, originating from Mogadishu, Barawa, Yemen, and most of all, from Hadramawt, settled on the East African coast. Renowned for their piety, they had great charisma. Often their first port of call was Pate where they founded lineages, as they did in Lamu and other towns in the region. During the seventeenth century most of these groups also settled on the rest of the coast from the Lamu archipelago, notably in the Comoros, especially the islands of Anjouan, Moheli, and Ngazidja, where they sometimes ruled small sultanates. These clans took part in the sea traffic and trade as far away as Indonesia. According to B. G. Martin and Randall Pouwels, from the sixteenth century on, they created complex trade networks that were run by lineages settled in various places on the coast where they played prominent roles in local politics.[56]

We can surmise that these networks were partly based on the Malagasy slave trade. Considering their experience in the slave trade with the Horn before 1500, as evidenced by Eric Vallet, Yemeni and Hadrami merchants probably reoriented part of their traffic towards the Swahili coast and Madagascar around that date. This hypothesis could explain the vitality of the trading connections between the Lamu archipelago, the Comoros, and Madagascar as shown by much of the evidence. This does not mean that the Hadrami and Yemeni migrants had been responsible for establishing the slave trade from Madagascar, for the Antalaotra port cities, which had Shirazi foundation myths like the Swahili coastal cities, had already been in existence since the end of the fourteenth century and sometimes earlier.[57] It thus appears that the Malagasy slave trade existed before the sixteenth century.[58]

Besides the Arabic and Swahili chronicles cited by Martin and Pouwels, the Portuguese sources attest to close trading links between the Swahili coast, the South Arabian peninsula, the Red Sea, Madagascar, and the Comoros. As early as 1570 Monclaro mentions the dense traffic between Pate and the Red Sea.[59] In the early seventeenth century Diogo do Couto clearly corroborates these connections. According to him, the island of Ngazidja was divided into twenty kingdoms, ruled by "Arab Moors" (*Mouros Arabios*—some perhaps were lineages of Hadrami and Yemeni origin) who had reached the "coast of Malindi" before settling on the island. Each year traders from "Mecca" (the Red Sea) came to the island to obtain slaves and various products.[60] As mentioned before, the Arab merchants going to the Comoro Islands mostly came from southern Arabia, and slaves were principally exported to that area, mainly to Mocha, Aden, al-Shihr, and Kishn.[61] For instance, a 1611 English account states that four small ships sailed each year to Mocha from the "coast of Swahell" loaded with slaves (purchased in Madagascar), ivory, and ambergris.[62] These port towns were the principal Arabian commercial centers linked to the East African coast before the advent of Oman as a naval power in the late seventeenth century. One of their functions was to re-export to the Red Sea and Egypt the products of the western Indian Ocean trade, like Indian cloth, and also slaves, as implied by some of the evidence: Piri Reis explicitly mentions Yemen and Jidah as importing Comoro slaves.[63] Merchants from Mogadishu, Barawa, Malindi, Mombasa, the Lamu archipelago, and of course the Comoros, traded in Madagascar, some of them certainly descended from the Hadrami and Yemeni lineages settled in those regions.

Two documents confirm this hypothesis more firmly. According to Barreto in 1667, the traders from "Mecca," Barawa, and Mogadishu who visited the port cities of Madagascar to buy slaves were "*cacizes*."[64] In Portuguese texts, this expression, transcribed from the Arabic *qasis* (priest), or its Swahili equivalent *kasisi*, usually refers to a Muslim religious figure, possibly a sharif or other person believed to have religious charisma. A statement by São Domingos in 1630 is even more explicit: "To this island of Pate come ships, on their way from Mecca to the island of Saint Laurence [Madagascar] with sharifs, who are their *cassizes* [*qasis*], and who spread their sect there, and take back many *Buques* [*Buki* —Malagasy], pagan children, to bring them to Mecca."[65] This extract sheds light on the connections between the Red Sea, the Lamu archipelago towns, and Madagascar or the Comoros. These trading networks appear to be partially run by sharifian groups, settled from the south of the Arabian Peninsula to the slave exporting lands. Even if evidence fails to identify the specific lineages that settled in Madagascar, there is no doubt that Swahili and Arab migrants settled there in the sixteenth and seventeenth centuries, attracted by trading opportunities.[66] Moreover, in the early eighteenth century, after the Sakalava conquest of northwestern Madagascar, links remained strong between the region and the Lamu archipelago. An Antalaotra tradition maintains that an Islamized Sakalava princess married an "Arab" from Pate.[67]

Chronicles and oral traditions dealing with the prestigious Hadrami and Yemeni clans that settled on the Swahili coast during this period date back to the late nineteenth and twentieth centuries. All insist on their fame and religious proselytism, their role as political mediators, or their decisive help to the Swahili against the Portuguese and the Oromo.[68] Trade, particularly the slave trade, was probably their main goal in settling in eastern Africa, but it is not surprising that such traffic would not be mentioned in traditions or written accounts from the late nineteenth century.

We do not have detailed information on the way the Swahili sold the slaves to the Arab merchants. Possibly the latter did not make the long journey to Madagascar and the Comoros, but rather obtained slaves in the Swahili port cities where they also purchased other products, chiefly ivory. The slave trade is rarely mentioned by the Portuguese in the sixteenth century, maybe because it was much less than it would become in the next century. Indeed, the Portuguese did not have a great interest in the slave trade. Before the end of the sixteenth century there are few accounts of the Swahili coast trade in the archives. These accounts deal mostly with the regions of Kilwa, Mozambique, and Sofala where the slave trade made up a minor part of the sixteenth-century trade. Yet we know that the two Ottoman expeditions, which sailed as far as Mombasa, visiting several ports along the way in 1585–1586 and 1588–1589, obtained slaves from the Swahili.[69] In the seventeenth century the Lamu archipelago dominated the Swahili slave trade from Madagascar and the Comoros; it appears to have been the main port of call for coastal slave traders, probably since the end of the preceding century. An estimated 2,000–3,000 slaves were said to be exported annually to the island of Pate, so the scale of the traffic was quite considerable. While sojourning in Pate in 1606, Gaspar de São Bernardino was told that "Arab Moors" had reached the city to purchase young slaves, and Nicolau de Orta Rebelo, who accompanied him, mentions in his own account that the ship that took them from Pate to Hormuz was loaded with many slaves.[70] In addition to the Portuguese evidence and Buckeridge's account, an English source dated 1645 states that slaves were cheap in Pate and Barawa.[71]

The preeminence of the Lamu archipelago as a redistribution port of Malagasy slaves can be explained by existing trading networks with Madagascar and the Comoro Islands, as well as its outlying position from Portuguese headquarters on the Swahili coast. From the early 1590s Mombasa was under the control of the Portuguese who often visited and patrolled the region located between the town and Mozambique until the late seventeenth century.[72] Arab ships certainly reached the outlying parts of the Lamu archipelago, because ships had to pay taxes in Mombasa, unlike Pate island (before the building of a custom house in Pate in 1633).[73] Lisbon complained that trading ships often frequented this region, which grew rich to the detriment of Mombasa.[74] Likewise Arab ships generally avoided Mombasa because of trade restrictions instigated by the Portuguese. Finally, the Portuguese probably opposed the selling of slaves by the Swahili to the Arabs, because of their systematic Islamization, which was denounced by many authors. Thus, as noted by Buckeridge, slaves were abundant and cheap on the whole coast, except in the places where the Portuguese prevailed.[75] As in the Comoros, the slave trade on Pate Island benefited from the reduced presence of the Portuguese who had been definitively expelled from the region in 1660.[76] Eventually all the factors favorable to the slave trade were linked: the Hadrami and Yemeni lineages settled in those areas where the Portuguese were not very influential, mainly the Lamu archipelago and the Comoros. We must add that other towns, principally Malindi and Mombasa, welcomed Arab slave traders in the beginning of the sixteenth century, followed by Barawa and Mogadishu in the seventeenth century. Probably Swahili and Comorian traders also went to Arabia or the Persian Gulf to sell slaves.[77] Bigger Swahili ships were able to sail to Arabia, and it seems very likely that, from time to time, the richest Swahili kings and traders sent their own ships to the western coast of India.[78]

It is difficult to estimate the scale of the Swahili slave trade between Madagascar and the regions of Mombasa and the Lamu archipelago. Because sources are so few for the sixteenth century, we may very likely underestimate the importance of slave traffic during that time. Yet it seems that the slave trade grew during the seventeenth century, for which we have more documentation. Portuguese sources comment more frequently on the slave trade by the Muslims. The growth of this trade was perhaps linked to the population growth of the towns in the Lamu archipelago in the seventeenth century, particularly Pate.[79] Various accounts support claims that merchants from the Red Sea, Barawa, and Mogadishu exported an estimated 3,000 slaves a year in the mid-seventeenth century from Madagascar.[80]

Slave export estimates are derived from accounts of the Malagasy highland trade, Barreto's account, the trade by ships from Pate Island, and Portuguese accounts of trade with Mombasa, Malindi, Barawa, Mogadishu and other Swahili coastal towns. Armstrong proposes a rough estimation ranging from 40,000 to more than 150,000 slaves exported from Boeny during the seventeenth century, which takes into account the whole non-European slave trade (Swahili, Comorian, and Arab).[81] In such a context, we suggest that the estimate for the Swahili trade may have been 2,000 to 3,000 slaves per year direct from Madagascar (in peak times), excluding the trade with the Comoros or by Comorians. Furthermore, such figures are credible when considering the loading capacity of East African ships or ships built elsewhere but used by Swahili merchants. For example, in 1506 two ships belonging to leading inhabitants of Kilwa were inspected by the Portuguese, each capable of transporting 180 slaves.[82] Likewise in 1616 a great Pate merchant, calling at Anjouan en route for Madagascar, took on board his ship 250 to 300 shipwrecked Portuguese.[83] An English document dated 1646 states that an Anjouan ship landed on the island with 500 slaves from Boeny, but this figure may be an overestimation.[84] Finally, some Swahili ships were big enough to be able to sail to Arabia, as mentioned above.

Prior to the eighteenth-century, slave traders (Portuguese, Swahili, Comorian, and Arab) also obtained slaves from the East African mainland. The Portuguese obtained slaves from the Kerimba Islands and the mainland populations of Mozambique, particularly the Makua, starting in the late sixteenth century. Besides the Malagasy slave supply networks,

Swahili traders also obtained slaves from the coastal interior. It is likely that Swahili from the north of this region also bought slaves, as stated by Santos.[85] When considered together, however, available sources show that the traffic in slaves was far below the scale of the slave trade in the eighteenth century. Previously, trade in ivory surpassed any other trade in the area.[86]

On the rest of the Swahili coast north of Cape Delgado, the slave trade with mainland communities was small, if it existed at all. This situation continued until the nineteenth century, except for the Kilwa region. So far no sources deal with the Swahili coast trade between 1500 and 1800, apart from some evidence of rare and minor exceptions like Katwa, a population of Somali origin that settled in the area between the Lamu archipelago and Barawa in the seventeenth century. According to Santos they specialized in captive women and eunuchs. In 1624 Lobo learned that slaves were sold in the Juba River area, in particular Katwa.[87] The Portuguese also owned Katwa slaves.[88] It is also possible that Oromo women from this region were purchased as concubines, and this continued into the nineteenth century.[89] This trade in very specific and expensive slaves remained secondary. As evidenced by numerous Portuguese documents, ivory, agricultural products, and other commodities were the main trades with groups in the hinterland.

In these areas Swahili traders never instigated war or razzia on the surrounding populations for the purpose of getting captives for sale. Swahili society was principally mercantile and not warlike. Merchants obtained slaves from other Swahili communities in Madagascar or the Comoros or from the mainland populations themselves in the Cape Delgado or Juba River areas. The Swahili city-states often appear as weak military powers, frequently attacked by their mainland neighbors, or else dependent on military forces recruited among the mainland people for their defense.[90] Examples of this abound. In any case, it would have been unwise for the Swahili to raid communities on the coastal mainland with whom they had close clientage ties, based on essential trade, political, and military alliances and payment of tributes.[91] These clientship relations sometimes resulted in the Swahili imposing tribute payments in slaves. According to the traditions of the Pokomo, a Bantu-speaking people residing on the banks of the Tana River south of Lamu, sometime before the nineteenth century Swahili from the Lamu archipelago had imposed on Pokomo villages under their authority a tribute of two boys and two girls from each big village and one of each for small settlements.[92] The presence of Pokomo smiths of slave origin in Siyu seems to confirm this.[93] Slave labor of this sort, however, cannot be compared to the Malagasy slave trade, although it amounted to an oppressive clientship, forming part of the complex relations of dependence. Such tribute arrangements were limited and very rare. Later, traditions assert that this tribute was replaced by payments in bags of rice.[94]

Unlike the southern Swahili coast in the eighteenth century, slave trade networks between the deep interior and the coast to the north of Kilwa did not develop during this era. We can surmise that conditions of the mainland trade routes, the political situation, and demographic dynamics of the area did not favor such a traffic, contrary to the situation in Madagascar, and later, the Mozambique and Kilwa regions. The demand for slaves was not sufficiently attractive to interest other areas of slave purchasing, for the Malagasy supply was large enough to meet existing demand.

PORTUGUESE AND INDIAN DEMAND

We turn from our discussion of the Arab slave demand to evaluate Portuguese involvement in the slave trade.[95] Apart from the Mozambique region, the Portuguese obtained many slaves in Sofala and its hinterland, whom they employed in their settlements in the area.[96] Between the end of the sixteenth century and the beginning of the seventeenth century a large number of slaves also came from the trade between Mozambique and the port cities of northwestern Madagascar, and sometimes from the Comoros.[97] This traffic was much smaller than the one run by the Swahili and the Arabs to supply the Muslim market, because the Portuguese presence on the shores of Madagascar was not as extensive or as regular.[98] The Portuguese also obtained slaves from the Swahili north of Kilwa. Most of the slaves were destined for Goa or other Portuguese settlements, where they were employed by the Portuguese administration as soldiers or sailors or sold as servants.[99] For instance between September 1623 and August 1626, 39 Africans were baptized by Augustinian priests in the Portuguese settlement of Muscat: three are described as Katwa, four as Malagasy, the remaining are only mentioned as "Cafres."[100] Zanzibar appears to have been one of the main areas of slave purchasing for the Mombasa Portuguese, a trade run by settlers established in Zanzibar and its Swahili inhabitants. It is possible that the slaves were born on the island as they were numerous according to Monclaro.[101]

It is difficult to estimate the scale of the Portuguese slave trade from the Swahili coast. Demand from India was small, probably around a few hundred slaves a year, as labor was abundant and cheap in India.[102] Furthermore, it is highly improbable, for religious reasons, that the Portuguese would have been involved in the slave trade with Arabia. Nevertheless, they doubtless obtained captives on the Swahili coast itself for local use as servants, manpower for the administration, and perhaps agricultural labor. The Portuguese living in Mombasa around 1630 owned many slaves, Malagasy, Katwa or imported from the Zambezi area.[103] Bocarro mentions that the Portuguese introduced slaves to Pemba for cultivation, as perhaps attested by an anonymous Pemba chronicle discovered at the beginning of the twentieth century.[104] The slave trade between the Portuguese and the Swahili or the Antalaotra certainly contributed to the increase of the East African slave trade, as suggested by Pearson.[105] But it was only a modest addition to the slave trade for Arabia, perhaps amounting to between a few hundred to one thousand slaves (at the maximum) per year intended for India or the Portuguese settlements in the Persian Gulf or on the coast. Moreover, the involvement of the Swahili in this trade was probably limited, since the Portuguese also obtained captives from non-Swahili populations on the mainland. The Portuguese maintained a monopoly on the Swahili coast trade; English and Dutch slave traders were confined to Madagascar.[106]

Indian merchants, both Muslim and Hindu (*Vania*), went each year to the Swahili coast where it is likely that they bought slaves from the Swahili. We know that African slaves were present in India, but the absence of evidence suggests that this traffic was very rare. A solitary account refers to the slave trade before the eighteenth century: in 1518 a ship from the Gujarat region, coming from Malindi and heading for Cambay, had slaves on board, although most of the freight was ivory and metals.[107] Much later, in 1777 the French slave trader Morice says that Surat merchants were involved in the Zanzibar slave trade, but those slaves may have been destined for the Persian Gulf where Indian traders were numerous.[108] African slaves were present on the western shore of India, outside the Portuguese settlements, but they were not numerous and most likely were exported from Arabia or the Persian Gulf and were born in the Horn.[109] Thus, it seems almost certain that no direct significant slave trade existed between the East African coast and India from the sixteenth century to the end of the eighteenth century.

THE ISSUE OF SLAVERY AND SLAVE IMPORTATION INTO SWAHILI SOCIETY

Probably the Swahili purchased slaves from Madagascar or the Cape Delgado and Juba areas for their own needs. Despite the fact that none of the scholars working on the Swahili coast has examined that matter, most of them suggest that there were small numbers of slaves in Swahili society before the nineteenth century.[110] Both the slave trade and the status of slavery in Swahili society before that time requires further exploration, particularly the modes of dependency and servitude in Swahili culture, and their importance in the socioeconomic organization of the city-states.[111] In this study we suggest that imported slaves, as distinct from clients from the hinterland, were also employed by the Swahili, which does not mean that their status in Swahili society was totally different from the status of mainland clients. The information in the Portuguese sources makes it difficult to distinguish between "slaves," who might actually be freeborn clients, from slaves who are kinless "absolute outsiders," that is captives from raided societies.[112] This problem stems from the fluidity and ambiguity of the status of dependent people in Swahili society: slaves were considered more like personal clients and much less like chattels.[113] Thus, for the nineteenth century, the distinction between slaves and other subordinates is difficult to perceive.[114] The terms for various kinds of subjection in the Portuguese sources include words like *negros*, *cafres* (from the Arabic *kafir*: infidel, pagan) and *escravos* (slaves), all of which often refer to clients as well as slaves.[115] Other expressions are less explicit, most of all *vassalos* (vassals), or *vassalos da terra firme* (vassals of the mainland), which designate mainland populations tied to a city on a clientship basis.[116]

Nevertheless, some sources are less ambiguous. Although generally it is not easy to distinguish the origin and the status of the individuals employed by Swahili patrons, some of them were probably slaves imported from Madagascar or the Cape Delgado region. Dependents and slaves were used in very diverse ways on the East African coast. They served as laborers in some Swahili towns. Some servants in elite households probably came from slave origins.[117] A 1773 Dutch account mentions, for instance, that the citizens of Anjouan "do not work, but have everything done for them by their slaves," in the houses as well as in the fields.[118] Slaves might also serve as bodyguards, sailors, craft workers, and sailors.[119] Among the Pokomo in Siyu some blacksmiths were slaves. The use of women slaves as concubines was certainly widespread. For example the mother of one of the sons of the king of Malindi in 1528 was a slave of "*Cafre*" origins.[120]

The majority of clients were almost certainly employed in agriculture,[121] but imported slaves were also employed. In particular a servile population occupied the islands of Pemba and Zanzibar. Perhaps this might be explained by the fact that the Swahili communities of those islands lacked contact with the mainland populations, so they had fewer mainland clients than the other city-states. Furthermore, the two islands were very fertile, particularly Pemba, which specialized in rice cultivation, and they traded agricultural products to Mombasa and other Swahili coast towns.[122] According to Bocarro, who wrote around 1634, the Pemba Swahili, like the Portuguese, had introduced "*Cafres*" to the island for cultivation.[123] The anonymous Pemba chronicle supports these remarks. In a rather confusing account, it states that some Portuguese, Shirazi, and Nabahani had settled on the island in the early seventeenth century. Each group came with numerous slaves who were settled on the agricultural lands of the island. It should be noted that these slaves were inherited along with other properties, which clearly indicates that they were actual slaves, not assistants or helpers.[124] We could perhaps see this chronicle as an account of the introduction of a kind of slave mode of production on the island; however, this account should be used with caution, for it might have been linked to specific nineteenth-century claims.[125] Kent assumes that the Swahili demand for Malagasy slaves might have been associated with their wish to develop rice-growing on the coast in order to be independent from the importation of Malagasy rice.[126] While we lack sources to support this hypothesis, it seems credible in light of Portuguese documentation. Apparently there was widespread use of slaves in the Comoros for domestic service and agricultural labor, which was certainly a consequence of the role played by the archipelago in the Malagasy slave trade. Two accounts, dated 1671 and 1673 respectively, mention the presence of slaves working on plantations of coconut trees and other fruit trees.[127] Further, among the rare documents dealing with the use of slaves on the Swahili coast, two letters written in 1598 by the king and the "Prince" of Pate are quite explicit, stating that the town inhabitants refused categorically and fiercely to accept the presence of Portuguese priests in the city for fear that the priests would convert the "slaves" to Christianity. At this time missionaries did indeed purchase slaves and then emancipated them. According to Pate officials, slaves were meant to help the inhabitants in cultivation and were thus essential to their prosperity.[128] Such slaves were certainly not mainland clients, as these latter would have been Islamized and so would not have been bought by the Portuguese priests. A Portuguese report states that in 1728 the islands of Mombasa, Pemba, and Zanzibar were inhabited by Muslims and pagan "captives" who had been bartered for cloth.[129] Later in the 1770s French and English accounts show that there were both free and slave peasants in the towns of Kilwa and Anjouan. In particular, Morice explains that on the island of Kilwa agriculture was done by "Moors" and "slaves," whereas the mainland was cultivated by "Moors" and "free Africans."[130] Thus, the existence of mainland clients of free status, working side by side with Swahili patrons, did not exclude the presence of slaves brought into the coastal towns by the slave trade. To meet the need for laborers in agriculture or domestic service, the Swahili may have diverted for their own use slaves originally meant for the Arabian trade. Very likely, part of the 2,000 to 3,000 Malagasy slaves, who yearly passed through Pate island during the second half of the seventeenth century, were absorbed by local demand. At this time Pate town underwent a great expansion and became the principal trading and political power on the Swahili coast after Mombasa.[131]

According to Pouwels, chattel slavery, as opposed to dependency based on client relationships, seems to have been introduced on the Swahili coast by foreigners: mainly Portuguese, Mazrui, and Nabahani, and this appears to be confirmed by the Pemba chronicle cited above.[132] Although the evidence for this is not conclusive, it is tempting to see a link between these newcomers in eastern Africa and the obvious (or accelerated) expansion of the slave trade and slavery in Pemba, Zanzibar, and the Lamu archipelago from the end of the sixteenth century. Nevertheless, it is extremely difficult to evaluate the proportion of imported slaves in Swahili society before the nineteenth century, and consequently, hard to suggest an estimation of the scale of the slave trade conducted in the Swahili towns. Yet it is clear that slave exports to these towns represented only a small part of the slave trade; most of it was intended for Arabia. There were abundant mainland clients who offered themselves for labor service to the Swahili.[133] Further study of East African coastal slavery prior to the nineteenth century will surely expand our knowledge on this subject.

OMANI INFLUENCE FROM THE LATE SEVENTEENTH CENTURY TO THE 1750s

During the second half of the seventeenth century Oman became a crucial trading partner on the East African coast, notably in the slave trade. Omani slave demand arose from Omani needs as well as demands from the Muscat trade. In 1650 the Portuguese were expelled from the town. Following this, in just a few decades Oman became one of the main maritime and mercantile powers in the Persian Gulf and the western Indian Ocean. Moreover, the sovereigns of Oman, called imams, took a larger part in the maritime trade and the economic development of the country.[134] Omani agriculture was mainly based on date palm plantations, a complex irrigation system, and slave labor. It underwent a remarkable expansion through the efforts of Imam Saif bin Sultan (1692–1711).[135] Chronicles record that he greatly developed agriculture. He owned one-third of Oman's plantations, ordered the planting of around 30,000 date palms and 6,000 coconut trees and renovated a great part of the irrigation system. Its complexity and extent, as well as the size of the plantations, required the importation of a large force of servile manpower. Saif is said to have owned 700 male slaves, according to one report, and 1700 slaves of both sexes according to another.[136] Furthermore, according to Barendse, from the 1660s the cultivation of sugar cane may have expanded in Oman. Based mostly on slave labor, the export of sugar from Muscat to the Persian Gulf might have boomed.[137] As elsewhere in Arabia, there were numerous uses for slaves as concubines, servants, sailors, or pearl divers after the conquest of the region by Saif bin Sultan.[138] Military slaves of African origin belonging to the monarchs were also numerous.[139] Sheriff estimates that imports may have amounted from 500 to 1,000 slaves per year in the eighteenth century.[140] It seems clear that local demand increased substantially by the end of the seventeenth century.

At this time Muscat became an entrepôt for the whole Persian Gulf, being ideally located for the merchandise of India and East Africa. We can assume that the town became an important center for the redistribution of East African slaves for the Persian Gulf, and that Omani traders provided themselves with slaves from the Swahili trading ports. From the 1660s onward Omani merchants visited the East African coast perhaps every year. Contacts were mainly with the Lamu archipelago, independent from the Portuguese since 1660. Pate, in particular, had very close political and economic links with Oman. Ivory and slaves were certainly the main trading products. At this time Pate was largely involved in the Malagasy slave trade.[141] For all these reasons, it is highly probable that the trading connections between Pate and Muscat were partly aimed to supply Omani demand for slaves.

During the early 1690s Oman imposed its sovereignty over the island of Pate. Hamilton, who had traveled to Oman, stated that in the 1720s the Pate trade in ivory and slaves was exclusively intended for Muscat. He observed that the purpose of the Omani conquest of the city-state around 1692 was to appropriate these two trades.[142] After the siege of Fort Jesus, the Portuguese base in Mombasa, from 1696 to 1698, the Portuguese were expelled from the Swahili coast north of Cape Delgado. Thereafter, Oman dominated the Swahili shore and put garrisons and factories in Kilwa, Zanzibar, Pemba, Mombasa, and Pate. At first Omani armed intervention in Mombasa was a military and trading alliance between the Omani faction in the town and some of the Mijikenda communities inhabiting the mainland to control the ivory trade.[143] Despite this, we can suppose that the control of the slave trade was an additional motivation for the Omani conquest, as Risso suggests.[144] Because of the expulsion of the Portuguese, documentary accounts are scarce, and thus it becomes difficult to get a clear understanding of the trade structures on the East African coast between 1698 and 1750. Clearly, the Omani dominated this maritime trade, with slaves comprising the second most important exported commodity, after ivory.

During the first half of the eighteenth century, northwestern Madagascar was still a slave exporting area, but this traffic decreased to the advantage of the Cape Delgado region and Kilwa. At the end of the seventeenth century, probably around 1685, the Bay of Boeny area was subjugated by Sakalava conquerors coming from the south of the island. The Antalaotra kept trading, but they were henceforth under the power of the Sakalava monarchs. During the first decades of the eighteenth century the trading port of Boeny (Masalajy) was progressively challenged by the Bay of Bombetoka, but the slave trade continued in both areas.[145] According to Dutch accounts dated 1694 and 1696, "Arab" traders bought numerous slaves in Boeny.[146] Moreover, according to an account in a 1708 French travel journal, Muscat merchants seem to have been the main slave purchasers in Antalaotra ports of trade.[147] Until the mid-eighteenth century the slave trade remained active in northwestern Madagascar, run by Swahili, Omani, European, and sometimes Sakalava traders.[148] Yet the Malagasy slave traffic to the East African coast appears to have diminished markedly during the eighteenth century, perhaps because military conflicts on the island decreased.[149] Thus, the slave trade between the Comoros and Madagascar continued on a small scale in the 1770s, but in the meantime the Comoro Islands ceased to be an important slave trading center. Although the Omani still visited the Bay of Bombetoka, they purchased very few slaves.[150] By the end of the century slaves were even imported from the East African coast by the Sakalava.[151]

Conversely, the slave trade on the coast from the Kerimba archipelago to Kilwa increased appreciably in the beginning of the eighteenth century. Afterwards it largely supplanted the Malagasy slave trade. Information gathered by Portuguese settlers in Mozambique and in the Cape Delgado islands shows that the Omani actively traded in the area, looking for ivory and slaves from the Swahili or the Yao who had developed important trading networks between the interior and the coast.[152] Ivory was the main commodity transported to the coast by the Yao, but we can reasonably assume that captives were also traded along these networks, which greatly expanded the scale of slave exports in the second half of the century. Between 1708 and 1711, the Omani were numerous north of Cape Delgado and sometimes in the Portuguese territory, where they traded with Kilwa.[153] There the Omani also obtained slaves from the Swahili. In 1698 the Omani accused the queen of Kilwa of helping Portuguese refugees and demanded that she deliver a hundred slaves to them. Later in 1711 she was charged with aiding the escape of slaves belonging to the Omani.[154]

On the northern coast, Hamilton stated that Pate also provided slaves to the Omani. Moreover, when the Portuguese succeeded in retaking Mombasa in 1728, they found "innumerable" slaves during the looting of the Omani ward. Several accounts record that about 500 Omani surrendered and that they had 1,000 male and female slaves in their service.[155] In 1729 the Portuguese were once again evicted from Mombasa. Until the 1770s no sources are available to assist in establishing an estimate of the slave trade on the Swahili coast, particularly in the main coastal slaving port of Kilwa; however, we know that Swahili traders were active north of the Kerimba Islands where they purchased slaves, ivory, and other products from the mainland populations or for the Portuguese and Luso-Africans inhabiting the area. These Swahili merchants came from Kilwa, Zanzibar, Mombasa, and Pate.[156] A 1754 report states that slave trading was their principal trade.[157] Although this traffic supplied slaves for the Omani living in East Africa and the Swahili themselves, its main purpose was certainly to supply the Muscat market, which had become the first outlet of the Swahili coast commodities of which slaves were prominent.[158]

While lack of sources makes it difficult to estimate the Swahili coastal slave trade in the first half of the eighteenth century, a few certainties emerge. We know that the Malagasy slave trade was important at the end of the seventeenth century and the beginning of the eighteenth century, but it was gradually supplanted by the increasing Swahili and Omani trade in Cape Delgado and Kilwa from 1698, mostly supplied by the Yao trading routes. By this time slaves were the second most important export from the coast, chiefly to Muscat. Thus, during the second half of the seventeenth century Oman established political domination over the Swahili city-states, which contributed to the reorientation of the slave trade networks. Probably these trade networks had been operated by lineages of Hadrami and Yemeni origins that had settled in the Swahili and Comorian towns and were largely oriented toward the Red Sea, but they began to be partially replaced by Omani with trading networks in Muscat. This trend increased in the last third of the eighteenth century, when Zanzibar, controlled by the Omani, centralized most of the slave trade. Swahili traders grew increasingly dependent on trade with Muscat. The Lamu archipelago, particularly Pate town, remained very active in the slave trade until the end of the eighteenth century, despite the drying up of the Comoros and Madagascar slave trade; Pate merchants often visited Kilwa and the Cape Delgado for slave trading.[159]

After 1689 the changing political and economic situations of the East African coast suggest that the slave trade decreased somewhat at the beginning of the eighteenth century. Omani domination did not always favor the trading interest of the Swahili who became increasingly dependent on the Muscat trade. Conflict frequently occurred between the Omani forces and some Swahili city-states from 1698 to 1727, sometimes degenerating into violent uprisings, particularly in Kilwa. The Swahili, once free from Portuguese suzerainty, resented the Omani occupying forces whom they accused of threatening their sovereignty and hindering freedom of trade. During the years 1700–1710 the Swahili also criticized the Omani for not sending enough merchant ships to the East African coast or for importing poor quality cloth, which prejudiced the Swahili trade.[160]

The coast trade with the Omani suffered severely from the 1720s to the end of the 1740s. This was partly due to internal affairs in Oman, for from 1719 to 1749 the sultanate was disrupted by several civil wars, which split the country into two rival factions in disputes about the succession of the imams. This had serious repercussions on the coast.[161] In the 1720s the Omani factions in the Swahili towns tore at one another, sometimes involving the Swahili in the struggles. The Mombasa Omani even attacked those settled in Zanzibar, and ships belonging to one faction were banned from the port towns controlled by the opposing faction or by local Swahili authorities.[162] This continued into the next decade. In 1734 Omani civil strife prevented ships from sailing to Mombasa, with the result that there was a shortage of cloth and other essential trade commodities for the Swahili towns. Again between 1739 and 1745 the Mombasa Omani did not receive reinforcements or textiles.[163]

CONCLUSION

This reevaluation of the Swahili slave trade has shown that it was already important before French and Omani demands for slaves stimulated its expansion in the second half of the eighteenth century. It seems that the traffic grew from the end of the sixteenth century and then declined a bit in the first half of the eighteenth century. This rise and decline occurred for several reasons. In the early sixteenth century the Portuguese began to take over the thriving gold and ivory trade of the southern Swahili coast in Sofala, Mozambique, and Kilwa. From the 1560s onward, they had established control over this area. Some Swahili merchants may have then turned to the slave trade to make up for the loss of this market. Another hypothesis is that the slave trade from the Horn of Africa, once important,[164] diminished in the second half of the sixteenth century, causing a rise in the Arab demand for slaves imported from the East African coast. As noted, slave trade networks existed between southern Ethiopia, where pagan populations were raided by Christians and Muslims alike, and the Red Sea.[165] Perhaps the Oromo invasion of the region in the mid- sixteenth century considerably disrupted these networks and cut off access. Recent research has rediscovered the networks of Muslim trading towns settled between the Red Sea and the Ethiopian highland, the vitality of their trade is now well evidenced. But we also know that these inland networks greatly declined after the mid-sixteenth century, as did Zayla.[166] The Yemeni and Hadrami may have then turned to the Swahili coast to obtain slaves, although it should be noted that the Horn slave trade continued during the following centuries.

Other factors contributed to the demand for servile labor. Portuguese settlements in Mozambique, Mombasa, and India demanded East African slaves for household service or agricultural manpower. In addition, the new prosperity of some Swahili city-states, mainly in the Lamu archipelago, required slaves to work as builders, sailors, and peasants or as status symbols of conspicuous consumption as concubines, servants, guards, and craftsmen. Moreover, agricultural development in Pemba and Zanzibar seems to have begun at this time and probably required a certain work force of peasants of servile origin – though limited in number and working alongside freeborn clients from the mainland. Recent Hadrami and Yemeni migrants settled on the coast may have sustained and strengthened slave traffic to Arabia for they had intimate knowledge of both the demand in Arabia and Red Sea towns as well as the supply networks in Madagascar, the Comoros, and the Lamu archipelago. They had also experience of slave trading from Zayla. Lastly, during the second half of the seventeenth century the trading and economic growth of Oman further stimulated an increase in the demand for slaves.

Because of the lack of sources, it is not possible to estimate the scale of the slave trade in the sixteenth century. Figures do exist in the seventeenth century historical documentation; however, these derive from scattered Portuguese and English sources that must be treated cautiously. A few scholars have offered estimates of the slave trade on the East African coast. Austen asserts that an average figure of 3100 slaves were yearly exported between 650 and 1920, but this covers such a large chronological period that his estimate seems questionable, more so because he does not cite his evidence. [167] Lovejoy makes the assumption that around 1,000 slaves were shipped each year to Arabia in the seventeenth century,[168] but this appraisal is not supported by the assessments given in contemporary documents. According to the estimation given for the Malagasy trade toward Boeny and the figures put forward by Buckeridge, Barreto, and the 1663 Portuguese account cited by Axelson, the Swahili slave trade from Madagascar amounted to between 2,000 and 3,000 slaves a year in the seventeenth century.[169] If we add to these figures the direct trade run by Arabs and Comorians in the Antalaotra port towns, we can suppose that the whole Malagasy slave trade amounted to around 2,000 to 5,000 slaves per year, not counting the European slave trade in the region. These estimates are corroborated by numerous sources of various origins, which very clearly show that slave trading was one of the main activities of the major port towns of northwestern Madagascar and the Comoros in the seventeenth century as well as between the Swahili coast and southern Arabia.

Thus, the scale of the global slave trade run by Swahili, Comorian, and Arab merchants, who provided themselves in Madagascar and the Cape Delgado and Juba areas, might have fluctuated between 3,000 to 6,000 slaves a year in the seventeenth century, which was - again - a peak period. However I favor a low estimate of around 3,000 to 4,000 because of the bias of the sources, particularly the Portuguese accounts.[170] About 4,000 slaves might be a possible figure for peak years only: it is impossible to be more precise.[171] This appraisal includes the slaves sold for local use in Arabia and the Persian Gulf, in the Swahili towns, and in the Portuguese settlements, but it excludes the slave trade directly run by the Portuguese with the Antalaotra or the non-Swahili populations of the mainland. Moreover, we cannot assess the proportion of slaves shipped from or to each area. The Arabian Peninsula and the Persian Gulf probably absorbed the majority of the captives, followed by the Swahili towns, and finally, the Portuguese settlements.

Even though these estimates must be considered as approximations, they are far below the transatlantic trade in the seventeenth century. Yet there is no doubt that the extent of this traffic had important socioeconomic consequences for East Africa. No doubt it exacerbated wars in Madagascar's interior. It is obvious that the slave trade took a very large part in the wealth of the Antalaotra port towns of northwestern Madagascar from the end of the sixteenth century. The slave trade, coupled with rice and cattle, stimulated urban growth in these towns in the fifteenth century through Swahili and Arab migration. The Comoro Islands may have experienced the same type of population growth at that time. Likewise, the rising prosperity of the Lamu archipelago merchants was mainly based on the ivory trade but also on the slave trade,[172] for its location offered opportunities for strategic connections with southern Arabia, Oman, and the mainland polities.[173] According to Pouwels, the Hadrami and Yemeni immigrants markedly contributed to the wealth of the Lamu archipelago,[174] and we can conclude that the slave trade took a significant part in this. Moreover, the

Swahili traffic in slaves offered an easily accessible servile labor source that might have sustained the beginning of a slave-based agriculture on Zanzibar and Pemba and, more generally, the development of a kind of servile dependency on the coast, although other factors also contributed to this development.

This reappraisal of the slave trade before 1750 demonstrates that it was based on firm networks well rooted in the economic life of some Swahili towns. Thus, the Swahili coast economy was ready to handle the expansion in the slave trade from the 1770s up until the second half of the nineteenth century. Further, the growth of the plantation economy on Zanzibar and Pemba in the first decades of the nineteenth century intensified demands for slaves; perhaps the roots of this servile labor are older than previously thought. It is hoped that future research will elaborate on the issues explored in this chapter.

Notes

1. This chapter is a revision of "Le commerce des esclaves sur la côte swahili, 1500–1750," *Azania* 38 (2003), 69–97. I would like to thank Laboratoire Mutations Africaines dans la Longue Durée, UMR 8054 CNRS-Université Paris 1, and l'Institut Français de Recherche en Afrique (IFRA), Nairobi, for financial support to conduct research in Lisbon and Kenya, and to present this paper at the conference on "Slavery, Islam and Diaspora," York University, Toronto, 24 October 2003. I also thank Randall L. Pouwels, Edward A. Alpers and Pier M. Larson for comments on earlier drafts. Naturally the views expressed herein are solely mine.
2. J. Middleton, *The World of the Swahili: An African Mercantile Civilization* (New Haven, 1992), 204.
3. Ibid., see the extensive bibliography.
4. On the nineteenth century, see F. Cooper, *Plantation Slavery on the East Coast of Africa* (New Haven, 1977); A. Sheriff, *Slaves, Spices and Ivory in Zanzibar: Integration of an East African Commercial Empire into the World Economy, 1770–1873* (London, 1987); and J. Glassman, *Feasts and Riot: Revelry, Rebellion, and Popular Consciousness on the Swahili Coast, 1856–1888* (Portsmouth, NH, 1995).
5. G. S. P. Freeman-Grenville, *The East African Coast, Select Documents from the First to the Earlier Nineteenth Century* (Oxford, 1962); idem, *The French at Kilwa Island: An Episode in Eighteenth-Century East African History* (Oxford, 1965); and R. Ross, "The Dutch on the Swahili Coast, 1776–1778: Two Slaving Journals," *International Journal of African Historical Studies* [hereafter *IJAHS*] 19 (1986), 305–60.

6. See E. A. Alpers: *The East African Slave Trade* (Nairobi, 1967); idem, "The French Slave Trade in East Africa (1721–1810)," *Cahiers d'études Africaines* 37 (1970), 80–124; idem, *Ivory and Slaves in East Central Africa: Changing Patterns of International Trade to the Later Nineteenth Century* (London, 1975); Freeman-Grenville, *The French at Kilwa*; E. B. Martin and T. C. Y. Ryan, "A Quantitative Assessment of the Arab Slave Trade of East Africa, 1770–1896," *Kenya Historical Review* 5 (1977), 71–91; and J. M. Filliot, *La traite des esclaves vers les Mascareignes au XVIII*[e] *siècle* (Paris, 1974).
7. R. Coupland, *East Africa and Its Invaders, from the Earliest Times to the Death of Seyyid Said in 1856* (Oxford, 1938), 17–35.
8. Alpers, *The East African Slave Trade*, 7; idem, "The French Slave Trade in East Africa," 82; and J. de V. Allen, "Swahili Culture Reconsidered: Some Historical Implications of the Material Culture of the Northern Kenya Coast in the Eighteenth and Nineteenth Centuries," *Azania* 9 (1974), 125. However it should be noted that Edward Alpers recently revised his views. E. A. Alpers, "Mozambique and 'Mozambiques': slave trade and the diaspora on a global scale," in B. Zimba, E. A. Alpers and A. Isaacman, eds., *Slave Routes and Oral Tradition in Southeastern Africa* (Maputo, 2005), 49-50.
9. G. S. P. Freeman-Grenville, "The Coast 1498–1840," in *History of East Africa,* eds. G. Mathew and R. Oliver, (Oxford, 1962), 1:152–55; and H. N. Chittick, "The East Coast, Madagascar and the Indian Ocean," in *The Cambridge History of Africa*, ed. R. Oliver (Cambridge, 1977), 3:184–85.
10. J. E. Harris, *The African Presence in Asia, Consequences of the East African Slave Trade* (Evanston, 1971), 3; Martin and Ryan, "Quantitative Assessment of the Arab Slave Trade of East Africa," 71–75; B. A. Ogot, "Les mouvements de population entre l'Afrique de l'Est, la corne de l'Afrique et les pays voisins," in *La traite négrière du XV*[e] *au XIX*[e] *siècle: documents de travail et compte-rendu de la réunion d'experts organiseie, ed. UNESCO* (Paris, 1979), 183–84.
11. Notably R. W. Beachey, *The Slave Trade of Eastern Africa* (London, 1976), 8; Sheriff, *Slaves, Spices and Ivory*, 31; M. N. Pearson, *Port Cities and Intruders: The Swahili Coast, India, and Portugal in the Early Modern Era* (Baltimore, 1998), 161–62; and M. Horton and J. Middleton, *The Swahili: The Social Landscape of a Mercantile Society* (Oxford, 2000), 84–85.
12. P. J. J. Sinclair and T. Håkansson, "The Swahili City-State Culture," in *A Comparative Study of Thirty City-State Cultures,* ed. M. H. Hansen (Copenhagen, 2000), 468–70; and T. Spear, "Early Swahili History Reconsidered," *IJAHS* 33 (2000), 278–79. These two recent articles stress the need for a better understanding of slavery before the nineteenth century.
13. See especially Freeman-Grenville, *Select Documents;* idem, *The French at Kilwa*; J. Strandes, *The Portuguese Period in East Africa* (Nairobi, 1961); E. Axelson, *Portuguese in South-East Africa 1600–1700* (Johannesburg,

1960); and idem, *Portuguese in South-East Africa 1488–1600* (Johannesburg, 1973).

14. R. L. Pouwels, "The East African Coast, c.780 to 1900 C.E.," in *The History of Islam in Africa*, eds. N. Levtzion and R. L. Pouwels (Athens, 2000), 259–60; and idem, "Eastern Africa and the Indian Ocean to 1800: Reviewing Relations in Historical Perspective," *IJAHS* 35 (2002), 395–96, 418; J. G. Prestholdt, "As Artistry Permits and Custom May Ordain. The Social Fabric of Material Consumption in the Swahili World, circa 1450 to 1600," *Working Papers* #3, Program of African Studies, Northwestern University, 1998, 23; T. Vernet, "Les cités-États swahili et la puissance omanaise (1650–1720)," *Journal des Africanistes* 72 (2002), 93, 96–97, 108; and idem, "Les cités-États swahili de l'archipel de Lamu, 1585–1810. Dynamiques endogènes, dynamiques exogènes," Ph.D. dissertation, Centre de Recherches Africaines, Université Paris 1 Panthéon-Sorbonne, 2005.
15. For instance, R. K. Kent, *Early Kingdoms in Madagascar, 1500–1700* (New York, 1970); P. Vérin, *Les échelles anciennes du commerce sur les côtes nord de Madagascar* (Lille, 1975); and M. Newitt, "The Comoro Islands in Indian Ocean Trade before the Nineteenth Century," *Cahiers d'Etudes Africaines* 89–90 (1983), 139–65.
16. For a global perspective on the historiography and the debates on the inter-African and Muslim slave trades, see O. Pétré-Grenouilleau, *Les traites négrières, essai d'histoire globale* (Paris, 2004).
17. "Zanj" is the name given by medieval Arab and Persian authors to the inhabitants of the East African coast.
18. G. H. Talhami, "The Zanj Rebellion Reconsidered," *IJAHS* 10 (1977), 443–61.
19. Ibid., 445–51; and C. Allibert, ed., *Textes anciens sur la côte est de l'Afrique et l'océan Indien occidental* (Paris, 1990), 66–68, 74, 92. For western Africa, see N. Levtzion and J. F. P. Hopkins, eds., *Corpus of Early Arabic Sources for West African History* (Princeton, 2000).
20. Ibn Battuta, *Voyages*, ed. C. Defremery and B. R. Sanguinetti (Paris, 1982), 2:94. Similarly, al-Masudi, who claims to have traveled on the coast around 915, does not cite the slave trade and focuses his account on the ivory trade. See Allibert, *Textes anciens sur la côte est de l'Afrique*, 75–86.
21. The Rasulid sultanate ruled Yemen and Hadramawt between 1229 and 1454. E. Vallet, "Pouvoir, commerce et marchands dans le Yémen rasulide (626-858/1229-1454)," Ph.D. dissertation, Université Paris 1 Panthéon-Sorbonne, 2006, 341-353, 467-468. My thanks to Eric Vallet for his insights on the slave trade to and from Rasulid Yemen.
22. In Zanzibar, Pemba, and the adjacent mainland, the Wadebuli traditions mention the presence on the coast of a powerful community before the sixteenth century, which seem to refer to Indians from the town of Daybul and the Sind region. They are said to have cruelly bullied the local people and forced them to work. According to Randall Pouwels, these traditions

suggest an early slave trade between this area and India, since trade networks between northwestern India and East Africa are evidenced at that time. Nevertheless, this remains a hypothesis, as there is lack of evidence to support this claim. The Wadebuli traditions and the early trade connections with India require more study. Pouwels, "Eastern Africa and the Indian Ocean to 1800," 396; personal communication with Pouwels; and Vernet, "Le commerce des esclaves sur la côte swahili," 74–75. Besides, it should be noted that most of the traditions dealing with the ancient rulers of Pemba, whatever their origin (Wadebuli, Shirazi, or Mazrui), insist on their cruelty. See W. H. Ingrams, *Zanzibar, Its History and Its People* (London, 1931), 140–44, 155. Furthermore, direct slave trading to India was almost nonexistent after the sixteenth century, as we will see.

23. Beachey, *Slave Trade of Eastern Africa*, 4; Talhami, "Zanj Rebellion Reconsidered," 457–61; and F. Renault and S. Daget, *Les traites négrières en Afrique* (Paris, 1985), 45–56. An increasing number of scholarly works are being published on the African diaspora in Asia and the Middle East. For instance see A. Catlin-Jairazbhoy and E. A. Alpers, eds., *Sidis and Scholars: Essays on African Indians* (Noida and Trenton, 2004); J. de Silva Jayasuriya and J.-P. Angenot, eds., *Uncovering the History of Africans in Asia* (Leyden, 2008).
24. C. Niebuhr, *Travels through Arabia, and Other Countries in the East* (Edinburgh, 1792), 2:219; and R. J. Barendse, *The Indian Ocean World of the Seventeenth Century* (Armonk and London, 2002), 260.
25. R. Brunschvig, "Abd," in *Encyclopédie de l'Islam* (Leyden, 1960), 1:33–34; Harris, *The African Presence in Asia*, 4; Cooper, *Plantation Slavery*, 26; and E. A. Alpers, "Africans in India and the Wider Context of the Indian Ocean," in *Sidis and Scholars*, eds. Catlin-Jairazbhoy and Alpers, 29–33.
26. G. de São Bernardino, *Itinerário da Índia por terra até à Ilha de Chipre* (Lisbon, 1953), 74; and T. de São Domingos, *Breve relação das christandades que os religiosos de N. Padre Sancto Agostinho tem* (Lisbon, 1630), f. 13v; and Sheriff, *Slaves, Spices and Ivory*, 37.
27. Brunschvig, "Abd," 26–34.
28. Vérin, *Les échelles anciennes du commerce*; G. Rantoandro, "Une communauté mercantile du nord-ouest: les Antalaotra," *Omaly sy Anio* 17–20 (1984), 195–210; C. Radimilahy, *Mahilaka: an Archaeological Investigation of an Early Town in Northwestern Madagascar* (Uppsala, 1998); P. Beaujard, "L'Afrique de l'est, les Comores et Madagascar dans le système-monde avant le XVIe siècle," in D. Nativel and F. Rajaonah, eds., *Madagascar et l'Afrique* (Paris, 2007), 48, 72-74, 77, 83-85.
29. Vérin, *Les échelles anciennes du commerce*, 519–79.
30. Vérin, *Les échelles anciennes du commerce*, 243–81; and Henry T. Wright et al, "The Evolution of Settlement Systems in the Bay of Boeny and the Mahavavy River Valley, North-Western Madagascar," *Azania* 31 (1996), 37–73.

31. Buki is the ancient Swahili name for Madagascar. In the early seventeenth century Couto mentioned that the Antaloatra called Madagascar "Ubuque" (transcription of *Ubuki*), in D. do Couto, *Da Ásia* (Lisbon, 1778), 7-4-5, 311–12. See also "Relação da jornada e descobrimento da Ilha de S. Lourenço...;" and "Roteiro da Ilha de S. Lourenço..." in *Os dois descobrimentos da Ilha de São Lourenço mandados fazer pelo Vice-Rei D. Jerónimo de Azevedo nos anos de 1613 a 1616,* ed. H. Leitão (Lisbon, 1970), 208, 308, 310. Most of Luís Mariano's writings have been published in French by Grandidier in the *Collection des ouvrages anciens concernant Madagascar* [hereafter *COACM*] (Paris, 1904), v.2, but due to the poor translation, I am using Leitão's edition for the texts included in it.
32. Vérin, *Les échelles anciennes du commerce*, 577–607.
33. Couto, *Da Ásia*, 7–4–5, 312; J. dos Santos, *Etiópia Oriental e vária história de cousas notáveis do Oriente*, ed. M. Lobato and E. Medeiros (Lisbon, 1999), 267; and "Diário da viagem da caravela Nossa Senhora da Esperança [1613–1614]" in Leitão, *Os dois descobrimentos da Ilha de São Lourenço*, 71.
34. "Relação da jornada e descobrimento da Ilha de S. Lourenço..." in Leitão, *Os dois descobrimentos da Ilha de São Lourenço*, 204.
35. "Hova" refers to the inhabitants of Imerina, or more generally in Imerina to the freemen who are not noble.
36. This trade is documented by Portuguese, English and French accounts, which all cite the name *Hova*. See "Relação da jornada e descobrimento da Ilha de S. Lourenço" in Leitão, *Os dois descobrimentos da Ilha de São Lourenço*, 207; "A Voyage in ye ship Frances from Mossambique for St. Lawrence [1640]" in S. Ellis, "Un texte du XVIIème siècle sur Madagascar," *Omaly sy Anio* 9 (1979), 157–158, 163; and Anonymous, "Mémoire sur les côtes orientales et occidentales d'Afrique contenant des instructions bonnes pour les navigateurs" (c.1696), Doc. 1, 25, Marine 3JJ342 Archives Nationales de France, Paris [hereafter ANF].
37. Ellis, "Un texte du XVIIème siècle sur Madagascar," 157.
38. Santos, *Etiópia Oriental*, 267.
39. Beaujard, "L'Afrique de l'est, les Comores et Madagascar," 77, 84.
40. For the Sada slave trade, see "Lettre du Père Luis Mariano, datée de Mozambique le 24 août 1619," *COACM* 2:312; and N. Buckeridge, *Journal and Letter Book of Nicholas Buckeridge 1651–1654*, ed. J. R. Jenson (Minneapolis, 1973), 46.
41. Newitt, "Comoro Islands in Indian Ocean Trade," 139–52.
42. "The Second Voyage of Captaine Walter Peyton into the East-Indies...in January 1614;" and "Observations Collected Out of the Journall of Sir Thomas Roe [1615]," in S. Purchas, *Hakluytus Posthumus or Purchas his Pilgrimes* (London, [1625–1626] 1965), 4:292, 315; "Relāche de Pieter van den Broecke aux īles Comores, en 1614," *COACM* 2:93; "Registre des conseils tenus pour le compte de la colonie anglaise de Madagascar (de W.

Courteen et Cie")," *COACM* 5:518; and Newitt, "Comoro Islands in Indian Ocean Trade," 149–50.

43. Piri Reis declared that, "They breed slaves like lambs and sheep." Quoted in C. Allibert, "Une description turque de l'océan Indien au XVIe siècle, l'océan Indien occidental dans le *kitab-i Bahrije* de Piri Reis (1521)," *Études Océan Indien* 10 (1988), 27.
44. Edward A. Alpers, personal communication.
45. Afonso de Albuquerque to King, 6 February 1507, *Documentos sobre os Portugueses em Moçambique e na África Central, 1497–1840* [hereafter *DPMAC*] (Lisbon, 1962–1975), 2:122–23; Allibert, "Une description turque de l'océan Indien," 21; Couto, *Da Ásia*, 7-4-5, 317; Santos, *Etiópia Oriental*, 267; "A Journall of the Third Voyage to the East India...Written by William Keeling [1608]," in Purchas, *Hakluytus Posthumus*, 2:515; "Relação da jornada e descobrimento da Ilha de S. Lourenço," in Leitão, *Os dois descobrimentos da Ilha de São Lourenço*, 207–08; "Lettre du Père Luis Mariano...24 août 1619," *COACM,* 2:312; Viceroy to King, Goa, 12 March 1623, Documentos Remetidos da Índia (hereafter DRI) 17, f.10, Arquivos Nacionais/Torre do Tombo, Lisbon [hereafter AN/TT]; E. Axelson, ed., "Viagem que fez o Padre Ant. Gomez, da Comp.[a] de Jesus, ao Imperio de de [sic] Manomotapa," *Stvdia* 3 (1959), 229; M. Barreto, "Informação do estado e conquista dos Rios de Cuama...11 de dezembro de 1667," *Boletim da Sociedade de Geographia de Lisboa* 4 (1883), 55; and J. C. Armstrong, "Madagascar and the Slave Trade in the Seventeenth Century," *Omaly sy Anio* 17–20 (1984), 213–16.
46. A. de Albuquerque to King, 6 February 1507, *DPMAC*, 2:120–23; Ellis, "Un texte du XVIIème siècle sur Madagascar," 157; and Buckeridge, *Journal and Letter Book*, 46.
47. Sources are plentiful about this trade; see for example: Viceroy to King, 27 December 1506, *As gavetas da Torre do Tombo,* v.X*: gav. XIX–XX, maços 1–7* (Lisbon, 1974), 364; Santos, *Etiópia Oriental*, 270; "A Journall of All Principall Matters Passed in the Twelfth Voyage to the East-India, Observed by Me Walter Payton [1612];" and "The Second Voyage of Captaine Walter Peyton into the East-Indies," both in Purchas, *Hakluytus Posthumus*, 4:183, 292.
48. Governor of India to King, Panaji, 4 December 1589, Archivo General de Simancas, Secretarias Provinciales, *Libro* 1551, 32/7, f.788, Instituto de Investigação Científica Tropical—Centro de Estudos de História e Cartografia Antiga, Filmoteca Ultramarina Portuguesa, Lisbon [hereafter FUP].
49. "Lettre de Luis Mariano sur sa mission à la côte ouest (vers juillet 1616)," and "Lettre du Père Luis Mariano...24 août 1619," both in *COACM* 2:213, 305, 311–312; Axelson, "Viagem que fez o Padre Ant. Gomez," 229; São Domingos, *Breve relação das Christandades*, f. 13v; and Buckeridge, *Journal and Letter Book*, 46.

50. J. Nogueira, *Socorro que de Moçambique foi a S. Lourenço contra o Rei arrenegado de Mombaça fortificado na ilha Massalagem,* ed. M. Barreto (Lourenço Marques, 1971), 65.
51. Vernet, "Les cités-États swahili de l'archipel de Lamu, 1585–1810," 199–205.
52. "Lettre de Luis Mariano...(vers juillet 1616)," and "Lettre du Père Luis Mariano... 24 août 1619," both in *COACM,* 2:213, 305; and Buckeridge, *Journal and Letter Book*, 46.
53. Buckeridge, *Journal and Letter Book*, 46; and Axelson, *Portuguese in South-East Africa 1600–1700*, 141.
54. "Lettre du Père Luis Mariano...24 août 1619," *COACM,* 2:305, 311–12.
55. A. de Beaulieu, *Mémoires d'un voyage aux Indes Orientales, 1619–1622, un marchand normand à Sumatra*, ed. D. Lombard (Paris, 1996), 70.
56. B. G. Martin, "Arab Migrations to East Africa in Medieval Times," *IJAHS* 7 (1974), 377–89; and Randall L. Pouwels, *Horn and Crescent: Cultural Change and Traditional Islam on the East African Coast, 800–1900* (Cambridge, 1987), 37–42. See also, Vernet, "Les cités-États swahili de l'archipel de Lamu, 1585–1810," 158–69, 179–80.
57. Vérin, *Les échelles anciennes du commerce*, passim; C. Radimilahy, *Mahilaka.*
58. The Portuguese reported the slave trade with Malindi and Mombasa during their first trip to the island in 1506; see A. de Albuquerque to King, 6 February 1507, *DPMAC,* 2:122–23.
59. "Relação (cópia), feita pelo Padre Francisco de Monclaro...da expedição ao Monomotapa, comandada por Francisco Barreto," *DPMAC,* 8:354–55.
60. Couto, *Da Ásia*, 7–4–5, 317. The Portuguese, and Couto himself, usually refer to the Swahili as "Moors of the Coast (of Malindi)," as opposed to the "Arab Moors" or the "Moors of Arabia," that is inhabitants of Yemen, Hadramawt, and Oman.
61. Santos, *Etiópia Oriental*, 267, 270; "Relâche de Pieter van den Broecke aux îles Comores, en 1614," *COACM*, 2:93; "Registre des conseils tenus pour le compte de la colonie anglaise de Madagascar," *COACM*, 5:518; and Newitt, "Comoro Islands in Indian Ocean Trade," 149–150. Some traders from Kishn (situated on the northeastern coast of Hadramawt) operated from the island of Socotra, which was ruled by the Kishn sultanate. Each year they sent ships to the Comoros to buy slaves and rice. "Observations of William Finch [1607];" and "A Journall of the Third Voyage to the East India [1608]" both in Purchas, *Hakluytus Posthumus*, 2:515 & 4:13–14.
62. This is the earliest mention of the name "Swahili" in an European document; the Portuguese never used the term. Sir H. Middleton, "The Sixth Voyage, Set Forth by the East Indian Company," in Purchas, *Hakluytus Posthumus*, 3:155.
63. Allibert, "Une description turque de l'océan Indien," 27.

64. Barreto, "Informação do estado e conquista dos Rios de Cuama," 55.
65. São Domingos, *Breve relação das Christandades*, f. 13v. Although it does not mention the slave trade, a 1624 document refers to a sharif merchant from Aden who came to trade to Pate. João de Velasco to André Palmeiro, Diu, 25 July 1624 in *Rerum Aethiopicarum scriptores occidentales inediti a saeculo XVI ad XIX,* ed. C. Beccari, (Rome, 1912), 12:81.
66. Kent, *Early Kingdoms in Madagascar*, 103–04; Martin, "Arab Migrations to East Africa," 387; and Newitt, "Comoro Islands in Indian Ocean Trade," 145.
67. C. Guillain, *Documents sur l'histoire, la géographie et le commerce de la partie occidentale de Madagascar* (Paris, 1845), 21–22.
68. Martin, "Arab Migrations to East Africa," 381; and Pouwels, *Horn and Crescent*, 40–42.
69. Estimates for 1585–1586 are from Couto, *Da Ásia*, 10–8, 185; and for 1588–1589, from Santos, *Etiópia Oriental*, 355.
70. G. de São Bernardino, *Itinerário da Índia*, 74; and N. de Orta Rebelo, *Un voyageur portugais en Perse au début du XVIIe siècle,* ed. J. Verissimo Serrão (Lisbon, 1972), 77, 85.
71. "Registre des conseils tenus pour le compte de la colonie anglaise de Madagascar," *COACM,* 5:445.
72. For a lengthy and revised study of Portuguese rule over the Mombasa coast, see Vernet, "Les cités-États swahili de l'archipel de Lamu, 1585–1810."
73. Notably Baltasar Marinho, Goa, 4 February 1634, f.7, transcription of a document from the Arquivo Histórico Ultramarino, Lisbon [hereafter AHU], located in Fort Jesus Museum Library, Mombasa.
74. King to Viceroy, Lisbon, 25 January 1614, in *Documentos remettidos da Índia ou Livros das Monções* (Lisbon, 1889), 9:t.3, 13.
75. Buckeridge, *Journal and Letter Book*, 46. It should be noted that corruption was rife and the customs did not work very well.
76. Vernet, "Les cités-États swahili et la puissance omanaise," 94.
77. For instance, the ships cited above, which went each year to Mocha, seem to have belonged to traders living on the Swahili coast. "The Sixth Voyage, Set Forth by the East Indian Company [1611]," in Purchas, *Hakluytus Posthumus*, 3:155. A 1613 document states that the inhabitants of Mohely "build barkes upon this island, and trade with them, alongst the Coast of Melinde, and Arabia, with slaves and fruits." "A Journall of All Principall Matters Passed in the Twelfth Voyage to the East-India [1612]," in Purchas, *Hakluytus Posthumus*, 4:183. Other documents dealing with the slave trade are less explicit, but seem to imply that some of the ships owned by East African traders sailed to Arabia.
78. For a full discussion, see Vernet, "Les cités-États swahili de l'archipel de Lamu, 1585–1810," 150–55. Perhaps these ships were not *mitepe*, which were the traditional Swahili ships.

79. Vernet, "Les cités-États swahili et la puissance omanaise," 93–97; and idem, "Les cités-États swahili de l'archipel de Lamu, 1585–1810," passim.
80. See Buckeridge's account; and Barreto, "Informação do estado e conquista dos Rios de Cuama," 55.
81. Armstrong, "Madagascar and the Slave Trade," 216.
82. Pero Ferreira Fogaça to King, Kilwa, 31 August 1506, *DPMAC,* 1:618–19; and Nuno Vaz Pereira to Fernão Cotrim, Kilwa, 14 January 1507, *DPMAC,* 2:36–37.
83. A. Bocarro, *Década 13 da história da Índia* (Lisbon, 1876), 1:636–37. Nevertheless, the ship was very packed and the Portuguese suffered as a result.
84. "Registre des conseils tenus pour le compte de la colonie anglaise de Madagascar," *COACM,* 5:515, 518.
85. J. Huygen van Linschoten, *Itineraìrio, viagem ou navegação para as Indias orientais ou portuguesas*, ed. A. Pos and R. Loureiro (Lisbon, 1997), 82; Santos, *Etiópia Oriental*, 252, 299–300; and Barreto, "Informação do estado e conquista dos Rios de Cuama," 35.
86. Alpers, *Ivory and Slaves*, 63.
87. Santos, *Etiópia Oriental*, 377–78; and J. Lobo, *The* Itinerário *of Jerónimo Lobo*, ed. D. Lockhart (London, 1984), 59.
88. João da Costa, "Titt.º dos christãos que se fizerão na christandade de Mascate pellos Rellegiozos de Nosso P.de de Santo Aug.º," Muscat, 22 August 1626, Manuscrito da Livraria n° 731, ff. 287-290, AN/TT; G.S.P. Freeman-Grenville, *The Mombasa Rising against the Portuguese from Sworn Evidence* (Oxford, 1980), 57.
89. C. Pickering, *The Races of Man and their Geographical Distribution* (Philadelphia, 1848), 211; C. Guillain, *Documents sur l'histoire, la géographie et le commerce de l'Afrique Orientale* (Paris, 1856), 3:537; R. Brenner, "Renseignements obtenus relativement au sort du Baron de Decken et informations géographiques sur le pays de Brava," *Annales des voyages, de la géographie, de l'histoire et de l'archéologie* (1868), 2:136; and M. Ylvisaker, *Lamu in the Nineteenth Century: Land, Trade, and Politics* (Boston, 1979), 119.
90. Vernet, "Les cités-États swahili de l'archipel de Lamu," 271–95, 303–40. The exception is Pate, which led military expeditions against the Katwa and the Bajun in the seventeenth century. These conflicts, however, were part of a much larger plan to conquer the whole area.
91. For example, the "*Muzungulos*" (Nyika/Mijikenda) of the mainland across from Mombasa described themselves as "vassals" of the king of Mombasa. They had to supply the city with grain while the king was expected to offer them cloth. Antoìnio Bocarro, *O livro das plantas de todas as fortalezas, cidades, e povoações do Estado da Índia Oriental,* ed. I. Cid (Lisbon, 1992), 2:37–40. For a summary of Swahili intergroup relations, see R. L. Pouwels, "The Battle of Shela: the Climax of an Era and a Point of Departure in the

Modern History of the Kenya Coast," *Cahiers d'Etudes Africaines* 123 (1991), 367–71, 381–82; Vernet, "Le territoire hors les murs des cités-États swahili de l'archipel de Lamu, 1600–1800," *Journal des Africanistes* 74 (2004), 381–411; and idem, "Les cités-États swahili de l'archipel de Lamu, 1585–1810," *passim*.

92. A. Werner, "Some Notes on the Wapokomo of the Tana Valley," *Journal of the African Society* 12 (1912), 366; and idem, "The Bantu Coast Tribes of the East Africa Protectorate," *Journal of the Royal Anthropological Institute* 45 (1915), 336.

93. H. Brown, "History of Siyu: The Development and Decline of a Swahili Town on the Northern Kenya Coast," Ph.D. dissertation, Indiana University, 1985, 180.

94. Werner, "Notes on the Wapokomo," 366.

95. According to Kusimba, the Portuguese raided and enslaved the Swahili and other communities. He assumes that some Swahili and other coastal groups would have taken refuge on the mainland. Kusimba, *The Rise and Fall of Swahili States* (Walnut Creek, CA, 1999), 163–71. In another article the same author hypothesizes, from very weak evidence, that the Tsavo region west of Mombasa, suffered severely from slave raiding from 1500 onward. See C. M. Kusimba, S. B. Kusimba, and D. K. Wright, "The Development and Collapse of Precolonial Ethnic Mosaics in Tsavo, Kenya," *Journal of African Archaeology* 3 (2005), 260–65. While Portuguese military repression was often violent in cases of uprisings against their authority, no sixteenth or seventeenth century document corroborates such speculation, although Portuguese authors often insist at length on Portuguese retaliation. The Portuguese never enslaved the coastal and mainland populations north of Mozambique Island. Instead they acquired slaves solely through trade. Besides, as mentioned above, there was almost no slave trade in the interior of the Mombasa area.

96. The first mention of the purchase of a slave is dated 1505. Pero de Anhaia to Manuel Fernandes, Sofala, 6 December 1505, *DPMAC* 1:318–21. After this date such references are numerous.

97. Santos, *Etiópia Oriental*, 299; "The Second Voyage of Captaine Walter Peyton into the East-Indies," in Purchas, *Hakluytus Posthumus*, 4:292; Ellis, "Un texte du XVIIème siècle sur Madagascar," 157; Buckeridge, *Journal and Letter Book*, 44; and Newitt, "Comoro Islands in Indian Ocean Trade," 150.

98. Newitt, "Comoro Islands in Indian Ocean Trade," 150; and Armstrong, "Madagascar and the Slave Trade," 216.

99. Linschoten, *Itinerário*, 82, 182; Santos, *Etiópia Oriental*, 335, 340; São Bernardino, *Itinerário da Índia*, 57; Bocarro, *O livro das plantas*, 2:42; and "William Alley: An English Visitor to Mombasa in 1667," in Freeman-Grenville, *Select Documents*, 190. In 1589 the towns of Faza, Siyu, and Pate were ordered to deliver twenty slaves per year for the galleys of the *Estado*

da Índia. Couto, *Da Ásia*, 10–11; Beachey, *Slave Trade of Eastern Africa*, 8; Pearson, *Port Cities and Intruders*, 161; and Alpers, "Africans in India," in *Sidis and Scholars*, ed. Catlin-Jairazbhoy and Alpers, 34–35, 56.

100. J. da Costa, "Titt.º dos christãos que se fizerão na christandade de Mascate," Muscat, 22 August 1626, Manuscrito da Livraria 731, ff. 287-290, AN/TT.
101. "Relação (cópia), feita pelo Padre Francisco de Monclaro," *DPMAC,* 8:346–47; and G. de São Bernardino, *Itinerário da Índia*, 50.
102. Linschoten, *Itinerário*, 182–83; Alpers, *Ivory and Slaves*, 95; and Pearson, *Port Cities and Intruders*, 161.
103. Freeman-Grenville, *The Mombasa Rising against the Portuguese*, passim.
104. Bocarro, *O livro das plantas*, 2:40; "Jambangome ms., An Arabic Chronicle of Pemba," in J. Gray, "Zanzibar Local Histories (Part II)," *Swahili* 31 (1960), 121–22.
105. Pearson, *Port Cities and Intruders*, 161.
106. Armstrong, "Madagascar and the Slave Trade," 217–29; and L. Mosca, "Slaving in Madagascar: English and Colonial Voyages in the Second Half of the XVII Century," unpublished paper presented at the Conference on the Siddis of India and the African Diasporas in Asia, Goa, January 2006.
107. Diogo Lopes de Sequeira to King, Cochin, 23 December 1518, *DPMAC,* 5:596–97.
108. Freeman-Grenville, *The French at Kilwa*, 107.
109. Harris, *The African Presence in Asia*, 34.
110. For a detailed discussion of the existence of slavery, see Randall Pouwels, "Battle of Shela," 375–81. For scattered references about slaves, see Freeman-Grenville, "The Coast 1498–1840," 152; Allen, "Swahili Culture Reconsidered," 125; Ylvisaker, *Lamu in the Nineteenth Century*, 20; and Horton and Middleton, *The Swahili*, 135.
111. See Pouwels, "Battle of Shela," 375–81.
112. C. Meillassoux, *Anthropologie de l'esclavage: le ventre de fer et d'argent* (Paris, 1986), 68–78.
113. Pouwels, "Battle of Shela," 376–77; and Glassman, *Feasts and Riot*, 80–95.
114. Glassman, *Feasts and Riot*, 94.
115. For instance, an account states that "slaves" were offered by the Sofala king to the Portuguese to help them to build a fort. J. Augur, "Conquista de las Indias de Persia & Arabia" (Salamanca, 1512), extract in DPMAC, 3:612. But J. de Barros indicates that they were "Cafres," apparently free and remunerated; in *Da Ásia* (Lisbon, 1552), 1-10-2, f.120v.
116. Such terms are often encountered in accounts dealing with the Mijikenda (Nyika), clients of Mombasa, and the Oromo, Katwa, and Bajun, tied to one or the other city of the Lamu archipelago.
117. Abdalla bin Ali bin Nasir, *Al-Inkishafi, Catechism of a Soul,* ed. J. de V. Allen (Nairobi, 1977), 64.

118. A century earlier Fryer already noticed that the heads of families of Anjouan had several slaves in the service of their households. J. Fryer, *A New Account of East India and Persia, Being Nine Year's Travels, 1672–1681,* ed. W. Crooke (London, 1909), 1:61. For references about field slaves, see Ross, "The Dutch on the Swahili Coast," 311.
119. In 1673 the king of Anjouan was surrounded by a guard of a dozen slaves. Fryer, *New Account of East India*, 1:62. In 1776 the bodyguards of the Kilwa king were both freemen and slaves; see Freeman-Grenville, *The French at Kilwa*, 177. In 1709 "captive *Cafres*" belonging to a Kilwa Swahili sailed on a trading ship to Cape Delgado. Manuel de Santo Alberto, Amiza, 18 May 1709, *Livros das Monções* (hereafter LM) 74A, 75/2, f.271, FUP. According to Morice, sailors of the East African coast were "Africans" of free or servile status; see Freeman-Grenville, *The French at Kilwa*, 146, 164.
120. Barros, *Da Ásia*, 4-3-4, 143. The poem *al-Inkishafi*, written around 1820 in Pate and dealing with the past fortunes of Pate's great men, states that they had "gay-robed women for their ease." Abdalla bin Ali bin Nasir, *Al-Inkishafi*, 64.
121. Allen, "Swahili Culture Reconsidered," 127–29; Pouwels, "Battle of Shela," 381–82; and Vernet, "Les cités-États swahili de l'archipel de Lamu, 1585–1810," 522–33.
122. Santos, *Etiópia Oriental*, 338; and Bocarro, *O livro das plantas*, 2:41–42. In 1686, under Portuguese sovereignty, as in 1711, under Oman, Mombasa was totally dependent upon Pemba rice for its food. See João Antunes Portugal to *Conselho do Estado*, Mombasa, 6 August 1686, LM 51B, 29/4, f.171; and anonymous to Mwinyi Juma bin Mwinyi Kaya (translation), Goa, 25 September 1711, LM 77, 25/2, f.107, FUP.
123. Bocarro, *O livro das plantas*, 2:42.
124. Gray, "Zanzibar Local Histories (Part II)," 121–26. The whole chronicle insists on slavery.
125. For a fuller discussion see Vernet, "Les cités-États swahili de l'archipel de Lamu, 1585–1810," 543–47. Presently research is being carried out by the author on the very interesting case of Pemba.
126. Kent, *Early Kingdoms in Madagascar*, 70, 186.
127. A. Sauvaget, "La relation de Melet du voyage de la Haye aux Indes Orientales," *Etudes Océan Indien* 25–26 (1998), 143; Fryer, *New Account of East India*, 1:66; and Newitt, "Comoro Islands in Indian Ocean Trade," 155.
128. Sultan Mohammed bin Omar to Francisco da Gama (translation), Goa, 22 October 1598, and Mohammed bin Mohammed "Bwana Mtiti," Prince of Pate, to Francisco da Gama (translation), Goa, 22 October 1598, *Miscelãnea Manuscrita da N. S. da Graça de Lisboa*, caixa 2, t.3, pp. 213-14 and 333, AN/TT.
129. A. de Brito Freire, "Jornaes de viagem na India, e regresso a Lisboa 1727 a 1732," cod.485, f.24, Biblioteca Nacional, Lisbon [hereafter BNL].

130. Newitt, "Comoro Islands in Indian Ocean Trade," 155; and Freeman-Grenville, *The French at Kilwa*, 170.
131. Pouwels shares this hypothesis; see "Battle of Shela," 381.
132. Ibid.
133. Vernet, "Le territoire hors les murs des cités-États swahili," 402–08; and Vernet, "Les cités-États swahili de l'archipel de Lamu, 1585–1810," *passim*. Thus, while the slave trade run by the Lamu archipelago merchants was flourishing, each town of the archipelago had "mainland vassals" who played essential political and economic roles in the area.
134. R. D. Bathurst, "Maritime Trade and Imamate Government: Two Principal Themes in the History of Oman to 1728," in *The Arabian Peninsula, Society and Politics*, ed. D. Hopwood (London, 1972), 98–103.
135. P. Risso, *Oman and Muscat, an Early Modern History* (London, 1986), 2–3, 13; and J. C. Wilkinson, *The Imamate Tradition of Oman* (Cambridge, 1987), 23–25.
136. Salīl ibn Razīk, *History of the Imāms and Seyyids of 'Omān, from A.D. 661–1856,* ed. G. P. Badger (London, 1871), 92; Risso, *Oman and Muscat*, 13–14; and Wilkinson, *Imamate Tradition of Oman*, 220–21.
137. However I have never come across evidence that corroborates this and thus one should take Barendse' assertion with caution. Barendse, *The Indian Ocean World*, 212.
138. Niebuhr, *Travels through Arabia*, 1:239; Bathurst, "Maritime Trade and Imamate Government," 102; and Risso, *Oman and Muscat*, 200.
139. A. Hamilton, *A New Account of the East Indies* (Edinburgh, 1727), 1:66. A Dutch account states that the ruling Imam in 1756 owned 500 "African slaves from Mombasa," whereas his predecessors had owned 4000 slaves. See W. M. Floor, "A Description of the Persian Gulf and Its Inhabitants in 1756," *Persica* 8, 1979, 179. A French account dated 1775 describes the black soldiers of Muscat as follows: "The infantry I saw is a mix of blacks from various lands, armed with guns… Their wages are 3 rupees per month… The guards are for the most Abyssinian… There is an army of around 4000 men, and the Imam can augment it up to 6000 men." Anonymous, "Sur l'archipel du nord de Madagascar…Sur Mascatte en Arabie," c.1775, C4–145 (Colonies, Seychelles), unfoliated, ANF. Slavery in Oman also needs further research.
140. Sheriff, *Slaves, Spices and Ivory*, 19, 37.
141. Vernet, "Les cités-États swahili et la puissance omanaise," 93–97.
142. Hamilton, *New Account of the East Indies*, 1:11–12; and Vernet, "Les cités-États swahili et la puissance omanaise," 97–98.
143. Vernet, "Les cités-États swahili et la puissance omanaise," 99–102.
144. Risso, *Oman and Muscat*, 119–20.
145. Vérin, *Les échelles anciennes du commerce*, 133–39, 272–79, 446–47; and Armstrong, "Madagascar and the Slave Trade," 215.

146. Armstrong, "Madagascar and the Slave Trade," 215.
147. J. de la Roque, *Voyage de l'Arabie Heureuse* (Amsterdam, 1716), 8.
148. "Relāche du navire *Le Barneveld*, de la compagnie des Indes Orientales... en l'an 1719," *COACM,* 5:32–33; "Journal du voyage du navire hollandais *De Brack*...en 1741," *COACM,* 6:110; and "Relation d'un voyage fait à Madagascar en 1751 par Louis Fort," *COACM,* 5:248–49.
149. The slave trade on the eastern and southern coasts of Madagascar also decreased in the second half of the eighteenth century, which led the French to seek slaves on the East African coast.
150. Newitt, "Comoro Islands in Indian Ocean Trade," 159–60; Ross, "The Dutch on the Swahili Coast," 310; and Freeman-Grenville, *The French at Kilwa*, 125, 190.
151. Vérin, *Les échelles anciennes du commerce*, 153.
152. Alpers, *Ivory and Slaves*, 63–64.
153. Manuel de Santo Alberto, Amiza, 22 May 1708, LM 73, 12/5, f.49; M. de Santo Alberto, Amiza, 18 May 1709, LM 74A, 75/1–2, ff.270v–271; and Queen of Kilwa, Sultani Fatima binti Sultani Mfalme Mohammed, to Mwinyi Juma bin Mwinyi Kaya (translation), Goa, 25 September 1711, LM 77, 23/2, f.98, FUP.
154. Mwinyi Juma bin Mwinyi Kaya to Bwana Dau bin Bwana Shaka, Mozambique, 15 August 1711, LM 77, 21/1–2, ff.87v–88, FUP.
155. Conde da Ericeira, "Noticias da India," cod.465, f.131v.; and A. de Brito Freire, "Jornaes de viagem na India," cod.485, f.5, BNL.
156. Vigoureux to the contrôleur général de la Compagnie des Indes, Port-Louis, Ile de France [Mauritius], 22 November 1736, Colonies C4–2 (Colonies, Ile de France), unfoliated, ANF; and "Memorias da costa d'Africa Oriental..., Sena, 21 May 1762," in A. A. de Andrade, ed., *Relações de Moçambique setecentista* (Lisbon, 1955), 214–15.
157. Francisco de Melo e Castro to Manuel de Souza e Brito, Mozambique, 19 May 1754, cod.1310, f.54, AHU.
158. Floor, "Description of the Persian Gulf and Its Inhabitants," 179.
159. Mwinyi Saveja wa Bwana Abakari wa Mwinyi Mupate to António Cardim Frois, Kilwa (1730), LM 97B, 81/5, f.594, FUP; F. de Melo e Castro to M. de Souza e Brito, Mozambique, 19 May 1754, cod.1310, f.54, AHU; António Teixeira Tigre to António Manuel de Melo e Castro, Ibo, 8 November 1790, doc. 36, caixa Moçambique [hereafter Moç.] 61, AHU; "Memorias da costa d'Africa Oriental..., Sena, 21 May 1762," in Andrade, *Relações de Moçambique setecentista*, 214; Ross, "The Dutch on the Swahili Coast," 341–45; Freeman-Grenville, *The French at Kilwa*, 176; and Vernet, "Les cités-États swahili de l'archipel de Lamu, 1585–1810," 482–84.
160. Alpers, *Ivory and Slaves*, 70–75; and Vernet, "Les cités-États swahili et la puissance omanaise," 101–08.

161. Bathurst, "Maritime Trade and Imamate Government," 103–05; and Risso, *Oman and Muscat*, 39–45.
162. Anonymous to João Bautista Lopes de Laure, Surat, 20 November 1724, Viceroy to King, Goa, 16 January 1724 & 1 January 1726 in A. B. de Bragança Pereira, *Arquivo Português Oriental (nova edição)* (Bastorá-Goa, 1940), 1-3-3, 279–80, 201–02, 313–14; Strandes, *The Portuguese Period in East Africa*, 278; and Vernet, "Les cités-États swahili de l'archipel de Lamu, 1585–1810," 388–90, 423–27.
163. José Barbosa Leal to King, Mozambique, 14 November 1734, doc.23, caixa Moç. 5; and Pedro do Rego Barreto da Gama e Castro to Diogo de Mendonça, Mozambique, 10 November 1745, doc. 15, caixa Moç. 6, AHU.
164. P. E. Lovejoy, *Transformations in Slavery: A History of Slavery in Africa* (Cambridge, 1983), 27; Renault and Daget, *Les traites négrières*, 47; and R. A. Austen, *African Economic History, Internal Development and External Dependency* (London, 1987), 59, 275.
165. Bertrand Hirsch, personal communication; E. Vallet, "Pouvoir, commerce et marchands dans le Yémen rasulide," 343-352; M.-L. Derat, "Chrétiens et musulmans d'Éthiopie face à la traite et à l'esclavage aux XVe et XVIe siècles" in *Traite et esclavage en Afrique orientale et dans l'océan Indien*, ed. M.-P. Ballarin, M.-L. Derat, H. Médard, T. Vernet (Paris, forthcoming). According to a Jesuit priest in 1556, more than 10,000 or 12,000 of these slaves were sold to the Turks or the Arabs in the Red Sea ports. But these figures may have been exaggerated by the priest who stated that they all had wanted to be Christianized. M. Hassen, *The Oromo of Ethiopia: A History 1570–1860* (Cambridge, 1990), 29–32.
166. Most of these Muslim cities were abandoned and forgotten. B. Hirsch and F.-X. Fauvelle-Aymard, "Cités oubliées, réflexions sur l'histoire urbaine de l'Éthiopie médiévale (XIe – XVIe siècles)," *Journal des Africanistes* 74 (2004), 299-314; T. Insoll, *The Archaeology of Islam in Sub-Saharan Africa* (Cambridge, 2003), 58-61.
167. Austen, *African Economic History*, 59, 275. Despite the lack of evidence, Austen's figures are often cited; see for instance, Pétré-Grenouilleau, *Les traites négrières*, 147–49.
168. Lovejoy, *Transformations*, 60.
169. Armstrong's appraisal supports this claim.
170. Considering that the Portuguese denounced the trade toward Arabia, which they probably overestimated. This rough estimate of 3000 to 4000 lowers my previous estimate published in "Le commerce des esclaves sur la côte swahili," 94.
171. My hesitations arise from the difficulty to estimate non-Western slave trades. As such, to my mind, the analysis of networks is much more important than "guesstimates."

172. Ivory was by far the main trade of the Lamu archipelago before the mid-nineteenth century, see Vernet, "Les cités-États swahili de l'archipel de Lamu, 1585–1810," passim.
173. Allen, "Swahili Culture Reconsidered," 125. This contradicts Allen's claim: "It is now generally agreed that slave trading did not play an important part in the northern Swahili economy before the nineteenth century."
174. Pouwels, *Horn and Crescent*, 49–54.

Chapter 5

QĀJĀR ḤARAM: IMAGINATION OR REALITY?

Behnaz A. Mirzai

This study of *ḥaram* life in Iran has been inspired by the paucity of accurate scholarship and literature on the subject. Most of what we know relies on two sources: biographies of Persian courtiers and European accounts. On the one hand, the discourse in western literature has been dominated by ideas about "orientalism" and the perception that the *ḥaram* or *andarūn* (women's quarters) was an oppressive institution. The *ḥaram* has been depicted as a polygamous sexually oriented space, where men maintained control over women. On the other hand, the conventional approach of Persian writers has been to focus on the lives of the *shāhs* and the elites and on foreign policy and political developments. Thus, studies have either misrepresented or ignored subalterns, based on the assumption that common people had no impact on the country's politics. I intend to redress these shortcomings by focusing on the *ḥaram*, with special attention to female slaves and eunuchs.

Although works produced by Persians and Europeans have provided many important insights into *ḥaram* life, they have tended to reiterate similar stereotypes. Be it the orientalists' ignorance of the local culture or the Persian proclivity to study courtier attitudes of dissatisfaction or admiration for the Qājār court, both present parallel approaches that ultimately overshadow our understanding of the true reality of *ḥaram* life. Yet we must study and analyze discourses about the royal Qājār court produced by the perspectives of both insiders and outsiders to reconstruct the world of the *ḥaram*.

In exploring *ḥaram* culture, a broad range of accounts should be considered, especially since studies of the *ḥaram* continue to be shaped by traditional literary models. We need to build a new model for understanding the reality of *ḥaram* life through time and space. Though not sufficient, historical descriptions can certainly give us an insight into, and a foundation from which to study, the *ḥaram* past. For instance, Sulṭān Aḥmad Mīrzā wrote his book *Tārīkh-i Ażudī* about *ḥaram* life. This book is a significant source for understanding the life of the first three Qājār kings based on the author's close observation. Also, a Sudanese slave was so enamored by Muḥammad Ḥasan Khān I'timād al-Salṭanih, a courtier of Nāṣir al-Dīn Shāh, that he married the slave when she came to Tihrān.[1] Another is Dust 'Alī Khān Mu'ayyir al-Mamālik, the grandson of Nāṣir al-Dīn Shāh.[2] His book takes us into the *shāh*'s *ḥaram* where he himself grew up. It deals with the personal life of Nāṣir al-Dīn Shāh, while also recording the life histories of individual slaves. Mu'ayyir al-Mamālik draws a detailed picture of the performance and duties of female and male slaves from an insider's perspective. The memoir of Tāj al-Salṭanih, the daughter of Nāṣir al-Dīn Shāh, recounts her personal life in a highly emotional way. She writes about the African *dadih* (female child-carers) who raised her: "the *dadih* must specifically be a black…the unfortunates became enslaved and are called '*zarkharīd*' [a *ghulām* or *kanīz* who is bought] and a means for their [the well-to-do] greatness."[3]

Jakob Edouard Polak, an Austrian physician in the court of Nāṣir al-Dīn Shāh, lived in Iran from 1851 to 1860. He wrote a two-volume book based on his observations.[4] Apart from general information on cultural, social, and medical conditions in Iran, a short section of Polak's work provides a detailed description of slaves of various races and their status. His work is significant for its observations of society and, especially the lives of the lower social classes.

By the late nineteenth century more descriptions of *ḥaram* life were published. Charles James Wills, a medical officer who visited the *andarūn,* describes various members and slaves in the *ḥaram*.[5] Similarly, Isabella Bishop, the English traveler and writer (and first female member of the Royal Geographical Society) wrote about the Persians, Kurds, and Africans she met in the *andarūn* of the *khān* (chief) of Qizil Uzen, a village in northern Iran.[6] Jean Baptiste Feuvrier, the French soldier who served as Nāṣir al-Dīn Shāh's personal physician also offers insights into the lives of slaves in the *ḥaram*.[7]

Given the significant position of the multifunctional *ḥaram* institution of the Qājārs, this study attempts to examine the links between the private and public spheres, the *bīrūn* and *andarūn*. I argue that the socially and hierarchically organized occupants of the *ḥaram* served as agents who connected the household with the outside world, the public, and imperial life. By using the term *ḥaram*, I refer to the large private quarters that were attached to the royal family. Thus, I exclude the petty households established by nonroyal slave-owners. I contend that "slavery" in the *ḥaram* differed from all other forms of slavery. My intention is not to idealize *ḥaram* life, but rather to portray an actual picture of the royal *ḥaram*, where slaves, eunuchs, servants, and women were not voiceless, oppressed figures, but active individuals without whom the political system could not function. Further, my study benefits from photographic evidence: pictures of *ḥaram* life taken by Nāṣir al-Dīn Shāh Qājār and others.

INDIVIDUALITY AND COLLECTIVITY

One of the most important ways to distinguish *ḥaram* slavery from domestic or agricultural slavery is the physical environment and architecture in which the slaves lived. Most Iranian houses were traditionally divided into two parts: the *bīrūnī* (exterior) apartment allocated to men and the *andarūnī* (interior) or *ḥaram* (the quarter of the house devoted to women).[8] *Andarūnī* was a private space for the intimate social life of family members. Gender separation within the inside and outside areas depended on blood relationships; thus, men were not permitted to enter the *andarūnī* rooms until the *quruq* when the *shāh* or eunuchs had sent out all nonrelated men.[9] The *bīrūnī* was a public space where social norms had to be observed. The *ḥaram* people were confined within a physically enclosed environment, and their freedom to maneuver and to have contact with the outside world was strictly limited. *Ḥaram* servants, however, liaised between the two areas, thus facilitating inside and outside contact. Reliance on this social structure separating the *bīrūnī* from the *andarūn* maintained the purity of the royal family. On the one hand, this system ensured, through the implementation of Islamic law, that the royal family's purity and popularity with the public were safeguarded. On the other hand, it secured the inside from any outside political threat.

The *ḥaram* was a community of individuals whose tasks responded to the needs of the group. Residents of the royal *ḥaram* were mainly women, children, slaves, and free servants guarded by eunuchs.[10] The master-slave relationship was based on power, which emphasized the importance of loyalty and respect. These were essential in elevating the slave's status and maintaining the security and authority of the master. Within the established triangular pattern of the system, the social relationship among *ḥaram* members relied on harmony. The main characteristics of *ḥaram* life were: the subjugation of a member's individuality to the group and the royal system; the strict control of relationships between the sexes by convention and customary discipline; and the predetermination of the boundaries that assigned the interaction of *ḥaram* members. Indeed, the monopoly of the master's power assured that his authority was understood by the occupants and not contradicted. Yet within the *ḥaram* institution, slaves created strategies to deal with their limitations and masters adjusted to the realities of these individuals' lives and personalities. My research examines the identity and status of the slaves brought into this system and explores their activities within the boundaries of the *ḥaram*.

Ḥaram slaves were both male and female, white and black. They were recruited for service in the royal court from within and outside the country. Some were purchased by the local governors and sent to the *ḥaram* as gifts, and some were "booty" taken in war. There were also tribal chiefs who sent their daughters to the royal court to maintain political alliances with the government. The advantage of the geographic removal of slaves and eunuchs was considered a guarantee of loyalty to the master. Devotion and social detachment may seem paradoxical, but psychological and economic factors ensured the maintenance of the master-slave relationship. Uprooted slaves adopted by the *shāh*, detached from all social support groups and political authorities, devoted themselves to the Qājārs. Their behavior, formed within the masters' institutions, shaped their identity as a single unit with shared objectives.

While documentary sources furnish us with general ethnographic details about *ḥaram* slaves, we know very little about their places of birth. Specific terms such as *bardih* and *bandih* mean slave. *Ghulām* referred to a male slave and *kanīz* to a female, do connote gender and status; and if they were African, the term *sīyāh* (black) was also used. In addition to these general categories, terms such as *Āfrīqā'ī*, *Ḥabashī*, *Zangī*, *Nubī*, *Sīdī*, or *Kāfarī* demonstrated that ethnicity, religion, and geographical point of origin were used to categorize African slaves.[11] The classification of slaves by the writers mentioned above was to some extent arbitrary and varied. Mary Sheil states that three ethnic groups of Africans were living in Iran: "Bambassees, Nubees, and Habeshees," (in contemporary terms, people from Tanzania, Nubia, and Ethiopia).[12]

The centralized bureaucracy of the Qājārs required a division of labor within the *ḥaram* system. Slaves and eunuchs were used for various purposes such as manual workers, entertainers, *ghulām-i shāhī* (bodyguards), *lalih* (male nurses), *dadih* (female nurses) and *pīshkhidmats* (confidential servants). They came from different religious backgrounds, including Christian and Jewish. Likewise they were ethnically and geographically

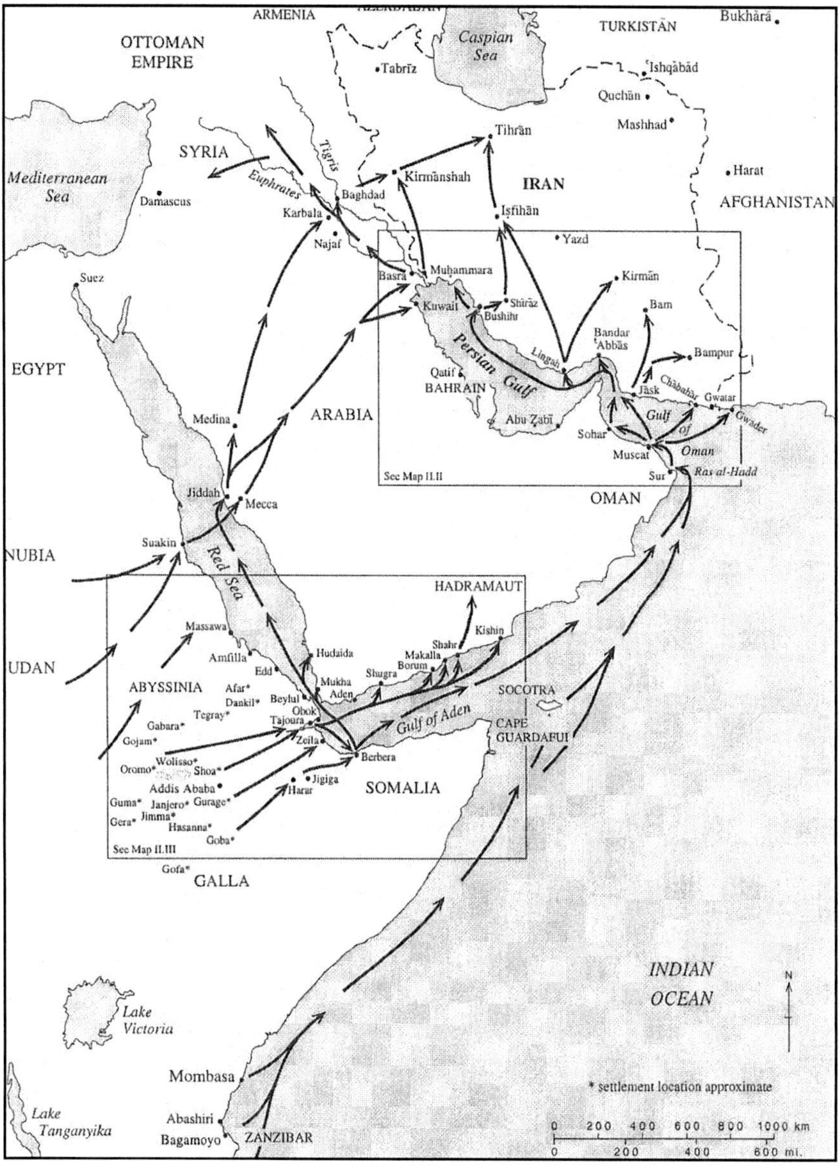

Map 5.1 Slave Trade of Iran

diverse: Turkoman, Kurd, Turk, Ādharī, Shīrāzī, Qazvīnī, Iṣfihānī, Georgian, Armenian, and Circassian. The servants of the *ḥaram* performed specific duties under the supervision of old guardians and eunuchs. Administrative and bureaucratic arrangements coordinated and organized the functional patterns of *ḥaram* occupants based on gender and ethnicity.

Some sources suggest that ethnicity determined the specific tasks of African slaves. Prevalent stereotypes divided Africans into two geographic types: East Africans from Zanzibar, Mombasa, and other towns on the Swahili coast, and northeastern Africans, including Nubians and Ethiopians. The first group was labeled as "lazy" servants, and for this reason, their price was lower. Men were employed as outdoor workers and field laborers, and women performed coarse household work. This apparent pattern of employment leads us to hypothesize that Persian families regarded the former group of Africans as investments. For this reason, they employed many cheap laborers in economic production and domestic work. By contrast, Africans from the northern and northeastern regions were considered to be brave and intelligent, and it is assumed that the most valued black *ḥaram* servants were Habashis recruited from this part of Africa. They were used as confidential servants in households and could be elevated to important positions. Habashi female slaves were often retained as concubines and were employed in the lightest duties in *andarūn*.[13] A parallel situation also applies to other ethnic groups— white Georgians and Circassians—who were renowned for their beauty and considered to be the most desirable of the *ḥaram* slaves. Such attitudes assisted in the process of the assimilation of certain ethnic groups.

Although the *ḥaram* occupants were ethnically diverse, they asserted their individuality within the context of established behavioral patterns. Hierarchical ranking within the organized social system determined the responsibilities of members of the community and shaped the relationships of heterogeneous members of the *ḥaram*. Gradually this system ameliorated any distinguishing ethnic characteristics of the slaves, underlining their dependency, but also permitting the formation of new identities. Within the framework of assigned tasks and activities, the members of the *ḥaram* could maneuver, interact with royal members, and forge links with the outside world. The existing coherence and structured domestication of the *ḥaram* allowed slaves and eunuchs to erect a framework that elevated their status and influence. Likewise, standardized patterns of employment paved the way for *ḥaram* inhabitants to occupy sensitive offices in the palace working for the central government.

VISUALIZING THE INVISIBLE: EUNUCHS, SLAVES, AND WOMEN

The position of the royal court was central to the growth and stability of the Qājār dynasty, the most important of the sociopolitical institutions. The *shāh* was the pivot around which the *ḥaram* system revolved. Having an established and extensive *ḥaram* was considered a mark of honor and dignity among the *shāhs* of his dynasty, built upon the principles of advancement, wealth, and luxury. The *ḥaram* relied on slaves being able to create alliances between the royalty and the outside world, since they communicated with foreign diplomats, doctors, teachers, and orientalists. Having easier access to internal and external resources, members of the *ḥaram* were able to live in a distinguished environment in which they participated in the arts, literature, fashion, politics, and entertainment. Even the lowest members of the *ḥaram* were inevitably exposed to the ideals of the royalty.

The domestic world of the *ḥaram* was inexorably connected to the Qājār government and inseparable from its politics. As such, attachment to the *ḥaram* within the Qājār sultanate could provide opportunities for popular respect and power. Alī Asghar Amīn al-Sultān, who was originally a Georgian slave, rose to the rank of prime minister in 1886.[14] Manūchihr Khān Muʿtamid al-Daulih, also a slave from Georgia, rose through the ranks to an elevated position in government, first appointed as *khaujih bāshī* (chief eunuch of the *ḥaram)*, then appointed as a minister, and finally promoted to governor of Iṣfihān.[15] Another Georgian slave, Khusru Khān Gurjī, brought to Iran by Āqā Muḥammad Khān, moved through the royal court to become the governor of Yazd, Kurdistān, Iṣfihān, and Qazvīn.[16]

Slaves, eunuchs, and servants formed a significant part of the royal court and, taken as a whole, were vital to the existence, function, and development of the Qājār government. The disciplined royal body guards were engaged in special palace ceremonies, many wearing military uniforms and bearing weapons.[17] Male slaves and free servants who inhabited royal households and palaces were considered the backbone of the state's military and administrative organizations. Sulṭān Masʿud Mīrzā, one of Nāṣir al-Dīn Shāh's sons and the governor of Iṣfihān and later of Fārs, Kurdistān, Luristān and Yazd, organized an army called the *Qazāq*. This group consisted of one hundred African slaves whose uniform consisted of a red felt coat, white trousers, polished black boots, a white fur hat, a golden belt, and a sword. They were drilled by two German military instructors.[18] Not all slaves were outfitted as grandly. For instance, when the Prince of Shīrāz arrived home, his slaves were described as follows:

"[C]rowds of cringing slaves and ragged troops were summoned from their peaceable occupations, to stand in mock array in the courts of the royal residence."[19]

Eunuchs played a central role in the sophisticated slave bureaucracy of the Qājārs. In fact, the development of Qājār bureaucracy reflects as much as anything else the autonomy gained by eunuchs in the outside world as within the *ḥaram*. Their activities and roles included some of the most important internal, domestic, and external state-related responsibilities. Eunuchs were called *khaujih* and bore the title *āghā* (English: great), a word applied before their name as a sign of respect and signifying eunuch status. Many eunuchs possessed vast political power and controlled a variety of state offices. For example, during the period of Constitutional Revolution (1905-11), when one of the *'ulamā* , Sayyid Muḥammad Ṭabāṭābā'ī, wanted to alert Muẓaffar al-Dīn Shāh to the chaos in the country, he wrote a letter through Ḥajjī Ghaffār Khān, which was given to the *mu'tamid al-ḥaram* (chief eunuch) who personally submitted it to the *shāh*.[20] Eunuchs played crucial socioeconomic and cultural roles as well as being critical agents in the enhancement and centralization of the Qājār's bureaucratic system.

Eunuchs were recruited and purchased from among the slaves to serve all ranks of nobility as well as wealthy merchants. They offered protection for the *andarūn* and warded off threats from adversaries.[21] Often their detachment from normal kinship ties made them viable candidates for a variety of political and administrative tasks in the *ḥaram*. Therein they were offered further opportunities for social advancement in advisory, protection, and educational capacities. Since the eunuchs' relationship with the *shāh* was based on total allegiance, mutual honor was established. Not only were they appointed to important government positions, but they were also given a variety of titles: *īshīk āqāsī bāshī* (grand chamberlain), *qullar āqāsī bāshī* (chief of *ghulāms*); *āghā bāshī* or *khaujih bāshī*[22] (chief of eunuchs); and *khaujih sarāyān*[23] (standing eunuchs).[24] Some of them, like the *āghā bāshī,* who controlled the *ḥaram*, had several other eunuchs working under them.[25] The Ethiopian Ḥāj Surur Khān was given to Nāṣir al-Dīn Shāh as a present by Niẓām al-Daulih Mu'yyir al-Mulk. He was so well respected that whenever he went for a walk, several other eunuchs usually accompanied him.

Eunuchs received an income. Their financial independence enabled them to gain authority and prestige. For example, Bashīr Khān, the *āghā bāshī*, was considered wealthy, earning T2,000 annually from Nāṣir al-Dīn Shāh. Born in Ethiopia, he had been brought to Iran as a child and ultimately married one of Muḥammad Shāh's (r.1834–1848) concubines.[26]

Eunuchs were responsible for protecting women and children in the *andarūn*. They regulated sexual practices and facilitated *ḥaram* functions. As intermediaries between women and outsiders, they guarded the honor and prestige of the royal family by distributing messages and information among the *ḥaram* inhabitants, bringing materials from the outside to the women inside, escorting guests from the *bīrūnī* and announcing their arrival to the *andarūn* (thus preserving Islamic cover),[27] preventing unauthorized men from entry, and safeguarding women's movements. For instance, Āghā Nurī Khān, the *I'timād al-ḥaram,* was responsible for women in the *ḥaram*, including granting entry and exit permission. Similarly, as eunuchs were considered to be the best horsemen, it was their responsibility to protect women outside the *ḥaram* as well. They accompanied the women in the streets, managed their horses, and kept umbrellas over their heads when it rained.[28] Three or four eunuchs served each of the first-rank wives of the *shāh*, while second-rank wives had one or two eunuchs and third-rank wives had none.

Women's reproductive role in the *ḥaram* was less emphasized than has been suggested. The overwhelming misrepresentation and fallacies associated with ideas about the lives of women in this world have been exacerbated by the Islamic tradition that denied outsiders access to *andarūn* space. Indeed, women established their own power within the gendered *ḥaram* space, based on customary and traditional social notions that allowed the empowerment of women within a male-dominated world.

Without the hierarchical system managed by *andarūn* women and the *shāh*'s wives, the *ḥaram* system could not have functioned. At the apex was the *shāh*'s mother.[29] A wife of royal origin, whose son had the right to take the throne, was considered first in rank and possessed a separate residence. This structure determined the significance and authority of the first-rank wife in relation to other members of the *ḥaram*. The senior wives of the *shāh* were next in rank. The majority of females in the *ḥaram,* however, were not the *shāh*'s legal wives. Some were chosen as his concubines,[30] some married government officials, and some were wives and concubines of other members of the royal family. Circassians and Georgians, called *gurji Juzali* (beautiful Georgian), were more likely to be chosen as the *shāh*'s companions. These women were considered "leisure" members, and were granted jewelry and houses. It has generally been assumed that most African female slaves came from Ethiopia. These women, the Habashi, were renowned for their intelligence and honesty, and were usually retained as concubines or employed as attendants in the *andarūn*.

Nāṣir al-Dīn Shāh's wives were categorized according to ranks described above and received regular stipends. The finances of the *ḥaram* came from the custom house through the office of the *i'timād al-ḥaram.* Anīs al-Daulih, one of the Nāṣir al-Dīn Shāh's wives, received T30,000 annually.[31] The highest-ranking of the *shāh*'s women received monthly stipends of T750, the second-rank T500–T200, and the third group T100–T150 each.[32] Through their attained wealth women could obtain considerable financial independence and exercise power in the *ḥaram.*

Female slaves were involved in household reproductive and administrative activities within the palace. They were maids, domestic servants, and menial labourers who performed the heavier duties inside the *ḥaram.* They served the *shāh*'s wives by doing the housework, including serving food to the *ḥaram.*[33] In their capacity as carers for the *shāh*'s children—working as *dāyih* (wet nurses) or *dadih*—they were regarded as second mothers.[34] They also served as female dignitaries who represented the interests of their mistresses.

Female slaves had the opportunity to rise to high positions and become close to the *shāh.* In this case, their residence was changed, their stipends rose, and the number of their servants increased. Moreover, if offspring of their relations attained governmental positions, their status benefitted their relatives. For instance, Muḥammad 'Alī Mīrzā, the eldest son of Fath 'Alī Shāh and the governor of Iranian Kurdistān, was the son of a female Georgian slave in the Qājār royal house.[35]

In contrast to the *shāh*'s wives, female slaves were less confined to the *ḥaram* compound. Their ability to move outside prescribed boundaries determined the limits of their freedom. They were more mobile and more independent in their access to the public domain. Through their enjoyment of a measure of freedom in time and space from the *ḥaram*, some acquired instinctive knowledge and artful manners that became an inspiration for the Qājār royalty. The *ḥaram* was a world of complexity encompassing all sorts of social life from politics to the arts. Within the domain of private space, its members projected their individuality and talents. They could elevate their status through their artistic talent, entertainment skills, diplomacy, housekeeping, and the demonstration of respectful subordination and affection to others. They could institute change in both the *ḥaram* and their own personal lives.

The close relationship that developed between slaves and freeborn members of the royal household reduced many of the prejudices and social boundaries of the *ḥaram.* Slaves were responsible for nurturing princes, training young girls, and educating royal children about science and good manners. Meanwhile, inside the *ḥaram*, young women were trained by senior women. They learned how to administer *andarūn* duties and maintain relations with the *shāh*, the royal family, and others. The slaves' children played with princes. ʿAyn al-Salṭanih, the grandson of Muḥammad Shāh, grew up with his own *kanīz*, Ṭāza Gul (the new flower), and studied in the same *maktab* (traditional school). When ʿAyn al- Salṭanih married, the *kanīz* was given to his wife, Gilīn Khānūm, after whose death she continued to work for him together with her husband Changīz.[36] Feelings of belonging to the royal family motivated many slaves and domestic servants to work collectively. Indeed, the Qājār *ḥaram* was represented as an extended family to its slaves and servants.

Theatrical entertainment and the artful manner of dance and musical performance have been seen as indicators of the *ḥaram* inhabitants' empowerment. Some *ghulām bachih* (child slaves) played musical instruments including the *dāyrih* and *dunbak* (two types of tambourine) and *santūr* (dulcimer).[37] Ṭūṭī was a dancing girl from Shīrāz, and the African Ḥājjī Qadamshād led a group of dancers.[38] In *ḥaram* culture sport was also popular. Eunuchs like Ḥāj Mubārak performed as wrestlers before the *shāh*.[39]

The *ḥaram* was an exclusive space where the inhabitants worked, congregated, exchanged information, and learned about society and politics. It was a safe domestic sphere where prestige and power were maintained for the Qājār family, largely through the efforts of servants and slaves who served as agents of communication between the *andarūn* and the *bīrūn*. This study has attempted to dispel the stereotypic representation and imagery of the secluded *ḥaram*. It emphasizes its active role within the palace. The relationship worked both ways: not only did newly recruited slaves and servants transform and revitalize the traditional culture of the *ḥaram*, but it facilitated the integration of the various social, religious, and ethnic backgrounds of slaves and servants into the *andarūn* culture. Their alliance formed a unified *ḥaram* culture that ensured social and religious norms. Dependency and empowerment were two inseparable factors in the slave-*shāh* relationship. The *ḥaram* institution and way of life became so ingrained that they remained an integral part of Iranian society even after the first abolitionist *farmān* in 1848 and lasted until slavery was finally abolished in 1928.

Notes

1. I'timād al-Salṭanih Muḥammad Ḥasan Khān, *Khalsih* (Tihrān, 1348), 11.
2. Dust ʿAlī Khān Muʿayyir al-Mamālik, *Yāddāshthāī az Zindigānī-yi Khuṣuṣī-yi Nāṣir al-Dīn Shāh* (Tihrān, 1362).
3. Tāj al-Salṭanih, *Khāṭirāt-i Tāj al- Salṭanih*, ed. Manṣura Ettiḥādīa and Sīrus Saʿdvandīān (Tihrān, 1361), 8.
4. Jakob Eduard Polak, *Persien, das Land und seine Bewohner* (Leipzig, 1865).
5. Charles James Wills, *In the Land of the Lion and Sun or Modern Persia* (London, New York, and Melbourne, 1891), 41–43.
6. Isabella Bishop [Isabella L. Bird], *Journeys in Persia and Kurdistan* (London, 1891), 2:181.
7. Jean Baptiste Feuvrier, *Trois ans a la cour de Perse* (Paris, 1900), 157; Muʿayyir al-Mamālik, *Yāddāshthāī az Zindigānī-yi Khuṣuṣī-yi Nāṣir al-Dīn Shāh*, 12; and Mas'ud Sālur and Iraj Afshār, *Rūznāmih-yi Khātirāt-i 'Ayn al-Saltanih (Qahramān Mīrzā Sālur)*, Ganjīnih-yi Khātirāt va Safarnāmih-hā-yi Īranī, 8-17 (Tīhrān, 1374), 872.
8. Feuvrier, *Trois ans a la cour de Perse,* 146. See also Shireen Mahdavi, "Women, Shi'ism and Cuisine in Iran," in *Women, Religion and Culture in Iran,* ed. Sarah Ansari and Vanessa Martin (Surry, 2002), 21–23.
9. Jakob Eduard Polak, *Persien, das Land und seine Bewohner* (Leipzig, 1865), 235.
10. S. G. W. Benjamin, *Persia and the Persians* (London, 1887), 104.
11. Sir John Malcolm, *Sketches of Persia* (London, 1827), 1, 19.
12. Lady Mary Sheil, *Glimpses of Life and Manners in Persia* (New York, [1856] 1973), 243.
13. Sheil, *Glimpses of Life and Manners*, 243–44; and Wills, *In the Land of the Lion and Sun,* 326–27. See also, Kemball to Sheil, 8 July 1842; Edwards to Kemball, 1842, pp. 207–11; and Kemball to Robertson and Sheil, 8 July 1842, FO 84/426, National Archives of the United Kingdom, Kew.
14. Abbas Amanat, *Pivot of the Universe: Nasir al-Din Shah Qajar and the Iranian Monarchy, 1831–1896* (Berkeley, 1997), 438.
15. Polak, *Persien,* 261; and James Baillie Fraser, *A Winter's Journey from Constantinople to Tehran* (New York, [1838] 1973), 2:16–17.
16. Muḥammad Taqī Lisān al-Mulk Sipihr, *Nāsikh al-Tawārīkh Tārīkh-i Qājārīya* (Tihrān, 1377), 3:1480.
17. Wills, *In the Land of the Lion and Sun*, 50.
18. Dust ʿAlī Khān Muʿayyir al-Mamālik, *Rijāl-i 'Ahd-i Nāṣirī* (Tihrān, 1361), 225.
19. Fraser, *Narrative of a Journey into Khorasan*, 103.

20. Mahdī Malikzādih, *Tārīkh-i Inqilāb-i Mashruṭīyyat-i Īrān* (Tihrān, 1335), 2:118.
21. Polak, *Persien,* 258; and James Bassett, *Persia, the Land of the Imams: A Narrative of Travel and Residence, 1871–1885* (London, 1887), 287.
22. See Muḥammad Ḥasan Khān I'timād al-Salṭanih, *al-Ma'āṣir va al-a'ṣār* (Kitābkhāni-yi Sanā'ī, 1307), 24.
23. See I'timād al-Salṭanih, *al-Ma'āṣir va al-a'ṣār*, 35. The *I'timād al-ḥaram* Ḥājjī Āghā Surur was the *khaujih bāshī.*
24. Qājārs were Turks; thus, many Turkish terms were used during this period.
25. Polak, *Persien,* 230.
26. Ibid., 258.
27. The words "*cet*" (Turkish) and "*buru*" (Persian) mean "go".
28. 'Ayn al-Salṭanih, *Rūznāmi-yi Khāṭirāt,* 794; Mu'ayyir al-Mamālik, *Yāddāshthāī az Zindigānī-yi Khuṣuṣī-yi Nāṣir al-Dīn Shāh,* 50, 70; and Polak, *Persien,* 254.
29. We know, for instance, that Mahd Ulyā, the mother of Nāṣir al-Dīn Shāh, was politically influential.
30. 'Ayn al-Salṭanih, *Rūznāmi-yi Khāṭirāt,* 1:1021.
31. Ibid., 1:1018–1020.
32. Mu'ayyir al-Mamālik, *Yāddāshthāī az Zindigānī-yi Khuṣuṣī-yi Nāṣir al-Dīn Shāh*, 18.
33. Ibid., 26.
34. Wills, *In the Land of the Lion,* 326; and Polak, *Persien,* 236.
35. J. P. Ferrier, *Caravan Journeys and Wanderings in Persia, Afghanistan, Turkistan, and Beloochistan* (London, 1857), 23.
36. 'Ayn al- Salṭanih, *Rūznāmi-yi Khāṭirāt*, 2:1753.
37. I'timād al-Salṭanih, *Yāddāshth-yi I'timād al-Salṭanih Marbūt bi Sāl-i 1300 H.Q.* (Tihrān, 1350), 43.
38. Malcolm, *Sketches of Persia*, 2: 149; and Mustaufī, *Sharḥ-i Zindigānī-yi Man*, 1:214.
39. Mu'ayyir al-Mamālik, *Yāddāshthāī az Zindigānī-yi Khuṣuṣī-yi Nāṣir al-Dīn Shāh*, 49.

Chapter 6

SLAVES IN A MUSLIM CITY: A SURVEY OF SLAVERY IN NINETEENTH CENTURY KANO

Mohammed Bashir Salau

While Islam and slavery coexisted in Kano by at least the medieval era, they were not as entrenched as they became in the nineteenth century.[1] The subjugation of the city by jihad forces in the early 1800s served as a major factor in strengthening and reinforcing the religion and the institution of slavery. These forces acted foremost as agents of Uthman dan Fodio and helped him integrate Kano and its environs into the vast Sokoto caliphate, founded following his declaration of jihad (holy war) in 1804.[2] Kano's conquest transformed it into a significant Muslim city in which the new rulers instituted a stronger morphological and legal Islamic system.[3] Despite the growth of Islamic culture among the nineteenth-century rulers of Kano, non-Islamic factors continued to influence developments in the city as well as in the Sokoto caliphate.[4]

Several scholars have examined the place of slavery in the caliphate, but few specifically focus on nineteenth-century Kano city even though detailed information exists for the era.[5] Of the few works on Birnin Kano, Heidi Nast mainly explores the relationship between gender and power in the settlement; hence only part of her analysis focuses on how Islam influenced the role of royal concubines in the palace.[6] Similarly, although Sean Stilwell offers the most comprehensive account of royal slavery in Kano city, he does not discuss much about nonroyal slaves or Islam.[7] This study will highlight the changing circumstances of both nonconcubines and nonroyal slaves within the context of Islamic reforms and the expansion of slavery in nineteenth-century Kano city society. The slave population in Kano increased significantly after the jihad, mainly through state-sponsored raids, although trade and kidnapping were also important means of enslavement. Slaves were used in virtually all aspects of the economy and society. While Islam influenced the process of slave acquisition, its religious strictures were loosely followed.

This study examines the conditions of slaves in nineteenth-century Kano city, including their acquisition, use, mobility, attitudes toward Islam, legal status, treatment, and resistance to slavery. In addition, it addresses how slave owners manipulated Islam as a means of social control. By 1800 Kano city may have contained a population of 30,000 permanent residents within its walls. There is no evidence to suggest that slaves constituted a significant proportion of this population before the jihad or that slavery flourished in Kano and its environs under the reign of Muhamman Alwali dan Muhamman Yaji (1781–1807).[8] The estimates of the city's population for the period following Alwali's reign largely derive from the accounts of contemporaneous European explorers and so must be treated with caution. Despite this, these figures indicate that the slave population had become very significant even before the mid-nineteenth century by which time the enslaved probably constituted half of the population. In 1824 visiting European explorers observed that more than half of Kano's 30,000 to 40,000 people were slaves,[9] while three years later Hugh Clapperton observed that there were thirty slaves to every free man in the city.[10] Commenting in the 1850s, Heinrich Barth indicated that the slave population in the city was about the same ratio as that of free men and described the slave presence then as "very considerable."[11] Another European writer, Charles H. Robinson, subsequently commented on the persistence of this population pattern in the last decade of the nineteenth century.[12] Thus, from the above estimates, it appears that it was only after the success of the jihad in 1807 that the slave population in Kano city rose dramatically.

Slave acquisition in nineteenth-century Kano city was inevitably conditioned by a mixture of factors, including Islamic law, which not only sanctions slavery but also approves of enslavement through jihad against nonbelievers.[13] It was natural that the nineteenth-century jihad movement and the subsequent wars of consolidation involving Kano led to the introduction of significant numbers of slaves into the city. The initial state-managed wars were largely confined to Kano and its environs. While these wars probably provided an opportunity for those already enslaved to secure their freedom or to escape from their masters, they also led to the introduction of many new slaves into the city.[14] The first emir, Suleiman (reigned 1807–1819, was not known to have many slaves in his palace and did little to encourage economic development in the city. His successor, Emir Ibrahim Dabo (1819–1846), however, initiated a huge expansion of slavery. Upon his accession, Dabo faced severe political and economic problems that prompted his reliance on slavery in the city and the emirate. For nine years he waged a series of vigorous campaigns to subdue rebel Fulani clan chiefs and to consolidate the emirate. In the course of these campaigns he restocked the palace with slaves, while the city retained many slaves brought in by war captains. Contrary to Islamic social law, which stipulates that believers in the faith should not be enslaved, a considerable number of these newly enslaved recruits were Muslims.[15] This loose adherence to Islamic principles concerning enslavement seems to have persisted into the late nineteenth century, although on a much reduced scale.[16]

The majority of foreign wars fought after the jihad took place after Dabo's regime. These skirmishes introduced more slaves into Kano city, predominantly non-Muslims from the Ningi region, which was constantly raided by Emir Usuman (reigned 1846–1855) and his successors: Emirs Abdullahi (reigned 1855–1883), Mohammed Bello (1883–1893), Mohammed Tukur (1893–1894), and Aliyu (1894–1903).[17] Various sources suggest that the wars against the Ningi peoples yielded a large number of war captives. For instance, in 1871 Emir Abdullahi and his allies attacked Warji and enslaved 5,200 people, while in 1895 Robinson noted that about 1,000 enslaved Ningi were brought back to the city from a single campaign.[18] Apart from the wars with peoples of the Ningi region, the late nineteenth-century rulers of Kano also fought other significant wars in Maradi, Damagaram, and other places, which introduced even more slaves into Kano and the emirate.[19]

Regardless of whether they were captured in the course of internal or foreign wars, enslaved prisoners brought into Kano were generally treated in accordance with Islamic theory. Although some were publicly executed at the various gates leading to the city, Muslim captives were mainly ransomed.[20] In the case of those enslaved, they were distributed according to the Hausa system of *humusi* (division of war booty) whereby the emir took one-fifth and the officers who took part in the campaigns shared the rest in adherence to Islamic law. In Kano and other parts of the Sokoto caliphate the strict application of this principle of booty distribution often proved abortive for two main reasons. First, some title-holding war captains such as the *sallama*, the *dan rimi*, and the *shamaki*, who were supposed to keep part of the slave booty, were themselves slaves and hence their share inevitably went to the emir(s). Second, since the emirs were often absent from the war front, individual nonslave warriors exploited such opportunites and appropriated some of their captives as personal slaves on the grounds that they were private booty.[21]

In the nineteenth century traders also brought slaves into Kano city. Predominantly Muslim, their business was greatly enhanced by the unprecedented level of state intervention that followed the establishment of jihadist regimes in Kano and the Sokoto caliphate. They traversed neighboring and distant settlements such as Borno, Adamawa, Bida, Bagarmi, and Gonja for business activities, which included trading in slaves.[22] By the mid-nineteenth century merchants had transformed Kano into a great centre of slave trading. One estimate reveals that by 1862 between 2,500 and 3,000 slaves were displayed daily for sale at the Kano market.[23] Although the majority of the slaves were ultimately reexported, a sizeable number were retained within the city.

The disposal of slaves at the Kano market was usually not handled by the itinerant traders but by resident slave dealers who lived mainly in the Dala and Koki wards of Kano where they operated a small house-to-house system of marketing resident slaves. Their main business dealings, however, centered on imported slaves at the Kurmi, Mandawari and Fase-Keyi markets where business transactions are said to have been tempered by Islamic regulations, especially following the jihad.[24] Thus, slave dealers (who appear to be predominantly Muslim males) revealed the true conditions of slaves to prospective buyers. Factors such as age, sex, origin, health, and demonstrated talent determined the price of a slave. Although the sale prices fluctuated considerably during the nineteenth century, usually the price of young women was a little higher than that of young men.[25]

Outside the acquisition of slaves through warfare and trading, Kano city also derived a smaller number of its slaves through several other means, especially kidnapping, but also through gifts and inheritance. Although Islam does not encourage the act, random slave kidnapping became particularly endemic within the Kano emirate whenever enforcement of sharia was lax and/or during periods of turmoil.[26] It appears that some of those seized during such times, particularly in the border regions, were ultimately enslaved in the city. Beside those kidnapped within the Kano emirate, strangers from other regions such as Bornu and Ningi were also seized, sometimes by relatives, and sold into slavery at Birnin Kano.[27]

Increased availability of slaves made more extensive use of slaves possible in nineteenth-century Kano. Further, after 1807, when the transatlantic slave trade was outlawed and external demand for slaves from the Atlantic economies declined, there was a concomitant rise in retaining slaves for use in the city and other parts of the emirate. Slaves were used in households where they carried out various tasks such as cooking, laundry, and cleaning. Eunuchs were employed as guardians of women. Slaves were also employed as field workers in a variety of agricultural environments: on small farms where they usually worked alongside their masters; on farms or plantations outside the city; or in multiple farms that made up the estates of wealthy slave owners. For instance, Tambarin Agalawa Yakubu, a wealthy kola importer who died in the early 1890s, managed the Makafi, Gonar Kuka, Allah Tayamu and Gonar Kofi farms located within the city walls of Kano as well as many plantations and small farm holdings outside the city. His fragmented holdings were characteristic of Kano emirate plantation development in the private sector during the late nineteenth century.[28]

Other Kano slave owners used their slaves in a variety of occupations. Influential merchants such as the renown Kundila involved their slaves in their trading activities (to the extent that trusted individuals were sent to distant lands to buy and sell on behalf of their masters) while the *Fatoma* (financiers) employed their slaves to provide various services, including livestock rearing for incoming traders. We know that a considerable number of the approximately 50,000 dyers occupied at some 15,000 dye pits in the Kano area at the end of the nineteenth century were slaves. Within the city, many slaves were engaged in spinning and weaving to supply this industry. Outside the textile industry, blacksmithing and other relatively minor industries, such as mat making and basketry, also engaged slaves in production.[29] More importantly, however, slaves were employed in various capacities in the Kano palace, including domestic and emirate administration, army service, and security.[30] In addition to their practical use, slaves (especially royal slaves) served as an important status symbol in nineteenth-century Kano. Barth perceived this, observing that in the passages of the emir's court "hundreds of lazy, arrogant courtiers, freemen and slaves, were lounging and idling…killing time with trivial and saucy jokes."[31] Taken together, slaves in their varied employment contributed to Kano city's enhanced participation in the desert-edge economy and the evolving "legitimate trade" across the Atlantic, but it was the orientation of the city's economy toward the desert-edge sector that, in addition to local custom and Islam, significantly influenced the master-slave relationship in the city.

Regardless of how and where the slave was employed, perhaps the most important factor in his or her social mobility in the emirate of Kano was Islam. The religion makes it compulsory for slave masters to provide their slaves with religious education and ultimately to convert them to Islam, by chastisement if necessary.[32] Slave masters facilitated slave education by providing instruction in the Quran, Arabic, and traditions of the Prophet. Further, as part of the conversion process, masters usually attempted to ensure that their slaves learned and abided by the Islamic code of conduct, including the observance of the five daily prayers and fasting. Once the slave had satisfied basic requirements of conversion, he or she usually participated in a ritual ceremony in which the slave was given a new name, marking the beginning of a new relationship with the master. It follows that the converted slave began to enjoy certain benefits that translated into an enhanced status beyond that of non-Muslim slaves. In related cases, Islam also enhanced the status of children born in slavery. Soon after delivery, such children were commonly given Muslim names in ceremonies usually sponsored by the slave masters, after which they were designated as *cucanawa* (second-generation slaves). Compared to purchased or captive slaves, the *cucanawa* enjoyed greater freedom of movement and other benefits.[33] For female slaves, another route toward mobility in emiral Kano was concubinage. Islam allowed a free man to marry a maximum of four wives simultaneously and also to posses as many concubines as his means allowed.[34] Largely under the influence of this injunction, concubinage became widespread in Birnin Kano. Once a slave woman became a concubine her status approximated that of a free-born wife in many respects, as was the case in other Muslim societies.

Besides concubinage, the Islamic principle that encourages every slave master to accept a slave's request to purchase his freedom and to assist him in acquiring the means to do so, contributed visibly to slave mobility in Kano city. There are abundant cases where slaves entered into agreements with their masters on the price to pay for their *murgu* (freedom). In many cases, slaves were able to make installment payments to their masters until they met the agreed purchase price, thereby securing their freedom.[35] Slaves could also explore other means of emancipation sanctioned by Islam.[36]

Although only a few slaves attained high office, primarily due to the avenues of mobility offered by Islam, their example provided even the lowliest slave with hope that fortune might, one day, turn in his favor upon conversion to Islam or the attainment of higher Islamic education. Such perceived opportunities for enhanced status or possibilities for emancipation may have contributed to the accommodative attitude of most slaves toward Islam.[37] Not only did slaves demonstrate this attitude, it appears that they also sought to influence the practice of the religion. For example, some royal slaves successfully pressured Emir Abdullahi Dabo to approve their marriages with free women, although their victory was short-lived, for after Dabo's death, Mohammed Bellow forced them to divorce their freeborn wives. Even though the Maliki law adopted in Kano city sanctions such union, the post-*jihad* rulers did not permit the practice.[38]

The legal status of slaves in emiral Kano city varied according to whether they were first- or second-generation, and this also had a religious connotation. Purchased or captured non-Muslim slaves could be punished or disposed of by their owner as he pleased. Children of male and female slaves belonged to the mother's owner, and owners could dissolve slave marriages. Where the owner took female slaves as concubines, the children were freeborn and thus legitimate heirs of their father. Further, their mothers became free upon the death of the owner. Other slave offspring were brought up as Muslims and were linked to the owner's family by quasi-kinship ties. Collectively, the aforementioned and other codes that governed slavery derived from the Maliki law that also operated in other parts of the Sokoto caliphate.[39]

The Maliki law that defined the legal status of slaves in the Sokoto caliphate generally and Kano city particularly also sanctioned the fair treatment of slaves. An owner, for example, was enjoined to share his food with his slaves, clothe them properly, not overwork them, and refrain from excessive punishment.[40] Despite the commitment of many rulers and Muslims to Maliki law, the history of slavery in Kano city, especially in the latter part of the nineteenth century, is replete with tales of harsh treatment of slaves due to several factors, including laxity in implementing the sharia and the inability of the slave population to reproduce itself naturally. A partial explanation for this development may perhaps be found in changing slave demographics. Early in the nineteenth century many slaves were not only Hausa but also Muslim, and hence probably treated well in accordance with Islamic principles. By the end of the century, however, non-Muslim slaves made up a large percentage of the slave population. It appears that this influenced a change in the nature of slave treatment. According to Imam Imoru, who obtained his Islamic education in Kano, "people had nothing but contempt for slaves. The slaves suffer: people look at slaves as worthless creatures, they do not consider them as human beings and treat them harshly."[41] Available oral data corroborates this point and there is other evidence that indicates that the treatment of newly captured and trade slaves (mostly at the market) was visibly inhumane.[42]

In the face of harsh treatment, slave status was always considered a disgrace regardless of the slave's attainment of high political office and/or access to economic advantages. "A slave is a slave for all that he is rich," states part of a proverb current in Birnin Kano and other parts of the Sokoto caliphate during the nineteenth century. Under such circumstances it is not surprising that tension between master and slave sometimes erupted in violence and outright resistance to slavery. In 1827 Clapperton reported from Kano that a merchant from Ghadames had been strangled in his bed. His female slaves were suspected of the murder since two or three similar cases had occurred before. Moreover, there were numerous cases of runaway slaves, while the number of town slaves who insisted on being sold was high. For their own part, trade slaves seized any opportunity to escape from the notorious slave-trading city or resisted in other ways, including refusing to work or engaging in deliberate work slow-downs. Even though slave resistance in Kano did not take the form of a general uprising, the palace slaves did mount a revolt during the reign of Abdullahi (1855–1883), but the aristocracy successfully contained it.[43]

Various reasons may explain why a general slave uprising failed to develop in Kano city before the end of the nineteenth century. First, violent treatment and the threat of harsh punishment may have kept slaves in check. Second, slave owners used Islamic propaganda to warn slaves about possible dreadful consequences that might result if slaves questioned the legality of their enslavement or fled their masters.[44] For example, Emir Ibrahim Dabo quoted verses of the Quran and Prophetic traditions that stressed the importance of loyalty to rulers.[45] Moreover, slave owners, as part of the indoctrination, relied extensively on charms and amulets made by Muslim scholars to deter slaves from active resistance.[46]

In conclusion, this study offers a preliminary examination of the relationship between Islam and slavery in nineteenth-century Kano. It seeks to bridge the gap in the existing literature on slavery and to highlight the detailed information submerged in a variety of documents that allow scholars to go beyond existing generalizations about slavery in the Sokoto caliphate. This investigation provides sufficient evidence to demonstrate that slavery was very widespread in Kano city, that it was more complex than previously assumed, and that it was typical of slavery in other parts of the Sokoto caliphate.[47]

Notes

1. M. G. Smith, *Government in Kano 1350–1950* (Boulder, CO, 1977), 129–30; and H. R. Palmer, "The Kano Chronicle," *Journal of the Royal Anthropological Institute* 38 (1908), 58–98.
2. For a history of the Sokoto caliphate, see Murray Last, *The Sokoto Caliphate* (London, 1967).
3. For the debate on what constitutes a Muslim city, see Janet L. Abu-Lughod, "The Islamic City-Historic Myth, Islamic Essence and Contemporary Relevance," *Journal of Middle East Studies* 19 (1987), 155–76; Ira Lapidus, *Muslim Cities in the Later Middle Ages* (Cambridge, 1967); and Albert Hourani and S. M. Stern, eds., *The Islamic City* (Philadelphia, 1970).

4. Abdullahi Mahadi, "The State and the Economy: The Sarauta System and Its Roles in Shaping the Society and Economy of Kano with Particular Reference to the Eighteenth and the Nineteenth Centuries," Ph.D. dissertation, Ahmadu Bello University, Zaria, 1982.
5. Studies on slavery in the Sokoto caliphate include Allan Meyers, "Slavery in the Hausa-Fulani Emirates," in *Aspects of West African Islam,* ed. Daniel F. McCall and Norman R. Bennet, Boston University Papers on Africa (Boston, 1971), 5:177–81; and P. E. Lovejoy, "Slavery in the Sokoto Caliphate," in *The Ideology of Slavery in Africa*, ed. idem (Beverly Hills, 1981), 200–43.
6. See Allan Christelow, ed., *Thus Ruled Emir Abbas: Selected Cases from the Records of the Emir of Kano's Judicial Council* (East Lansing, MI, 1994).
7. For further details, see Heidi J. Nast, *Concubines and Power: Five Hundred Years in a Northern Nigerian Palace* (Minneapolis: London, 2005); and idem, "The Impact of British Imperialism on the Landscape of Female Slavery in the Kano Palace, Northern Nigeria," *Africa* 64 (1994), 34–73 See also Sean Stilwell, "The Kano Mamluks: Royal Slavery in the Sokoto Caliphate, 1807–1903," Ph.D. dissertation, York University, 1999; idem, "Power, Honour, and Shame: The Ideology of Royal Slavery in the Sokoto Caliphate," *Africa* 7 (2000), 394–421; and idem, "Culture, Kinship, and Power: The Evolution of Royal Slavery in Nineteenth Century Kano," *African Economic History* 27 (1999), 137–75.
8. Smith, *Government in Kano*, 261.
9. Dixon Denham, *Narrative of Travels and Discoveries in Northern and Central Africa in the Years 1822, 1823 and 1824 by Major Denham, Captain Clapperton and the Late Doctor Oudney...* (London, 1826), 281.
10. Hugh Clapperton, *Journal of a Second Expedition into the Interior of Africa* (London, 1829), 171.
11. Heinrich Barth, *Travels and Discoveries in North and Central Africa Being a Journal of an Exhibition Undertaken under the Auspices of H.B.M.'s Government in the Years 1849–1855* (London 1965), 143–44.
12. Charles H. Robinson, *Hausaland; or Fifteen Hundred Miles Through the Central Soudan* (London, 1896), 113.
13. J. S. Hogendorn, "Slave Acquisition and Delivery in Precolonial Hausaland," in *West African Culture Dynamics: Archaeological and Historical Perspectives*, eds. R. Dumett and B. K. Schwartz (New York, 1980), 477–93; and Philip Burnham, "Raiders and Traders in Adamawa: Slavery as a Regional System," in *Asian and African Systems of Slavery,* ed. James L. Watson (Berkeley, CA, 1980), 43–72.
14. Smith, *Government in Kano,* 201.
15. See *Government in Kano,* 233–35, Smith oversimplifies this by referring to this category of people largely as "Hausa".
16. Interviews with Mallam Idrisu Danmaiso, Hausawa ward, Kano, 7 August 1975; and Alhaji Isyaku Yakasai, Kano, 6 August 1975, Yusuf Yunusa Col-

lection. The Yunusa Collection consists of interviews recorded on cassette tapes in 1975. They have been deposited at the Northern History Research Scheme of Ahmadu Bello University Zaria, and at Harriet Tubman Institute of York University, Canada. Tubman Institute. They are also available on CDs or in digital format at the Tubman Institute.

17. For more details on the raids on the Ningi region, see Adell Patton, Jr., "An Islamic Frontier Polity: The Ningi Mountains of Northern Nigeria, 1846–1902," in *The African Frontier*, ed. Igor Kopytoff (Bloomington, IN, 1987) and Smith, *Government in Kano*, 274–77.
18. This is not to suggest that all those enslaved through foreign warfare were retained in Kano; however, Robinson's statements indicate that a significant number of war prisoners ended up there, although in most cases this was temporary. See *Hausaland*, 130–31. For details of the Warji raid, see Paul Lovejoy, Abdullahi Mahadi, and Mansur Ibrahim Mukhtar, "C. L. Temples, Notes on the History of Kano," *Sudanic Africa: A Journal of Historical Sources* 4 (1993), 7–76.
19. Yusuf Yunusa, "Slavery in the Nineteenth Century Kano," B.A. essay, Department of History, Ahmadu Bello University, Zaria, 1976; and Smith, *Government in Kano,* 276–78.
20. Interviews with Dan Rimin Kano, Kano city, 12 & 30 December 1975, Yusuf Yunusa Collection.
21. Ibid; and Mahdi Adamu, "The Delivery of Slaves from the Central Sudan to the Bight of Benin in the Eighteenth and Nineteenth Centuries," in *The Uncommon Market. Essays in the Economic History of the Atlantic Slave Trade,* eds. H. A Gemery and J. S. Hogendorn (New York, 1979), 167.
22. For more details on the role of the state in trade during the nineteenth century, see Mahadi, "State and the Economy."
23. Yunusa, "Slavery in Nineteenth Century Kano," 10. The number of slaves displayed for sale at Kano varied considerably.
24. Interview with Sani Shu'aibu, Hausawa ward, Kano, 22 August 1975, Yusuf Yunusa Collection.
25. Yunusa, "Slavery in Nineteenth Century Kano," 12.
26. John Weir Chamberlain, "The Development of Islamic Education in Kano City, Nigeria, with Emphasis on Legal Education in the Nineteenth and Twentieth Centuries," Ph.D. dissertation, Columbia University, 1975, 126.
27. Yunusa, "Slavery in Nineteenth Century Kano," 6.
28. See Paul Lovejoy, *Transformations in Slavery: A History of Slavery in Africa* (London, 2000), 201–08; and idem, "Plantations in the Economy of the Sokoto Caliphate," *Journal of African History* 19 (1978), 341–68. Lovejoy suggests that this was as a result of the increasing implementation of the Islamic principle on inheritance and emancipation.
29. For more details on the use of slaves in Kano city, see Yunusa, "Slavery in Nineteenth Century Kano;" and Mahadi, "State and the Economy."

30. Stilwell, "Kano Mamluks."
31. Barth, *Travels,* 1:494, 497.
32. Khalīl ibn Isḥāq al-Jundī, *Mâliki Law; Being a Summary from the French Translations of the Mukhtaṣar of Sîdî Khalîl, with Notes and Bibliography, ed. and trans.* F. H. Ruxton, Napoleìon Seignette Perron, and Ernest Zeys (London, 1916).
33. Stilwell, "Kano Mamluks;" and Yunusa, "Slavery in Nineteenth Century Kano," 27.
34. For a detailed discussion of the institution of concubinage in the Sokoto caliphate, see Paul Lovejoy, "Concubinage in the Sokoto Caliphate," *Slavery and Abolition* 21 (1990), 159–89.
35. Yunusa, "Slavery in Nineteenth Century Kano," 30.
36. For instance, some were able to secure their freedom through deathbed acts of emancipation sanctioned by Islam.
37. Individual slaves must have resisted incorporation into Islam. For this, some may have been executed, exported, or punished in various ways while others may have succeeded in running away. In the face of such realities, most probably preferred accommodation to their new circumstances.
38. Stilwell, "Culture, Kinship and Power," 137–75; and Smith, *Government in Kano,* 294–95, 303.
39. E. R. Yeld, "Islam and Social Stratification in Northern Nigeria," *British Journal of Sociology* 2 (1960), 116.
40. For more details, see al-Jundī et al, *Maliki Law.*
41. Douglas E. Ferguson, "Nineteenth Century Hausaland: Being a Description by Imam Imoru of the Land, Economy and Society of His People," Ph.D. dissertation, University of California at Los Angeles, 1973. Imam Imoru's account of slave treatment contradicts those of Barth and some subsequent writers. The reason for the different interpretation has been detailed in Lovejoy, "Slavery in the Sokoto Caliphate."
42. Interview with Hauwa, Gwangwazo ward, Kano emirate, 11 July 1975, Yusuf Yunusa Collection.
43. See A. G. B. Fisher and H. Fisher, *Slavery and Muslim Society in Africa: The Institution in Saharan and Sudanic Africa and the Trans-Saharan Trade* (London, 1970), 140; and Palmer, "Kano Chronicle," 131.
44. Interview with M. Muhammadu, Bakin Zuwo, Kano, 9 October 1975, Yusuf Yunusa Collection.
45. Mahadi, "State and the Economy," 424.
46. Yunusa, "Slavery in Nineteenth Century Kano;" and interview with Alhaji Wada Shahuci, Kano emirate, 18 July 1975, Yusuf Yunusa Collection.
47. For the most comprehensive account of slavery in the Sokoto caliphate so far, see Lovejoy, "Slavery in Sokoto Caliphate." For an uncritical treatment of slavery in Kano, see Yunusa, "Slavery in the Nineteenth Century Kano."

Chapter 7

ISLAM, ETHNICITY AND SLAVE AGITATION: HAUSA "MAMLUKS" IN NINETEENTH CENTURY YORUBALAND

Olatunji Ojo

From the mid-nineteenth century slaves in Yorubaland were increasingly associated with insurrection and crime. Such incidents became more regular after 1850. Slaves, especially Hausa, known as Gambari, were associated with armed burglary, weapons possession, and assault with dangerous weapons. These violent crimes prompted the authorities of many Yoruba towns to enact laws that ordered the expulsion of resident Gambari population. Those who opted to remain were forced to carry passports and provide proof of 'legitimate' employment.[1] Those who failed to comply with these requirements were subjected to various punishments, including death.

Why were the Hausa specially targeted? Scholars examining the circumstances of these anti-Hausa laws have placed them within the context of socioeconomic change in the Yorubaland of the 1890s. They argue that the robberies were connected to military demobilization and the transformation of former combatants into bandits. Similarly, the notion of "Hausa thieves" was linked to commercial rivalry between Yoruba and Hausa kolanut traders as well as disputes arising from the excesses of Hausa soldiers in the service of British imperialists.[2] This study argues that these explanations do not sufficiently explain why Yoruba-speaking peoples, who made up the bulk of demobilized soldiers and ex-slaves and who suffered similar adjustments, were not similarly stigmatized. Second, the adjustment crises of the 1890s do not explain similar tensions during the first half of the nineteenth century. In fact, I suggest that analysis will reveal anti-Hausa sentiment going back to the 1810s. In doing so, this chapter examines the links between Yorubaland and the Islamic world and how shifts in these connections changed ethnic prejudices. As background, this study explores the context of problems arising from slavery, the slave trade, and changing relationships between the Yorubaland and Hausaland. In effect, the 1890s crime wave provided an avenue for the Yoruba to punish Hausa residents for a perceived reversal of fortunes. The connection to the past, as well as the focus on religion and slavery, enable us to reevaluate studies on Islam and slavery in Nigeria that have often centered on political units whose nature and organization were predominantly Islamic. The relationship between Islam and slavery in non-Muslim societies, such as Yorubaland, is yet to be fully appreciated.

ISLAM AND THE DELIVERY OF HAUSA SLAVES TO YORUBALAND

Not later than the sixteenth century Yorubaland was integrated into the Islamic world of West and Central Sudan.[3] Over the next three centuries this link facilitated the commercial exchange of slaves, kola nuts, munitions, pepper, imported salt, beads, cowries, cotton products, and other commodities for horses, textiles, leatherworks, mineral salts used for medical purposes, and natron (mixed with tobacco or snuff to add taste), and grain.[4] By the eighteenth century, however, Islamic influence from Hausaland had intensified in Yorubaland through long-distance traders and the importation of a large number of slaves.[5] The eastward expansion of the trans-Saharan trade route into Central Sudan, along with the political transformation of the region, allowed Yorubaland to play a very active role in the Central Sudan-Atlantic slave trade. Of special interest were slaves whose captivity coincided with the increased pace of Islamic revivalism in the Central Sudan. These slaves did not come out of Oyo's expansion into the Central Sudan, but as a result of internal wars among the various Hausa states. The importation of a large number of Muslim slaves by "Yoruba infidels" became one of the factors that propelled the attempt to extend the Sokoto religious wars or jihad (1804–1830s) southward.[6]

Rather than reduce the number of enslaved Muslims, however, the jihad apparently increased the number of Muslim and non-Muslim slaves from the Central Sudan. The expansion of Muslim slave exports had far reaching implications at home and abroad. This is evident in the frequent

Hausa slave agitations in Bahia, Brazil, and Sierra Leone, where many slaves were settled.[7] The sale of slaves thus increased the commercial position of Oyo, and its major port towns, Rakka (or Ogodo) in the interior, and Porto Novo, Lagos, and Badagry on the Atlantic coast.[8]

Apart from those who were sold into the Atlantic trade, many were retained within Yorubaland, and the number increased with the decline of the Atlantic slave trade. By the late eighteenth century, such Yoruba towns as Ilorin, Kuwo, Gbanda, Kobayi, Agoho, Kobe, Ikoyi, Oyo, Lagos, Badagry, Iseyin, and the districts of Egbado and northern Egba had substantial Muslim communities.[9] Muslims served in various capacities and were engaged as traders, slaves, scholars, and herders. Among the slave population, Muslims were a special class, having occupied important roles and having supported their non-Muslim Yoruba owners in the enslavement of fellow Muslims. Slaves of northern origin served in the cavalry, the elite wing of the military, and were also employed as barbers, rope-makers, cowherds, physicians, textile makers, farmers, and amulet makers.[10] These functions remained important throughout the century. In 1854 a Christian priest was told "the Mohammedans have their living by selling charms. Their patrons were the chiefs who did this for success in battle, riches, and long life among others."[11] Another contemporary writes:

> The chief reason why chiefs especially kings wish themselves long life is because plots are often hatched against them, either by their brothers…hence there is often civil war among them to which they often fall victims. And therefore when [a] title is given to one, although he accepts it with joy, he must now resort to Mohammedan and heathen diviners for charms to bury in his house, to hang to the roof of his house or round his body for protection.[12]

Increasingly many Yoruba believed that the Muslim amulets were more powerful than those made by the local medicine man. Soon it became popular for warlords to invite top Muslim clerics into their household for blessings before going to battles. Muslim charm makers also doubled as Islamic teachers and traders, which increased the interactions between them and the warlords.[13]

YORUBALAND, HAUSA SLAVES, AND THE AFTERMATH OF SOKOTO JIHAD

The Sokoto jihad had other consequences for Yorubaland. To prevent the enslavement of Muslims, jihad leaders enacted laws to stem the tide of Hausa slave exports. According to Paul Lovejoy, Sokoto decided to "maintain inspection points on its frontiers to look for Muslims who had been wrongly enslaved."[14] Attempts were also made to punish non-Muslim societies whose state of unbelief, it was argued, underpinned their participation in the enslavement of Muslims. This involved wars against non-Muslim states and granting freedom to enslaved Muslims. As some writers put it, the jihadist agenda was to "dip the Koran in the sea,"[15] a euphemism for the total conquest, Islamization, and incorporation of Yorubaland into the Sokoto caliphate. It was this decision that shaped the overall Hausa-Yoruba relationship in the nineteenth century, influenced Hausa slave resistance, and ultimately influenced the ethnic identity of slaves in Yoruba communities.

The second dimension was that shortly after the breakout of the Sokoto jihad, reform agitation also began among Muslims in Yorubaland. Abdullah Salih (Alimi), a cleric with strong ties to Sokoto, and Solagberu, a Yoruba clergyman, soon emerged as powerful Muslim voices in Yorubaland. They provided leadership to challenge the evils in their society.[16] Even though their popularity among the commoners operated against the interest of Yoruba power brokers, their expertise in warfare and Islamic medical science and support base in the military increased the demand for their presence in the palaces of Yoruba rulers. Consequently, a faction of the ruling elite, led by army chief Afonja of Ilorin, allied with these preachers in his plot to weaken Oyo and further his own cause.[17]

Having been promised protection against their former masters, slaves in Oyo revolted in 1817, after which they fled to Afonja's base in Ilorin. Because Ilorin was located on the trade route between Oyo and Sokoto, most slaves who seized the opportunity to rebel were from Central Sudan and hoped to return to their old homes.[18] For many of them the flight represented a sort of *hijra*, prescribed for Muslims whose faith was compromised by "sinful" regimes. The movement of slaves to Ilorin was buttressed by ethnic, religious, and class considerations. While Islam bound Alimi and Solagberu together, the latter shared the Yoruba ethnic bond with Afonja. Thus, most fugitive Hausa settled under Alimi and the Yoruba with Solagberu. These considerations would prove decisive factors in Ilorin's history. The 1817 revolt developed into a major uprising when, in 1823 the Alimi-Hausa alliance overthrew the Afonja-Yoruba party.[19] Following the victory of the Muslims in Ilorin, the town became the base of Muslim advancement into Yorubaland. From then onward, Hausa-Yoruba conflicts were associated with ethno-religious differences.[20]

Events in Ilorin had a major impact on Oyo politics and economy. Apart from slaves, Oyo also obtained the backbone of its military from the importation of horses and horse handlers from the Hausa states. Thus, a reduction in the supply of slaves and horses to Oyo also meant a decline in its military strength.[21] With a weakened military, Oyo's ability to check the encroachment of Sokoto warriors into its domain as well as Hausa interference in internal affairs was seriously compromised.

Second, Islamic militarism spawned a generation of armed brigands, consisting of Muslim militants (*jama'a*) and lawless Yoruba youths, the young glories or jackals (*ògo wẹẹrẹ*) who fanned out, waging wars and pillaging various Oyo towns and villages.[22] Ilorin's military successes against Oyo blocked the northern slave trade, which greatly reduced slave exports from the Central Sudan and stimulated the slave trade among Yoruba-speaking peoples. The collapse of the Old Oyo kingdom accelerated the political crisis in Yorubaland and exposed the intensity of "ethnic" rivalries among Yoruba states and the rate at which one group recruited slaves from among the others. Because bandits also engaged in slave raiding, this changed the ethnic composition of Yoruba towns and of the slaves sold by the Yoruba. For instance, as people fled Oyo in search of security, incoming refugees and the evolution of a culture of conspicuous consumption among Yoruba freebooters further heightened ethnic divisions, social tension, and conflict over land. The shift was accentuated by the emergence of Lagos as the most important slave port in West Africa, thereby drawing Yorubaland into the slave trade. The closeness of Lagos to Yoruba markets spread the frontiers of slave raiding further into the interior, thereby increasing the level of violence associated with slave recruitment. The ensuing crises underscored the importance of ethnicity in the pattern of slave recruitment.[23]

The dilemma for the authorities of Yoruba towns, at least in the early decades, was how to differentiate between Muslims who wanted to practice their religion and those who sought to overthrow the state. As a result, the power elite feared and distrusted radical Islam because of its role in the overthrow of Oyo and the subsequent sociopolitical upheavals throughout the Yoruba-speaking region. Muslims, slaves and freeborn, encountered hostility and even were persecuted. For instance, Oyo clamped down on its Muslim population during which many people, mostly Central Sudanese, were killed, imprisoned, or quickly sold into the Atlantic slave trade.[24] In Ibadan, to prevent the development of a Muslim community, the only mosque in the town was destroyed in the 1830s.[25] For this reason very few Hausa slaves were subsequently retained in areas previously under Oyo rule or settled by Oyo refugees, and explains why they were concentrated in the coastal districts of Lagos, Badagry, Ijebu, and Egba.[26]

Having failed to dislodge the Hausa from Ilorin, Oyo authorities sought alliance with any power that could help against its enemies.[27] Thus, when Clapperton traveled through Oyo territory between December 1825 and January 1826, a rumor spread rapidly that he was going to make peace between the rebelling Hausa slaves and the king of Oyo.[28] Clapperton himself gave impetus to this belief when he told one of the provincial chiefs "that if the King [of Oyo] made a good friend of the King of Eng[land] he would send him every thing he wanted that if ships could come up the Quara [Niger] there would be an end to the war immediately." These statements demonstrate Oyo's desire for allies against Sokoto. Hence, it was not surprising that its chiefs were more interested in the "great guns" than Clapperton's accounts of England's scenery. Alaafin Majotu even went to the extent of prolonging Clapperton and Lander's stay in Oyo and promised Lander, if he would live there, a wife, the position of prime minister, and the post of army chief.[29]

Unlike the 1820s and the 1830s, when Sokoto's cavalry operated freely and easily in the northern Yorba plains, the movement of Oyo's population into the forest and hilly regions reduced the impact and intensity of cavalry warfare. This also reduced the scope of resistance among slave soldiers. Consequently, future slave agitations shifted away from overtly political to low-scale, often personal, and religious forms, which is evident in the Islam-*orisa* religious and political split between Hausa slaves and their Yoruba owners. Islam provided an ideological platform for Hausa slave resistance, and even allowed them to refuse to serve under either the Yoruba *olorisa* or the small Christian elites.

On the other hand, the *orisa* religion operated as an ethno-judicial tool for the Yoruba to justify class and ethnic differences, punish offenders, and improve personal and communal welfare. Out of religious conviction, Hausa slaves often refused to participate in *orisa* activities. Clapperton and Lander remarked on the religious divide between Hausa slaves and their owners. At a reception organized for Clapperton in 1825, unlike the host Adele whose "principal men…had a dram each—with what relish they sucked it round their mouths keeping it in as long as they could," the "Mohametans from Haussa…refused, passing it all ways to others when the glass was offered to them."[30] At Abeokuta in 1856 a Fulani slave was found alone having refused to eat from the food his owner had offered to an *orisa*.[31] Similar information came from Ibadan, one of the leading Yoruba Muslim cities. In 1859 some Fulani cattlemen employed by Ibadan chiefs visited the CMS mission under David Hinderer. According to Mrs. Hinderer's journal, these Fulani who lived together said "*iya* (mother) we are alike, we are strangers in this country; we both speak a different language from this people (Yoruba), so we are one." They condemned *orisa* worship: "We cannot bear to look upon these foolish idols which the people here trust in. We are not half-Mohammedans like many here (Ibadan)."[32]

It is interesting how Central Sudanese slaves wove together the identities on which they and the European Christians stood in cultural opposition to the Yoruba. Their identities were based on language, ethnicity, belief in a global proselytizing religion, and sometimes, skin color. In each category, Muslims and Christians were minorities, outsiders, and "antislavery." Paradoxically, these shared beliefs were also at the root of the split between Muslims and Christian missionaries. Each party held its religion to be superior to the other. Thus, when Bowen tried to convert his Fulani language teacher to Christianity, the teacher Jato, a Fulani slave at Abeokuta, cancelled the classes claiming that his master's cattle demanded more attention.[33] At Ibadan, when Mrs. Hinderer preached to her Fulani guests, the latter "quickly began to talk about the weather and other things."[34]

To the Yoruba therefore, people who shared these characteristics were easily marked as outsiders and fair game. Thus, in 1866 a Hausa slave was chosen to replace an Ijesa soldier-slave as victim for human sacrifice. Even though the Ijesa's military background might have helped him because the Yoruba were loath to dispose of their soldier slaves, some of the expressions they used suggested that ethnicity was a bigger factor in his freedom. According to some Abeokuta chiefs, the Ijesa was "one of us" and the Hausa was a "foreigner."[35]

YORUBA CONSTRUCTION OF "GAMBARI" ETHNICITY

There were two layers in the naming of Central Sudanese slaves in Yorubaland. The Yoruba used terms such as "Bariba", "Tapa", "Gambari" "Hausa", "Kannike"; and "Gara" or "Agatu" to describe Borgu, Nupe, Hausa, Kanuri and Igalla/Idoma slaves respectively. The multiplicity of terms for Central Sudanese slaves also showed that the Yoruba-speaking people were aware of the multiethnic nature of these slaves' homelands. That some of these terms penetrated into the Atlantic world suggest that such slaves were probably sold by Yoruba traders, passed through Yorubaland en route to the Atlantic coast, or enslaved alongside Yoruba-speaking slaves in the Americas through whom the names were passed on to white slave owners.[36] Not later than the second half of the eighteenth century, however, the more embracing term "Gambari" had been adopted as a generic name for Central Sudanese people.

We do not have sufficient evidence on the origin of the term "Gambari." There is a Kambari ethnic group located close to the commercial intersection between the Hausa, Yoruba, Wangara, and Borgu network whose people served as porters in the Hausa-Yoruba trade. Since the Yoruba were located in the southern Niger valley, it is not impossible that the Yoruba knew about the "Gambari," a probable corruption of Kambari through operations on the Niger.[37] Because of the high visibility of Hausa in the Yoruba-Central Sudanese trade, it appears that the Yoruba began to associate the term "Gambari" with Hausa who constituted the largest component of the Central Sudanese population.

Since ethnicity also implies language, geography, and culture, ethnic identification of slaves is not always precise. Those referred to as Hausa or Gambari apparently included slaves from outside the core Hausa states. This was also the case in the nineteenth century, when the spread of Hausa influence through commerce and religion broadened the meaning of Hausa or Gambari. During this period more Hausa traders and slaves began to settle in or pass through Yorubaland, as the Hausa language became the lingua franca of the Central Sudan.[38] This process of "Hausa-ization" introduced terms that referred to the Hausa language and its speakers, people under the Sokoto regime, and people from across the River Niger as "Gambari."

Although Central Sudanese slaves came from a variety of ethnic origins, they often referred to themselves or were referred to as "Hausa," "Gambari," or Muslim slaves when fighting for their freedom. The "Hausa-ization" of Central Sudanese slaves contrasted sharply with the situation in their homeland where religious and ethnic differences had resulted in their original enslavement. This is not a strange paradox, for it confirms one of the diasporic peculiarities where identity indicators tend to have broader meaning than in the homeland.[39]

Religion also played a unifying role, bringing in people from outside the Central Sudan. Indeed, it did not take long for brigands of Yoruba origin to be identified as "Hausa" so as to benefit from opportunities open to the latter. For instance, Crowther attributed the destruction of many Oyo towns in the 1820s to the banditry of "Eyo" Muslims. In 1841 and 1857 he met several Yoruba in the service of the Nupe army. They spoke fluent Yoruba, Hausa, Nupe, and Fulani, and people called them Fulani.[40] So throughout the century, ethnicity and religion constituted strong ideological considerations connected to the recruitment and status of slaves, as well as important platforms for political change.

Christian missionaries in Yorubaland also compounded the nature of Hausa ethnic identification. They often equated Muslims with Hausa, and fair-skinned Africans with Fulani or Moors.[41] This multilayered meaning of Hausa is confirmed in Clapperton's journal. He recorded that when he arrived in Badagry, en route to the Central Sudan, he was visited daily by "natives of Haussa—some of who are Fellatas [Fulani], Negroes [Blacks] and one Showa Arab from Bornou."[42] Thus, in nineteenth-century Yorubaland the terms Hausa and Gambari suggested a dual process of "being" and "becoming" Hausa as well as a geographical, linguistic, commercial, political, and religious references. The Gambari were therefore people who spoke either the Hausa language or pledged allegiance to Sokoto caliphate.[43] It is in this sense that in 1899 Major Francis C. Fuller, the second British resident officer at Ibadan, described the "Gambari" as "belonging to any tribe beyond the [River] Niger."[44]

HAUSA SOLDIERS, YORUBA CIVILIANS: BRITAIN AND THE INVENTION OF TRIBALISM

Just as Ilorin provided an escape route for Hausa slaves, another development along the Atlantic Coast provided a similar, if not greater opportunity, for Hausa slave resistance. We have shown how British interests in the Central Sudan resulted in the missions of Clapperton and the Lander brothers from 1825 to 1830, followed by a joint British-CMS Niger valley mission in the 1840s and 1850s. The import of these missions and their modest antislavery instance was not lost on Hausa slaves serving in Yorubaland. Thus, both the British and many Hausa in Yorubaland who had been settled there as slaves shared common antislavery and anti-Yoruba sentiments.[45]

British authorities seized on the real and perceived differences between the Yoruba and Hausa slaves to recruit the latter into the colonial service as porters, interpreters and soldiers. One of the first tests of the Hausa-Yoruba divide employed by the British was during the Central Sudanese Mission led by William Balfour Baikie in March 1859. Baikie, plausibly in furtherance of the British antislavery campaign sent out his assistant Crook, who also happened to be a Nupe-Saro to recruit porters for the journey. Crook knowingly spread the information among Central Sudanese slaves in Lagos and by that "stole" them from their masters. More runaway slaves joined the entourage at Abeokuta. Overall scores of Central Sudanese slaves, estimated at 150–200, abandoned their owners and joined the Baikie party.[46] Within a few days, a second party led by John Hawley Glover again set to leave Lagos for the Rabba to join Baikie. Like Baikie, Glover ordered one of his Hausa servants Shanee (Yoruba & Hausa: Sani) to recruit porters. As the news of the Mission's departure from Lagos spread in the city and neighboring Yoruba towns, another 250 slaves including those belonging to Oba Dosunmu and a leading Lagos merchant and politician, Madam Efunporoye Tinubu, most of Nupe and Hausa origin joined Glover's mission to the Niger.[47] What these Hausa slaves wanted was not wage labor, but to use the British expeditions as avenues to returning to their homeland. As the news of these fugitive crises spread, Hausa slaves in Abeokuta and Ibadan also began to abandon their owners. When Lagos and Abeokuta slaveowners tried to retrieve their slaves from these entourages, the situation degenerated into an exchange of gunfire between the two groups. For the courage displayed by Hausa slaves in repelling the Yoruba, it was no surprise that when a colonial constabulary was to be created during the 1860s, the British authorities decided that the Hausa were best suited for this institution. They were considered to have the physique expected of a soldier. Official records described them as "well-built and lithely…many of them averaging nearly six feet in height…hardy, active, of a cheerful disposition" and loyal to constituted authority.[48] These attributes were reinforced by the historical success of Muslim warriors in Africa in the course of Islamic expansion and state formation, so the Hausas were seen as heirs to the Islamic tradition of warfare. Two officers who personified this phase, both of whom served as administrators of Lagos, were Henry Stanhope Freeman (1862–1863) and Glover who acted briefly for Freeman in 1862 and served as substantive administrator from 1863 to 1872. Glover, in addition to understanding the Hausa-Yoruba tension reinforced his opposition to the Yoruba by recruiting some Hausa porters and brought them to Lagos on his way to assume office as administrator of the government Nigeria in 1863. This group formed the core of Glover's colonial military force.[49] According to Freeman,

> this force should be raised here [Lagos] either of Houssas exclusively or of Houssa and Cape Coast men mixed. The Houssas… come from the interior…and have no tie binding them to the inhabitants of the coast save that of slaves to their masters. They are however the best fighting men the tribes on the coast possess. When Lagos was taken in 1852 [sic] Houssa slaves defended it…When once they throw off the yoke of slavery they bear no goodwill to their former masters and would stand by us to the last.[50]

Hence, for many decades the Nigerian army was also called the "Hausa Constabulary," "Glover's Hausas," or "The Forty Thieves."

What we see here is a conscious policy to emphasize the Hausa-Yoruba divide. A dispatch to the colonial office provides evidence of this policy. Commenting on the ethnicity and status of slaves in Lagos, Freeman identified two categories: (1) slaves appertaining to the soil and (2) slaves bought from the interior. According to him, both categories were domestic slaves but the latter were numerous and frequently sold into foreign slavery and therefore more detached from their Yoruba owners. Their principal aim was to redeem themselves and return to their country. Unfortunately only a few succeeded, since on "the slightest show of discontent such a slave was sold off to some distant market probably for exportation." The slaves of the soil, however, were better off, being in their own country under more benign conditions of servitude. Despite Freeman's inadequate knowledge of slavery in Yorubaland, he was right in identifying the odds stacked against Hausa slaves. "Slaves of the soil," a metonym for Yoruba slaves, were not too far from their natal homes, the farthest being Ekiti, Ijesa, Oke (Upper) Ogun, or places located within a 300-mile radius of Lagos. More than that, they shared certain ideological aspirations with their owners, having come from the same cultural zone. Slaves from the interior did not have these advantages. Some came from as far away as Borno and Sokoto, between 1,000 and 1,500 miles from Lagos, making the possibility of flight back home more difficult.

Another factor was that some of these Hausas were originally not enslaved in Lagos. Hundreds among them were runaway slaves from Whydah, Porto Novo, Abeokuta, or Epe, who escaped to Lagos after it fell to Britain in 1851, and others had returned from Brazil and Sierra Leone. Rather than escaping to freedom, however, some had been recaptured and re-enslaved by Yoruba people. As far as the British and the Hausas were concerned, the Yoruba slavers were nothing more than kidnappers. Hence, Freeman's calculation that these Hausa and Muslims would work hard for their liberty was well founded.[51]

After several decades of inaction in the Yoruba interior, the Lagos government embarked on an aggressive policy targeted at promoting free trade and asserting British supremacy. This required the pacification of the many Yoruba war camps and the arrest of warlords. Once again the British called on its Hausa agents, the soldiers and porters. Hausa slaves proved capable allies for these assignments, both of which had a positive impact for the abolitionist cause. On their journey to the Yoruba interior in 1886 the officers charged with ending the Kiriji war (1877–1886), Henry Higgins and Oliver Smith, traveled with an escort of fifty Hausa soldiers, 2500 ball cartridges, a seven-pounder gun, and a rocket launcher. According to Governor Fred Evans, the troops were not intended to overawe the Yoruba, but to safeguard the commissioners.[52] This was a half-truth. More than providing security to the commissioners, the necessity for Hausa soldiers was conveyed in an 1893 official statement. During the year Governor Gilbert Carter and a guard of Hausa soldiers toured parts of Yorubaland during which they destroyed the last Yoruba war camps. At Ibadan,

Carter requested the establishment of a military base and the deployment of two maxim guns and ammunition, and if possible, the new and superior machine-gun. In his words "there is no doubt that these guns are much needed, not necessarily for use, but it has been found that the mere sight of them has a soothing effect upon the native mind."[53] It is possible to gauge the impact of these military demonstrations on Yorubaland. Higgins and Smith's visit put pressure on Ondo authorities as to set in motion the process for the abolition of human sacrifice.[54] It was also not a coincidence that the treaties that ended the Yoruba wars were signed on these two occasions of military demonstration. Within the next decade Hausa slaves participated in the occupation of Ibadan; the bombardments of Ijebu, Oyo, and Ejinrin; and the imposition of low market prices at Ondo.[55]

HAUSA "WIVES": ETHNICITY AND FEMALE FUGITIVE SLAVES

British imperialism provided the opportunity for Hausa slaves to broaden their opposition against Yoruba slave owners. Unlike the earlier period when each slave tried to redeem himself/herself, the post-1890 period witnessed a more covert attempt to establish families and kin groups, and in some cases, Hausa enclaves. What provided this opportunity was the establishment of military barracks in some Yoruba towns. With Hausa dominating the military, the Hausa language became the official language of the Nigerian army. Thus, during the early decades of the colonial era, military barracks in Yorubaland were also called "*ago Hausa*" (Hausa camp). These camps often allowed Hausa soldiers to capitalize on the poor communication between local authorities and the new government, and the awe in which British officers were held, to abuse the system.[56] Between 1894 and 1901 reports from British officers—Major Frederick Lugard and Captains Robert Lister Bower and Gerald W. Ambrose—included accounts of impostors posing as government messengers. According to Ambrose, the impersonators only required "a delapedated [sic] pair of boots, a red fez or cap, a shirt and dark trousers" and "an old uniform, no matter of what regiment" to give them the semblance of absolute legitimacy since the people could hardly differentiate between genuine and fake officers.[57]

Because of the weakness of the antislavery crusade, Hausa soldiers seized on personal initiative to facilitate redemption of slave wives. One such initiative was the way that soldiers used "unauthorized actions" to help in the destruction of slavery.[58] They allowed military camps to be used as havens for fugitive female slaves, which illustrate links between gender, religion, marriage, and ethnicity. From the inception of British imperialism in Yorubaland, the local authorities premised their support for Britain on the assurance that the British would not tamper with existing institutions. This included guarantees that soldiers and traders would not take their wives and slaves away, and that runaway slaves would be restored to their owners.[59] Despite this assurance, many slaves still escaped to British territories and the barracks, where some fugitive wives married soldiers or returned to their native homes with the soldiers' help. In 1897 the case of one sergeant Galadjimo [Galadima?] who lured a female Hausa slave to the barracks was reported to the British resident, Major Bower. Court transcripts show that Galadima's action was common among Hausa soldiers, and that runaway Hausa female slaves often "demanded for the protection accorded to other Hausa female relations of soldiers." In settling the case, the British officer ordered the woman to pay her redemption fee to become free.[60]

In a related development, two incidents in the Ondo district further illustrate the links between slavery and ethnicity. In the first case, Mekunserun claimed he had bought two Hausa female slaves, Adisatu and Lade, from Amodu, a Hausa slave dealer at Iwo. Shortly afterward, a Hausa soldier seized the women and took them to the barracks. Even after Captain Bower had restored the women to their owner, they escaped again; Adisatu to another Hausa soldier, Private Musa Kanu; and Lade to the acting traveling commissioner of Igbobini, Major Ewart. In his judgment, Ewart restored the women to Mekuserun, but allowed Kanu to redeem Adisatu for £5.[61] In the second case, Fatumo, a Nupe slave wife of Awoyele's late father, rather than be inherited by a relation of her owner-husband, informed Awoyele that she had married Private Abba Kanu. Her decision to marry Kanu was also supported by the traveling commissioner, who asked Kanu to redeem her for £5.[62]

These cases are significant because they highlight the divergent motives of British officials, African soldiers, and female slaves. The women believed in the liberation ideology of the British government; this might explain Fatumo's decision for refusing to be shared out as property. Yet, the British were ambivalent on the issue of abolition and the poorly defined antislavery laws. Administrative ambivalence left major decisions to the whims of individual officers, which might explain Adisatu and Lade's escape from Ibadan (Bower's jurisdiction) to Igbobini (Ewart's jurisdiction). Hausa soldiers fully exploited their position to intimidate Yoruba slaveholders and keep them from reporting the loss of their slave wives. The behavior of Galadima, Musa Kanu, and Abba Kanu—all Hausas and most likely ex-slaves—represented a continuous pattern of Hausa slave resistance in Yorubaland. Furthermore, since the women involved were Hausa, it is plausible that ethnicity, common slave experience, and a desire to get back to their homelands rather than marriage were the main motives in the alliances they formed.

CONCLUSION

The Islamic jihad contributed to the demise of the Oyo kingdom and simultaneously boosted Muslim resistance to slavery. The jihad provided a common cultural ideology around which slaves from the Central Sudan were mobilized. These included the imposition of a supranational government based in Sokoto, the spread of the Hausa language, and wider acceptance and glorification of Islam. By 1817 Central Sudanese in Yorubaland responded to these "ethnic" indicators radiating from their homelands. More than in Central Sudan, where these same instruments were used to justify enslavement and where the Central Sudanese would have seen themselves variously as "Kenuwa," "Afunu", and "Akenci" for the Hausa,[63] "Beriberi" for the Kanuri, "Kakanda" for Nupe, and "Ardnawa" or "Ganega" for non-Muslims, slaves from this region reversed the process and used these tools to oppose the same institution. Muslim slaves imbued with this ideology fled from their masters and sought refuge with Sokoto and European establishments such as the jihadists and the West African Frontier Force. It is this dialectic reversal, which in many Yoruba minds, despite their deep internal differences, turned every Central Sudanese slave into a Hausa or Gambari, a Muslim, and perhaps, an armed robber.

Problems arising from slave control were genuine concerns both to the Yoruba overlords and their Hausa slaves. As we have shown above, the abilities of Hausa slaves to resist corroborate Lovejoy's study of slave resistance in the Central Sudan. According to him, although slave rebellion was less likely where runaway slaves were frequent, flight might not prevent slave revolts, especially when slavery merges with ethnicity. In other words, when slaves from common cultural backgrounds found themselves in concentrated locations, ethnic solidarity could lead to group action.[64] These cultural indicators were available to the Yoruba "Hausa-Mamluks." The Yoruba wars and the possibility of being sold into international slavery or killed in religious ceremonies made it difficult for Hausa slaves to contemplate massive flights. As soon as Hausa slaves were concentrated in Oyo, and with Muslim states only a few miles away, revolt became an attractive option. Similarly, in the coastal states, distance from home and the possibilities of re-enslavement in the Oyo region made flight a difficult venture. Hence, with years of frustration, the Hausa allied with the British in the conquest of Yorubaland, gradually turning military camps into "slave villages." This study also shows that resistance took two approaches: one overtly political and involving group action, and the second more low-key, personal, and spiritual. For example, through the Oyo slave revolt, the destruction of Old Oyo, and service in the British army, the Central Sudanese actively responded to sociopolitical changes, hitting at Yorubaland from both north and south. This suggests slave awareness that slavery was a violent institution, which required some element of violence to overthrow it. That violence—political and imperial—was couched in the terms of civilizing missions: *orisa* worship must give way to either Islam or Christianity. This attitude is closely tied to a passive, but most likely frequent, form of resistance. Hausa slaves refused to join in *orisa* worship, they refused to consume alcohol, and they rejected conversion to Christianity.

Notes

1. See Francis C. Fuller, Resident Officer's journal, 24 and 27 July and 30-31 August 1897; Alfred Ehrhardt, Resident Officer's journal, 10 and 19 January, 13-16 May, 6 and 26 June, 23 and 26 July, and 1 and 16 August 1898; and Fuller, journal, 20 and 21 January 1899 in Ibadan Provincial Papers [hereafter IbaProf] 3/6, National Archives of Nigeria, Ibadan [hereafter NAI].
2. Isaac B. Akinyele, *Iwe Itan Ibadan ati die ninu awon ilu agbegbe re bi Iwo, Osogbo, Ikirun* (Ibadan, [1911] 1980), 122-38; Abner Cohen, *Custom and Politics in Urban Africa: A Study of Hausa Migrants in Yoruba Towns* (Manchester, 1969), 103–13; Toyin Falola, "From Hospitality to Hostility: Ibadan and Strangers, 1830–1904," *Journal of African History* [hereafter *JAH*] 26 (1985), 65–66; and Ruth Watson, "Murder and the Political Body in Early Colonial Ibadan," *Africa* 70 (2000), 25–48.
3. John D. Y. Peel, *Religious Encounter and the Making of the Yoruba* (Bloomington, IN, 2000).
4. See Robin Law, *The Oyo Empire c.1600–c.1836: A West African Imperialism in the Era of the Atlantic Slave Trade* (Oxford, 1977), 211–17.
5. Peter Morton-Williams, "The Oyo Yoruba and the Atlantic Slave Trade, 1670–1830," *Journal of the Historical Society of Nigeria* [hereafter *JHSN*] 3 (1964), 25–45; Law, *Oyo Empire*, 211–36; Mahdi Adamu, "The Delivery of Slaves from the Central Sudan to the Bight of Benin in the Eighteenth and Nineteenth Centuries' in *The Uncommon Market: Essays in the Economic History of the Atlantic Slave Trade*, eds. Henry A. Gemery and Jan S. Hogendorn, (New York, 1979), 163–80; and M. Adamu, "The Aftermath of the Jihad in the Central Sudan as a Major Factor in the Volume of the Trans-Saharan Slave Trade in the Nineteenth Century" in *The Human Commodity: Perspectives on the Trans-Saharan Slave Trade*, ed. Elizabeth Savage, (London, 1992), 111–28.

6. See Muḥammad al-Amīn ibn Muḥammad and Edward J. Arnett, *The Rise of the Sokoto Fulani, Being a Paraphrase and in Some Parts a Translation of the Infaku'l Maisuri of Sultan Mohammed Bello* (Kano, 1922), 16.
7. Pierre Verger, *Trade Relations between the Bight of Benin and Bahia Seventeenth to Nineteenth Century* (Ibadan, 1976); João Reis, *Slave Rebellion in Brazil: The Muslim Uprising of 1835 in Bahia* (Baltimore, 1993); and Paul E. Lovejoy, "Background to Rebellion: The Origins of the Muslim Slaves in Bahia," *Slavery and Abolition* 15 (1994), 151–80.
8. Law, *Oyo Empire*, 211–36; and Adamu, "Delivery of Slaves from the Central Sudan."
9. See Hugh Clapperton, Journal, 16–20 January 1826 in *Hugh Clapperton into the Interior of Africa: Records of the Second Expedition, 1825–1827,* eds. Jamie Bruce-Lockhart and Paul E. Lovejoy (Leiden, 2005). See also Richard Lander and John Lander, *Journal of an Expedition to Explore the Course and Termination of the Niger* (New York, 1832), 1:17, 36–37, 45; Samuel Johnson, *The History of the Yorubas from the Earliest to the Beginning of the British Protectorate* (Lagos, [1921] 1976), 193–94; Ajayi K. Ajisafe, *History of Abeokuta* (Bungay, Suffolk, 1924), 100; Tajudeen G. O. Gbadamosi, *The Growth of Islam among the Yoruba 1841–1908* (London, 1978), 1–87; and Peel, *Religious Encounter*, 187–214.
10. Johnson, *History*, 123, 193; and Law, *Oyo Empire*, 183–99.
11. J. T. Kefer, journal, 3 September 1854, CA2/059, section IV: Africa Missions, Church Missionary Society Archive [hereafter CMSA] (microfilm, Marlborough, 1997).
12. Samuel W. Doherty, journal, 8 February 1877, CA2/035, CMSA.
13. See Daniel Olubi, journal, 3 December 1877, CA2/075, CMSA. In 1877 Oyewo, the son of Are Momoh Latoosa, the ruler and most important slaveholder in Ibadan history, completed a four-year Islamic education at Iseyin.
14. See Paul E. Lovejoy, "The Bello-Clapperton Exchange: The Sokoto Jihad and the Trans-Atlantic Slave Trade, 1804–1837," in *The Desert Shore: Literatures of the African Sahel,* ed. Christopher Wise (Boulder, 2000), 201–27, and Humphrey J. Fisher, "A Muslim William Wilberforce? The Sokoto Jihad as Anti-Slavery Crusade: An Enquiry into Historical Causes" in *De la Traite à L'esclavage du XVIIIeme au XIXeme*, ed. Serge Daget, (Nantes, 1988), 2:537-55. On West African notions of enslavement see Ahmad Baba, *Mi'raj al-Su'ud: Replies on Slavery,* annotated and tr. John O. Hunwick and Fatima Karrak (Rabat, 2000); and Robin Law, "Legal and Illegal Enslavement in West Africa in the Context of the Trans-Atlantic Slave Trade," in *Ghana in Africa and the World: Essays in Honor of Adu Boahen,* ed. Toyin Falola (Trenton, NJ, 2003), 513–33.
15. Thomas Bowen, *Adventures and Missionary Labours in Several Countries in the Interior of Africa from 1849–1856* (London, [1857] 1968); and Johnson, *History*, 288.

16. See Samuel Crowther to Rev. William Jowett, 22 February 1837, appendix III, in Frederick Schön and Samuel Crowther, *Journals of the Rev. Frederick Schön and Mr. Samuel Crowther: Expedition Up the Niger in 1841* (London, [1842] 1970), 322–23.
17. On factional conflict in Oyo, see Law, "The Constitutional Troubles of Oyo in the Eighteenth Century," *JAH* 12 (1971), 25–44.
18. Bruce-Lockhart and Lovejoy, eds., *Hugh Clapperton into the Interior of Africa*, 189– 90.
19. This date is based on information collected by Clapperton in 1825 that the crisis at Ilorin started two years earlier. See journal, 17 December 1825 in *Hugh Clapperton into the Interior of Africa,* ed. Bruce-Lockhart and Lovejoy. These developments fit into the second phase of Murray Last's three-phase classification of Islamic movements in West Africa. See his overview, "Reform in West Africa: The Jihad Movements of the Nineteenth Century," in *History of West Africa,* eds. J. F. Ade-Ajayi and M. Crowder, (London, 1985), 2:15–35. Last argues that the populism that gave success to Uthman Dan Fodio was limited to Hausaland. Without such a popular basis, military superiority of the jihad forces outside Hausaland was effective only on the plains amid small-scale, relatively non-centralized societies. Where the Islamic populist movement was introduced, but involved an element of local nationalism, such as in Oyo, the result was a reformed, yet independent, government hostile not to Islam but to the claims of the Sokoto caliphate.
20. Crowther to Jowett, 22 February 1837. Details of the crisis in Oyo have been treated by Johnson, *History*, 178–283; Idowu A. Akinjogbin, "The Prelude to the Yoruba Civil Wars of the Nineteenth Century," *Odu*, 2nd series 1 (1965), 24–46; Law, *Oyo Empire*, 245–302; Law, "Chronology of the Yoruba wars," 211–22; Law, "Constitutional Troubles of Oyo," and Law, "The Northern Factor in Yoruba History" in *Yoruba Civilization*, eds. I. A. Akinjogbin and G. O. Ekemode, (Ile-Ife, 1976), 103–32; Joseph A. Atanda, "The Fall of the Old Oyo Empire: A Reconsideration of Its Causes," *JHSN* 5 (1971), 477–90; Atanda, "Comments on 'A Little New Light on the Collapse of the Alafinate of Yoruba'," in *Yoruba Historiography,* ed. Toyin Falola (Madison, 1991), 105–21; Wande Abimbola, "The Ruins of Oyo Division," *African Notes* 2 (1964), 16–19; and Abdullahi Smith, "A Little New Light on the Collapse of the Alafinate of Yoruba" in *Studies in Yoruba History and Culture: Essays in Honour of Professor S. O. Biobaku,* ed. G. Olusanya (Ibadan, 1983), 42–71.
21. On Oyo horses, see Clapperton, Journal, 28, 34, 56; and Lander and Lander, *Journal of an Expedition*, 190. In 1863 Richard Burton described Abeokuta as having the "poorest ponies, 12 hands or so high…one was however a Borneo [sic] horse with the high withers that characterise the breed (28 bags or £25)…Good horses used to be brought down…from Yoruba (Oyo); since the war, however, the Ilorins and Ibadans…have laid an embargo and prohibitory duty upon exporting them… Ponies formerly cost 2 bags (36s) the

same now sell for 15–20 bags. Arab horses cost between 200–300 dollars." By 1890, a 15-hand horse cost not less than seven prime slaves (£70). See Burton, *Abeokuta and the Camaroons Mountains: An Exploration,* (London, 1863), 1:155–56 and Alvan Millson, "The Yoruba Country, West Africa," *Proceedings of the Royal Geographical Society (PRGS)*, vol. 13, no. 10 (Oct., 1891), 578.

22. On the *jamaa* and *ògo wẹ̀ẹrẹ*, see Johnson, *History*, 193–202; Crowther to Jowett, 22 February 1837; and H.F.C. Smith, D.M. Last and Gambo Gubio, "Ali Eisami Gazirmabe of Bornu," in *Africa Remembered: Narratives by West African from the Era of the Slave Trade,* ed. Phillip C. Curtin (Madison, 1976), 199–216.
23. Olatunji Ojo, "Warfare, Slavery and the Transformation of Eastern Yorubaland c.1820–1900," Ph.D. dissertation, York University, 2003, chapter 2.
24. Lander and Lander, *Journal of an Expedition*, I:278–79 and Smith, Last, and Gubio, "Ali Eisami," 289–316. Clapperton and Lander met Muhammad b. Hajj 'Umar Ghamzu, a Libyan and leader of the Arab community in Sokoto previously detained at Oyo for three years after the 1817 revolt.; see Edward W. Bovill, *Missions to the Niger* (Cambridge, 1964-66), IV:678-83.
25. Akinyele, *Iwe Itan Ibadan*, 46. The Muslims established a separate community, some two to three kilometers away, named *Imalefalafia* (Muslims for Peace).
26. Rev. James Johnson, "Annual Report, 1877" CA2/056, CMSA; and "Evidence of Rev. James Johnson," enc. in Denton to Chamberlain (confidential), 4 June 1898, CO 147/133, National Archives of the United Kingdom, Kew [hereafter NAUK].
27. Schön and Crowther, *Expedition Up the Niger in 1841*, 317–18.
28. Clapperton, Journal, 16 and 17 December 1825.
29. Clapperton, Journal, entries for December 1825–January, 1826. The ploy was to deny the Sokoto caliphate any benefit that an association with Britain could bring.
30. Clapperton, Journal, 1 & 8 December 1825.
31. Bowen, *Adventures and Missionary Labours*, 137.
32. C. A. Hone and D. Hone, eds., *Seventeen Years in the Yoruba Country: Memorials of Anna Hinderer Gathered from Her Journals and Letters* (Piccadilly, 1872), 198–99. A reference to Muslim slaves' belief about the superiority of Islam over Yoruba religion is also contained in Bowen, *Adventures and Missionary Labours*, 137. From Ondo, Charles Phillips wrote: "Few Mohammedans. I have only seen five resident Mohammedans in the whole country since I came in 1877. Three of those are Ondo slaves and they do not scruple to join in the idolatrous rites of their Master." See "Address Delivered at Missionary Meeting Held in the Schoolroom, Faji, Lagos, 28 February 1879," Phillips Papers, 1/3/3, NAI.
33. See Bowen, *Adventures and Missionary Life*, 133–34, 188–205. Bowen's original mission was to preach in the Central Sudan. Unfortunately, he could

not proceed because of the frequent wars there and in Yorubaland. Jato was a Fulani from Sokoto, previously a soldier from his scars (wounds), mulatto colored, tall, handsome and intelligent. He taught Bowen about 250 phrases. He served in Abeokuta from about 1836 until he died around 1852 or 1853. When Bowen decided to visit Ilorin in 1855, he met stiff opposition throughout the planning stages and during his entire stay in the town.

34. Hinderer, diary, 26 July 1859, in Hone, *Seventeen Years*, 198.
35. James A. Maser, journal, 21 July 1866, CA2/068, CMSA.
36. On Aoussa (Hausa), Gambary, Taqua (Tapa), and Barba (Bariba) slaves in Saint Domingue, Trinidad, and Brazil see David Geggus, "Sex Ratio, Age and Ethnicity in the Atlantic Slave Trade: Data from French Shipping and Plantation Records," *JAH* 30 (1989), 23–44; Verger, *Trade Relations,* 285–93; Lovejoy, "Background to Rebellion," 151–80; John Washington, "Some Account of Mohammedu-Sisëi, a Mandingo, of Nyáni-Marú on the Gambia," *Journal of the Royal Geographical Society* 8 (1838), 448–54; and "Ethnic-Regional Origins of African-Born Recruits of the Fifth West India Regiment, 1798–1808," in Roger Norman Buckley, *Slaves in Red Coats: The British West India Regiments, 1795–1815* (New Haven, CT, 1979), based on WO 25/656, NAUK.
37. On Kambari, see Richard F. Burton, *Abeokuta and the Camaroons Mountains: An Exploration* (London, 1863), I:227; John Milum, "Notes of a Journey from Lagos up the River Niger to Bida, the Capital of Nupe and Ilorin in the Yoruba Country, 1879–80," *Proceedings of the Royal Geographical Society* 3 (1881), 36; Bowen, *Adventures and Missionary Labours*, 198–99; Samuel Crowther and John C. Taylor, *The Gospel on the Banks of the Niger: Journals and Notices of the Native Missionaries Accompanying the Niger Expedition of 1857–1859* (London, [1859] 1968), 56; and F. P. Conant, "Peoples of Kontagora and Zuru: Kambari," in *Peoples of the Middle Niger Region Northern Nigeria*, Ethnographic survey of Africa, pt. 15 (London, 1960), 21–29. On Wangara see Lovejoy, "The Role of the Wangara in the Economic Transformation of the Central Sudan in the Fifteenth and Sixteenth Centuries," *JAH* 19 (1978), 173–93.
38. In the mid-1850s the Hausa language was described as the French of Central Africa. Cf. William B. Baikie, *Narrative of an Exploring Voyage Up the Rivers Kwora and Binue Commonly Known as the Niger and Tsadda in 1854* (London, [1856] 1966), 69. On the application of Hausa to ethnicity, religion, and commerce, see Crowther and Taylor, *Gospel on the Banks of the Niger,* 101; and Paul E. Lovejoy, *Caravans of Kola: The Hausa Kola Trade 1700–1900* (Zaria, 1980).
39. See David Eltis and David Richardson, eds., *Routes to Slavery: Direction, Ethnicity and Mortality in the Transatlantic Slave Trade* (London, 1997); Sylviane A. Diouf, *Servants of Allah: African Muslims Enslaved in the Americas* (New York, 1999); Michael A. Gomez, *Exchanging Our Country Marks: The Transformation of African Identities in the Colonial and Antebellum South*

(Chapel Hill, NC, 1998); Kristin Mann and Edna Bay, eds., *Rethinking the African Diaspora: The Making of a Black Atlantic World in the* Bight of Benin and Brazil (Portland, OR, 2001); Linda Heywood, ed., *Central Africans and Cultural Transformations in the American Diaspora* (Cambridge, 2001). Paul E. Lovejoy and David V. Trotman, eds., *Trans-Atlantic Dimensions of Ethnicity in the African Diaspora* (London, 2003); and Jose C. Curto and Paul E. Lovejoy, eds., *Enslaving Connections: Changing Cultures of Africa and Brazil during the Era of Slavery* (Amherst, NY, 2004).

40. Crowther to Jowett, 22 February 1837, appendix III, in Schön and Crowther, *Journals*; and Crowther and Taylor, *Gospel on the Banks of the Niger*, 100, 126–27.
41. A generic term for North Africans.
42. Clapperton, Journal, 4 December 1825.
43. See Crowther and Taylor, *Gospel on the Banks of the Niger,* 100. It is in this sense that the Yoruba of Ilorin and Nupe passed as Hausa.
44. Fuller, Journal, 21 January 1899, IbaProf 3/6, NAI.
45. Henry Stanhope Freeman to Duke of Newcastle, 6 & 9 May 1864, CO 147/6, NAUK.
46. Baikie, in command of the Niger Expedition, to Earl of Malmesbury, 11 May 1859, FO 2/32, NAUK; Freeman to Newcastle, 31 December 1863, CO 147/4, NAUK; and E. Adeniyi Oroge, "The Fugitive Slave Crisis of 1859: A Factor in the Growth of Anti-British Feelings among the Yoruba," *Odu* 12 (1975), 42–43.
47. 'Memo' enclosed in Brand to Russell, 5 May 1860, FO 84/1115, NAUK; Henry Townsend to Henry Venn, 30 April 1859, CA2/085b, CMSA; and Oroge, "Fugitive Slave Crisis of 1859," 44–48.
48. Kirk-Greene, "Preliminary Note," 129; and A. Haywood and F. A. S. Clarke, *The History of the Royal West African Frontier Force* (London, 1964), 89.
49. Lady Glover, *Life of Sir John Hawley Glover* (London, 1897), 78–80; A. C. G. Hastings, *The Voyage of the Dayspring: Being the Journal of the Late Sir John Hawley Glover* (London, 1926); and W. D. McIntyre, "Commander Glover and the Colony of Lagos, 1861–1873," *JAH*, 4 (1963), 57–79. See also E. Adeniyi Oroge, "The Institution of Slavery in Yorubaland with Particular Reference to the Nineteenth Century," Ph.D. dissertation, University of Birmingham, 1971, 337–58; Orogoe, "Fugitive Slave Crisis of 1859" 40–54; and Oroge, "The Fugitive Slave Question in Anglo-Egba Relations 1861–1886*,"* *JHSN* 8 (1975), 61–80.
50. Freeman to Russell 1 July 1862, FO 84/1175, NAUK and Freeman to Newcastle, 31 December 1863, CO 147/4, NAUK. In 1864 Glover mobilized 250 men from the 4th and 5th West Indian Regiment and Lagos Hausa Constabulary in his attack on the Egba. See Saburi O. Biobaku, *Egba and its Neighbours 1830–1874* (Oxford, 1957), 76.
51. Freeman to Duke of Newcastle, 9 October 1862, CSO 1/1/1, NAI.

52. Instructions to Henry Higgins and Oliver Smith (signed Fred Evans), 14 August 1886, enc. 8 in dispatch #32, British Parliamentary Papers [hereafter PP] C4957, LX:125.
53. Gilbert S. Carter to Ripon, 11 December 1893, CSO 1/1/13, NAI.
54. King, Head Chiefs and Chiefs of Ode Ondo to Moloney, 31 July 1886, enc. 5 in dispatch #33, Evans to Granville, 24 August 1886, PP C4957, LX:131–33. Also see Olatunji Ojo, "Slavery and Human Sacrifice in Yorubaland: Ondo, c.1870–1894," *JAH*, 46 (2005), 379–404.
55. Carter to Knutsford, 8 February 1892, CSO 1/7/5, NAI; and Carter to Ripon 18 January and 15 August 1894, CSO 1/1/14, NAI. In August 1894 the maxim gun was brought to Mapo, the city center, to welcome Governor Carter. Mapo was within a half-kilometer radius of the compounds of the leading Ibadan warlords. See Phillips, diary entries from January to October 1887, Phillips Papers 3/2; entries for 29–30 March 1898, Phillips' diary, Phillips Papers 3/8; and entry for 29 June 1898, traveling commissioner's journal, Ondo Div 8/1, all in NAI.
56. Entry for 25 September 1897, Erhardt's journal, enclosed in McCallum to Chamberlain, 2 November 1897, CSO 1/1/20, NAI. See also Akinyele, *Iwe Itan Ibadan*, 123 & 127; and Nathaniel D. Oyerinde, *Iwe Itan Ogbomoso* (Jos, 1934), 126.
57. Margery Perham and Mary Bull, eds., *The Diaries of Lord Lugard: Nigeria, 1894-1895 and 1898* (Evanston, Ill., 1963), 4:264–65. See also W. Gerald Ambrose, "Annual Report on Northeast District," in *Lagos Annual Report 1901–1902* (Lagos, 1902), 220. Captain Bower, the traveling commissioner in the Yoruba interior, arrested and jailed twenty impostors between 1893 and 1894.
58. Oroge, "Institution of Slavery," 375–78.
59. Entries for 24 December 1873, 2 January & 25 May 1875, Young's journal, CA2/098, CMSA; and entry for 30 September 1878, Phillips' journal, Phillips Papers 1/3/1, NAI.
60. F. C. Fuller to colonial secretary, 3 December 1897; and Henry E. McCallum to colonial secretary, 8 December 1897, CSO 1/1/20, NAI.
61. Adisatu was recognized as a second wife, but Lade remained in her status as a trader-slave. See Ewart, journal, 22 & 28 April 1898, Ondo Div 8/1, NAI.
62. William Macgregor to Chamberlain, 19 June 1900, CSO 1/1/30, NAI.
63. Interview with Mohammed Abdelkadir, Toronto, 12 October 2003.
64. Paul E. Lovejoy, "Problems of Slave Control in the Sokoto Caliphate," in *Africans in Bondage: Studies in Slavery and the Slave Trade*, ed. P. E. Lovejoy (Madison, WI, 1986), 235–72; and "Fugitive Slaves: Resistance to Slavery in the Sokoto Caliphate," in *In Resistance: Studies in African, Caribbean, and Afro-American History,* ed. Gary Y. Okihiro (Amherst, MA, 1986), 71–95.

Chapter 8

RANSOMING CAPTIVES IN THE SOKOTO CALIPHATE

Jennifer Lofkrantz

In the closing years of the nineteenth century a military party led by Mahe, the son of ʻAbd al-Raḥmān, the eleventh sarkin musulmi of Sokoto, was returning home after what was, until this point, a successful expedition against Jan Tullu.[1] Accompanying Mahe was Barayi Zaki, a grandson of ʻAbd al-Raḥmān through one of his daughters. Mahe's expeditionary force successfully captured Jan Tullu, but was pursued by Sarkin Doso Na Mailaya and some French troops intent on rescuing Jan Tullu.[2] In the ensuing skirmish, Mahe managed to escape, Jan Tullu was rescued, and Barayi Zaki, the sarkin musulmi's grandson, was captured and held for ransom by the French troops.[3] This event reveals key elements in the practice of ransoming in nineteenth-century Sokoto caliphate. First, Barayi Zaki was captured during an incident that combined aspects of military raiding and traveling. Second, recognizing the high status of their captive as a grandson of the sarkin musulmi, Barayi Zaki's captors knew that they could profit much more from ransoming him back to his grandfather than by selling him as a slave or killing him. As befit his status, his captors set Barayi Zaki's ransom price at twenty pairs of *tsamiya*, twenty *kore* cloths, forty *wawa* cloths, twenty *kudi da kudi* cloths, three youths, and two girls. Third, through indirect means the captors let it be known who they were holding and what they wanted for his safe return, thereby opening communication links.

Ransom, or payment for the return to freedom of an individual recently captured and facing enslavement, was an important feature of slavery in

Islamic West Africa, and in particular, the Sokoto caliphate. The nineteenth century was a period of intense insecurity and warfare in western and central Sudan, which led to considerable enslavement. Enslavement, undertaken for political reasons, was fundamental to the socioeconomic structure of the societies of the Muslim regions of West Africa. Warfare, even the *jihāds* that were perpetrated in the hope that Islamic unity would usher in a better political world, generated slaves. In regions of enslavement there was a corresponding level of insecurity and instability, which allowed space for kidnapping and raiding that were not necessarily motivated by ideology or politics, but simply for the private and economic reasons of the captors. Ransoming served as a safety net for Muslims, like Barayi Zaki, who were captured in war or otherwise seized and threatened with sale into slavery.

While ransoming was practiced throughout West Africa, the most important feature that distinguishes it in nineteenth-century western and central Sudan from non-Muslim regions of West Africa is that Islamic law sanctioned ransoming and redemption. According to the Mālikī school of law, and most others, there were six legitimate options for dealing with prisoners of war: enslavement, execution, exchange against Muslim prisoners, taxation, free release, and ransom. Further, ransoming was encouraged as a means to secure the freedom of captured fellow Muslims. As the well-known fifteenth-century jurist Muḥammad al-Maghīlī advised, "if wealth abounds he [the prince] will preserve a surplus in the treasury for possible emergencies, for building mosques, *ransoming captives*, discharging debts, marrying women, aiding pilgrims and other necessities" (author's italics).[4] Aḥmad Bābā does not address the question of ransoming directly, but it is possible to infer from *Mi'rāj al-Su'ūd* that he preferred that freeborn Muslims held by other Muslims reattain their freedom through free-release. He believed that Muslims who could be proven to be free Muslims should not to be enslaved under any circumstances and should be freed immediately, if confirmed to be of free origin.[5]

'Uthmān ibn Fūdī strongly opposed the ransoming of prisoners held by his forces, but favored the ransoming of his captured followers. In the early years of the *jihād* this made sense since it was not strategic to release, even on payment of a large ransom, supporters of the regimes he was trying to overthrow. His close friend Muḥammad Tukrur instructed in his 1789 admonitory poem "Busuraa'u" that prisoners could be kept as slaves, sold for horses, or made to pay tribute, but does not mention that prisoners could be ransomed.[6] Nevertheless, in *Bayān wujūb al-hijra 'ala 'l-ibad*, 'Uthmān ibn Fūdī makes clear that when captured, his followers should be ransomed, stating unequivocally that "the redemption [ransoming] of Muslim captives is obligatory."[7] In this text, 'Uthmān ibn Fūdī also discussed protocols concerning the payment of ransom. He paraphrases the discussion in both Juzayy's *al- Qawānīn* and Khalīl b. Isḥāq al-Jundī's *Mukhtaṣar* on ransom payments. While both scholars agree that Muslims are obligated to ransom captive fellow free Muslims, they differ slightly on who was responsible for paying the ransoms. According to Juzayy, the payment of a ransom is first the responsibility of the captive. If the captive is unable to raise the ransom fee, then the imam should pay the ransom first out of the state treasury, second from raising the money from the Muslim community, and third by compelling non-Muslims to pay the fee. In contrast, Khalīl argues that the ransom fee should first be raised from the *fay'*, second from among the Muslim community, and lastly from the captive's own assets.[8] Although 'Uthmān 'ibn Fūdī does not state in *Bayān wujūb al-hijra 'ala 'l-'ibad* who he thinks bears the primary responsibility for making ransom payments, it is clear that he strongly believed that captive Muslims must be ransomed.

Muḥammad Bello agreed with his father's opinion regarding the importance of ransoming captive Muslims and with the decision not to allow the ransoming of their enemies. In *Risāla ilā ahl al-ḥaramayn al-sharīfayn wa ilā ahl al-mashriq,* Bello states that it was incumbent upon Muslims to free fellow Muslims who were wrongly enslaved; in other words, individuals who were loyal to the jihadist forces. Further, like his father, but unlike his uncle, 'Abdullāhi ibn Fūdī, Bello was against the ransoming of enemies or prisoners of the Sokoto caliphate. He indicated this in an undated letter he sent to Yakubu Bzymin Bauchi, the founder of the Bauchi Emirate, in which Bello advised that it was more preferable to execute prisoners than to ransom them. He gave this advice through the retelling of the story of the victory over Tabūk and the subsequent discussion about the fate of the captives. According to Bello, Prophet Muḥammad told his companions that in regard to the prisoners, there were three acceptable choices: ransom, enslavement, or death. He went on to say that initially the Prophet Muḥammad favored ransoming; however, 'Umar argued that the prisoners should be killed on the grounds that captives did not deserve to be either ransomed or enslaved and that they should be killed so they would no longer be a threat to Islam. After a vigorous debate among the companions, Allāh descended a Qu'rānic verse that said to kill the prisoners. In advising Yakubu Bauchi on what to do with the captives in his custody, Bello counseled that his decision must be based upon the will of Allāh, and on the interests of Islam and of justice.[9]

In the early years of the Sokoto caliphate the predominant opinion within the caliphate was against ransoming of prisoners held by their forces; however, there were dissenting opinions. Most prominently,

'Uthmān ibn Fūdī's brother, 'Abdullāhi ibn Fūdī, favored the ransoming of prisoners. In *Tazyīn al-waraqāt,* he argued that prisoners should be allowed to pay ransom and that the ransom money should be included in the booty.[10] Indeed, 'Abdullāhi ibn Fūdī habitually gave safe-conduct to select prisoners, most likely to organize ransom payments for themselves as well as for other remaining captives. As jihadist leaders solidified their power and the Sokoto caliphate became dominant within the region, the practice of not ransoming captives relaxed. In *Magana Hausa* (1885), James Frederick Schön mentions that the captors of high-status children relished the opportunity to negotiate ransoms with the captives' relatives.[11] Likewise in late nineteenth-century Ilorin, captives, regardless of their religious identity, were regularly ransomed.[12] Even so, in the last half of the nineteenth century it was still easier for Muslims to be ransomed than for non-Muslims. For example, in this time period, while many enslaved prisoners brought to Kano were executed at the various city gates, Muslim captives were, for the most part, ransomed.[13]

Due to the form of warfare practiced in central Sudan and the political economy of the Sokoto caliphate, the wrongful capture and enslavement of Muslims continued throughout the nineteenth century, despite vigorous condemnations of the practice. With the founding of the Sokoto caliphate, 'Uthmān ibn Fūdī's *jihād* in central Sudan launched a period of political, religious, and economic change in the region. The impact of the *jihād* led to increased insecurity, an expansion of warfare and raiding, the proliferation in enslavement, and therefore an increase in ransoming. According to *Tadhkirat al-Nisyān*, raiding for both goods and people was an important component of warfare in western and central Sudan from at least the Moroccan invasion of Songhay in 1591.[14] A common military technique in the establishment of the Sokoto caliphate, which was also used in subsequent *jihād* movements, was to raid a particular village or town and enslave whoever was not killed in the fighting.[15] Describing the first attack on Gobir, 'Uthmān ibn Fūdī states that, "we met them and put them to flight, and burnt their houses. We killed their males, and took their women and children. They scattered."[16] In *Tanbīh al ikhwā alā ard al-sūdān*, 'Uthmān ibn Fūdī argues that, "the aiming to get booty should not be counted against a man if he has fought to make God's law supreme." Booty, in terms of captives, was a main motivator for Bello's troops. After one expedition in Gobir his troops were ready to desert because they did not receive what they perceived to be a more equitable share of the captives.[17] Moreover, as 'Uthmān ibn Fūdī observed in *Kitāb al-farq*, booty was one of the seven income sources for the public treasury; the others being the land tax, the poll tax, the tithe, inheritance, and property with a missing or no owner.[18]

Further, the political economy that developed in the Sokoto caliphate was based on slavery, and so depended on the continual influx of new slaves as laborers and soldiers. Therefore, there was a persistent drawing of slaves from the emirates, which at times swept up free Muslims who were not supposed to be enslaved.[19] Despite vigorous condemnations of the practice, caliphate officials could not stop this from happening. In his poem "*Busuraa'u,*" Tukrur asserted that there were five categories of unbelievers: those who do not know the Qu'rān, those who mock the Sunna, those who practice false religions, those who do not pray, and *those who sell free individuals without a just reason*" (author's emphasis).[20] In *Masā'il muhimma* (1802), 'Uthmān ibn Fūdī found it necessary to forbid the sale of any Fulani on the basis that the Fulani had long been recognized as Muslims.[21] Likewise Bello repeated his father's injunction against enslaving Fulani in his *Miftāh al-Sadād*, despite the fact that Bello did not consider all Fulani to be Muslims.[22] While the senior leadership of the Sokoto caliphate tried to discourage the enslavement of recognized free Muslims, calling those who engaged in the practice "unbelievers," there was not much the state could do to prevent it. Instead of simply releasing free Muslims illegally enslaved, the Sokoto caliphate condoned their ransoming by families and friends. The ransoming of free Muslims benefited many groups: the religious authorities who had ethical and religious objections to the enslavement of free Muslims; the state officials who could not prevent illegal enslavement; the holders of wrongly enslaved free Muslims who were compensated for the loss of their investment; and the wrongly enslaved free Muslim who regained his or her freedom. In this way, ransoming in Sokoto served as an outlet to secure the freedom of the wrongly enslaved and a vehicle for the compensation of the owners.

Raiding and ransoming of individuals continued through the late nineteenth century and into the early twentieth century. As an undated letter (most likely from the 1890s) from Emir Abubakar of Katsina to Sarkin Musulmi 'Abd al-Raḥmān demonstrates, the collection of booty was still important. He wrote that "Allah granted the power to go to the country of Maradi and I myself went with my army to a village called Ungwar Mata, which we sacked and burnt, and in which we found much booty by Allah's will and your blessing."[23] The French resident in Tessaoua reported in 1903 that throughout the late nineteenth century, communities throughout northern Gobir had been constantly raided for captives and goods on behalf of Gobir officials.[24] Baba of Karo recounts that in her youth (the 1890s or the early twentieth century), the ruler of Kontagora, Ibrahim Nagwamase, also known as Mai Sudan, and who continuously raided the Katsina-Zaria region, also sent raiding parties into her region of southern Kano.

While the actual raiders always sold their captives, it was often possible to trace their sales and to ransom kidnapped individuals; Baba's account omits mention of tracing and ransoming people except for her relatives.[25] In cases involving people, it is unlikely that either side would have entertained the possibility of ransoming captured slaves while the prospects of ransom negotiations for free individuals would have depended on their status and wealth. Moreover, besides the taking of captives through warfare and their subsequent enslavement or ransom, the insecurity caused by politically motivated warfare and raiding created space for nonpolitically motivated raiding for economic gain or criminal intent. Brigandage was technically illegal. Muhammad ibn Zayd al-Qayrawānī in *Risālah* advocated stiff penalties for *muḥāribūn* (brigands), especially if a person was killed during a raid.[26] Yet official warfare and raiding conducted on behalf of the caliphate also allowed individuals to raid, pillage, and kidnap on their own behalf. These individuals could then make a profit from their captives by either selling them as slaves or ransoming them back.

In the mid-1850s, as a consequence of Bello's war with other Hausa states and Borno, the Lander brothers noted that: "many thousands of his [Bello's] men, fearing no law, and having no ostensible employment, are scattered over the whole face of the country. They commit all sorts of crimes; they plunder, they burn, they destroy, and even murder, and are not amenable to any earthly tribunal for their actions."[27] This continued throughout the century. In the 1890s and early 1900s the notorious pillager Kaoura, reputed to have unlimited audacity, operated between Gobir and Maradi. In 1904 he was reported as holding approximately 250 female slaves and a number of free women taken during his raids.[28] Likewise in the same time period it was observed that Abu Senouchi was making large profits from raiding villages and caravans along the Komadougou River. Many of his captives he sold as slaves, but it is probable that many of these kidnapped individuals were also ransomed.[29]

Due to political insecurity, raiding of caravans was also common, which also provided opportunities to kidnap people for ransom. One of the inherent risks of being part of a caravan was the prospect of being raided. For example, Bello's correspondence acknowledged the problem of the pillaging of caravans to the north of the Sokoto caliphate, especially by the Tuareg Kel Gress, while in the 1850s the roads in and out of Zinder were notorious for attacks on small caravans.[30] In 1902 the French found it necessary to inform Gobir officials that they must do more to prevent the Gobirawa from attacking caravans.[31] Not all individuals taken captive during a raid on a caravan would have been considered eligible for ransoming. Caravans were composed of people of various statuses. Caravan workers included slaves, trade slaves, porters, and teamsters as well as merchants of varying degrees of wealth.[32] While a wealthy merchant had a good chance of being ransomed, free porters and teamsters did not, and slaves and trade slaves still less.

While caravaners risked being captured, enslaved, or held for ransom, the traders and their trade routes provided vital communication links between captors and those willing to pay a ransom. Upon capture individuals marked for enslavement were quickly moved away from the location of their capture to suppress communication between the captive and his or her family and friends; however, communication between captor and the friends and families of candidates for ransom was encouraged to facilitate successful negotiations for ransom. From at least 1600 Muslim traders dominated long-distance trade within West Africa. Dyula networks dominated trade in the western Sudan and Hausa trading networks in the central Sudan. Muslim trading networks also operated across the Sahara into North Africa, and after the fifteenth century these linked the Maghreb with the European posts on the Atlantic coast.[33] These trading networks allowed for the flow of information including news on captives, as we can see in the case of Barayi Zaki.

Once a person had been located and his or her availability for ransom was ascertained, it was necessary for the captor and those who wanted to pay the ransom to conduct negotiations. Usually this entailed the use of a mediator or broker. Throughout Muslim West Africa there was a tendency for political or government officials to serve in this capacity, suggesting official sanction for ransoming.[34] For example, when Mahommah Gardo Baquaqua was enslaved for the first time, around 1820 in northern Asante, his brother used a broker to arrange his ransom.[35] Gustav Nachtigal vividly described the ransom negotiations that he witnessed between the Jagada and the Arinda Dirkonma:

> a few days later the surviving members of the expedition returned, and confirmed the melancholy nightmare. On the very same day a near relations of Adama, the chief of the Jagada, who was the most loyal supporter of the Arabs in Borku, was sent to Ennedi, both to get reliable news about the fate of each individual, and also to conduct negotiations for ransoming the prisoners... A fortnight later, about the middle of July, there appeared an emissary from the Bidyat Gordoi from the tribe of the Arinda Dirkoma, and therefore a Teda man, many of whom lived in the western valleys of Ennedi to present the conditions

> for releasing the prisoners, while our envoy remained behind as a hostage.[36]

The importance of mediators in ransom negotiations is further indicated by mid-nineteenth-century correspondence between the scholar Siḍi Mahmūd and Abūbakar Atikū ('Uthmān ibn Fūdī's son and the third sarkin musulmi of the Sokoto caliphate). Siḍi Mahmūd had written to Abūbakar Atikū about the fate and ongoing ransom negotiations of a group of captive Muslims. Atikū responded that he too was very concerned about these prisoners whom he also wanted ransomed. He added that he was waiting for the return of a certain individual before taking further action.[37] It appears that this particular person may have been the mediator between Atikū and those holding the prisoners. Baba of Karo recalled that at the end of the nineteenth century ransom negotiations for the return of her uncle's wife and children involved both the Sarkin Zarewa and the emir of Katsina as mediators.[38] In the case of Barayi Zaki, contact between his captors and his family was made through Sarkin Bayaro Abdullahi in a letter addressed to 'Abd al-Raḥmān, informing him that:

> your son [grandson Barayi Zaki] is in Doso and the Christians have put a heavy ransom on him. They have stipulated for twenty pairs of trousers—(Tsamiya)—twenty black Kano cloths Kore), forty cloths (wawa), and twenty cloths (Kudi da Kudi)—in all a hundred also three youths and two girls. This is the ransom which they have imposed, for your information.[39]

Ransoming was a successful practice because the captors knew that family and friends were willing to go to great lengths to raise ransoms for captured individuals, usually set at more than the person would fetch if sold as a slave. Ransoming benefited both the captive and the captor: the captive regained his or her freedom and previous status, and the captor often gained more than the market price for a slave. Baba of Karo's account of the ransoming of her father's wife Rabi in the 1890s exemplifies the profit of ransoming. Rabi was taken in a raid, sold in Katsina to Malam Maicibi of Maska, where she was located by her family. Maicibi had bought her for 100,000 cowries, an average price for a young female slave, but demanded a ransom of 400,000 cowries for her return, four times her worth as a slave.[40] Similarly Baba of Karo relates that her paternal uncle Ubangida lost his pregnant wife and three children in the same raid. He paid 400,000 cowries for his wife, 400,000 for his three children, and 400,000 for his unborn child.[41]

The high cost of ransoming in the Sokoto caliphate was echoed throughout the region. In the 1860s the 'Awlād Sulaymān demanded ten camels or the equivalent for the release of one man, but was satisfied with less, if the prisoner's family was not rich enough.[42] At the end of the nineteenth century the ransom price in Kayes was two slaves; in Bakel and Sumpi it was double the selling price; and in Segu, Sokolo, and Timbuktu it was at the discretion of the owner.[43]

Captors holding individuals for ransom capitalized on the belief that people valued freedom, especially of relatives, and were therefore willing to pay more than the market value of a slave to achieve that freedom. Two cases in Medine in 1890 and one from Bougouni Cercle in 1900 show this to be true. In one of the Medine cases, a father paid fourteen oxen, six guns, and two pieces of guinea cloth as ransom for his son. In the second case, the father paid five oxen and two *gros d'or*.[44] At the time prime male slaves were worth no more than 300 francs. In the Bougouni Cercle case, a woman from the village of Kan paid a ransom of three slaves and four guns for her old and sick husband.[45] Since old men, especially those who were sick, did not command much on the slave market, the people holding this man captive obviously got a much better price for him from his wife than they would have if they had sold him as a slave.

Due to the high cost of ransoming, the practice of ransoming was often limited to the elite, such as Barayi Zaki and his family, who had the ability and means to negotiate and pay ransoms. For example, Tuareg raiders always returned captured Kado nobles from Anzourou upon payment of a ransom.[46] In late-nineteenth-century Sahara, caravan chiefs, whose families were more likely to have the money to ransom them back were targeted for kidnapping and ransoming.[47] Likewise Baba of Karo's family was able to ransom kidnapped family members because they had the means to do so.

A case from early 1889 near Kita further illustrates the importance of status in ransoming and regaining freedom. In this instance people from Masina had pillaged a caravan near Kofoulou in either February or March 1889. They killed the caravan chief and took ten prisoners. Eventually, according to the March 1889 Kita cercle report, some prisoners were returned, most likely on payment of ransom, but the women were kept.[48] The killing of the caravan chief was most likely an accident since he would have commanded a high ransom. It is intriguing that no women were returned. There are a few possibilities for this. Although it is unlikely, the women may have been viewed as very valuable by the pillagers and their captors were therefore unwilling to ransom them back. Perhaps there were free women among the captured women for whom the captors demanded a particularly high ransom, but those raising ransom money could only raise enough money for the men whom they viewed as more valuable. Most probably the women were already enslaved, either as personal slaves and porters of the caravan traders, or as trade slaves who were being transported for sale. If they were indeed slaves, then buying replacement slaves offered a cheaper alternative. So it seems likely in this case that the individuals of free status were ransomed back and those already enslaved were not.

Finally, returning to the case of Barayi Zaki, we can see how his situation fits into the context of ransoming in the late nineteenth century. He was a high-status male whose family valued his freedom and had the means for him to regain it. Indeed his family had long advocated ransoming as a legitimate means for regaining the freedom of captured Muslims. Moreover, his captors were aware of his status and knew they could profit from ransoming him. Bayari Zaki was captured during a military skirmish, a common means of acquiring individuals for ransom. A third party with both political and personal ties to his family made the initial contact to negotiate a ransom. Sarkin Bayaro Abdullahi's letter to his brother Sarkin Musulmi 'Abd al-Raḥmān does not indicate whether a ransom was paid for the return of Bayari Zaki. What we do know for certain is that by 1927 Bayari Zaki was living freely in Denge. Paying the ransom would have been the quickest, easiest, and most assured way of obtaining his release.

Notes

1. Mahe held the honorary title of *sarkin mafara* and was given the governorship of Dendi by his father.
2. It is unclear whether the French troops were Europeans, Africans, or both.
3. Sarkin Bayaro Abdullahi to the Sarkin Musulmi 'Abd al-Raḥmān, undated in H. F. Backwell, *The Occupation of Hausaland 1900–1904; Being a Translation of Arabic Letters Found in the House of the Wazir of Sokoto, Bohari, in 1903* (London, 1969), 23–24.
4. Muḥammad al-Maghīlī, *Taj al-din yajib 'ala-mulūk*, trans. T. H Baldwin (Beyrouth-Liban, 1932), 21. Al-Maghīlī most likely wrote this treatise for Mohammad Rumfa, Emir of Kano (1463–1499).
5. Aḥmad Bābā, *Mi'rāj al-Su'ūd*, annotated and trans. John Hunwick and Fatima Harrak (Rabat, 2000).
6. Muhammad Tukrur, "Busuraa'u," verses 759–61, in J. Haafkens, *Chants Musulmans en Peul*: *Textes de l'heìritage religieux de la communauteì musulmane de Maroua, Cameroun* (Leiden, 1983).
7. 'Uthmān ibn Fūdī, *Bayān wujūb al-hijra 'ala'l-'ibad*, ed. and trans. F. H. El Masri (Khartoum, 1978), 123.
8. Ibid., 123.

9. See Boubou Hama, "Journal novembre 1964 à mars 1965," 397–400, Archives Nationales du Niger [hereafter ANN], Niamey, Niger. For more on the story of Tabuk as related in Hausa oral history, see Dalhatu Muhammad, "The Tabukū Epic in Hausa: An Exercise in Narratology," in *Studies in Hausa Language, Literature and Culture: Proceedings of the Second Hausa International Conference*, eds., Ibrahim Yaro Yahaya, Abba Rufa'i, and Al-Amin Abu-Manga (Kano, 1982), 397-416.
10. 'Abdullāhi ibn Fūdī, *Tazyīn al-Waraqāt*, 122–30. He further explores this issue in *Diya' al-sultan wa ghayrihi min al-ikhwan*. See Paul Lovejoy, "The Bello-Clapperton Exchange: The Sokoto Jihad and the Transatlantic Slave Trade," in *The Desert Shore: Literatures of the Sahel*, ed. Christopher Wise (Boulder, 2001), 209.
11. J. F. Schön, *Magaìna Hausa. Native Literature or Proverbs, Tales, Fables and Historical Fragments in the Hausa Language* (London, 1885), 164–65.
12. Ann O'Hear, *Power Relations in Nigeria, Ilorin Slaves and Their Successors* (Rochester, 1997), 39.
13. Interview with Dan Rimin Kano, 12 and 30 December 1975, Yusuf Yunusa Collection, deposited in the Northern History Research Scheme of Ahmadu Bello University Zaria, and the Harriet Tubman Institute, York University, Toronto.
14. Octave Victor Houdas and Edmond Benoist, *Tedzkiret en-nisīan fī akhbār molouk es-Soudān*. Documents arabes relatifs aì l'histoire du Soudan (Paris, 1966).
15. Hadj Sa'id, "Histoire de Sokoto, "in *Tedzkiret en Nissian fi akhbar moulouk es Soudan, ed. Octave Victor Houdas and Edmond Benoist* (Paris, 1966), 205.
16. 'Uthmān ibn Fūdī, *Tanbīh al ikhwā alā ard al-sūdān* in H. R. Palmer, "An Early Fulani Conception of Islam (Continued)," *Journal of the Royal African Society* 53 (1914), 191.
17. Sa'id, *Histoire de Sokoto*, 306–07.
18. See M. Hiskett, "'*Kitab-al-farq'*: A Work on the Habe Kingdoms Attributed to 'Uthman dan Fodio," *Bulletin of the School of Oriental and African Studies* 23 (1960), 571.
19. For more on the slave mode of production, see Emmanuel Terray "Long-distance Exchange and the Formation of the State: The Case of the Abron kingdom of Gyaman," *Economy and Society* 3 (1974), 315–45; and Paul E Lovejoy, *Transformations in Slavery*, 2nd ed. (Cambridge, 2000).
20. Tukrur, "Busuraa'u," verses 8–15, in Haafkens, *Chants Musulmans en Peul*, 147.
21. Mervyn Hiskett, *The Sword of Truth* (New York, 1973), 77.
22. See Lovejoy, "The Bello-Clapperton Exchange," 205.
23. Sarkin Katsina Abubakar to Sarkin Musulmi of Sokoto, 'Abd al-Raḥmān, undated, in Backwell, *Occupation of Hausaland*, 34.

24. Résidence de Tessaoua, Rapports politiques mensuels 1903, Mois de mars, 1.E11.21 1903, ANN.
25. Baba of Karo and Mary F. Smith, *Baba of Karo, a Woman of the Muslim Hausa* (New Haven, 1981), 67–75.
26. Muhammad ibn Abī Zayd al-Qayrawānī, *Risalah*, trans. Leon Bercher, 3rd edition (Algiers, 1949), 263.
27. Richard Lander and John Lander, *Journal of an Expedition to Explore the Course and Termination of the Niger, with a Narrative of a Voyage down that River to Its Termination* (New York, 1858), 1:282.
28. Residence de Tessaoua, Cercle de Zinder, Rapport politique du mois de Juin, 1E.34 1904, ANN.
29. Cercle de Gouré, Compte rendu suivant de tournée effectuée dans les territoires du Nord de la Komadougou par le Chef de Bataillon Mouret, 1908, 1E5.11 1908, ANN.
30. See Muḥammad Bello to Wachar, undated, in Boubou Hama, Journal de 2 mars 1968 au 6 mai 1969; and Muḥammad Bello to Sidi Mahmūd, undated, in ANN 282–84; and James Richardson, *Narrative of a Mission to Central Africa, Performed in the Years 1850–51, under the Orders and at the Expense of Her Majesty's Government* (London, 1853), 2:225.
31. Rapport politique sur les sultanats du Tessaoua, du Gober et du Maradi (mois du Janvier), 1E1.16 1902, ANN.
32. See M. B. Duffill and Paul E Lovejoy, "Merchants, Porters, and Teamsters in the Nineteenth-Century Central Sudan," in *The Workers of African Trade,* ed. Catherine Coquery-Vidrovitch and Paul E Lovejoy (Beverley Hills, CA, 1985), 150. See also E. Ann McDougall, "Camel Caravans of the Saharan Salt Trade," in ibid., 99–121.
33. See for example, A. Adu Boahen, "The Caravan Trade in the Nineteenth Century," *Journal of African History* 3 (1962), 349–59; Edward Bovill, *The Golden Trade of the Moors* (Oxford, 1958); and Ghislaine Lydon, "On Trans-Saharan Trails: Trading Networks and Cross-Cultural Exchange in Western Africa 1840s–1930s," Ph.D. dissertation, Michigan State University, 2000.
34. See Jennifer Lofkrantz, "Ransoming Policies and Practices in the Western and Central Bilād al-Sūdān c1800–1910," Ph.D. dissertation, York University, 2008.
35. Robin Law and Paul E Lovejoy eds., *The Biography of Mahommah Gardo Baquaqua* (Princeton, 2001), 131.
36. Gustav Nachtigal, *Sahara and Sudan*, trans. Allan B Fisher and Humphrey J Fisher (London, 1980), 2:377–78.
37. Abūbakar Atikū to Siḍi Mahmūd, undated in Hama, Journal de 2 mars 1968 au 6 mai 1969, 279, ANN.
38. Baba of Karo and Smith, *Baba of Karo,* 69.
39. Sarkin Bayaro Abdullahi to the sultan of Sokoto, Sarkin Musulmi Abderrahman, in Backwell, *Occupation of Hausaland,* 23–24.

40. Baba of Karo and Smith, *Baba of Karo*, 72–73; and Paul E Lovejoy, "The Characteristics of Plantations in the Nineteenth-Century Sokoto Caliphate," *American Historical Review* 84 (1979), 1269. For conversions, see David C. Tambo "Sokoto Caliphate Slave Trade in the Nineteenth Century," *International Journal of African Historical Studies* 9 (1976), 216.
41. Baba of Karo and Smith, *Baba of Karo*, 69.
42. Nachtigal, *Sahara and Sudan*, 2:378.
43. See K14: Captivité au Soudan. Rapports sur les captivités dans les cercles du Soudan, 1894, Archives Nationales du Sénégal, Dakar, Sénégal [hereafter ANSD]; K19: Enquête sur la captivité. Rapports sur la captivité dans les cercles de la Sénégambie-Niger 1904, ANSD; and Rapports sur la repression de la traite des esclaves en Haut- Sénégal- Niger Cercles de Bamako, Bandiagara, Bongouni, Djenne, Kayes, Medine, Nioro, Segou, Sokolo, 1894–1904, FA 1E 156, Archives Nationales du Mali, Koulouba, Mali [hereafter ANMK].
44. Justice Indigene Correspondance Cercle de Medine 1887–1905, Medine le 22 aout 1890, FA 2M 22, ANMK. One *gros* was equal to 1 *drachma,* which was equal to 1/8 ounce; hence 2 *gros d'or* was equal to ¼ ounce of gold.
45. Justice Indigene Correspondance Cercle de Bougouni 1896–1920, Bougouni, le 22 mai 1900, FA 2M 7, ANMK.
46. Jean-Paul Olivier de Sardan, *Quand nos pères étaient captifs: Recits paysans du Niger* (Paris and Nubia, 1976), 32–34.
47. Note sur les rezzous Marocains Tombouctou 1906, FA 1E 16; and Note sur les rezzous Marocains Tombouctou 1906, 1D 59 10, ANMK.
48. Rapports politiques et rapports de tournées, Cercle de Kita 1883–1905, Kita 15 octobre 1889, FA 1E 47, ANMK.

Chapter 9

DEBATING SLAVERY AND ABOLITION IN THE ARAB MIDDLE EAST[1]

Amal N. Ghazal

At the turn of the twentieth century, *ulama* were faced with a number of socioeconomic transformations that required a legal perspective to legitimize or delegitimize them. One of those transformations was the movement to abolish the institution and practice of slavery. So far studies of slavery in the modern Middle East are few.[2] They reveal little about the political and socioeconomic dynamics that led to the abolition of slavery in the Middle East, and even less about the debates stirred up among the circles of *ulama*, many of whom believed the abolition of slavery was a concern. They have dealt mostly with official Ottoman policies on abolition and the different views held by Ottoman officials, and in some cases, Ottoman poets and writers.[3] Although Ottoman officials invoked Islam and the *shari'a* to justify their policies, their views did not necessarily represent those of the *ulama* who were more sharply divided on this issue.

This study seeks to expose two opposing perspectives on abolition among *ulama* in the Arab Middle East and to situate their arguments within the legal context that shaped them. It argues that the debate over the legitimacy of abolition between two opposed circles of Arab *ulama*, one conservative and anti-Salafi and the other Salafi reformist, was rooted in a discourse shaped by two legal traditions with serious political and social ramifications: one based on *taqlīd* (imitation) and the other on *ijtihād* (independent interpretation of legal sources). While conservatives adhered to *taqlīd,* reformers embraced *ijtihād* in an attempt to accommodate what they considered inevitable socioeconomic and political developments in their societies. Far from presenting a uniform view on the topic, this study reveals the divergent views that Arab *ulama* held toward abolition.

Taqlīd means accepting a legal opinion without knowing or investigating its origin or basis. This doctrine, while shunned in the early centuries of Islam, established itself over time as the accepted intellectual norm in the field of Islamic jurisprudence. When Muslim reformers in the nineteenth century launched their attack on that doctrine, they faced a storm of criticism from a number of *ulama* who viewed *taqlīd* as sacred dogma and who deemed the doctrine of *ijtihād* promoted by reformers as a religious innovation and an "unorthodox" practice. *Ijtihād,* the opposite of *taqlīd,* is a juristic methodology used by *ulama* to search for a legal opinion on novel issues. It is carried out by "a coherent system of principles through which a qualified jurist could extract rulings for novel cases. From the ninth century onwards this was universally recognized by jurists as the sacred purpose of *usul al-fiqh* (legal theory)."[4] That ceased to be the case in the twelfth century, when the doors of *ijtihād* were announced officially closed. The rationale behind this move was that with the establishment of complete schools of law there was no need to speculate on new legal issues. At the practical level, however, *ijtihād* remained a practice to which *ulama* resorted on a daily basis although it functioned under other names. The debate over the necessity of officially opening the gates of *ijtihād* had been slowly emerging since the eighteenth century and reached a boiling degree by the end of the nineteenth century with the rise of the reform movement known as the Salafiyya.[5] Salafis argued for the need to reinstate *ijtihād* as an essential element of Islamic jurisprudence and considered the reintroduction of *ijtihād* into the scope of daily life a precondition for the betterment and advancement of Muslim societies. It would allow Muslims to integrate themselves into modern life and negotiate their space within it. More significantly, it would open the gates for a dialogue between Muslims and European Christians.[6] Reformers acknowledged the fact that exposure to western civilization had become an inevitable reality for Muslims. *Ijtihād* would enable them to assimilate new ideas, concepts, and manners streaming from Europe. Also, it would allow the *ulama* to regulate that encounter. Ultimately, *ijtihād* would be the tool that would filter and channel into Muslim societies what was considered permissible and beneficial from European civilization and ideas.

The literature on modern Islamic thought has repeatedly highlighted this reformist trend as it represented the "modernist" impulse of Islam and reflected its "accommodative" nature, thus befitting a "progressive" notion of historical development along European lines. While the Salafiyya movement and its advocacy of changes and assimilation was by no means new in Islamic history or unique to the nineteenth and twentieth centuries; nevertheless, its vigor and impact at the time drew the attention of many researchers. This excessive focus on that movement, at the expense of others, has given the prevalent impression that Islamic thought at the turn of the century was *only* reformist, progressive, and accommodating. Despite the vigor this movement enjoyed, it was fiercely opposed by a conservative anti-Salafi movement that considered Islamic reformism a religious heresy and condemned reformers as the "Protestants" of Islam whose aim, anti-Salafis stated, was to please Europeans, annihilate Islam, and abolish the *shari'a*. The most contentious point in the debate between Salafi reformers and conservative anti-Salafi was *ijtihād* and the call to reopen its gates. If *ijtihād* for reformers was a necessary tool to modernize and rebuild the glorious role of Muslims in world civilizations, it was nothing but blasphemy in the eyes of the conservatives and an attempt to destroy Islam. While reformers sought reconciliation between the Muslim tradition and modern European civilization, conservatives generally turned a deaf ear to all calls for rapprochement. For them, Europe was a wholesale evil; assimilating aspects of its modernity was to make a deal with the devil. Not only were European social manners or political theories categorically refused by conservatives, but so were European dress codes, languages, sciences, and any idea that originated from Europe, the abolition of slavery being no exception.

European criticism of the practice of slavery in Muslim societies and the association it made between this practice and Islam itself generated many responses among Muslims.[7] Reformers were generally receptive to this criticism. Although they rebuked the idea that the malpractice of slavery was rooted in religion itself as European critics argued, they admitted that the persistence of slavery in Muslim societies should be reconsidered and that the religious basis that justified its existence should be reevaluated. Since they believed that the Qur'anic text was open to reinterpretation and its meaning could be determined by current social and political factors, they did not hesitate to reexamine the verses pertaining to slavery. For conservatives, that was an unthinkable matter, since the meaning of the verses was fixed and not a variable that could be open to speculation or subject to reassessment.

Here I present examples of the arguments made by both groups of *ulama* and outline their opposite perspectives on slavery and abolition. My main sources are excerpts from the Arabic press in addition to a commentary by one of the most influential conservative scholars, Yūsuf al-Nabhānī.

Al-Manār journal, published in Egypt between 1898 and 1935, and run by Salafis, represented the views from the reform camp. *Al-Haqā'iq*, published in Syria between 1910 and 1912, advocated the conservative perspective.[8] Yūsuf al-Nabhānī (d. 1932) was an archenemy of the Salafiyya movement. His career as an editor for the official Ottoman newspaper *al-jawā'ib* and later, as a judge, was built through his connections to a conservative network of Arab *ulama* who enjoyed the support of the Ottoman Sultan 'Abd al-Hamīd II.[9] Al-Nabhānī was a prolific writer whose works included a renowned collection of eulogies for Prophet Muhammad, a treatise on the danger of missionary schools, antireform polemics, praise poems for Sultan ʹAbd al-Hamīd II, and a comparative essay on Islam and Christianity. It was in this latter work, which contrasted Islamic beliefs to Christian ones, that his views on slavery appeared.[10] The booklet was divided into three sections: a comparison of divine attributes in Islam to those in Christianity; a comparison of Prophet Muhammad's attributes to those of Jesus Christ; and an elaboration on the purpose of the *shari'a* with emphasis on selected rules. One of the rules he highlighted was the *shari'a* perspective on slavery. Given the context in which al-Nabhānī discussed the topic, it is clear that he was aware of the nature of accusations made by European abolitionists against slavery in Muslim societies. His primary motive was to refute their argument that Christianity embraced emancipation because it was more humane than Islam.

Al-Nabhānī maintained that slavery was legal because people were naturally divided into the rich and the poor, the strong and the weak. As a result, the prosperity of the world depended on the interrelationship between those groups or classes of people. The rich, he argued, were physically weak and in need of the assistance of strong slaves, whose purchase God had permitted to help the rich. Slaves, he continued, needed a master who provided for them and treated them like his own children, "since noble people would treat their slaves the same way they would treat their own children, following the example of the Prophet."[11] When listing the sources of slaves, al-Nabhānī admitted there was only one source: a war against non-Muslims, during the course of which the decision to enslave captives or free them should be made by the leader of the Muslim community alone and not by individuals.[12] Meanwhile, he acknowledged that Islam allowed the emancipation of slaves and considered it an act for which Muslims would reap many rewards. He emphasized that God forbade unjust acts toward slaves and warned against overworking them; reminding his readers that those who freed slaves and treated them well would receive heavenly rewards.

Al-Nabhānī then resorted to mapping out the legal ground justifying slavery's existence. Slavery as discussed in the *shari'a*, he argued, was of great benefit to human kind, being an old practice found in previous communities and long permitted by God. As for Europe's pursuit of the abolition of slavery, Europeans aimed at winning "the hearts and minds of the Sudanese unbelievers to control their land afterwards."[13] As a result, he refused to accept abolition on human terms but rather considered it as part of western colonial policies in Africa. He doubted European motives, wondering why Europeans abolished slavery when they realized that slaves and their owners were in need of each other and were "a blessing to each other."[14] At this point, al-Nabhānī's pro-slavery argument took another turn and acquired a new dimension. If the socioeconomic structure regulating the slave/slave-owner relationship justified slavery in the eyes of al-Nabhānī, so did the spiritual and personal well-being of slaves that accrued as a result of enslavement. Slavery, as al-Nabhānī outlined it, became a watershed in the life of a slave, dividing it into two phases: one before enslavement and one after. Before their enslavement, slaves lived in miserable conditions and were ignorant about God, life, and the afterlife. After they were enslaved, they converted to Islam, became content, and acquired knowledge of matters pertaining to life and the hereafter. They reached a stage of which they never dreamt, as was the case with the Mamluks. In al-Nabhānī's view, the emphasis should not be on their status as "slaves" but as "Muslims" and this "Muslim" identity overshadowed the "slave" identity. Thus, slavery represented an opportunity for captives to embrace Islam, which, in turn, served as the slaves' ladder for spiritual and social satisfaction.

In contrast, those slaves who were forced into freedom despite the will of their masters, he continued, ended up in forced labor. Some were unable to carry out their tasks; others had improper shelter and "lived a life not even suitable for dogs."[15] As a result, freedom through forced emancipation, he argued, harmed them more than it harmed their masters. He concluded by restating his rationale to defend slavery based on economic disparities and by declaring that God, in his great knowledge about the affairs of this world, allowed slavery for reasons that might not be known to human beings. This last statement is a testimony to al-Nabhānī's legal framework that doubts the ability of human reasoning, as required by *ijtihād*, to gain full insight of the Qur'anic text or to redefine certain concepts and rules in the *shari'a*. Similar arguments were also made in the pages of *al-Ḥaqā'iq*.

Al-Ḥaqā'iq, the other source on conservative views, ran an antiabolition piece in 1911, reprinted from another journal entitled *al-Balāgh* and signed by a certain Muḥammad Rāghib.[16] The reprinted piece responded to a previously published pro-abolition article by Aḥmad al-Maḥmasānī in a journal called *al-ḥaqīqa*. Al-Maḥmasānī argued that a major achievement of European civilization was the manumission of slaves and the abolition of slavery. That achievement, he added, was inspired by Islam, which had opened the doors wide open for European nations to take those steps toward abolition since Islam, according to al-Maḥmasānī, predicted or rather encouraged abolition. How Islam inspired Europe in this regard was an issue the author chose to leave open for speculation. He quoted the following prophetic *ḥadīth* as promoting the abolition of slavery:

> Gabriel kept asking me to take care of my neighbor until I thought he [the neighbor] would be one of my inheritors; he kept asking me to take care of women until I thought divorce was forbidden; and he kept asking me to take care of slaves until I thought a day would come when they would be all emancipated.[17]

To the objective eye, the *ḥadīth* in itself, as is the case with verses pertaining to slavery, does not call for immediate emancipation of slaves. Such a meaning is rather reductive, depending on the interpreter's personal opinion. Rāghib, for example, did not understand the *ḥadīth* in a similar way. First, he refuted al-Maḥmasānī's interpretation of the *ḥadīth*, and outlined what he believed were the real European intentions behind the call to abolish slavery. He accused al-Maḥmasānī of misunderstanding the *ḥadīth*, declaring that if God had wanted slavery to be abolished, He could have asked Muslims to abolish it in a direct way. It was too important a matter for the Prophet to be ambiguous about and not to deal with in a straightforward manner. Because manumission was part and parcel of a coherent legal system in which the sinner could be punished by being ordered to free his slave(s)—as in cases of breaking an oath or accidental death—slavery, Rāghib insisted, could not be abolished.[18] The intent of the *ḥadīth* was rather to encourage Muslims to treat slaves well and not to abolish slavery altogether. Moreover, he did not believe that Europeans abolished slavery for the sake of humanity as they claimed. Their real intentions, he argued, were to divide the Muslim world, to weaken and destroy the power of its rulers, and to stop the spread of Islam. Nothing, he explained, testified to the reality of those intentions more than the "present war," alluding to the Italian invasion of Tripolitania in 1911. To achieve those goals, Europeans had to abolish slavery, especially after they had realized that "the one hundred thousand slaves who arrived in Muslim lands every year ended up converting to Islam, became free, and then married, thus increasing the number of Muslims."[19] Some of them went back to their original countries and attempted to convert their own people. According to Rāghib, this enraged Europeans who used abolition as a way to slow down the spread of Islam.

This, however, was not the only factor that infuriated Rāghib. If al-Nabhānī feared negative outcomes of abolition on the economic system or the social and religious well-being of slaves, Rāghib was more concerned about the implications of abolition on the social order and moral values of Muslim societies. Men who were unable to marry free women for financial reasons resorted to concubines who, he believed, played a crucial role in increasing the number of Muslims. As a result, Muslim men were able to satisfy their needs within permissible limits. That was not the case anymore now that slavery was outlawed. He regretfully commented that "had slavery been kept permissible no one would have sinned or taken paths that were destructive to the *umma* (the Muslim community)."[20] At the end of his commentary, he wondered why Muslims felt the need to please Europeans to the extent of asking for the abolition of slavery and even going as far as interpreting the aforementioned *ḥadīth* in a way that appealed to Europeans. He repeated his original statement that slavery was an established rule in Islam and should not be abolished.[21]

Rāghib emphasized the relationship between slavery and conversion on the one hand and slavery and social morality on the other hand. He believed that it was in the best interest of the *umma* not to follow the lead of Europe if the *umma* were to maintain its social integrity and expand its realm. Europe could only be viewed as an "enemy" whose motivation should always be questioned and whose policies were aimed at corrupting Muslim societies and annihilating Islam. Since conservatives believed that criticism of slavery emanated from Europe and that abolition was a European idea, they left no room for bargaining. In their eyes, Europe was only seeking ways to win its battle against Islam, with abolition as one of its weapons. Reconsidering the meaning and purpose of the *ḥadīth* or Qur'anic verses to conform to the movement toward outlawing slavery was not only against the tradition of *taqlīd* but also a miscalculation that would ultimately lead to European victory over Islam.

Salafi reformers, though they shared some concerns with conservatives, were more willing to discuss issues raised by Europeans and to use a higher level of religious pragmatism in responding to criticism. The reformers' take on abolition proved how far they could go with that pragmatism, as excerpts from the reformist newspaper *al-Manār* demonstrate. *Al-Manār*'s comments and opinions on slavery appeared in its *fatawa* (legal opinion) section, to which Muslims from all corners of the Muslim world sent inquiries asking for *al-Manār*'s legal opinion or perspective. In addition to the *fatawa*, there was one article on slavery featuring the opinions of 'Abd al-Raḥmān al-Kawākibī, Muhammad 'Abduh, and Muhammad Rashīd Riḍā on the subject. Al-Kawākibī (1849–1903) was of Syrian origin and left for Cairo in 1898, after he fell out of favor with the Ottoman authorities. In Cairo he frequented the circle of the prominent reformer Muhammad 'Abduh and wrote for *al-Manār*, edited by 'Abduh's disciple Rashīd Riḍā. He was critical of the Ottoman Sultan 'Abd al-Hamīd II and his advisor Abū al-Hudā al-Ṣayyādī, with whom al-Nabhānī was once associated.

Al-Kawākibī wrote his opinions on slavery after he had visited East Africa in 1901. They were published after his death by Rashīd Riḍā in *al-Manār* in 1905.[22] Al-Kawākibī wrote in response to criticism raised by an unidentified source against an international conference held in Zanzibar on slavery.[23] In his reply, he focused on how limited the slave trade between East Africa and the Middle East had become, thanks to European intervention. The few slaves who still went to the Hijaz left with pilgrims heading to Najd, and to a lesser extent, Yemen, with very few entering Syria, where, al-Kawākibī indicated, there were no more male slaves. Al-Kawākibī supported abolition, but also condemned the hesitant Ottoman policies in this regard, offering some suggestions on how to end the trade completely. He blamed the Ottoman rulers for closing their eyes to whatever remained of the slave trade and urged European powers to apply more pressure on Ottoman officials to take the requisite steps to end it.[24]

To state his legal opinion on slavery in Islam, al-Kawākibī referred to the opinion of a friend "who is among the Arab Muslim *ulama* and among the most celebrated freemen and political writers."[25] According to Riḍā, al-Kawakibī was referring to none other than the prominent reformer Muhammad 'Abduh who might not have been equally as critical, openly at least, of the role of the Ottoman court in perpetuating slavery. There is no doubt, however, that his reflections on slavery had a strong impact on someone like al-Kawākibī. 'Abduh recognized that Islam sanctioned slavery as other religions did, but Islam, being the most civilized in its legal system, did not attempt to abolish it at once.[26] Rather, it tried to close the circle around it until it had become obvious that the objective of the *shari'a* was to abolish slavery gradually. 'Abduh listed the following examples in support of that objective:

1. The *shari'a* restricts slavery and allows it only among those born to slave parents and among prisoners of war who are non-Muslims, non-Arabs, and non-relatives.
2. It considers illegal slavery one of the most forbidden acts in Islam, second only to committing a homicide.

3. It rules that emancipation of a slave in some cases is the only way certain sins can be washed away or forgiven.
4. It makes emancipation the only atonement for a sin of worship.
5. It makes the pledge to emancipate [slaves] as one of the most important pledges one can make.
6. It provides emancipation as a means through which a broken oath can be forgiven.
7. It considers emancipation as the best way to show grace to God and to ask for safety.
8. It allows for emancipation to be included in a person's will and as a result, God would reward that person by saving him from hellfire.[27]

In addition, 'Abduh continued, Islam required Muslims to free as many slaves as they could, so that slavery would gradually disappear. He based his argument on his belief that the *shari'a* came to defend liberty and freedom. He presented the following proofs:

1. Slaves are emancipated once they claim to be free because freedom is the original state of human beings. It is the owner's duty, and not that of a slave, to prove such a claim to freedom was false.
2. Enslavement does not deny slaves the right to claim freedom.
3. Emancipation occurs once the slave owner guarantees it, even if he was not serious about his proclamation, was drunk, or was forced to make such a proclamation.
4. Women slaves are emancipated once they give birth to a child. At this point they cannot be sold again and should be emancipated upon their master's death.
5. A concubine's testimony to the identity of the father of her child guarantees her freedom, even if the master denies fatherhood.
6. A partial owner of slaves who emancipates his share compels others to emancipate their share as well.
7. A judge's decision to free a slave is executed even if his decision is considered unjust.
8. The caliph of Muslims has the right to emancipate all slaves if he considers them illegal slaves, even if his decision contradicts with other schools of jurisprudence. The caliph can take any measure that limits slavery because freedom is the ultimate purpose of the *shari'a*.

'Abduh's emphasis on freedom as a concept embedded in Islamic religious thought appeared in another context as well. In *al-Balad*, his commentary on chapter ninety of the *Qur'an*, 'Abduh provided an explanation of the verse mentioning manumission, referred to in terms of *fakku raqaba* (literally meaning "freeing a neck").[28] 'Abduh emphasized that the prophetic *ḥadīth* encouraging manumission was at a *tawātur* level, one of the highest classifications, lending the *ḥadīth* an authority matching or equaling that of a Qur'anic verse. This, he insisted, bore witness to the inclination of Islam toward freedom and its aversion to captivity and slavery.[29] Elucidating the word *aqaba* immediately preceding *fakku raqaba,* 'Abduh stated that it stood for a difficult path to take; if taken, however, it led to salvation. 'Abduh implied that manumission, or perhaps abolition, might be a difficult decision to take but once taken, it guaranteed happiness in life and the afterlife.

After stating 'Abduh's opinions, al-Kawākibī carried on with his own elaboration on the topic. The major reason for the perpetuation of slavery, he continued, was the subjective and self-serving application of the *shari'a* by tyrant rulers. In an indirect way, al-Kawākibī hinted that the customs and lifestyle of Ottoman rulers necessitated the existence of slavery.[30] It was the duty of Muslim *ulama* to put an end to it. As for the practice of purchasing female slaves for domestic services, al-Kawākibī maintained that it was dispensable and an unnecessary act of arrogance, whereby common people imitated their corrupt rulers. The *shari'a*, as well as its scholars, he concluded, was grateful to Europe for abolishing slavery. For that policy to be more effective, al-Kawākibī, quoting 'Abduh, suggested the following measures:

1. Europe should use its "literary" influence to denounce the presence of black slaves as well as white female slaves in [Ottoman] palaces.
2. Europe should ask eastern rulers to follow the steps of European rulers in declaring their legal marriage and denouncing any successor to the throne who is the fruit of an illegal marriage.
3. Europe should ask its ambassadors in Istanbul, Tangiers, Tehran, Kabul, and its consuls in Tunisia, Egypt, and Jedda (not Mecca) to inquire with muftis from different schools of jurisprudence and in plain Arabic, about the *shari'a*'s perspective on the enslavement of human beings by purchasing, stealing, or capturing them. This inquiry would reveal that Istanbul did not allow the *ulama* in Mecca to provide an honest answer on the issue of abolition.[31]

Following those suggestions, Ridā provided his own opinion on slavery, "considered by Europeans one of the vices of Islam, in sharp contrast to their civilization that had requested the emancipation of all slaves."[32] In response to that criticism, Ridā pointed out that Islam neither sanctioned slavery nor made it a duty or a *sunna* (a voluntary act sanctioned by the prophetic tradition). It simply provided a legal framework for something that already existed.[33] His opinion was repeated time and again in *al-Manār* where he answered questions pertaining to slavery in Islam and Muslim societies. A Parisian correspondent submitted a list of eleven questions, four of them directly related to the issue of slavery, which Ridā answered carefully.[34] After defining slavery and showing the legal differences between a slave and a free person, Ridā clarified Islam's position on slavery. The structure of his argument was similar to that of al-Nabhānī though its end result was different. Slavery, he argued, existed because of a mutual interest between slave owners and slaves, with each depending on the other. A sudden abolition could corrupt a social structure and harm both slaves and their owners.[35] Although Islam did not explicitly call for abolition, the *shari'a* imposed restrictions and regulations on slavery as a prelude to bringing it to an end. Ridā then outlined what he considered the steps taken by the *shari'a* to encourage people to free their slaves, quoting from several *ḥadīth*s supporting his argument. "Had Muslims and their rulers who succeeded the Guided Caliphs followed the rules of the *shari'a* properly," he added, "slavery would have been abolished in the first century of Islam." With that claim, Ridā held Muslims, and not the *shari'a* per se, were responsible for the existence of slavery. While the *shari'a* pointed toward the direction of abolition, Muslims ignored those instructions.

Al-Manār received another question from its deputy in Kuwait who asked for clarification on how slavery was addressed, not in the *Qur'an*, but in both the Old and the New Testaments.[36] The purpose of the question, according to the inquirer, was to refute the accusations of barbarity and inhumanity against Islam. Ridā examined sections from the Testaments that referred to slavery and concluded that Islam remained the most merciful among other religions in its treatment of slaves. Moreover, he emphasized that while other nations made enslavement obligatory, Islam did not. Instead, Islam provided it with a legal framework and opened the door for emancipation.

Another question came from an Egyptian inquirer asking if there was a difference between black slaves and white slaves and whether the blackness of slaves was a basis to differentiate them from the free persons.[37] Ridā responded to the query about skin color first, ridiculing the idea that enslavement and freedom were associated with skin color. He stated that, in principle, all human beings should be free. He referred to a saying attributed to 'Umar bin al-Khaṭṭāb, the second Caliph, confirming his statement.[38] Slavery, he said, had its origins in the struggle between the weak and the strong, whereby the latter tried to control the former. Upon capture, prisoners of war used to be killed, but later on, prisoners were enslaved instead. Slavery developed into a universal practice and all ancient laws acknowledged it, thus making it into a social necessity. When Islam came, it could not outlaw slavery at once as it did with gambling, adultery, and adoption for example, but it did outlaw malpractices such as humiliating or overworking slaves.[39] Again, Riḍā listed the many laws encouraging emancipation and stated that enslavement in some cases was of benefit to defeated communities, especially to women who had nowhere to go. He condemned the selling of both Circassian females and Sudanese boys by their parents. Those who bought them, he continued, did not have legal ownership of them.[40] It was the duty of the ruler to put an end to such a practice. As for the difference between the free man and the slave, he replied that they were equal in terms of faith and piety and that an enslaved person could be closer to God than a thousand free men. Because the slave was dependent on his master, the *shari'a* exempted him from some obligations such as attending the Friday congregation, performing pilgrimage, participating in *jihad,* or paying *zakāt* (obligatory tax).[41]

In 1922, *al-Manār* received a letter from Singapore inquiring about Chinese concubines bought from their families.[42] Riḍā, in his answer, emphasized that freedom was an innate condition for all individuals and nations and reiterated the aforementioned statement attributed to 'Umar bin al-Khaṭṭāb in that regard. He regretted that slavery had become a social institution, plaguing several societies to the extent that its abolition would have created chaos. When Islam came with its "reform," however, it provided several opportunities to free slaves. The reason it did not impose a complete ban on enslavement, he elaborated, was because Muslims would then be the only people to be enslaved by their enemies if defeated in a battle. To maintain balance, Muslims did not abolish slavery until all warrior states decided to do so, as was the case with the Ottomans who agreed to abolish slavery after other nations had done the same. He reminded the inquirer that although slavery was permitted, it was not a "duty" that Muslims had to perform. He then reinstated his condemnation of the kidnapping and buying of Chinese, Circassian, and black slaves, warning that this was not permissible under the *shari'a*. Moreover, Riḍā declared that sexual intercourse with those female slaves could be considered as an explicit act of adultery.[43]

A close examination of the arguments made by both the antiabolition and the proabolition *ulama* reveals not only common concerns but also deep disparities in their stands toward slavery. Both groups were engaged in the discussion in response to European criticism of slavery in Muslim societies and of the alleged role the *shari'a* had played in perpetuating and legitimizing slavery. Both stated that Islam was more humane and merciful in its treatment of slaves in comparison to other religions. Both argued that slavery had become such an integrated institution in societies that Islam could not abolish it at once. Furthermore, their arguments were firmly grounded in the two major sources of Islamic law, the *Qur'an* and the *ḥadīth*. Though both referred to the same sources, each used them differently and even paradoxically, in order to conform to each group's beliefs and religious dogmas.

The conservatives accepted neither the premises of European criticism nor its objectives. They portrayed slavery in positive terms, emphasizing its role in providing socioeconomic balance in societies. Most important for them was how the agency of slavery served to convert the enslaved, thus increasing the number of Muslims. This was a crucial factor in what they considered an ongoing clash between Europe and Islam. Abolition of slavery would dry up one source of conversion to Islam and would, as a result, tip the balance in favor of Europe. They believed that religious texts did not grant any legitimacy for abolition. If the text was not clear and explicit in its advocacy of abolition, it could not be reinterpreted to meet new developments. No previous interpretation of the *Qur'an* or the *ḥadīth* had proposed abolition and thus, based on the *taqlīd* tradition, this issue could not be reconsidered in light of a different historical context. The meaning of the verses or the *ḥadīth* could not vary to accommodate changes that had occurred in the institution of slavery, and definitely not for the purpose of appeasing Europeans or imitating them. By adhering to the traditional interpretation of the religious text, conservatives aspired to protect Islam from what they deemed as another colonial enterprise aimed at defeating Islam and weakening Muslims, this time through the abolition of slavery. Thus, the conservative approach, dictated to a large degree by their animosity toward the west and their unwillingness to reexamine laws in the *shari'a*, shaped their reactionary rhetoric toward abolition and restricted their legal maneuvering.

The abolitionist arguments of al-Kawākibī, 'Abduh, and Riḍā reflected their own beliefs and agenda. Abolition fit within their Islamic reform campaign that promoted concepts of freedom and liberty on the one hand and attempted to integrate them into the *shari'a* on the other. They regarded Islamic law as a dynamic body of regulations subject to reflective interpretations, providing enough room to promote new ideas. The meaning of verses and *ḥadīth* pertaining to slavery was stretched to argue that abolition was not only promoted by Islam but also ordained by it. The objective behind regulating slavery, limiting its sources, and encouraging emancipation of slaves was to put an end to the practice. If the abolition of slavery was considered a "civilized" act and a necessary one, and since a legal pro-abolition argument could be made, reformers did not hesitate to argue in favor of it. After all, one of the main objectives of the reform movement had always been to relive that moment of the past when Islam was considered the bearer of human civilization, even if it entailed acknowledging past wrongdoings and misinterpretations of Islamic law. Those shortcomings could be redressed since, as reformers maintained, the verses of the *Qur'an* and the *ḥadīth* possessed an "evolutionary" meaning which could extracted from the text through *ijtihād*.

Notes

1. My interest in this topic originated during a seminar on Islam and Slavery taught by Professor Ann McDougall at the University of Alberta. I thank her for the interest she has generated in this topic.
2. The few studies available deal mostly with slavery and the slave trade during the Ottoman period. See for instance, Ehud R. Toledano, *Slavery and Abolition in the Ottoman Middle East.* (Seattle, 1998); idem, *The Ottoman Slave Trade and Its Suppression, 1840–1890* (Princeton, 1982); Y. Hakan Erdem, *Slavery in the Ottoman Empire and its Demise, 1800–1909* (London, 1996); and Alan Fisher, "Chattel Slavery in the Ottoman Empire," *Slavery and Abolition* 1 (1980), 25–45. More general works on slavery in the Middle East include the following: Shaun E. Marmon, ed., *Slavery in the Islamic Middle East* (Princeton, 1999); Bernard Lewis, *Race and Slavery in the Middle East: An Historical Inquiry* (Oxford, 1992); and Daniel Pipes, *Slave Soldiers and Islam* (New Haven, 1981).
3. For example, see Toledano, *Slavery and Abolition,* chapter 4.
4. Wael Hallaq, "Was the Gate of Ijtihad Closed?" *International Journal of Middle Eastern Studies* 16 (1984), 5.
5. For example, see Rudolph Peters, "Ijtihād and Taqlīd in the 18th and 19th Century Islam," *Die Welt des Islams* 20 (1980), 131–45.
6. For more information, see Muneer Goolan Fareed, *Legal Reform in the Muslim World: The Anatomy of a Scholarly Dispute in the 19th and the Early 20th Centuries on the Usage of Ijtihād as a Legal Tool* (San Francisco, 1996).
7. This oft-quoted criticism is that of the French Cardinal Lavigerie in July 1888, when he condemned Islam for the evil of slavery in Central Africa.

His statement generated several responses, the best known of which was that of the French-educated Egyptian Aḥmad Shafiq Bey who wrote a book entitled, *L'esclavage au point de vue musulman* (1891). The Lebanese journal, *Thamarāt al-funūn* (*Fruits of Knowledge*), for example, ran a number of articles in its pages criticizing Lavigerie and refuting his argument. These articles included the reply of the Ottoman minister Jawdat Pasha, translated into Arabic by Aḥmad 'Izzat al-'Ābid, the influential Damascene advisor in the Hamidian court. See especially *Thamarāt al-Funūn* 15 (1888), 712, 713, 716, 722.

8. For more information on *al-Haqā'iq*, see David Dean Commins, *Islamic Reform: Politics and Social Change in Late Ottoman Syria* (Oxford, 1990).
9. Amal Ghazal, "Sufism, Ijtihād and Modernity: Yūsuf al-Nabhānī in the Age of 'Abd al-Hamīd II," *Archivum Ottomanicum* 19 (2001), 239–71.
10. Yūsuf al-Nabhānī, *Sa'ādat al-anām fi ittibā' dīn al-islām wa tawḍīḥ al-farq baynahu wa bayna dīn al-naṣara fī al-'aqā'id wa al-aḥkām* (*Happiness in Following the Religion of Islam and Clarifying the Difference between Islam and Christianity in Terms of Beliefs and Rules*) (n.p., 1908).
11. Ibid., 42.
12. Al-Nabhānī referred to the battles of Mecca and Ḥunayn, when captured enemies were treated as slaves and allocated to Muslims who participated in battle; however, the Prophet Muhammad released and returned them all upon the intermediacy of their leaders.
13. al-Nabhānī, *Sa'ādat al-anām*, 42.
14. Ibid.
15. Ibid.
16. *Al-Haqā'iq* 10 (1911), 369.
17. Ibid.
18. Ibid., 370.
19. Ibid., 371.
20. Ibid.
21. Ibid., 373.
22. See *al-Manār* 8 (1905), 854–60. The letter is also reprinted in Muhammad Jamal al-Ṭahhān, ed., *Al-a'māl al-kāmila lil-Kawākibī* (Beirut, 1995), 259–64.
23. Ibid., 548. Al-Kawākibī visited Zanzibar and East Africa in 1901.
24. *Al-Manār* 8 (1905), 855.
25. Ibid.
26. Wilfrid Scawen Blunt included a translation of a letter sent by 'Abduh reiterating similar views in his *Secret History of the English Occupation of Egypt; Being a Personal Narrative of Events* (London, 1924), 193–94. Blunt quotes 'Abduh as saying, "...the Mohammedan religion not only does not oppose abolishing slavery as it is in modern time, but radically condemns its continuance."

27. *Al-Manār* 8 (1905), 856–57.
28. Muhammad 'Abduh, *Tafsīr juz' 'Ammā* (Cairo, 1967), 89.
29. Ibid.
30. Ibid., 262.
31. *Al-Manār* 8 (1905), 857.
32. Ibid., 860.
33. Ibid., 861.
34. *Al-Manār* 13 (1910), 741–42.
35. Ibid., 743.
36. *Al-Manār* 17 (1914), 658–61.
37 *Al-Manār* 20 (1917), 19–22.
38. The saying attributed to Caliph 'Umar, and frequently referred to by abolitionists, is: "Since when do you enslave people while they were born free?"
39. Ibid., 19.
40. Ibid., 21–22.
41. Ibid.
42. *Al-Manār* 23 (1922), 31–33.
43. Ibid., 33.

Chapter 10

THE *BORI* COLONIES OF TUNIS

Ismael Musah Montana

INTRODUCTION

This chapter examines *bori*-centered *diyar* (households) in the social and communal organization of enslaved West African communities designated "Sudani-Tunis" in nineteenth-century Tunis.[1] This study is of particular importance within the context of slavery, ethnography, and ethnicity in the Maghreb. It takes an approach similar to Allen Meyers's study of the origins of the *abid al-Bukhari* (slave soldiers) of Mawlay Ismail ibn al-Sharif (1672–1727). In his examination of the origins of *abid al-Bukhari* and their relation to black slaves brought from the western Sudan, Meyers distinguishes *abid al-Bukhari* from Africans from the Sudan and states that, contrary to popular misconceptions, a significant proportion of *abid al-Bukhari* were actually local Moroccans who did not originate from the Sudan.[2] This differentiation of *abid al-Bukhari* from the Sudanic Africans is atypical; yet few scholars have attempted to confront the historical and structural distinctions that existed among blacks and slave groups in the Maghreb region. Similarly to Meyers, I argue that compared to the preexisting freed slaves whose history predates the Husaynid era (1705–1957), as well as the native-born blacks known in Tunisia as "*shwashin*", the "Sudan-Tunis" constituted a distinctive new wave of enslaved West Africans. Further, I maintain that although the importation of this class of slaves into the regency may well have started under the Turkish ruler, Yousef Dey (1610–1637), who built the *souk el-Berka* for the sale of black slaves,[3] it was mainly under the Husaynids that the bulk of this class of predominantly Kanuri and Hausa slaves was brought into the regency. In fact, the systematic importation of these slaves began around 1738, shortly before the reign Ali Bey I (1740–1756), and peaked during the reign of Hammuda Pasha (1782–1814). In the mid-nineteenth century, Ahmed Bey (1837–1855) outlawed this trade. This new wave of enslaved West African slaves can be distinguished from other groups (for example, from the older generation of slaves whose history predated the Husaynids) in three main ways. First, the enslaved West Africans established networks of self-help religious practices centered on the Hausa *bori* cult. Second, their patterns of social, communal, and organizational structures differed. Third, they were the class of slave, which Ahmed Bey in 1846 had declared to be "illegally enslaved" on the grounds that it was effectively impossible to differentiate which of these slaves was legally enslavable, and in cases of doubt, the presumption should favor the right of liberty.[4]

Relying upon *Hatk al-Sitr Ammā Alayhi Sudāni Tunis min al-Kufr*[5] and other contemporary accounts, this chapter differentiates these enslaved West African communities from the *shwashin* (older generations of freed slaves) through *bori* colonies and the pattern of social organization that has made the West Africans the subject of numerous fascinating firsthand accounts.[6] Additionally, the chapter considers the extent to which West Africans were acculturated into Tunisian society through the institution of *bash agha* attached to the Husaynids' administrative bureaucracy.

THE *BORI* "COLONIES" AND CORPORATE ORGANIZATION

A remarkable characteristic of the enslaved West African communities was the pattern and structure of their communal households. Throughout the regency, West Africans formed separate communities and established corporate organizations according to their ethnic and geographical places of origin. These ethnic household organizations, in turn, organized a set of colonies related to *bori* ritual cycles. At the turn of the nineteenth century, al-Timbuktawi viewed these colonies as a clearly identifiable characteristic of the West African communities; however, all the ethnic households and communal organizations observed in Tunis were not unique to the Sudanese communities in the regency.[7] Elsewhere in the Maghreb and parts of the Ottoman Empire, where a large number of the same class of West Africans were domestic slaves, similar religious communal households and corporate organizations have been noted by several scholars as being one of the main features of black slaves imported to these regions.[8] In the case of the Regency of Tunis, the local structure of West African households and corporate organizations were centered on communal households called *dar* (pl. *diyar*). The term "*dar*" could mean both the household and the family that bears a single name of the *dar* as well as the building in which they reside. Thus, a *dar* may bring several generations together in one unit even if all the extended family members do not reside in that particular *dar*.

It is an accepted tradition among *bori* adepts and descendants of the West Africans that in the first decade of the eighteenth century, up to fourteen *diyar* existed in the Regency of Tunis.[9] Al-Timbuktawi reported that outside of Tunis, in towns such as Sousse in the Sahel, Kairawan in central Tunisia, and Sfax in the south, there were several small communal *diyar* as well.[10] He noted that ten *diyar* in Tunis bore West African communal characteristics: they housed "numerous *bori* deities and had other objects pertinent to the *bori*, including the matamores, banners, snakes and *bori* musical instruments such as the *kambri* (*gumbiri*)" which the *bori* communities regarded as a sacred instrument.[11] Al-Timbuktawi did not provide details about the size and locations of these *diyar*, but he indicated that they provided shelter for several newcomers—mainly slaves—brought from the Sudan. The *diyar*, indeed, served to integrate West Africans into the social fabric by means of affiliation into a corporate community, the members of which were collectively liable for supporting one another.

As indicated on the map of Tunis, a schematic pattern of the *diyar* at the time of al-Timbuktawi's sojourn in Tunis was loosely structured around ghetto-like compounds that clustered around the medina in the city of Tunis. Within the vicinity of the medina, many *diyar* were located in *homats* (residential quarters), specifically, around Halfaouin in Bab Swaiqa and Bab Djedid in the western suburb of the medina. J. S. Woodford identifies these as mainly residential quarters during the eighteenth and nineteenth centuries.[12] Populated mostly by a diverse group of foreigners of common origin and similar economic status, most of the people residing in such quarters were seasonal workers from neighboring countries such as the *Wargliya* (from Wargla in southern Algeria), *Trabelsiyya* (from Tripoli), and *Fezzazina* (from Fezzan in modern Libya). In addition, these quarters housed some Tunisians nationals, especially groups from the same *bled* (village) living and working in Tunis. According to Woodford, the location and actual settlements in Tunis where foreigners lived were all strictly regulated by the beys. Husaynid policy aimed to control foreign nationals, including recently enslaved blacks imported to the regency, just as they did with the local population. As Abun-Nasr and N. S. Hopkins also point out, this policy of containment of foreigners and the Tunisian populace

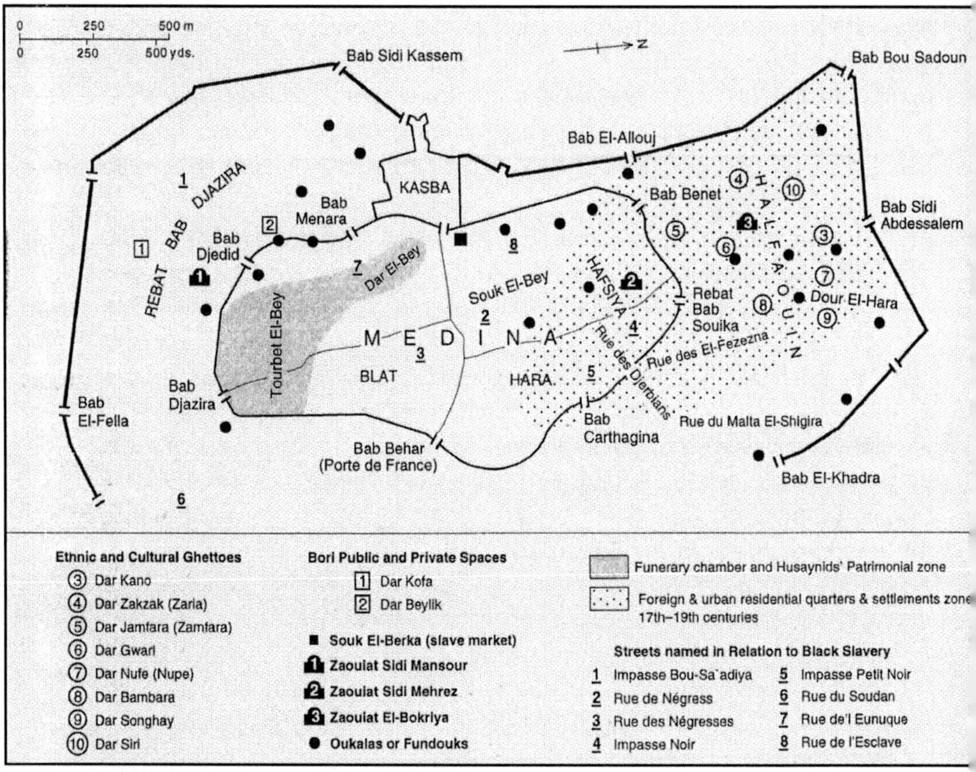

MAP 10.1 Tunis

encouraged concentration of foreign groups in particular quarters of the medina.[13]

It appears that *bori* colonies began to emerge in the regency in the first half of the eighteenth century. It is clear that one of the *diyar* that laid the foundation of the *bori* colonies can be dated from this period or slightly later; none can be securely dated to an earlier period. The oldest *diyar* can be traced back to the period of Ali Bey I (1740–1756), nephew and heir apparent to Husayn b. Ali. Due to the interest of urban historians in the old city of Tunis, the location of Dar Kofa is indisputably located and points to its military and political origins (see map)[14] Abdel Mejid al-Sabai, author of some private reports on the Husaynid era dated its appearance to military policies of Ali Bey I, stating that Dar Kofa was built between 1738 and 1739, following his rebellion against his uncle Husayn b. Ali (after the latter altered the succession of Ali Bey I in favor of his son Mohammad in

1724).[15] Al-Sabai recounted that following the defeat of his uncle, Ali Bey I recruited black slaves from the *bilad as-Sudan* to create his own regiment to counterbalance the full-fledged Turkish janissary drawing support from Algerian deys in support of Husayn's faction. After resorting to mercenaries from the Zwawa ethnic group in Algeria, Ali Bey commissioned the importation of slave soldiers directly from the *bilad as-Sudan*, which were designated *bawwaba* (palace guards).[16] The bey built several public houses for these regiments and assisted them in establishing their private *nawadi* (clubs). According to al-Sabai, "Each of these clubs was called *kofa*, and only the Sudanic black soldiers assembled in these clubs practice their own customs secretly." Even though his account provides no further details about these secret customs, his account may be the first evidence to document *bori* in the regency. Since these regiments were imported from the *bilad as-Sudan en masse*, it seems sensible to attribute the appearance of *bori* in the regency to the *bawwaba* regiments as well as to consider it as one of the common cultural elements of their diasporic experience. As a diasporic community, they no doubt felt the need to foster and construct a support network. Because of its strong connections with all spheres of life, religion was a major cultural element in life in the diaspora, allowing enslaved Africans to preserve ties with their homelands while empowering themselves in alien lands with mutual support. The *bawwaba,* possibly originating in Hausaland, may have invoked the Hausa *bori* as their medium of religious expression in Islamic North Africa.[17]

The nineteenth century Tunisian chronicler Ibn Abi Diyaf singled out Ali Bey I as the sole Husaynid ruler to employ black slave soldiers from *bilad as-Sudan*.[18] Ibn Abi Diyaf states that Ali Bey I designated his troops as *bawwaba* and clearly distinguished them from the existing military corps by providing them with stylish military uniforms and training them as his personal standing army ready for deployment in his wars.[19] In Ibn Abi Diyaf's mind was the idea that the *bawwaba* were modeled after the famous *abid al-Bukhari* of the Moroccan Sultan Mawlay Ismail; however, according to M. G. Smith, this represented a central element of Hausa political organization.[20] Part of the function of the *kofafi* was to act as the official intermediary between the king and the general populace without direct administrative control over the communication they regulated. Comparatively speaking, since the duties of the kofa are comparable with those of the *bawwaba*, then, it is likely that the *bawwaba* might have derived from the same *kofafi*, an already established professional military regiment in the Sudan.

Al-Timbuktawi offered an alternative account of Dar Kofa as originating in the Sudanic community of Tunis.[21] He speculated that Dar Kofa was *habus* (charitable property) that had been endowed in the name of a former slave, a woman named Kofa.[22] Although it is not clear who this woman might have been or even if she existed, it is clear that by 1807 Dar Kofa was no longer a secret club of the *bawwaba* regiments, but rather a communal center that provided social and religious space for West Africans. The claim that Dar Kofa might be an endowment named after a female ex-slave also suggests a gender shift and transfer of this household from the male-dominated *bawwaba* to the *bori* priestesses whose rise to prominence coincided with the reign of Hammuda Pasha.[23] In 1756, after nearly three decades of exile, Husayn b. Ali's faction regained the throne from their Bashiyya rivals. After this, the influence of the *bawwaba* in manning Dar Kofa is unclear.[24] By the time al-Timbuktawi was in Tunis in 1808 or 1809, Dar Kofa had attained its high status and importance in housing the *sarkin gida*, the holiest of the *bori* deities in Tunis, and its association with *bori* priestesses. Al-Timbuktawi's description of this household reveals that it was the largest unit of the West African *diyar* in Tunis, and was also a focal point of communal and religious life of its slave community. As such, he equated assembles of the Sudanese slaves who convened in Dar Kofa, especially during the month of *Sha`aban*, with pilgrims performing the *hajj*.[25]

Writing in 1886, al-Ḥashāishī included Dar Kofa among the ghetto-like residences in Tunis that were inhabited solely by foreign nationals.[26] He also described Dar Kofa as a *dar al-umumi* (public compound), noting that its residents were exclusively *Sudani*, that is black slaves.[27] Similarly, in 1914 Tremearne identified Dar Kofa as Hausa, a *gidan jamaat* (house of the community), and referred to it as "the elementary social unit" of each *bori* community.[28] Other households that made up the Hausa colonies in Tunis, according to Tremearne's account, were *gidan tsafi* (house of medicine) and *gidan kuri* (house of *kuri*). Tremearne viewed all the Hausa colonies that he described as part of *gidan jamaat*, because it was a temple: however, by the first quarter of the twentieth century the importance of Dar Kofa had diminished. Further information obtained from descendants of the *bori* communities confirmed that Dar al-Askar (household of soldiers) was another name for Dar Kofa, attesting to its connection with the *bawwaba* regiments.[29]

Another of the oldest *bori* colonies was Dar Beylic, which can be dated back to the eighteenth century. The etymology of this household suggests a connection between the Husaynids and recent West African slaves, but al-Sabai, who first reported on these households, made no mention of Dar Beylik among the *nawadi* (secret clubs) where Ali Bey's West African regiments secretly practiced their religion. Al-Timbuktawi, who was the first to mention Dar Beylic, did so in passing.[30] Tremearne attributes Dar Beylik to "one of the cousins of the Beys who owned a private temple."[31] While the origin of Dar Kofa suggests a connection between recent Sudanese settlers and the beylical authorities, Dar Beylik indicates the likelihood that the Husaynids Beys not only encouraged *bori* but embraced it as well.[32] Their attitude to *bori* was by all accounts contrary to that of the *jihad* leaders in the central Sudan who banned the cult. Like the Husaynid rulers of Tunis, some Karamanli in Libya also tolerated, if not encouraged, *bori* rites.[33]

By the first decade of the nineteenth century additional *bori diyar* were established as a set of complementary colonies that housed West Africans of common origin or similar ethnolinguistic background. Accordingly, these ethnic- and linguistic-based households were subordinate units to Dar Kofa, but unlike Dar Kofa, which served as the main temple and socioreligious space of the black community, the ethnically-based *diyar* served principally as shelters for slaves and hostels for pilgrims and travelers from West Africa. Located in the residential quarter (see map), each household recognized a *bori* pantheon whose spirits were pertinent to the ethnic background of those living in it. Both al-Timbuktawi and Tremearne described ethnic and linguistic *diyar* comprised principally of slaves of West African origin. Of this group, slaves ethnically associated with Hausaland formed the majority according to the regional distribution of the *diyar*. For instance, by 1807 the number of households affiliated with Hausa included Dar Kano, Dar Gwari, Dar Janfara (Zamfara), Dar Zakzak, (Zaria), and Dar Nufe (Nupe), altogether five out of seven households.[34] In addition, Al-Timbuktawi identified non-Hausa households, Dar Bambara, Dar Songhay, and one of "Bornouis" (from Borno). Of these, the largest was the "Bornouis", although it formed only one household, Dar Jamaat, as recorded in al-Hachaichi's account of the late 1880s. Al-Timbuktawi also noted another household known as Dar Siri.

Later accounts of the *diyar* suggest a clear shift in the structure of *bori* colonies from being ethnolinguistically centered to being associated with particular *bori* chief priestesses, especially during the 1860s, a period that followed the abolition of slavery in Tunisia. Al-Hachaichi, for example, clearly delineates such additional characteristics of the *diyar* following this shift. He discusses a number of ethnolinguistic *diyar* that were not described by al-Timbuktawi. It is not known if these *diyar* existed in the first decade of the nineteenth century, or if they did, if their structure was the same as reported by al-Hachaichi. The *diyar* were regionally-based households with which people identified on the basis of specific cities or ethnic groups from the *bilad as-Sudan*, including Wadai, Dar Fur, Baghirmi, and Kawar, and not only the seven reported by al-Timbuktawi.[35] Each *dar* had a *bori* priestess who possessed the same ethnicity or had originated from the same town after which a household was named. Moreover, al-Hachaichi also listed households named after particular *bori* priestesses, including Dar Arifat Baghirmi (household of the Baghirmi priestess), Dar Arifat Darfur (household of the Dar Fur priestess), Dar Arifat Bambara (household of the Bambara priestess), Dar Arifat Songhay (household of the Songhay priestess), Dar Arifat Bornu (household of the Borno priestess), and Dar Arifat Ziriya (household of the Algerian priestess). Dar Arifat Ziriya was the household occupied by fugitive and freed slaves from Algeria who moved to the Regency of Tunis following the abolition of slavery in 1846. One household that is not mentioned in the sources, but which according to *Stambali* adherents is Dar Saraa, did exist and might have been identified with al-Timbuktawi's Dar Siri, a house believed to have been inhabited by non-Muslims who refused to convert to Islam.[36]

THE SOCIAL ORGANIZATION OF THE "SUDAN-TUNIS"

The unique characteristics of the enslaved West Africans of Tunis cannot be fully appreciated without considering their communal life and social organization. These West Africans governed themselves according to organizational modes brought with them from the *bilad as-Sudan*. Hausa aristocratic titles such as *sarki* (king), *magajiya* (female head of a household) or *inna* (female patrons of a household) prevailed in the internal organizational structure of their support networks. To an extent, titles of Kanuri origin such as *galadima* (deputy of the *sarki*) were integral to these networks; however, similar to the structure of *bori* in the regency, Hausa cultural influence dominated their social organization.[37] This is evident, for example, in the hierarchy of titles such as *magajiya* or *arifa* (chief priestess) that were prevalent in the *bori* and the self-help networks centered on the *bori* colonies. Other titles, notably *galadima* and *sarki*, were more pragmatic and served as focal points between these communities and their host Tunisian society in wider interpersonal relations. Hence, a *galadima* functioned as spokesperson for the diverse *Sudanic* West African communities comprised of "Sudan-Tunis."

Throughout the nineteenth century all West African *diyar* and communal organizations were represented by a *galadima* functioning under the leadership of *sarkin bayi* (chief of slaves). The main duties of a *galadima* consisted of supervising *diyar* in a manner pertinent to the *diyar*'s ethnic membership. As a representative of his ethnic group in the *humats* residential quarters, the *galadima* would appear before the *sarkin bayi*, for example, to secure a *tezkiret* (a special permit) from beylical authorities to enable his ethnic group to partake in *bori* annual *ziarats* (pilgrimage and homage) to the shrine of Sidi Saad.[38] As well, when a local Tunisian family required a *bori* ceremony, usually to drive away evil spirits, the *galadima* would act as an agent for the *bori* cult and would, in turn, dispatch invitations to cult members, who for the most part came from his own ethnic background.[39] Furthermore, when a newcomer (including a group of voluntary migrants) arrived from the Sudan, or when emancipated slaves could not find their niche in Tunisian society, the *galadima* would assign them to a *dar* of their ethnic background.[40]

In fact, the *galadima*'s function in the Regency of Tunis was very similar to their counterpart in the Hausaland. Smith explains that in eighteenth and nineteenth century Hausaland, a *galadima* acted as deputy to, and sometimes served as, the official head of the dynasty.[41] Likewise, in the Regency of Tunis, *galadima* served as deputies to the *sarkin bayi*. Each *galadima* was responsible for his respective membership and served as intermediator between them and the *sarkin bayi*. While Smith points out that in eighteenth- and nineteenth-century Hausaland the position of *galadima* was reserved for eunuchs, but was later held by those of noble lineage, it is not clear what the case of appointment of a *galadima* was in Tunisia. Compared to the *arifa*, however, who could only settle internal disputes among the female members of the *bori* communities,[42] the *galadima* was responsible for reporting all disputes among the slaves to the *sarkin bayi* (also known as *bash agha*). The *galadima* also worked closely with the *caid abid* (the Beylik-appointed officials over the slaves who collected taxes).[43]

In matters relating to the regency and the beylical authorities, the Sudanese were under the supervision of the *sarkin bayi*. In the bey's courts and within the beylical bureaucratic administration, he held an official title called *bash agha*, or in local terms, *al-Hakim fi al-Qishrat al-Sawda* (the governor over the black skinned). The office of *bash agha* was part of the official machinery of the state and, therefore, played the most important role in Sudanese social organization in relation to the Husaynid state. The exact period in which this title was introduced into the regency is not known, but Louis Frank, the French physician who served Hammuda Pasha and lived there from 1802–1806, gave an eyewitness account of the black slaves he encountered, which reveals that by the late eighteenth century the institution of *bash agha* already existed in the regency.[44] It is likely that the Husaynids, and not the Muradids, first introduced *bash agha* as a bureaucratic position involving matters related to black slavery.

Usually the person who held this official title was a black eunuch; indeed, Frank describes the *bash agha* as the bey's "premier eunuch" who was fluent in the languages of the black slaves whom he served as chief judge and governor because not all blacks spoke Arabic.[45]

As a representative of black slaves in the bey's court, the *bash agha* was designated chief magistrate over the black slaves and was vested with sweeping jurisdictional authority. Among his principle functions was the settlement of disputes arising among Sudanese slaves; however, his juridical function and influence also extended to settling disputes between these slaves and Tunisian citizens. As Frank observes, "if a slave finds a means of taking refuge with the *bash agha*, the owner of that slave cannot regain possession of that slave without making a payment of six piastres to the *bash agha* who takes it upon himself to put an end to the disagreement between slave and the master."[46] Indeed, the fact that the office of the *bash agha* was attached to the bey's palace in Bardo suggests the importance of the position. Thus in matters relating to black slaves, the bey consulted the *bash agha*. This is shown in the record of bey correspondence and petitions. As the chief responsible for the black slaves in the regency, we see from the records of the *mejba* (tax returns) that copies of the tax returns were deposited in his office.[47] The *bash agha* supervised several *caids abid* (slave officials) appointed for the collection of the tax on slaves throughout the regency. By the late 1880s, however, this institution was abolished by the French during the protectorate because it was no longer deemed necessary.

Having been brought as recent *abid* (slaves), the religious, social, and communal lives of the enslaved West Africans, unlike those of the older generation of freed slaves in the regency, such as *shwashin*, were usually patterned on religious and cultural elements derived freshly from their homeland, the *bilad as-Sudan*. Whereas the Sudanese were principally *bori* practitioners, and by and large followers of the black slave saint Sidi Saad, most *shwashin* did not associate with the *bori* cult and *Stambali* ritual circles. Likewise, the *shawshin* were far more integrated into Tunisian society, and compared to the West Africans, more clan-like. Unlike the West Africans who lived apart in *bori* colonies headed by *galadima*, the *shwashin* were headed by shaykhs, a pattern of social organization modeled after the local segmentary structure. They occupied villages in the remote parts of southern Tunisia that are identified as *urush el-riqaq* (slave principalities).[48]

Notes

1. On the Sudan-Tunis communities, see Ismael Musah Montana, "Ahmad Ibn al-Qadi al-Timbuktawi on the *Bori* Ceremonies of Sudan-Tunis," in *Slavery on the Frontiers of Islam*, ed. P. E. Lovejoy (Trenton, NJ, 2003), 177–79.
2. Allan R. Meyers, "Class, Ethnicity, and Slavery: The Origin of the Moroccan *Abid*," *International Journal of African Historical Studies* 10 (1977), 428. On black slaves and the bori cult in Tunis, see Ahmed Rahal, *La communauté noire de Tunis: thérapie initiatique et rite de possession* (Paris, 2000).
3. See Ibn Abi Dinar al-Kairawani, *Al-Mu`nis fi Akhbar Ifriqiya wa-Tunis* (Tunis, 1968), 206. Arthur Pelligrin, attesting to Abi Dinar's account of the genesis of the Tunis slave market, attributed it to the Turkish administration. He concluded that Yusef Dey built the slave market solely for the sale of black slaves. Hence from its beginning, this market was exclusively reserved for "commerce des esclaves noirs." Pelligrin, "Le vieux de Tunis: les noms de rue de la ville arabe," *Bulletin économique et social de a Tunisie* 66 (1952), and idem, *Le vieux Tunis: Les noms de rues de la villes arabe* (Tunis, n.d.), 23.
4. On the slave trade and abolition of slavery in Tunisia, see Ismael Musah Montana, "The Trans-Saharan Slave Trade, Abolition of Slavery and Transformation in the North African Regency of Tunis, 1759–1846," Ph.D dissertation, York University, 2007.
5. Ahmad b. al-Qadi Abi Bakr b. Yusuf b. Ibrahim al-Timbuktawi, *Hatk al-Sitr Ammā Alayhi Sūdāni Tunis min al-Kufr* (Piercing the Veil; Being an Account of the Infidel Religion of the Blacks of Tunis) (Tunis, 1813), ms., Bibliothèque nationale de Tunisie, Tunis; and also Fatima Harrak and Mohammad El-Mansur, *A Fulani Jihadist in the Maghreb: Admonition of Ahmad Ibn al-Qadi al-Timbukti* (Rabat, 2000).
6. Louis Frank, *Tunis, description de cette régence* (Paris, 1850); and J. J. Marcel's review of this work in *l'Univers pittoresque: histoire et description de tous les peuples de leurs religions, moeurs, coutumes, etc...* (Paris, 1850); al-Timbuktawi, *Hatk al-Sitr*; Muḥammad ibn Uthmān Ḥashāishī, *Al-Ādāt wa-al-taqālīd al-Tūnisīyah: al-hadīyah aw al-fawāid al-ilmīyah fī al-ādāt al-Tūnisīyah* (Tunis, 1994); A. J. N. Tremearne, *The Ban of the Bori: Demons and Demon-Dancing in West Africa* (London, 1968); and idem, "*Bori* Beliefs and Ceremonies," *Journal of the Royal Anthropological Institute of Great Britain and Ireland* 45 (1915), 23–68.
7. Al-Timbuktawi, *Hatk al-Sitr*, 7, folio a. See also Montana, "Al-Timbuktawi on *Bori* Ceremonies," 178–79; and Muḥammad ibn Uthmān Ḥashāishī, *Al-Ādāt wa-al-taqālīd al-Tūnisīyah: al-hadīyah aw al-fawāid al-ilmīyah fī al-ādāt al-Tūnisīyah* (Tūnis, 1994); Muḥammad ibn Uthmān Ḥashāishī, *al-Riḥlah al-ṣaḥrāwīyah abra arāḍī Ṭarābulus wa-bilād al-Tawrāq* (*Voyage*

au pays des Senoussia à travers la Tripolitaine et les pays Touareg) (Tunis, 1988).

8. See John O. Hunwick, "Black Africans in the Mediterranean Islamic World," in *The Human Commodity: Perspectives on the Trans-Saharan Trade*, ed. Elizabeth Savage (London, 1992), 5-36.
9. Interview with el-Cheikh Hammadi el-Bidali Abdel Hamid (Hammadi's son), and Abel Majid Tunis at Sidi Abdel Salem, Tunis, 23 August 2000.
10. al-Timbuktawi, *Hatk al-Sitr*.
11. See Montana, "Al-Timbuktawi on *Bori* Ceremonies," 179–81.
12. J. S. Woodford, *The City of Tunis: Evolution of an Urban System* (Outwell, Wisbewch, Cambridgeshire, England, 1990), 102; and Jamil Abun-Nasr, "The Tunisian State in the Eighteenth Century," *Revue de l'Occident Musulman et de la Méditerrannée* 33 (1982), 35.
13. See Abun-Nasr, "The Tunisian State in the Eighteenth Century," 35; and N. S. Hopkins, "Traditional Tunis and Its Transformations," *Annals of New York Academy of Social Science* 220 (1974), 427–32.
14. Jellal Abdelkafi, *La Médina de Tunis: Espace Historique* (Tunis, 1989).
15. See Rachad Limam, *Siyassat Hammouda Pacha fi Tunis* (Tunis, 1980).
16. Liman, *La Politique de Hammouda Pacha*, 241.
17. On Africans and their religious experience in the Islamic lands of the Mediterranean, see John O. Hunwick, "The Religious Practice of Black Slaves in the Mediterranean Islamic Lands," in *Slavery on the Frontiers of Islam,* ed. P. E. Lovejoy (Princeton, 2004), 149–50.
18. Ibn Abi Diyaf, *Ithaf ahl-al-Zaman*, 2:122.
19. See Jamil M. Abun-Nasr, *A History of the Maghrib in the Islamic Period* (Cambridge, 1987), 179–80.
20. M. G. Smith, *Government in Zauzau, 1800–1950* (Oxford, 1960), 79.
21. al-Timbuktawi, *Hatk al-Sitr*; and also Montana, "Al-Timbuktawi on the *Bori* Ceremonies," 179.
22. al-Timbuktawi, *Hatk al-Sitr*.
23. See Rachad Limam, "Some Documents Concerning Slavery in Tunisia at the End of the 18th Century," *Revue d'Histoire Maghrebine* 8 (1981), 349–57; and idem, *Siyassat Hammouda,* 302–03.
24. On the succession crisis between Ali Bey I and Husay b. Ali's faction, see Mohamed-Hédi Chérif, *Pouvoir et société dans la Tunisie du Husayn bin Ali: 1705–1740* (Tunis, 1984); and Abun-Nasr, *History of the Maghrib*, 173–74.
25. Montana, "Al-Timbutawi on the *Bori* Ceremonies," 180.
26. Ḥashāishī and Marzūqī, *al-Riḥlah al-ṣaḥrāwīyah abra arāḍī Ṭarābulus wa-bilād al-Tawrāq*, 174–75.
27. Ibid.; and Ḥashāishī, *Al-Ādāt wa-al-taqālīd al-Tūnisīyah*, 300.
28. Tremearne, *Ban of the Bori*, 269.

29. Interview with Hammadi el-Bidali, Tunis, 23 August 2000.
30. al-Timbuktawi, *Hatk al-Sitr*.
31. Tremearne, *Ban of the Bori*, 23.
32. See Montana, "Al-Timbuktawi on the *Bori* Ceremonies," 179.
33. Tremearne, *Ban of the Bori*, 23.
34. See Montana, "Al-Timbuktawi on the *Bori* Ceremonies," 179.
35. Ḥashāishī, *al-Riḥlah al-ṣaḥrāwīyah*, 174.
36. Interview with Hammadi el-Bidali, Tunis, 23 August 2000.
37. See Tremearne, *Ban of the Bori*, 22; and idem, "*Bori* Beliefs and Ceremonies," 67.
38. For Tunisian state regulation of the Sudanese ziyaret to the shrine of Sidi Saad through the institution of *bash agha*, see Yaḥyá, *Al-Ādāt wa-al-taqālīd al-Tūnisīyah,* 212–13.
39. Interviews with Abdelmajid Bornaoui, Tunis, 19 July 2001; and Habib Al-Jouini, Tunis, 17 July 2001.
40. Interviews with Habib Al-Jouini, Tunis, 17 July 2001; and Abdelmajid Bornaoui, Tunis, 24 July 2001.
41. Smith, *Government in Zauzau,* 38–39.
42. See Frank, *Tunis*, 119.
43. See dossier 425, carton 36, Lettres des Caid de Sahel, Correspondences des Caids, Archives du Gouvernment Tunisienne.
44. Frank, *Tunis*, 119; Robert Brunschvig, "Abd," in *The Encyclopaedia of Islam* (Leiden, 1960), 35; and G. Zawadoski, "Le role des Nègres parmi la population Tunisienne," *En Terre d'Islam* (2e trimester, 1942), 147.
45. Frank, *Tunis*, 119.
46. Ibid.
47. See Registres fiscaux et administratifs [Tax Census Records], 1853–1860, Archives du Gouvernment Tunisienne.
48. See Mohammad Al-Hedi al-Juwayli, *Mujtama'atun li al-dhakira, Mujtama'atun li'al nisyan* (*Societies to Be Remembered, Societies to Be Forgotten: A Monograph on the Black Minority in Southern Tunisia*) (Tunis, 1994).

Chapter 11

THE SERVILE POPULATIONS OF THE ALGERIAN SAHARA, 1850– 1900

Benjamin Claude Brower

INTRODUCTION: SAHARAN SLAVERY IN THE FRENCH COLONIAL ARCHIVES

The trans-Saharan slave trade, which furnished much of the Mediterranean world with slaves, has received a good amount of attention from historians wishing to understand its volume and economic importance.[1] With the exception of Tuareg societies, however, knowledge of the practices of slavery in the Sahara remains sketchy. From the researcher's point of view, the ample documents produced by the early French presence in Algeria and the French interest in the area to the south make the lands that eventually became the Algerian Sahara an attractive place to begin this work.[2]

The French occupation of the northern reaches of the Algerian Sahara began in the 1840s. In 1852 the French firmly established their presence with the occupation of the oasis of Laghouat. French control moved southward piecemeal in subsequent decades, a process completed with the violent seizure of the oases agglomerations in the Tidikelt, Touat (Tuwāt), and Gourara (Gurāra) between 1899 and 1901. During the fifty-year interval, the French administration created a large documentation base on the region. This archive is richest in the data needed to undertake socio-economic studies. The administration was less interested in understanding cultural questions, and while they ardently desired to know about the political inclinations of Saharans, their analysis frequently fell far short of the mark (a notable failure was the routing of the 1881 Flatters mission). Nevertheless, French policy makers undertook considerable research on questions of political economy, and they also assessed the military capacities of the people to the south. Their data came from scientific expeditions, military operations, a network of spies and informants, and most importantly, interviews with Algero-Saharan traders and migrant workers.[3]

European sources on slavery in the Middle East and Africa are notoriously treacherous. For example, the documentation generated by missionary societies such as the *Pères blancs* has been criticized for factual inaccuracies and its political agenda, one served by exaggerating slavery.[4] The legacy of Edward Said alone encourages us to take such cautions seriously, but the rich amount of material in colonial archives, as affected as it may be by *le mal de voir*, should not be rejected out of hand.[5] A thorough knowledge of the archive and an analysis of the contexts in which sources emerged is a first step of critical reading strategies. This essay illustrates these and will remain attentive throughout to Dominick LaCapra's call for *Quellenkritik* (the critique of sources), that is to say, "documents are texts that supplement or rework 'reality' and not mere sources that divulge facts about 'reality'."[6]

The French colonial archive includes sources representing three different groups: the French administration, Saharan slave owners and slave traders, and servile populations. The first group includes documents written by French administrators (generally military officers) or explorers on official missions to the Sahara. While the opinions of this group concerning slavery were far from homogenous, certain generalizations can be made. First and foremost, in the second half of the nineteenth century, the French administration sought to minimize the importance of slavery in the lands it managed or hoped to control in the near future. In 1848 the provisional government of the Second Republic forced the abolition decree upon a reluctant group of administrators in Algeria who feared upheavals if they enforced the letter of the law in the volatile colony. They responded with equivocation: publicly colonial authorities took a strong stance in favor of abolition, while privately they attacked abolitionists as "philanthropists" and counseled accommodation with slavery and the slave trade. In some cases, officers went so far as to explicitly order subordinates to refuse to take notice of slavery in their jurisdictions.[7] This was the "eyes-closed" response to slavery, a quasi-official policy whereby local French administrators made accommodation with slavery and the slave-trade in their jurisdictions with the tacit or explicit authorization of their superiors. The goal was to not rile slave owners, local notables on which the French depended, and avoid the payment of reparations. Accommodating slavery was easy enough in northern Algeria, a place known as the Tell, where slavery was limited. But the Sahara presented a different case. Here, the slave trade was economically important, representing a good part of the wealth of trans-Saharan commerce. Moreover, slavery and the racial hierarchies it engendered marked a servile class of people of color who provided the labor essential for date-palm agriculture in the oases. French administrators recognized the importance of slavery in the Sahara. To curry favor with local notables and to appease policy makers worried about the political complications of abolition and slavery, they downplayed slavery as a benign institution that could be tolerated.

A second group of texts are documents addressed by Saharan notables to the French administration. For much of our period, this group was internally divided and looked toward expanding French influence with a mixture of determined opposition, anxiety, and, for some, hope that the French would advance their interests. However, all were heavily invested in the status quo and united in their fear that French control would compromise their relations with subordinates and even cause them to loose their slaves. As we shall see, Saharan notables devised various strategies to protect their social capital and property in the emerging new regime. These included anticipating and exploiting French ambivalences concerning abolition and redeploying the colonial vocabulary of mutual economic interest and its rhetoric of stability and order to maximum effect.

The final group of sources includes the acts and voices of servile populations as recorded by French administrators and explorers. The archive here is slim. Only the accidental or the extraordinary made its way into print (or more rarely, photographs), and several languages and layers of translation often obscure these texts. Moreover, as in many cases where the dominant give voice to the dominated, the reporters' affective responses, biases, political projects, and fantasies are often imbedded in these accounts. Nevertheless, careful work can reveal historically valuable information. These sources show servile people asserting positive identities through festivals, narratives, and skilled work. And in dramatic actions such as flight, we see the oldest and most dangerous example of resistance. These documents also provide hints pointing to the thousands who worked within the boundaries of their social position, skillfully deploying their limited tools to amass social and economic capital in a physical place, the desert, which produced rare surpluses and even rarer opportunities for the lowest strata. On the whole, the archive contains examples ranging the spectrum of the human drama, from heroic acts of resistance, to measured tactics of self-preservation, to resignation in the face of domination so total that agency was impossible.

HARATIN AND SLAVES, THE SERVILE POPULATIONS OF THE OASES

The warp and the woof from which were woven the complex patterns of oasis society are difficult to schematize. The half-century leading up to direct French rule was an especially dynamic period that makes hazardous the attempt to sketch social categories. Social divisions were marked and hierarchies formed in multifaceted ways. Real and imagined kinship relations were the foundation of oasis society. Yet language, political alliances and factions (*Ṣaff*), religious affiliation (Muslims, polytheists, Jews; Sufi order affiliation), gender, age, and physical characteristics, among many others, figured in the composition of the social fabric. One Saharan trader, when asked to describe the people who lived in the Touat region reported simply: "Touat is inhabited by five different people: the Blacks—who are the most ancient in the land—the Tuareg, the Zenatah (Berber speakers), the Arabs, and the Jews."[8]

A primary social marker, arguably the most important, was the divide that marked the beginning of the servile populations. The servile included two main groups. First were people who were legally free but whose status was circumscribed by social practices. They are generally known by the Arabic term *Ḥarāṭīn* (sing. *Ḥarṭānī*). The second were individuals who were the property of others and the recently emancipated or immediate descendents of those who had been. Social practice tended to amalgamate both under the Arabic word for slaves, *`Abīd* (sing. *`Abd*) for men and *imā'* (sing. *ama*) for women, or any of the various euphemisms used to denote slaves in the Sahara.[9] Whenever French reporters came across such people they called them either "*esclaves,*" or more commonly "*nègres*," using the term that French authors preferred for African slaves of color. (I translate *nègre* in this article as "Negro" in quotations and in my own voice as "slaves/freed slaves," reflecting the ambiguities.) Haratin and slaves both played an economically essential role in the Algerian Sahara, and the division of labor helped mark the social divide of Saharan society. Although labor patterns varied, the majority of physical labor associated with agricultural production in the oases was the duty of servile populations.[10]

A question that vexed colonial ethnographers, and continues to trouble Saharans, is the origins of the Haratin. For some they are the descendents of people forced north across the desert as slaves. Others say they come from free migrant ancestors who, over time, settled the isolated points of water in the desert. Still others claimed the Haratin are the original inhabitants of the Sahara who were later subjugated by Berberphone and Arabophone peoples. Etymology is of little help. In the Arabic dialects of the Maghreb, Haratin is a word that refers to things of mixed or base origins, or those lacking definite form such as a mixed breed horse or a parcel of land without clear title.[11] The corresponding Berber (Tamazight) term, *Ahardan* (pl. *Ihardanen*) is equally obscure and most likely comes from Arabic.[12] Adding to the confusion are the varieties of names by which these people were known in the different oases. In the Souf and at Ouargla, Haratin were called *Ouçfane,*[13] and in local parlance the free blacks of the Oued R'hir were called *Hachachna* and they claimed an Ethiopian origin.[14] In the Berber dialects spoken by the northern Tuareg, they were known as *Ashardan* meaning "mulatto"[15] or *Izzeggayen,* the "reds" or "copper-colored people."[16]

In these debates over origin what emerges with striking clarity is that the Haratin of the oases—in the nineteenth century and today—reject a slave genealogy. Most assert that they are the Sahara's original inhabitants or the descendents of free migrants.[17] As one nineteenth-century observer noted, "To call a Hartani a Negro or a freed slave is an absolute insult."[18] To call someone "son of a slave" was among the most injurious affronts and could lead to the wronged party seeking judicial recourse.[19]

Contested by the social actors themselves, the borders within the servile populations are difficult to map through colonial sources. Moreover, the historically unprecedented situation of French colonialism and the threat of abolition further obscured social relations. There is ample evidence suggesting that slave owners and traders misrepresented the status of servile people to their French interlocutors, claiming that enslaved people were free in order to retain their property in an age of abolition. In particular, masters claimed enslaved women as their wives to thwart abolition.[20] Indeed, many of the violations that illegally deprived Africans of their freedom in earlier centuries—like enslaving free-born Muslims, a violation that jurist Ahmad Baba had condemned in a seventeenth century fatwa—continued in the period prior to French conquest and afterwards.[21] Moreover, physical markers, especially skin color, were seen by many as *prima facie* grounds for enslavement of Africans of color, with the spurious myth of Ham cited as justification.[22] In other words, the same difficulties that historians and anthropologists have found further south greet the researcher in the Algerian Sahara. Furthermore, in the case of the French documents, we have to deal with the added problem of the term "Negro" that, as noted above, could mean both slaves and their immediate descendants.

SERVILE LABOR

Historian John Hunwick has posed the question of the importance of slaves to the labor systems in North Africa: "How were African slaves employed and under what conditions did they labour and live?"[23] Historians agree that slaves in the rural Tell were an insignificant part of the work force. "Algerian slaves were seldom used for agricultural labor," Allan Christelow tells us.[24] Instead, wealthy families exploited slaves narrowly within the household as domestic servants and concubines. New research may give us a better picture of this world one day. In the desert societies to the south, however, we know that slave and servile labor was a major element of the economy. Slaves and Haratin pulled water from the wells, dug and repaired the underground system of tunnels (*foggāras*) that provided water, and did the skilled work of digging artesian wells.[25] They irrigated, fertilized, and tilled the gardens; and they pollinated, pruned, and harvested the dates. Domestically, the toil of servile women ensured the viability of many Saharan households. Slave women, especially the young or those who had musical or artistic talents, were a key part of gift exchange: they routinely made up part of the tribute paid to foreign leaders or to religious elites such as heads of the Sufi orders.[26] Slaves were also an important investment, and merchants reaped handsome profits buying and reselling captives.

From their first contact with French authorities, Saharan leaders repeatedly stressed the importance of servile labor to their economic well-being. Some of the most important records come from the negotiations undertaken by General de la Roque, commandant of the Division of Constantine, with factions favorable to the French at In Salah (Tidikelt) in the 1890s. These opened with Roque's meeting with Mohammed ben Ahmed of the Ouled Mokhtar in May 1894.[27] The Saharan notable hoped to work out a deal with the French and ensure a favorable position for his clan after the French occupation. The Tidikelt had thwarted French advances for many decades and had gained a reputation for staunch resistance. Nevertheless, many felt that French expansion was imminent, and some, such as ben Ahmed, sought to negotiate terms that would preserve or expand their economic and political power. Ben Ahmed's secret meeting with General de la Roque earned him the title of the French governor (*`Amel*) of the Ouled Mokhtar. This position ensured him a handsome pension and gifts, and he hoped to have a secure place in the leadership of the Tidikelt after the French conquest. Although he found the title agreeable, ben Ahmed was clear in what he expected of the French:

1) Leave us our fortunes and possessions, our rights of property and inheritance as they currently exist in our customs.
2) Do not change the organization of our society and families (djama`a [council] and tribes).
3) Respect the customs and traditions in place among us and do not alter our relations with our servants.[28]

Governor General Cambon reported to de la Roque his agreement with these demands. "We will respect the customs of his country, the castes, the relations between masters and servants, the quasi-feudal organization," he wrote.[29] Two years later, another notable from In Salah, Abd el-Kader ben Ahmed ben Kouider representing the Ouled Dahane, came to Constantine on a similar mission. Ben Kouider was more explicit about the importance of resolving the issue of slavery and abolition. The anti-French faction, led by the Ba Djouda clan, had been using this question to exploit fears of masters and rally support for their cause. Ben Kouider was charged by their rivals to get a categorical response from the French on the issue of abolition. General de la Roque, however, was primarily interested in discussing political arrangements and payoffs and was therefore ill-prepared to respond to ben Kouider's questions on slavery. "He speaks on this subject," de la Roque related, "with remarkable competence and many times he left me in a quandary."[30] After responding to the French general's queries on the political sympathies of local people and on commerce, ben Kouider pressed him on the issue of slavery.

> Now that I have responded to your questions, allow me to present two issues of great importance: In the Tidikelt, Negroes alone work, to emancipate them would mean the ruin of the country. Your plans on this subject are not known to us, and we would like to be able to reassure our people on your intensions.[31]

Hoping to assuage the French general's concerns, ben Kouider implied that this servitude was not harsh and suggested that it did not fall under the bounds of the 1848 abolition.

> We have no slave markets: the Negroes I'm talking about are nearly all born in the area. They have houses, villages. They work for us, we do not sell them, and it seems to me that they do not fall under the interdiction imposed upon all French subjects to possess Negroes.[32]

Ben Kouider finished by stressing the importance of a favorable resolution to further negotiations: "I respectfully ask that you reflect well on this question, because it is of the utmost importance to us."[33]

In other words, ben Kouider was telling the general that what he feared most in a French occupation was the social upheaval that would follow if French implemented the 1848 abolition decree. To avoid this, he skillfully blurred the line between slaves and free clients. We do not have a record of the original conversation. The French translator used the term "Negro," thus we assume ben Kouider was speaking of slaves and their descendents. He did not speak about Haratin, a word the French translator would have used. But the "Negroes" of the Tidikelt had not been purchased; they lived in separate villages and were born in the region. Either this was an accurate representation of social reality, or ben Kouider wished to create in de la Roque's mind the impression that there were no slaves *per se*, but only a laboring group of "Negroes." He is unequivocal, however, concerning their importance. Their work was central to the economic vitality of the oases, and he could guarantee his support of a French invasion only if a deal was struck on this matter. De la Roque for his part was already convinced and had assured Governor General Cambon two years earlier: "Don't worry about the slavery question, it won't give us any problems."[34]

Ben Kouider's claims should be considered carefully. Slave sales did, in fact, occur in the Tidikelt, if not within the walls of towns at In Salah, then nearby. French documents show that the Zoua, a saintly clan who lived in a nearby oasis agglomeration, served as intermediaries in a trade that smuggled captives from the Niger Bend for sale in the French-administered Mzab in the 1880–1890s.[35] While it is probable that the servile class ben Kouider referred to was not part of this trade,[36] the image he presented of loyal, free servants is undermined when we consider that his visit to Constantine was actually prompted by the flight of several "Negroes," people ben Kouider wished to have returned. These individuals had stolen camels and fled their masters on a dangerous trip north where they hoped to find refuge in territories under French rule. To ensure French cooperation, ben Kouider implied the runaways were like all other laboring peoples of In Salah, namely, legally free but servile. Why they would flee, and more importantly, why he would ask the French to return them is not explained. Large populations of Haratin from the oases had migrated to the Tell and lived and worked there unmolested for years.[37] Moreover, if ben Kouider was concerned about the loss of the camels, why did he not insist on the animals' return (as was often done in the case of theft and raids) rather than that of their thieves? The French administrators did not pose such questions because they were eager to prove their good intentions and solidify ben Kouider's position vis-à-vis his rivals. Instead, Cambon himself ordered the fugitives returned. Knowing this order violated the spirit of 1848 abolition decree, the governor general justified his actions by arguing that the runaways were "after all only thieves."[38]

WORK, REMUNERATION, AND PROPERTY OWNERSHIP

Given these attempts to obscure the status of servile people, the researcher has to seek other evidence in the colonial archive to mark social distinctions. Categories that are more visible in documents, like the division of labor and property ownership, help better understand the social structure of the servile classes. Here the colonial sources can be quite helpful. As early as 1861, the French began to study the labor systems of the Algerian Sahara.[39] And by the close of the century they produced elaborate studies of population and property ownership designed to help future administrators establish fiscal policy when the oases were occupied.

These documents show that the Haratin of the oases were tied to patrons in unequal economic and political relations. They worked in a system similar to the sharecropping regime of the Tell known as *khammès*.[40] Haratin were expected to turn over four-fifths of the harvest to their patron, although practice varied widely, as discussed below. In addition, Haratin had to work on periodic collective works projects, a corvée called the *touïza.* This work was devoted to foggara repair, well digging, and irrigation canal upkeep.[41]

Haratin women figured differently in the labor system. I have found no reports of the wives or daughters of Haratin owing labor to their patrons: it appears as if all their work was devoted to the needs of their family unit. The sexual division of labor for both female Haratin and slaves/freed slaves appears to have been strictly demarcated, with women responsible for domestic work and men tending to agricultural labor. The archives here are sparse, however, and future research may alter this picture.

Slaves did similar sorts of work but in most cases entirely for their owner's benefit. Male slaves were also called upon for military service (there is evidence to suggest that Haratin also performed this duty). They served in particular as assassins for masters who did not wish to engage directly in violence against their enemies.[42] They also owed their master loyalty and submission. Slave women undertook the same domestic tasks as Haratin women, and some also labored in the small textile industries of the oases.[43] A major difference between the two, however, was that enslaved women were subject to the sexual advances of their masters.

Indeed, colonial documents report that sub-Saharan women were the objects of great sexual fascination on the part of Saharan notables. A French officer researching slavery in the eastern Algerian oases wrote,

> The young nubile black woman was in high demand—virgins were very expensive—in fact they were attributed with many charms and qualities. Experts in the arts of love, it was said, and very prolific with whites, they were recommended to those who, despite their efforts, had not been able to obtain descendants with women of their own race. To cure the '*coups de pied de Vénus'* [syphilis] it was enough to spend one night with them.[44]

Frenchmen in the Sahara shared this sexualized view of African women of color.[45] And unlike the other female populations of the oases, these women of color (freed slaves and perhaps Haratin) were made sexually available to French soldiers, including Algerian auxiliaries from further north. Writing from In Salah in 1906, one officer reported, "Since the occupation of In Salah, the troops have intimately mixed with the inhabitants; marriages with locals are the general rule for French and indigenous military men."[46] That many of these unions were not "marriages" in the typical sense is testified to by the fact that the children born to these women were called "parasites," and they suffered extremely high rates of mortality.

The remuneration of Haratin was complex and varied widely. A portion of the harvest (dates, fruits and vegetables) was the base remuneration. For the dates, a Hartani laborer would, in principal, receive one-fifth of the harvest, but evidence for actual allotments is rare, and there were many variances from this norm. These differences responded to the wealth and social status of patrons and their relationship with the Haratin, as well as differing patterns of property ownership, local traditions, the abundance of the harvest, and, perhaps most importantly, the source of water. Lands irrigated by springs, artesian wells, and foggaras required less daily labor than wells, and remuneration schemes reflected this.[47]

The most precise figures on this count come from the 1930s and 1940s. Much had changed since the French occupation at the beginning of the century, including the end of the eyes-closed policy. While these numbers should not be seen as representative of earlier periods, they give some idea of how remuneration varied, given the sources of water. In the Souf region of southeastern Algeria, a Hartani laborer working in gardens irrigated by artesian wells would receive 2–2.5 kilograms of dates per palm tree.[48] Given the fact that on average the date-palms of the Algerian Sahara produced 20–50 kilograms per irrigated tree, this was a low payment and reflects the minimal labor needed in these gardens. At Timimoun, an oasis largely irrigated by the foggaras, the dependent laborer had the right to a tenth of the wheat and barley harvest; a third of sorghum (*bechna*); and a fifth of the dates, garden vegetables, and figs.[49] In addition, for the difficult and skilled work of palm fertilization, the Hartani received one cluster of dates (2–3 kilograms) for every three palms pollinated.[50] The Hartani at El Goléa, working lands irrigated by artesian wells, was entitled to 50 percent of the grain crop, garden fruits, and vegetables, and one cluster of dates for each palm tree pollinated.[51] In the Oued R'hir a Haratin family would receive one-fifth of all the products of the palm tree (dates, *djerid, lif, chebka,* explained below) and a third of the grains and garden produce (fruits and vegetables).[52]

Livestock also figured in the remuneration for Haratin labor or as a gift to a slave. A master or patron might offer an adult sheep or goat, or the young borne by a specific female. This was especially common during the wet stage of desert climate cycles when livestock numbers peaked.[53] Many Haratin owned donkeys; but few camels, which were less suited to oasis work.

Haratin also received by-products of oasis agriculture as part of their remuneration. From the date-palm, they might get up to 50 percent of the palm sap (*legmi*) that was used to produce a fermented alcoholic drink. A Hartani could also expect part of the green palm leaves (*djerid*) that were woven into baskets, eating plates, and barriers to keep desiccating desert winds and sands out of garden plots.[54] They also received the palm fiber (*lif*) that was used to fill mattresses, make ropes, fashion the saddle bags (*chebka*) used to transport dates, and make saddle padding (*haouïa*) for mules and camels.[55] Finally, a portion of the male palm blossoms, so highly sought at the time of fertilization, might also form part of a Hartani's recompense.[56]

The slave, for his or her part, could expect material sustenance from the master. This included food and clothing. The diet of slaves in the Souf consisted of dates with *chichi* (coarsely ground barley) along with the various seasonal garden crops grown in the shade of the palms.[57] In principal, a slave's clothing allocation consisted of a new shirt and *gandūra* (tunic) each year and a new wool *burnūs* (wool cape) every ten years.[58] Masters offered gifts as incentive for hard work; they might consist of the dates produced by a specific palm or the offspring of a ewe or nanny-goat.[59] With certain exceptions (viz. concubines), slaves were responsible for their own shelter and generally slept in rudimentary huts in the gardens or under the elements. Both slaves and Haratin could expect their master/patron's hospitality (*ḍiyāfa*) on holidays. Slaves might also receive a portion of the date harvest from their master as a gift or in recompense for loyalty or exceptional work. For example, a master might give a slave the entire production of a certain palm tree for a given period or more simply several charges of dates at harvest.

Nevertheless, slaves had few legal property rights. Although there were provisions that allowed a slave to accumulate capital for manumission, the rule in the Sahara seems to have been "that which is property cannot be proprietor."[60] There were variations, of course. For example, an 1880 report notes that slaves of El Goléa were entitled to keep gardens and could save the money made from the sale of their produce.[61] Unfortunately, few documents in the French archive speak in detail about this important question.

HARATIN PROPERTY OWNERSHIP

Many Haratin families counted real property among their other resources. Here the French archive proves especially helpful. After occupying the southwest oasis groups—the Tidikelt, Touat, and Gourara—in 1899–1901, the French administration called upon the local council or djama`a (*d̲jamā`a*) of each community to undertake a census in 1906. They classed their findings with regards to categories we might call "ethnicity" (categories based on language, kinship, religious prestige [*shurfā*]), gender, age, and wealth. They also included property ownership. While inevitably Saharans tried to conceal some of their property holdings from French eyes, the administration was able to register the owners of the date-palm trees, the basic unit of taxation. These figures were published in 1908 by Alfred-Georges-Paul Martin, a military interpreter of the Indigenous Affairs service.[62]

The census showed substantial Haratin palm tree ownership. In the Gourara, for example, of 353 palm owners, 96 were Haratin (27%). For the Touat, the census listed 744 total owners, 265 of which were Haratin (35%). In the Tidikelt, the census reported 453 total owners, 100 of which were Haratin (22%). Each Haratin family, however, owned few trees. In the Gourara an overwhelming majority, 81 out of 96 (84%), owned less than 100 palm trees, and 43 of the poorest families owned only 20–30. The richest Haratin were three families who owned more than 150 trees each. For the Touat the proportions were similar, with 259 of 265 (97%) owning less than 100 trees, and the largest single segment, 111 families (42%) owned only 40–50 palms. In the Tidikelt, Haratin holdings deviated somewhat. Although there were few Haratin property owners (only 22%), a greater percentage had larger holdings: 69 percent possessed more than

100 palms each. Of these families, 10 percent had substantial holdings numbering over 300 trees.[63] Overall, Haratin represented 28 percent of total property owners in the southwest oases with the highest proportions in the Touat and the lowest in the Tidikelt. However, their holdings were small. In the Touat and the Gourara only 9.5 percent of Haratin owners held more than 100 palms each.

Date-trees were, of course, not the only source of property, and it should be kept in mind that access to large amounts of privately held water determined yields. In the southwest oases, Haratin controlled less than 8 percent of the total irrigation waters, and in the Tidikelt, where there were large Haratin holdings, they controlled only 2.7 percent of the available water.[64] For the entire region, Martin reminds us that although Haratin represented three-fifths of the total population (19,412 of 49,101), and more than a quarter (28%) of them owned date-palms, Haratin owned less than a tenth of available real property and water rights.[65]

What do these numbers represent in terms of actual wealth? At the turn of the nineteenth century, the subsistence threshold for a family of four adults (man, wife, adult daughter, and dependent) and three children was 100 palms.[66] Ninety palms gave the family food for six months; the grain cultivated in their shade provided another three months of nourishment. The family had to meet the remaining three months needs by selling the offspring of the household's livestock (usually a nanny-goat).[67] The family's needs for clothing, sugar, tea, and other goods went unpaid and had to be fulfilled through remunerated labor or bartering of the garden produce.

Holdings of less than fifty palms were inadequate for a family's subsistence, and those in this category incurred substantial debts to survive. The example of Ahmed ben Abdallah, a Hartani living in the Touat, is illustrative.[68] His family consisted of five adults and eight children and he owned forty palms. In a good year, the family could live two and a half months from their date harvest. The cereals cultivated between the palms gave them another three months of food supplies during optimal conditions. The family met the balance of their subsistence needs with loans and remunerated labor. The French occupation increased their financial burden substantially with annual taxes of fourteen francs. Under French rule, this Haratin family averaged fifty francs a year in debts to pay for taxes and food.

When one considers the chronic problem of crop failures due to droughts, insect predation, and blight, the precariousness of such a family becomes all the more apparent.[69] One French commentator at the end of the nineteenth century was frank in his assessment of the material condition of the Haratin.

> Today the Haratin constitute the most unfortunate race of the Touat; they have retained only their pride and their intelligence and do not want to be confused with the Negro, slave or freed. The food and clothing of the slave is assured, he is the thing of the master, the Hartani is nothing; he has to work to live, but work is not assured him. The slave is riveted to the chain of the master who feeds him; the Hartani is chained to misery.[70]

A patron might aid Haratin with relief or loans to fulfill part of the social contract of the oases, a contract that emphasized reciprocal solidarity, dependence, and inequality. However, Haratin were outside of their patron's immediate kin and did not represent any direct economic investment worthy of upkeep. This placed Haratin on the margins of oasis society where they were the first to feel the adverse affects of colonial rule. Before the French occupation, these included economic harassment and raids, the burden of supporting refugees/rebels from the Tell, and economic disruptions due to war and banditry. As our commentator remarked in the years before the French conquest:

> The country is full of beggars and as soon as a caravan from the North arrives in an oasis…it is literally assailed by old people dying of hunger, scrawny children crying in misery, half-clothed women holding out their hands; all are Haratin.[71]

After the French army occupied the southwest oases, the lot of the Haratin changed little. French rule meant new taxes and colonial authorities entrusted each djama`a with the responsibility of distributing this new burden among the local population. Not surprisingly, they placed most of it upon the Haratin who were forced to pay a fixed tax directly to the djama`a from which the French received their required allotment.[72] Apparently, the administration held true to the terms of the 1894 deal worked out by ben Ahmed and ben Kouider, ensuring the notables' social and economic ascendency.[73]

POPULATIONS OF HARATIN AND SLAVES/ FREED SLAVES

This final section will present a short survey of some the main demographic studies concerning slave and Haratin populations undertaken by the colonial administration. The French demographic figures for the Algerian Sahara in the nineteenth century are sporadic. An individual explorer might give population figures for a given oasis where he sojourned, but the 1848 abolition decree led the administration to excise slave counts from the oases under their direct administration (up to 1899 this included Touggourt, El Oued, Ouargla, the Mzab, and Laghouat). They could be frank, however, about the slaves living in the three oases groups of the southwest that still remained outside of French rule—the Gourara, Touat, and Tidikelt. Here, in the 1890s the French administration undertook a series of studies to understand their economic resources and military capacities, information need by military planners. Administrators drew their information from reports brought back by sympathetic traders and travelers, as well as spies, who were sent on specific espionage missions. The fruits of these efforts provide the first detailed breakdown of the population by categories that were supposedly provided by their informants. These included: "Berbers," "Arabs," "Shareef" (Shurfā), "Haratin," and people categorized as "Negroes." The French were especially interested in having reliable figures of slaves as they had become sensitive to the possibilities to foment social discord between masters and slaves and deploy it towards their own ends. For example, in the Gourara, the French commander in the neighboring Mzab made a deliberate effort to raise the expectations among slaves that they would benefit from French rule by offering runaways safe haven and jobs in his jurisdiction.[74]

There were three principal studies in the 1890s. One was authored by Camille Sabatier, a civilian explorer, one-time deputy from Oran, and a promoter of the trans-Saharan railroad, and it was based on research he undertook in 1891.[75] Although widely cited at the time, this work is of little value to the historian. Sabatier wildly inflated population estimates to garner support for an expansionist policy by creating visions of weighty tax registers.[76] More useful are two works authored by military administrators from the Sahara. Commandant Victor Deporter at Ghardaïa (Mzab) published the first in 1890 and Commandant François Godron authored the second in 1894.[77] Godron's study, to the best of my knowledge, was restricted to internal administrative circulation and was never published.

These two surveys gave widely divergent total population figures. Whereas Deporter estimated the total population of the southwest oases at 191,319, Godron came back with an incongruent figure of 32,070.[78] More consistent was the proportion of Haratin and slaves/freed slaves. Deporter figured that these servile groups made up 47 percent of the total population, while Godron found 44 percent. The two reports demonstrated less agreement about the percentages of slaves/freed slaves but were still very close to each other: Deporter estimated that 18 percent of the total population were slaves or freed slaves, while Godron set this number at 13 percent. The djama`a census of 1906 set the total population of the oases at 49,101. The number of servile population in 1906 remains close to the earlier studies: 48 percent of the total population was classed as either Haratin or slaves and freed slaves. There is, however, a notable decline of slaves: they were enumerated as only 8 percent of the total population, half of Deporter's figure. This is unsurprising, given the sudden illegality of slavery and a growing French desire to see it end.[79]

CONCLUSION

The stories told and the data contained in the French colonial archive is worth the historian's attention. It tells much about the people, conditions of work, and terms of servitude in the Sahara. We can see, for example, that prior to the French occupation, servile groups represented more than 40 percent of the total population in the southwest oases, and slaves/freed slaves made up about 15 percent of this number. Their toil made settled life in the desert possible; on this basic fact, the sources are unequivocal. They were responsible for the bulk of agricultural labor and were a vital element of the Saharan economy. Moreover, the French archive provides rare details concerning slavery, patterns of social stratification, and sources of desert wealth. In the case of the servile Haratin, the French archive gives the outlines of a social relation that was not only unequal but highly exploitive.

For those seeking the unvarnished reconstruction of the past, however, the colonial sources will disappoint. Their information is rarely firsthand, hardly exact, and prone to distortion. The problems associated with the ubiquitous and problematic category "Negro" have been highlighted in this essay: we cannot know exactly how many of these people were the property of others. But there are other difficulties, and the lesson of General de la Roque's negotiations with potential allies at In Salah is illustrative of the need for a thorough knowledge of the archives' conditions of production and a circumspect reading of its information. Saharan notables were the primary sources for the French data, and in an age of abolition they had a vested interest in misrepresenting social realities. When we consider the agenda of French reporters, who often shared the same goals as the slave owners, the task of critical analysis becomes all the more important.

Yet this critical work need not look only for twisted truths or misrepresentations. Researchers should be attentive to the ways that this archive, the basis of nearly sixty years of colonial rule, played an important role in the social restructuring that occurred in the period leading up to and following the French occupation. The categories existing in French discourses, however inaccurate, developed in a complex dialogue with Algero-Saharan interlocutors, and it was through these categories that colonial power eventually flowed. In other words, the researcher should be attentive to the ways that the archive's language became a constitutive part of new forms of social value and differentiation, and it should not be judged as only reflective or distortive of reality. Here we are reminded of Frantz Fanon's observation: "the colonist is right when he says he 'knows' them. It is the colonist who *made* and *reproduces* the colonized subject."[80] While the colonial archive certainly misrepresented its others in the interest of domination, it played an important role in restructuring actual social relations and identities.

APPENDIX

Table 1. Victor Benjamin Deporter's Estimates, 1888–1889

Gourara	Total Population	73,564
	Haratin	17,913
	Slaves/freed slaves	13,099
Touat	Total Population	95,008
	Haratin	33,227
	Slaves/freed slaves	17,624
Tidikelt	Total Population	22,747
	Haratin	6,224
	Slaves/freed slaves	4,194
Aoulef	Total Population	7,340
	Haratin	2,240
	Slaves/freed slaves	1,415

Source: Victor Benjamin Deporter, *A propos du Transsaharaien. L'extrême sud de l'Algérie. Le Gourra, le Toaut, In-Salah, le Tidikelt, le pays des Touareg Hoggar, l'Adrar, Tin Bouctou, Agadès, 1888–1889* (Alger, 1890).

Table 2. François Godron's Estimates, 1894

Gourara	Total Population	15,288
	Haratin	4,155
	Slaves/freed slaves	1,950
Touat	Total Population	9,322
	Haratin	2,650
	Slaves/freed slaves	1,835
Tidikelt	Total Population	7,460
	Haratin	1,860
	Slaves/freed slaves	1,420

Source: François Godron, "Renseignements sur les populations du Gourara, Touat, Tidikelt: zaouïas, ordres religieux, soffs," El Goléa, 16 mai, 1894, CAOM 22 H 55.

Table 3. Djema'a Census 1906

Gourara	Total Population	20,473
	Haratin	8,127
	Slaves/freed slaves	1,909
Touat	Total Population	17,492
	Haratin	6,474
	Slaves/freed slaves	1,611
Tidikelt	Total Population	11,136
	Haratin	4,811
	Slaves/freed slaves	854

Source: Djama`a Census (1906), in A.-G.-P. Martin, *A la frontière du Maroc: Les oasis sahariennes* (Paris, 1908).

Notes

1. John Wright, *The Trans-Saharan Slave Trade* (London, 2007).
2. Information from Dennis D. Cordell, conversation with the author, 11 January 2002.
3. An early example of this type of research is E. Carette, *Du commerce de l'Algérie avec l'Afrique centrale et les états barbaresques* (Paris, 1844).

4. Eve Troutt Powell, "The Silence of the Slaves," in *The African Diaspora in the Mediterranean Lands of Islam,* ed. John Hunwick and Eve Troutt Powell (Princeton, 2002), xxvi.
5. Henri Moniot ed., *Le mal de voir, ethnologie et orientalisme: politique et épistémologie, critique et autocritique* (Paris, 1976).
6. Dominick LaCapra, *History and Criticism* (Ithaca, 1985), ii.
7. Discussed in part III of Benjamin Claude Brower, *A Desert Named Peace: The Violence of France's Empire in the Algerian Sahara, 1844-1902* (New York, 2009). See also Dennis D. Cordell, "No Liberty, Not Much Equality, and Very Little Fraternity: The Mirage of Manumission in the Algerian Sahara in the Second Half of the Nineteenth Century," in *Slavery and Colonial Rule in Africa,* ed. Suzanne Miers and Martin Klein (London, 1999), 38–56.
8. Cid el-Hadj Abd el-Kader ben Abou Bekr et-Touaty, "Le Sahara et le Soudan, documents historiques et géographiques," trans. Abbé Bargès, *Revue de l'Orient* 13/1 (février 1853), 73-91.
9. R. Brunschvig, "Abd," *The Encyclopaedia of Islam,* vol. 1 (Leiden, 1960-2004), 24.
10. The cities of the Mzab varied somewhat from this rule. See Donald Charles Holsinger, "Migration, Commerce and Community: The Mizabis in Nineteenth-Century Algeria," Ph.D. dissertation, Northwestern University, 1979.
11. G. S. Colin, "Hartani," *Encyclopaedia of Islam,* v. 3 (Leiden, 1960-2004), 231.
12. Rachid Bellil, *Les oasis du Gourara (Sahara algérien)*; v.1: *Le temps des saints* (Paris, 1999). In the Zenāta dialect of Berber spoken in the Gourara region, Haratin are known as *isemghan* (sing. *asemgh*).
13. Emile Dermenghem, *Le pays d'Abel: Le Sahara des Ouled-Naïl, des Larbaā et des Amour* (Paris, 1960), 80; and Capitaine Leselle, "Les noirs du Souf," manuscript, n.d. [ca 1957] 20 X 1 Centre des archives d'outre mer [hereafter CAOM].
14. Jean-Jacques Pérennes, *Structures agraires et décolonisation, les oasis de l'Oued R'hir (Algérie)* (Alger, 1979), 23.
15. Colin, "Hartani," 231.
16. Fendou Agg Ameni to Père de Foucaud, 22 Sarat (1913) in Lionel Galand, ed., *Lettres au Marabout: Messages Touaregs au Père de Foucauld* (Paris, 1999), 134.
17. Bellil, *Les oasis du Gourara.*
18. N. Lacroix and H.-M.-P. de La Martinière, *Documents pour servir à l'étude du Nord-ouest Africain. Réunis et rédigés par ordre de Jules Cambon*; v.3: *Les oasis de l'extrême sud algérien* (Alger, 1897), 170.
19. Majda Tangi, *Contribution à l'étude de l'histoire des 'Sudan' au Maroc du début de l'islamisation jusqu'au début du XVIIIème siècle* (Villeneuve d'Ascq, 1994), 388.

20. See documentation in 12 H 50 CAOM.
21. Ahmad Baba, "*Mi'rāj al-Ṣu'ūd* Aḥmad Bābā's Replies on Slavery," annotated and translated by John Hunwick and Fatima Harrack, *Textes et documents* (University Mohammed V, Institute of African Studies) 7 (2000): 7-65.
22. Letter of Mustapha ben Ismaël, 24 janvier 1840, cited in *La révolution de 1848 en Algérie,* ed. Marcel Emerit (Paris, 1949), 37.
23. John O. Hunwick, *West Africa and the Arab World: Historical and Contemporary Perspectives. The J. B. Danquah Memorial Lectures. Twenty-third Series–February 1990* (Accra, 1991), 26.
24. Allan Christelow, *Muslim Law Courts and the French Colonial State in Algeria* (Princeton, 1985), 119.
25. This work is described in Ludovic Ville, *Voyage d'exploration dans les bassins du Hodna et du Sahara* (Paris, 1868); and Ludovic Ville, *Exploration géologique du Beni Mzab, du Sahara et de la région des steppes de la province d'Alger* (Paris, 1872).
26. The first mention of tribute made to the sultan of Morocco appears in 1861. This came when Commandant Colonieu visited the Gourara. Fearing that the French officer was the avant-garde of a French invasion, In Salah sent 5,000 francs and twenty slaves to the sultan of Morocco to ask for his protection. Capitaine Massoutier, "Conférence sur les questions sahariennes, 1891," Laghouat, 17 mars 1891, 22 H 35, CAOM. In 1886 the leaders of In Salah again sought aid from the Sharifian monarchy, worried about repercussions they might suffer for the murder of the French officer Lieutenant Marcel Palat. The Moroccan leader, Hassan I, reassured them and told them to send "négresses et parfum." The following month the khalifa of Tafialet, the sultan's brother, was more specific and told them that Moroccan protection would cost one hundred slave girls and fifty kilograms of gold and perfume. Periodic tribute in young women continued throughout the 1890s. See rapport mensuel, cercle de Ghardaïa, octobre et novembre, 1886; and rapport mensuel, octobre 1891, 76 I 3, CAOM.
27. GGA to Général de la Roque, #990, 15 avril 1894, 22 H 54, CAOM.
28. Ben Ahmed to GGA, 20 mai 1894, 22 H 54, CAOM.
29. GGA to Général de la Roque, #990, 15 avril 1894, 22 H 54, CAOM.
30. Général de la Roque to GGA ("Confidentielle"), Constantine, 16 mai 1896, 22 H 54, CAOM.
31. "Renseignements fournis par Abd el-Kader ben Ahmed ben Koudier, 10 au 15 mai 1896," 22 H 54, CAOM.
32. Ibid.
33. Ibid.
34. Général de la Roque to GGA, 1 juin 1894, 22 H 54, CAOM.
35. Brower, *Desert Named Peace*.

36. Paul Soleillet, "Exploration du Sahara central: voyage de M. Paul Soleillet d'Alger à l'Oasis d'In Çalah," Paris, 20 décembre 1875, F17 3007/2, Centre d'accueil et de recherches des Archives nationales [hereafter CARAN].
37. "Etat du mouvement des corporations indigènes dans les territoires civils pendant l'année 1845," in Ministère de la Guerre, *Tableau de la situation des établissements français dans l'Algérie, 1845–46,* Tome IX (Paris, 1846), 96–97. These people worked as house painters, porters, domestic servants, and garbage collectors. In 1845 there were 2,540 migrant blacks in the Algerian cities under French control.
38. "Note," GGA to Commandant de la Division d'Alger, n.d. [ca. May–June 1896], 22 H 54, CAOM.
39. Ville, *Voyage d'exploration.*
40. Massoutier, "Conférence sur les questions sahariennes," 22 H 35, CAOM.
41. Comandant Voinot, "Le Tidikelt, étude sur la géographie, l'histoire, et les mœurs du pays," In Salah, 20 avril 1905, 1 H 1032, Service historique de l'Armée de Terre [hereafter SHAT].
42. For example, when Paul Soleillet attempted to visit In Salah in 1874 he was warned by local leaders: "If you do not leave, we will send slaves to kill you." "Déclaration d'Adour ben Lakhdar," n.d., 4 H 7, CAOM. Another example comes from Lieutenant Palat's murder in 1886, when it was reported that the Ba Djouda of In Salah sent slaves to kill the explorer on his ill-fated attempt to travel from Algeria to Timbuktu. Letter of Mohammed ben Abderrahman, aka Yucef ben Attia, not addressed, n.d. [ca. August 1886], 4 H 12–17, CAOM.
43. Jean Delheure, "Le travail de la laine à Ghardaïa," *Revue de l'occident musulman et de la Méditerranée* 27 (1979), 5–74 ; Emile-Félix Gautier, "L'industrie des tentures dites 'Dokkali' au Gourara et au Touat," Alger, 1913, Bibliothèque AOM B2501, CAOM; Capitaine Chardenet, "Rapport sur le mouvement commercial du Tidikelt," In Salah, 26 août 1900, 22 H 59, CAOM; "Travail et emploi des laines par les indigènes," in E. Du Champ, *Le pays du Mouton. Des conditions d'existence des troupeaux sur les hauts-plateaux et dans le sud de l'Algérie* (Alger, 1893), 529–33.
44. Leselle, "Les noirs du Souf." The belief that sexually transmitted diseases could be cured by intercourse with an African woman reoccurs in Commandant Mercadier's interview with Griga, a former slave. See F.-J.-G. Mercadier, *L'esclave de Timimoun* (Paris, 1971), 91.
45. See E.-F. Gautier, *Sahara algérien* (Paris, 1908), 248; and Théodore Pein, *Lettres familières sur l'Algérie* (Alger, 1893), 491.
46. Rapport annuel de 1906, In Salah, 29 novembre 1906, 23 H 102 CAOM.
47. Gilbert Grandguillaume, "Régime économique et structure du pouvoir: Le système des foggara du Touat," *Revue de l'occident musulman et de la Méditerranée* 13–14 (1973), 437–57.
48. Leselle, "Les noirs du Souf." Many of the palms in the Souf were, however, irrigated by subwaters. These "bour" palms needed little day-to-day atten-

tion, but if the water table dropped, the roots would have to be excavated and trees lowered, a labor-intensive operation. Claude Bataillon, "Les Rebaia, semi-nomades du Souf," in *Nomades et nomadisme au Sahara* (Paris, 1963), 116; Auguste Cauneille, *Les Chaanba leur nomadisme: Evolution de la tribu durant l'administration française* (Paris, 1968), 177.

49. Gautier, *Sahara algérien*, 242. The task of building the foggaras was monumental. In the Touat agglomeration alone, one French observer counted 2,000 kilometers of tunnels.
50. Robert Capot-Rey, *Le Sahara français* (Paris, 1953), 357.
51. Ibid.
52. Pérennes, *Structures agraires,* 41.
53. Capitaine Métois, "L'élevage du mouton au Tidikelt," In Salah, 31 mai 1904, 24 H 109, CAOM. See also "Rapport du Lieutenant Cannac sur l'emploi du crédit pour encouragement à l'élevage du dahman dans le poste de el Aoulef—Bas Touat—Ksour ouest du Tidikelt," 1909, 24 H 109, CAOM; and "Station d'élevage ovin de Tadmit," n.d. boite 006, Séries agriculture, Archives nationales d'Algérie, Algiers.
54. Leselle, "Les noirs du Souf."
55. Ibid.
56. Capitaine Lô, "Les foggaras du Tidikelt," *Travaux de l'Institut de recherches sahariennes* XI (1954), 50; and Leselle, "Les noirs du Souf."
57. Rapports trimestriel, Annexe d'El Oued, 3e trimestre, 1885; 1e trimestre, 1886; 2e trimestre, 1891; and 4e trimestre 1891, 16 K 5–12, CAOM.
58. Leselle, "Les noirs du Souf."
59. Ibid.
60. Ibid.
61. "Relation sur une partie du voyage effectué par la Mission du transsaharien, du 17 janvier au 9 mars 1880," 28 mai 1880, 4 H 8–10, CAOM.
62. A.-G.-P. Martin, *A la frontière du Maroc: Les oasis sahariennes* (Paris, 1908).
63. According to a local tradition recorded by a French officer in 1905, the Haratin of Aoulef commanded enough resources in ca. 1800 to throw off the tutelage of their masters, the Ouled Zenane, and establish an independent settlement at Kasba el-Harratin. The effort failed and the ksar was in ruins when the French arrived. Comandant Voinot, "Le Tidikelt. Etude sur la géographie, l'histoire, et les mœurs du pays," In Salah, 20 avril, 1905. SHAT 1 H 1032.
64. Martin, *Les oasis sahariennes.*
65. "Monographie sur l'arrondissement d'In Salah," 1963, 1 H 2107 dossier 2, SHAT. Haratin and slave/free slave property ownership increased under French rule, when possibilities for remunerated labor increased. Servile groups invested their earnings in palm trees.
66. Martin, *Les oasis sahariennes*, 232.
67. Ibid. The kid could be exchanged for one camel load of dates.

68. Ibid.
69. At the turn of the century, a disease known as the *bayoudh* ravaged palms in the Tidikelt. The devastating blight wreaked havoc here until the 1930s. In one case, a palm grove that originally numbered 30,000 trees had only 8,000 surviving trees in 1937. P. Santini, "Contribution d'un médecin à l'étude de *bayoudh* maladie du palmier-dattier," *Archives de l'Institut Pasteur d'Algérie* XV (1937), 51–57.
70. Lacroix et Martinière, *Documents pour servir à l'étude du Nord-ouest Africain*, 169–70.
71. Ibid., 234.
72. Rapport annuel de 1906, In Salah, 29 novembre 1906, 23 H 102 CAOM.
73. All the same, notable power did not go uncontested. For example, in 1909 the Haratin of the Tidikelt staged a strike, refusing to harvest dates until they received better working conditions and increased pay. Rapport annuel de 1909, 23 H 102, CAOM.
74. Affaires indigènes to GGA, 10 août 1893, 22 H 38, CAOM. The French officer, Colonel Didier, reasoned that providing safe haven to escaped slaves, who "form the large majority of the population," will win their brethren over to the French side. "Given that they are more or less oppressed, [they] cannot see in any other than a good light the support that we give to the weak, support that they can solicit for themselves if we come among them." Affaires indigènes to GGA, #576, 7 juillet 1893, 22 H 38, CAOM.
75. Camille Sabatier, *Touat, Sahara et Sudan: étude géographique, politique, économique et militaire* (Paris, 1891). Reports of his scouting missions include, "Itinéraire de Figuig au Touat, Vallée Oued Messaoura," 1876, 22 H 32, CAOM; and "Rapport de M. Sabatier," Saïda, 2 janvier 1880, 4 H 8–10, CAOM.
76. See the critique of these early works in E.-F. Gautier, *La conquête du Sahara: Essai de psychologie politique* (Paris, 1910).
77. Victor Benjamin Deporter, *A propos du Transsaharien. L'extrême sud de l'Algérie. Le Gourara, le Touat, In-Salah, le Tidikelt, le pays des Touareg Hoggar, l'Adrar, Tin Bouctou, Agadès, 1888–1889* (Alger, 1890); and François Godron, "Renseignements sur les populations du Gourara, Touat, Tidikelt: zaouïas, ordres religieux, soffs," El Goléa, 16 mai 1894, 22 H 55, CAOM.
78. Deporter includes the oasis agglomerations at Aoulef with a population of 7,340; Godron does not.
79. Martin A. Klein, *Slavery and Colonial Rule in French West Africa* (Cambridge, 1998), 252–55. As a point of comparison, Klein estimates that slaves represented 21 percent of the total population in the Haut Senegal-Niger Bend region, and he calculates that *rimaibe* and other freed, but servile, classes numbered upwards of 50% of the total population.
80. Frantz Fanon, *The Wretched of the Earth*, trans. Richard Philcox (New York, 2004), 36; translation modified, original italics.

Chapter 12

BELLAH HIGHWAYMEN: SLAVE BANDITRY AND CRIME IN COLONIAL NORTHERN MALI

Bruce S. Hall

INTRODUCTION

Raiding and banditry were fundamental aspects of nomadic life in the southern Sahara and along the desert edge in the period before European colonial occupation.[1] The patterns of banditry and raiding, and the culture that valorized these actions, persisted well into the colonial period; they have survived, to some extent, right down to the present day.[2] Thus, it is hardly surprising that one of the tactics used by slaves in nomadic society to gain their freedom, or more generally to improve their lives, would follow similar cultural patterns. Indeed, in an area such as the Niger Bend where new socioeconomic opportunities for slaves were limited in the colonial period, banditry and other property crimes committed by servile people were a constant problem for the colonial administration. This chapter uses the lens of banditry to explore the changing relationship between the colonial state, pastoralist slaveholding elites, and slaves in the Niger Bend under French colonial rule. It argues that the changing nature of the relationship between pastoralist masters and their slaves was mediated, in part, through banditry and crime.

Slave bandits were not social rebels in Hobsbawm's sense, but they were not strictly criminals.[3] Instead banditry was one means among others for slaves to gain a certain independence from their masters. As such, one can detect shifts in slave banditry over the course of the colonial period from an activity sanctioned by masters and undertaken partly for their benefit to attacks increasingly directed at former masters and their property. The changes in slave banditry coincide with the evolution of slavery as it was practiced in precolonial times into new colonially-sanctioned forms of servility.

One of the consequences of the changes in master-slave relationships was that the ideology that underpinned slavery based in Islamic law became increasingly racialized, and this tended to make local ideas of racial difference much more explicit. Racial ideas have a long pedigree in the Sahel, and long predate the arrival of Europeans. Writers in the desert-edge areas in the Western Sahara and Sahel frequently invoked the basic racial distinction between *bīḍān* and *sūdān*, or "whites" and "blacks". But racial markers tended to be used to describe those people on the other side of the desert-edge borderland and in many cases this appellation stood in for more specific information on ethnic or linguistic affiliation. While it is certainly the case that racial terms attained a certain prominence in the identity of "white" Arab and Tuareg groups in the precolonial period, in local texts it is rare to see racial labels employed within these societies to distinguish, for example, between nobles and slaves.[4]

During the colonial period, ideas about racial difference were deployed in a much more systematic way by members of the elite slave-holding strata of Tuareg and Arab societies as a component of their strategies to maintain control over servile people. Colonialism presented certain challenges to the system of domination that had operated in the precolonial period. The colonial occupation of West Africa ended the slave trade that had filled the demand for slaves in the Niger Bend and other desert-edge areas. In slave systems that allowed for the manumission of slaves, the cutting off of supplies of new slaves to replace freed ones presented significant difficulties to those who wished to maintain the viability of slave-based economies. The French regime in the Niger Bend was ambivalent at best about reforming local slave systems, and many administrators went out of their way to ensure that existing slaves remained subject to their masters throughout the colonial period. Despite the intentions of the colonial state, however, new opportunities did open up for servile people in the slowly-developing colonial wage economy, and this further undermined the control held by slave masters. The response of masters was to rely more heavily on Islamic legal principles to justify and maintain their supremacy. The ideology of a fundamental difference between masters and slaves was further strengthened during the colonial period by sahelian elites who adapted local and French ideas about "race" to act as social markers within Arab and Tuareg societies. By emphasizing racial difference, slaves and freed slaves were effectively denied the status of free persons, and hence, the possibility of social and economic autonomy within nomadic societies.[5] The colonial state played an important role in ensuring that "blacks" in Arab and Tuareg societies, all of whom the French considered to be of slave origin, could not attain autonomy. The older patriarchal ways in which nomadic slaveholders represented their relationship with slaves was gradually replaced by a new "topsy-turvy" world in which slave circumventions of social hierarchy were met with increasingly racialized reactions and violence.[6]

Here, we will focus on a social category called the "Bellah". In the Niger Bend this term is both all-encompassing and imprecise, referring in general to "black" slaves and former slaves of the Tuareg, and constituting the largest component of the pastoralist population in northern Mali. The term "Bellah" is itself the product of the history we are considering here. Its imprecision is the result of a larger racialization of social status over time, so that servility and blackness are conflated, making all black members of Tuareg society Bellah, and assigning to all Bellah a slave origin. In today's usage, the Bellah are simply the former slaves of the Tuareg. As such they are similar to the Haratin in Mauritania.[7] It is worth pausing briefly to note that, in fact, not all Bellah were of slave origin and not all slaves in the Niger Bend were Bellah.[8] Furthermore, knowing whether a particular Bellah encountered in the historical sources was a slave, a freed slave still attached to his or her master, or a person completely independent of any servile ties is very difficult. In the colonial documents, "Bellah" became an ethnoracial appellation that could mean slave, freed slave, or even just a Tamashek-speaking "black" person. Its use always implied servility.

The Bellah constituted the majority of the nomadic population in the Niger Bend. Whether as slaves or as vassals, the Bellah were burdened with fulfilling most of the labor requirements in Tuareg society, and consequently, they were degraded culturally as people lacking in honor. Yet in the precolonial and early colonial period Bellah had often participated in raiding with, or on behalf of, their masters, and in banditry more generally. Because slaves were among the most common objects of booty in these raids, it was not uncommon for Bellah themselves to kidnap or capture slaves, who, as newcomers to the enslaving social situation, would hold a lower status than their captors (especially when the captured slaves were women or children). The extent to which Bellah bandits were able or willing to act independently in the precolonial period is not clear. Some independent action may have occurred, especially in the case of more autonomous Bellah vassal communities, but more commonly they seem to have acted as proxies for their masters. It is as agents of their masters that Bellah banditry is popularly understood in the Songhay-speaking sedentary communities that had been a target of nomad exactions before the establishment of firm colonial control in the 1910s. Bellah acts of banditry were commonly attributed to their masters.[9]

The colonial period created a new situation for slaves and Bellah groups, but many Bellah remained in servile relationships with their masters, who collected their taxes on behalf of the colonial state (and also continued to collect Bellah taxes for their own purposes) and who were the owners of herds and of fertile land farmed by Bellah on behalf of their masters. The effective denial of property to Bellah groups ensured that poverty was widespread, and that some Bellah would resort to the age-old strategies of banditry and theft on their own initiative. Over time, as the bonds between Bellah and their masters were loosened, the pattern of Bellah banditry and crime became more indiscriminate, sometimes targeting the same nomadic elites who had previously directed Bellah actions. Bellah banditry took diverse forms. One common pattern was that of highway robbery, in which small bands of highwaymen would steal the possessions of a traveler. In other cases, larger Bellah groups raided villages or herds, or absconded with animals entrusted to them, and then claimed that their actions were legitimate because their masters had stolen from them. Toward the end of the colonial period, this became a very serious problem (for masters) and resulted in numerous raids and counter raids between Bellahs and their purported masters.[10]

After World War II, Bellah banditry came to be seen in much more explicit racial terms. The colonial state and nomadic elites had developed a racialized conception and justification of their control over resources and servile Bellah in the Niger Bend. As late as 1949, a circular from the governor-general in Dakar on the Bellah question stated:

> It is a striking observation that populations living in servile conditions are to be found in the Saharan and Sahelian zones of West Africa, where all attempts at liberation are blocked by particular difficulties: [viz.] the existence of a nomad population of the white race which, for historical and physical reasons, ...can hardly be forced to perform manual labor.[11]

As the colonial system of servile Bellah labor began to break down, and as Malian nationalists began attempting to exploit the persistence of "slavery" in the north for their own political ends, the actions of Bellah bandits began to look like racial rebellions to the colonial administration. It is, I think, no accident, that in this period there was an increase in what appears to be racialized violence, including lynchings and castrations, directed against Bellah bandits and criminals.

Three different angles of this story will be discussed: first, the importance of continued relations of servility to the colonial political economy that was set up in the Niger Bend; second, the changing relationships between masters and slaves in nomadic society as seen through the prism of "race" and Islamic law; and third, the banditry and criminality of Bellahs and the reactions that this produced from nomadic elites and the colonial state.

SLAVERY AND THE DESERT-SIDE COLONIAL POLITICAL ECONOMY

The main problem faced by the colonial regime in the Niger Bend was insecurity generated by endemic raiding carried out by nomadic groups. At the end of the nineteenth century powerful Tuareg confederacies dominated the region. The nomads proved to be a very difficult population to subdue, and the French were constantly fearful of nomad revolts throughout the colonial period. From their earliest encounters with the Tuareg, when in 1894 a whole column of colonial soldiers was massacred outside of Goundam by opposing Tuareg forces, French administrators treaded carefully.[12] One former French administrator, who spent fifteen years working in the Niger Bend, characterized the colonial perspective on the nomads as both a preoccupation with surveillance and a romantic attraction for the nobility of nomadic life and culture.[13] Managing the problem of insecurity played a large part in determining the shape that the French colonial state would take in the Niger Bend, but sympathy for the nomads also contributed to a policy toward nomads that was based on creating alliances with the most important nomadic groups in the territory, and on a colonial political economy that favored the interests of nomadic elites.

There were two main patterns of raiding during the colonial period. The first type was the raids of the so-called "Grands Nomades" that provoked a great deal of French anxiety. The Niger Bend, and especially the area around Lake Faguibine to the west of Timbuktu, was a constant target of the "Grands Nomades" of the Sahara (Reguibat, Chambas, etc.) who lived in areas outside colonial control, and of various local dissidents who allied themselves with these groups. Only in the mid-1930s were these raids finally suppressed definitively. The second kind of raiding and banditry was more local and typically involved local nomads raiding animals, kidnapping servile people, and stealing various possessions from neighboring—usually subordinate—groups. As late as 1957 the French colonial state was ordering that kidnapped children and stolen goods be returned to a group of Bellah by their Kel Antessar masters who had raided them in a dispute over payment of taxes.[14] The suppression of both types of banditry was, in French eyes, a fundamental requirement for the political stability and economic development of the territory.

The colonial state entered into alliances with local nomadic elites to protect its territory from the incursions of the "Grands Nomades" and to ensure that local nomads would not cooperate with the bandits or rebel against colonial authority. It did this, in part, by creating special military units that could operate in the desert and that were manned by nomads (*méharistes*, *goumiers*). It also relied very directly on information provided by allied nomadic groups, and on the active collaboration of nomadic fighters, organized along tribal lines under their own chiefs, in combating raids.[15] The achievement of a modus vivendi with powerful nomadic elites, which the French felt to be necessary to ensure the political stability of the Niger Bend, included an assurance that the social hierarchy of nomadic society, including slavery, would be respected.[16] French policy in the Niger Bend was designed to eliminate nomadic domination of the Songhay-speaking sedentary population, and thus weaken nomadic power, but at the same time, it was meant to permit continuing nomadic control over servile people in their own societies, and hence, give them incentives to cooperate with the colonial authorities. The Niger Bend was not an important economic zone in the French Soudan, let alone in the larger scheme of French possessions in West Africa. The colonial state was more preoccupied with maintaining peace than in developing the local economy. Colonial labor needs were filled most easily by a system of indirect procurement in which chiefs were required to provide a certain number of laborers or recruits for military service. The continued control of nomadic elites over servile members of their society served these interests.

The ways by which Bellah were recruited into colonial service reveals the extent to which the French actually encouraged tighter control over Bellah groups by nomadic elites. During the First World War, the French forcibly recruited large numbers of Africans into the military. In the Niger Bend, military recruitment for overseas service fell exclusively on "blacks," both Songhay-speakers and Bellah. Village chiefs sent the Songhay recruits, although it was not uncommon for eligible young men to flee to avoid the draft.[17] In 1918 French propaganda for voluntary enlistment actually attracted several "white" nomads who presented themselves for military service. They were rejected for racial reasons; among the nomad population, military recruitment for overseas service was exclusively for Bellah. Fear that recruitment of "white" nomads would provoke rebellion and overt colonial racism, determined French nomad policy.[18] The means by which Bellah were recruited was often brutal. In 1918 ten Bellah recruits were drowned crossing the Niger River at Iloa (20 kms from Timbuktu) when the canoe that was transporting them sank. They died because they were tied in groups of five by a rope around their necks while being taken to Timbuktu by a French officer. This small colonial scandal led to a French investigation that concluded with an indictment of the way Tuareg nomads delivered Bellah "recruits" to colonial posts, comparing it to the slave trade within West Africa before colonial rule was established.[19]

French policy toward nomads also had an economic dimension. In the first decade of colonial occupation, French administrators developed a broad policy designed to encourage agricultural development in the Niger Bend based on freeing the Songhay-speaking sedentary population from the exactions of the nomads and encouraging the nomads to sedentarize their servile people. There was great regional variation in the success of these objectives. There were areas of the Niger Bend that had suffered greatly from the thirty years of insecurity that followed the wars between the forces of al-Hajj Umar Tal and Ahmad al-Bakkay al-Kunti in the 1860s. When the French arrived in the riverine region southwest of Timbuktu, they found that the sedentary population had been scattered and reduced in numbers by insecurity. The sedentary population that remained in the area lived in villages located on islands in the river or floodplain, having abandoned their previous sites of habitation because of the constant threat of raids.[20] With the establishment of the colonial state in the area, people began returning to the region and reestablishing themselves at abandoned village sites. As one colonial report described the situation:

> In effect, since the French occupation, the people see the peace being reborn little by little. They have decided to come back to their country of origin and the villages are beginning to rise again. It will require many years still before these villages regain the prosperity that they must have had previously if one judges from the existing ruins.[21]

Initial contacts with the French, however, seem to have been understood by sedentary people as little different from the raiding and looting they had grown accustomed to, and it was not until the first decade of the twentieth century that enough confidence was established for agricultural production to begin to recover. In some areas this did not happen until the 1910s.

The key factor in the regional differences in agricultural production was the nature of adjacent nomadic power and the degree to which tribute was collected in an ordered and predictable manner. The "bread basket" of the Niger Bend in the second half of the nineteenth century and in the early decades of French rule was the lake region to the west of Timbuktu, especially in the area around Lake Faguibine. Here a strong Tuareg group known as the Kel Antessar ensured a sufficient level of security for extensive agriculture to occur. They also developed a more or less regular system of taxation or tribute with sedentary Songhay chiefs. By way of contrast, in the area along the Niger River to the east of Timbuktu where rival Tuareg groups had played out their hostilities by raiding riverine communities, sedentary people did not even eat grain. What little cereal that they did grow was for Tuareg patrons or raiders and the agriculturalists survived by fishing and gathering wild plant foods. Their lack of agricultural production and their inability to store food resulted in a catastrophe for the sedentary people of this region during the famine years of 1913–16 when French administrators reported that over half the sedentary population east of Timbuktu had perished.[22]

The sedentarization of the Bellah in agricultural villages was long a dream of the colonial administration. In 1906 an administrator at Timbuktu was able to predict:

> The Bellah will be, for a while, the sharecroppers of the Tuareg, who are too keen on keeping them to molest or abandon them. The farming villages would create the first sites of sedentarization and would perhaps avoid, by their rational development, the crisis that threatens the nomads. We would thus not have to face a [military] repression [of the nomads] that would destroy their race, the only one capable of controlling the bush. Despite everything, [the nomads] are sympathetic because of their pride and attachment to their ancient customs from the old world of the nomad.[23]

In only two areas of the Niger Bend did this policy produce any significant nomad-directed Bellah agriculture before the end of World War I, both around Lake Faguibine where the Kel Antessar settled their Bellah seasonally and in the lake region of the Gourma where the Kunta settled their servile people in more permanent agricultural villages. It was the leaders of the Kel Antessar and Kunta who first understood the advantages that cooperation with the French offered them. Unsurprisingly their leaders increased their political and economic power more than any other nomadic group under colonial rule. Elsewhere Bellah were put into existing agricultural villages on a seasonal basis, but most Bellah who remained in their masters' service continued to fulfill traditional labor roles in nomadic society as animal herders or domestic laborers. There were ways in which Bellah could leave their masters, even if only seasonally. New wage opportunities developed in towns such as Timbuktu where a large Bellah population developed and sharecropping opportunities existed to some extent in some Songhay villages. Only toward the end of the colonial period would significant new opportunities arise in the Niger Bend when irrigation schemes were opened up at Diré and on Lake Horo, but even when Bellah migrated to take up wage work or petty commerce, their masters followed and demanded a share of wages for themselves.[24]

In an attempt to balance their two main political objectives in the Niger Bend, to ensure security, and to encourage at least moderate economic development, the French sought to divide the fertile floodplain of the Niger Valley between the Songhay-speaking sedentary agriculturists and the pastoral nomads, assigning the tenure rights of lands worked by the Bellah slaves to their nomadic masters. In effect, French policy freed one segment of the servile population from pastoral control while at the same time encouraging a landed relationship between pastoral overlords and their former slaves and servile people. The result was a conflation of different tributary status positions within nomadic societies and the effective creation of a larger group known as the "Bellah."

SLAVEHOLDER VIEWS ON RACE, SLAVERY AND ISLAMIC LAW

Slaveholding elites in the Niger Bend had always relied on Islamic law to regulate, at least in theory, the practice of slavery. The vast majority of the extant written material on slavery produced in the region falls well within established Islamic legal frameworks. There are, however, several exceptional local texts that were written in response to North African racial attitudes that apparently conflated blackness of skin with slavery. These texts open a rare window on wider sahelian perceptions of the relationship between "race" and slavery.

It is unusual in precolonial documents to find discussions of the qualities that were thought to adhere to people of different racial categories; however, in a remarkable text authored at the beginning of the seventeenth century, the celebrated Timbuktu jurist Ahmad Baba, who died in 1627, discussed the qualities of black people in the context of slavery. Ahmad Baba had been taken into forcible exile in Morocco after the successful Moroccan invasion of the Niger Bend in 1591.[25] In Morocco he found himself confronted with a much more racialized discourse on slavery than he was accustomed to in Timbuktu, and this moved him to write a rebuttal of what he considered to be the false ideas of North Africans about black people from sub-Saharan Africa. A debate had arisen in the sixteenth century in North Africa about whether all black Africans were by definition non-Muslims, and therefore, whether they had permanent slave status regardless of later conversions or professions of Islam. In response, Ahmad Baba, who was of Ṣanhāja Berber origin and therefore "white" in local terms,[26] wrote a lengthy treatise on slavery and its peculiar relationship to sub-Saharan Africa and blackness of skin. In this work, he refuted the popular North African idea that equated blackness with slavery by pointing out that certain African ethnic groups had converted to Islam without compulsion, and that therefore these Africans were equal with all other Muslims as far as Islamic law was concerned. Consequently, they were not legitimate targets of enslavement. In this text, Ahmad Baba also refutes the myth of the curse of Ham that was apparently widespread in North Africa at the time as a popular justification for the enslavement of Africans; however, in defending black Muslims against popular attitudes in North Africa, he sometimes reveals how he shared contemporary Arabo-Berber notions of the inferiority and "enslaveability" of black Africans. For example, he appears to embrace certain stereotypes about black Africans, remarking at one point on their "objectionable characteristics and uncouthness, and their servile nature."[27]

It is interesting that the most explicit discussion of race in local precolonial Arabic texts was provoked by an exposure to North Africa. Ahmad Baba's essential argument is that the North Africans just do not understand West Africa, and hence they make serious mistakes regarding who can and cannot be legitimately enslaved. For someone such as Ahmad Baba, the abiding divide between people in West Africa is not their "race," but their qualities as free Muslims or as slaves. There is already some overlap between the qualities of slave-ness and blackness, but as yet there is no equivalence. The degree to which North African ideas about race affected the thinking of people in the southern Sahara and Sahel, especially after the Moroccan conquest of Songhay, remains an interesting question.[28]

When the French arrived in the Niger Bend, they brought with them their own ideas about "race." In an odd way, these new colonial ideas reflected the old because they were derived, at least in part, from French experience in North Africa, and hence, bore at least some resemblance to the racial notions rejected by Ahmad Baba in seventeenth-century Morocco.[29] In the event, it was clear to local elites in the Niger Bend two hundred years after Ahmad Baba that the French did not understand race any better than the North Africans. The French were predisposed to equate race with social position and to assume that blackness meant servility, especially in nomadic society.[30]

Precolonial Arabic texts did at times make the distinction between blacks and whites, but this did not generally apply to racial differences within Arabo-Berber society. In a number of apparently precolonial texts describing specific instances of conflict in Arabo-Berber society, there are detailed accounts of the members of the two parties to the conflict. These texts tend to describe a list of named individuals and, at the end, include the Haratin (or "free blacks") and the slaves. The writers of these histories quite naturally assumed the hierarchical social relationship that existed in Arabo-Berber society and there is some evidence that there was a kind of moral economy of honor with regard to the treatment of one's inferiors. What is important is that the servile categories are named and that "race" is not invoked.

At the beginning of the colonial period, the same basic distinction continued to be made and the same terms (*bīḍān/sūdān*) were used to describe what we might think of as racialized ethnic difference. For example, in a local history written around 1906 describing the confrontation between an Arab group called the Berabish and the French army at the end of the nineteenth century, the author describes the arrival of a French military force in a village and the subsequent expulsion of its inhabitants: "They entered the village and when morning came every one appeared and [the French] said: "We don't want any people [here] whether they are Blacks or Arabs. But the Arabs remained for the rest of the day gathering their possessions until night came, and then they left to join their people. Then, after that, the Touareg came."[31] In this case, it appears that the blacks in question are Songhay-speakers and not directly affiliated with the Berabish. In this example, there is a significant amount of discursive continuity with texts produced during the precolonial period that indicates that we should not think of the changes in racial thinking as an "invention of tradition."[32] It should be noted that the term "*sūdān*" is much more common in these texts than the term "*bīḍān*", which is employed less often. Writers of local histories, for example, tended to use the ethnic or patronymic labels when describing nomadic groups. This is largely because the vast majority of authors were themselves members of either Arab or Tuareg society.

Texts written in the early colonial period introduce explicit elements of "race" into descriptions of different social categories within nomadic societies. In another local history describing the tribulations of a Tuareg group called the Iglād in the face of French occupation, the author describes a situation in which all the Iglād have fled the Niger Valley: "From Timbuktu to Gao, among the Whites and the Blacks there was not a single Iglād remaining except Muhammad Mustafa."[33] Here, the element of "race" is introduced to describe blacks and whites in Iglād society, and this is new. From the perspective of the numerous local histories of the conflicts between the French and Arabo-Berber groups, colonialism had overturned the existing social order. In the same text quoted above on the Iglād, which is devoted to the question of legitimate authority and who, among the Iglād can rightly exercise this authority, the author has the leader of the Iglād, who has submitted to the French, make the following speech to the local French commandant at Bourem:

> Listen to what I say to you Lieutenant and do what you want after that. You know that since we have kept the peace for the Christians and been taken under their protection and given them the *jizya*[34] that we had never before seen, you have reversed our social statuses and made the freeman into a slave and the slave into a freeman, the noble into a commoner and the commoner into a noble, the princes into subjects and the subjects into princes, for no reason. There is no reason for us to give [the French] the *jizya* when they do not leave us in the circumstances in which they found us, when the slave was a slave, the freeman a freeman, the subject a subject, the commoner a commoner, the prince a prince, the noble person noble and the base person base. So that when they had a request they could ask one of the nobles and they could carry out the request if they were able, but [because of the changes] they are [now] incapable of executing the order.[35]

The Iglād leader goes on to say that because of the destruction of the natural order at the hands of the French, they are unable, any longer, to carry out the orders of the French in collecting the *jizya* or in anything else. Although the "natural order" represented in this passage may be, in part, a racial order, it is not stated in explicitly racial terms. But from the perspective of the nomadic elites, maintaining the "traditional" social hierarchy would require new ideas. Discourses about race served these purposes, in part at least, because they could be made to correspond to some extent to French racial ideas, which could be exploited for nomadic interests.

The colonial state created its own system of justice to police property rights and protect property holders. The colonial state became the arbiter in all matters of property crime and thus the role of the Islamic judge in this domain was greatly reduced except in the case of Islamic judges working directly for the colonial state. Over time, even the role of official Islamic judges in criminal cases was reduced and their domain of activity was largely limited to civil cases of inheritance, divorce, and so forth. It has been suggested that elsewhere in the Sahel the imposition of a system of colonial justice worked to the advantage of desert-edge elites, and that consequently cases involving slavery were quite deliberately brought by these elites before colonial tribunals instead of traditional Islamic jurist.[36] Those issues that remained in the Islamic system reveal something about how these same slave-holding elites sought to codify changing relations between masters and slaves in the colonial period.

The Niger Bend is one of the areas of West Africa with the longest and deepest Islamic traditions. It is certainly one of the richest areas in terms of the sheer volume of extant Islamic documents. From a sociological perspective, one can see that Islam was especially important in commercial towns such as Timbuktu and among certain nomadic groups that were able to turn reputations for extraordinary religious knowledge and piety into larger political and economic networks that overcame, if only temporarily, the fractious segmentary tendencies of the nomads. The development of Kunta power in the nineteenth century is the best example of this.[37] The role that Islamic law and Muslim jurists played in regulating slavery in the precolonial period was probably greatest in communities where Islamic learning was most developed. Certainly the greatest volume of documentation on slavery was generated in commercial settings such as Timbuktu, although this may be partly a result of the accessibility of manuscripts there today. Much of this urban material on slavery deals with personal status issues (purchase and sale of slaves, manumission, inheritance, *waqf* [religious endowments] of slaves, and issues of personal behavior toward slaves, etc.).

Here we will consider a large collection of legal opinions issued by the last great Kunta scholar of the Niger Bend, Shaykh Bāy b. Sīdī `Amar al-Kuntī, who exercised significant religious influence on both nomads and sedentary communities from his desert *zawiya* in the Azawad in the first three decades of colonial rule. Unfortunately there are no dates given for individual opinions so all that can be said is that these issues arose sometime between 1895, when he took control of the *zawiya*, and 1929, when he died. The advantage of using this collection though, is that there are almost a thousand legal opinions by the same author, so it presents a fairly full picture of the various issues that were thrown up by the early colonial period in the Niger Bend and brought to this well-known Islamic jurist. We will confine ourselves here to those questions that pertain to slavery (perhaps four or five percent of all cases in the collection.)

In any premodern collection of Islamic legal opinions, we must expect to find numerous questions relating to slavery. Some questions in the collection of Shaykh Bāy could just as easily have been posed in precolonial times and appear to bear little connection to the changes wrought by colonial occupation. For example, there are a number of questions about the religious observances of slaves and whether it is incumbent on masters to force their slaves to pray.[38] There are also a large number of questions about female slaves, especially concubines. It is probably true that as in Mauritania, domestic female slaves were least likely to gain their freedom.[39] A variety of situations concerning concubines are described in questions but it is difficult from these sources alone to pinpoint a relationship to the new situation of colonialism. There are a number of other questions, however, that suggest changes in the relationships between slaves and masters. The very fact that these cases were brought before an authority such as Shaykh Bāy is indicative that there were new problems that required answers. Two discernable categories of questions suggest change: questions about slaves and money and/or taxation and questions about wayward slaves who had left their masters.

Dozens of questions can broadly be classified as concerning economic issues. Not all of them reflect the changes in the political economy ushered in by colonialism, but at least some indicate that slaves were finding wage-earning opportunities outside nomadic society. One questioner asks whether the money earned by his slave belongs to the slave or the master.[40] Another asks whether the wages earned by a female slave who carried the legal status of a religious endowment (*waqf*) belongs to the endowment's beneficiaries.[41] There are also several questions about how wages for service should be paid. In one case, a questioner asks about a situation in which a laborer refuses to complete his farm labor in a "garden" until he has been paid his wages.[42] The laborer is almost certainly a former slave. Another set of questions concerns whose responsibility it is to pay taxes on wages paid to a slave. Several questioners ask whether a master can take his slave's money to pay the slave's taxes. Shaykh Bāy's response in this case is to argue that a slave's money should not go toward his taxes but to his manumission.[43] We can speculate that this may have amounted to the same thing, and likely led to formal manumission in some cases so as to collect taxes from slaves. Certainly this was how the colonial taxation system operated. Since the colonial state expected masters to collect taxes from their slaves, just as nomadic chiefs were held responsible for collecting the taxes of all their subjects, including Bellah, it is logical that slaves would be pushed into economic activities on behalf of their masters. There are several questions in the collection that appear to relate to the renting out of slaves for such a purpose.[44] Taken together, these cases suggest that one of the changes of the first decades of colonial rule was that some masters put their slaves to work in the monetary economy, quite probably under pressure from colonial demands for taxes.

We know from a variety of sources that some slaves left their masters during the first decades of colonial rule. This collection does not help to quantify this process, but it does give some clues about how some slave masters responded. One question is repeated in slightly different ways a number of times. It concerns slaves who have left their masters to live somewhere else (in one case it is with the sedentary people along the river). The question is a religious one: Do the marriages of these slaves become invalid since they have left the people of religion (their masters) without permission and they are consequently no longer under the protection (*dhimma*) of their masters who are responsible for their religious practice? Shaykh Bāy's answer is that their marriages are invalidated by such actions and their marriages become adultery in such a situation.[45] Several other cases concern slaves who have run away with their master's money and the questioner is asking about how bounty hunters should be paid.[46]

The mosaic that can be pieced together from this brief accounting of legal opinions is anything but definitive. Nonetheless, these sources do at least point to the fact that some slave masters sought to transform their slaves into more economically viable clients, and that these slave masters sought ideological, cultural, and/or religious justifications for their continuing domination over slaves. For the nomads of the Niger Bend, slavery was an essential part of the Islamic code that governed their lives and defined their social system.

BELLAH BANDITRY AND CRIME

The responses of servile people to the new situation created by colonial rule were varied. Some slaves left their masters, but the majority seems to have remained in some degree of servility. The development of significant wage labor opportunities was so limited that it was not until after World War II that there was any serious disruption to the nomadic elite's control over Bellah labor. As late as the 1950s apparent cases of slaves being sold in Arabia by Tuareg pilgrims to Mecca caused a minor scandal in the French press.[47]

The absence of a dramatic exodus of slaves forces us to look more carefully in less obvious places to detect the changes in the lives of slaves and servile people. One such source is the colonial justice records, which, in the case of the Niger Bend, are full of instances of banditry, highway robbery, and other forms of theft. Although it is difficult to be precise, a conservative estimate would be that three-quarters of all cases during the colonial period involve servile perpetrators.[48] The cases range from instances of individual theft to organized bands of Bellah descending on herds or villages. Because these cases typically contain relatively little Bellah testimony, it is difficult to tease out the different motivations behind these acts. Furthermore, the fact that instances of theft and brigandage run through the entire colonial period should make us wary about attributing too much change to this type of economic activity. For example, in 1909 there is a case of a slave who arrived at the "village de liberté" of Timbuktu demanding to be admitted and bringing with him the animals of his master. For this act, which we might interpret as "social banditry," the slave received one year in prison.[49] On the other hand, in a case from 1939, a small band of Bellah raided a sedentary village in the Gourma, apparently at the behest of their masters. According to one of the witnesses, "every time the Bellah cause trouble it is because their masters push them to do it."[50]

The social significance of Bellah banditry is perhaps easier to discern by gauging the reactions that it generated. One level of reaction can be read in the punishments meted out by the colonial state. There was, unsurprisingly, a great disparity in the sentences handed down for the same crime, depending on the perpetrator's social status. A Bellah who killed his master in whatever circumstances was often given a long sentence or the death penalty. Masters who killed their slaves or servile underlings tended to receive relatively light sentences. For example, in a 1909 case involving the Tengérégifs,[51] a Tuareg master killed his Bellah shepherd because the shepherd had refused to milk the cows for his master or to take them out to graze. Despite the fact that the master killed his Bellah with a lance while mounted on horseback, he was convicted of involuntary manslaughter and sentenced to one year in prison because his actions were judged to have been provoked and accidental.[52] In cases in which those they were attacking killed Bellah bandits, claims of self-defense usually resulted in acquittals.[53] Most cases of even the most low-level theft committed by Bellah resulted in six months to a year in prison. In cases of highway robbery, the sentences were often much stiffer. In one example from 1920, a group of three Bellah attacked a traveler, killing him and stealing the goods he was carrying. One of the perpetrators was sentenced to death, the other two to fifteen years each in prison.[54]

Beyond the colonial state itself, the actions of Bellah bandits sometimes generated retaliatory violence from local victims. As mentioned above, there were periodic cases in which attackers were killed either while committing their crimes or after their apprehension. In one case in 1943, a Bellah was killed and another seriously injured by three Tuareg men who beat them after having successfully searched for the perpetrators of an act of robbery. In another case of a similar nature, two Bellah were apprehended in similar circumstances and tied to a horse, which dragged them to their deaths. In both cases the Tuareg perpetrators were convicted of murder and sentenced to long prison sentences.[55] In both cases the Bellah who had committed the acts of banditry were still in relationships with a "master". In both cases the killings occurred in the presence of many people, in villages where the Bellah lived, and seem to have been motivated in part by a desire to teach a lesson to other Bellah. That these very public incidents of retaliatory violence occur in the early 1940s, just a few years before serious problems broke out between Bellah and their masters over Bellah demands of emancipation and independence suggest that Bellah crime was also a barometer of social tension and the degree of exploitation in the larger relationship between the Bellah and their masters. These crimes might be seen as transgressions that are in some way rehearsals for the struggle to come. The violence that these acts engendered in response against the Bellah delineates in emphatic, now necessary, ways the border that was not to be crossed.

The line was crossed and in the late 1940s and early 1950s, as more and more Bellah groups demanded that the colonial administration grant them their independence, and that they be allowed to keep that animals which their masters had entrusted to them. This produced a considerable amount of violence in the years after World War II until independence in 1960.

CONCLUSION

During the 1950s the issue of "race" seems to emerge suddenly into the open in the Niger Bend. Not only was the "Bellah question" finally resolving itself in the Bellah agitation for freedom and autonomy, but noble Tuareg groups started preparing, or so they said, to leave the territory and move to "white" Arab countries. Other Arab and Tuareg elites conspired with members of the French military to separate the Niger Bend from what would become southern Mali so as to maintain nomadic hegemony in a new Saharan territory that would remain under French rule: the Organisation commune des régions sahariennes or OCRS.[56] Malian nationalists also began to use local racial issues in their electoral campaigns. But "race" was not new to the Niger Bend, nor were these issues of Arabo-Berber hegemony and colonial manipulation. What was new was that slavery's very slow death had finally arrived, to be replaced in local discourse with the politics of "race".

Notes

1. I use the term "nomad" and "nomadic" advisedly. This is a common term used in Mali to talk about these groups and it is the term that was used by the French colonial administration. In fact, most Tuareg and Arabs are more accurately described as semi-nomadic or transhumant pastoralists.
2. The "Tuareg revolt" in northern Mali and Niger of 1990–1995 was frequently understood as a form of banditry that drew on preexisting traditions among the Saharan "nomads." For a discussion of this, see Hélène Claudot-Hawad, "Bandits, rebelles et partisans: vision plurielle des événements touaregs, 1990–1992," *Politique Africaine* 46 (1992), 143–49.
3. The foundational text on "social banditry" is Eric Hobsbawm, *Primitive Rebels. Studies in Archaic Forms of Social Movement in the 19th and 20th Centuries* (New York, 1963). For a somewhat skeptical view of how Hobsbawm's ideas have been applied to Africa, see Donald Crummey, "Introduction: 'The Great Beast'" in *Banditry, Rebellion and Social Protest in Africa*, ed. idem (London, 1986), 1–29; and Ralph Austen, "Social Bandits and Other Heroic Criminals: Western Models of Resistance and Their Relevance for Africa" in ibid., 89–108. On the banditry of runaway slaves, see Paul E. Lovejoy, "Slavery in the Sokoto Caliphate," in *The Ideology of Slavery in Africa*, ed. idem (Beverly Hills, 1981), 230; and idem and Jan Hogendorn, *Slow Death for Slavery. The Course of Abolition in Northern Nigeria, 1897–1936* (Cambridge, 1993), 41–50.
4. James Webb, *Desert Frontier: Ecological and Economic Change along the Western Sahel, 1600–1850* (Madison, 1995); and Raymond Taylor, "Of Disciples and Sultans: Power, Authority and Society in the Nineteenth-Century Mauritanian Gebla," Ph.D. dissertation, University of Illinois at Urbana-Champaign, 1996, 3. James Webb has probably made the most sweeping attempt to analyze the development of racial identities along the desert-edge in the Western Sahara. He argues that progressive desiccation of the Sahara after the sixteenth century pushed Arabo-Berber pastoralists into ever greater competition with black Africans along the southward-moving ecological frontier of the desert, and that this led to a tendency to racialize Western Saharan identities. Because the environmental change allowed the pastoralist groups to increase their power over black African agriculturalists, it was the Arabo-Berber pastoralists who began to use racial identity as an ideological justification of their position. Raymond Taylor has made a similar argument on a more local scale, arguing that Western Saharans in southwestern Mauritania began using the label *bīḍān* to identify themselves in the eighteenth century to distinguish themselves from neighboring black African groups. See also my article on this subject, Bruce S. Hall, "The Question of 'Race' in the Pre-colonial Southern Sahara," *Journal of North African Studies* 10, No. 3-4 (2005), 339-67.

5. A similar process occurred in Mauritania. See Urs Peter Ruf, *Ending Slavery: Hierarchy, Dependency and Gender in Central Mauritania* (Bielefeld, 1999), 35–36. On French attitudes about "race" in Saharan society, see Benjamin Acloque, "Embarras de l'administration coloniale: la question de l'esclavage au début du XXème siècle en Mauritanie," in *Groupes serviles au Sahara. Approche comparative à partir du cas des arabophones de Mauritanie*, ed. Mariella Villasante-de Beauvais (Paris, 2000), 105–07.
6. The idea of a "topsy-turvy world" resulting from changes in the relationships between masters and slaves under colonial rule comes from a Hassaniyya poem recorded in the 1950s in Mauritania, where a very similar process had occurred. H. T. Norris, *Shinqiti Folk Literature and Song* (London, 1968), 30. E. Ann McDougall has made use of this poem in "A Topsy-Turvy World: Slaves and Freed Slaves in the Mauritanian Adrar, 1910–1950," in *The End of Slavery in Africa*, eds. Suzanne Miers and Richard Roberts (Madison, 1988), 362–88. Some have argued that Tuareg practices and justifications of slavery were different from those among Arabophone Saharans, and that the Tuareg relied less on principles drawn from Islamic law than Arab-speaking groups. A good treatment of the somewhat idealized representations of slavery in Tuareg society is Hélène Claudot-Hawad, "Captif sauvage, esclave enfant, affranchi cousin. La mobilité statutaire chez les Touaregs," in *Groupes serviles au Sahara*, ed. M. Villasante-de-Beauvais, 238–41; and Claudot-Hawad, "Identité et altérité d'un point de vue touareg. Eléments pour un débat," in *Touaregs et autres Sahariens entre plusieurs mondes. Définitions et redéfinitions de soi et des autres*, ed. H. Claudot-Hawad (Aix-en-Provence, 1996), 14.
7. As in the case of the Haratin, the origins of the Bellah are obscure. Some—perhaps the majority—are of slave origin, but others, especially certain pastoralist Bellah groups, appear to have never been enslaved. For a recent discussion of the origins of the Haratin in the Maghrib see Chouki El Hamel, "'Race', Slavery and Islam in Maghribi Mediterranean Thought: The Question of the Haratin in Morocco," *The Journal of North African Studies* 7 (2002), 29–52,
8. The term "Bellah" is apparently of Songhay origin. The Songhay distinguish between the Bellah and slaves in their own society who are called *tam* in the generic sense and *baññа* and *koŋŋo* for male and female slaves. In Tamashek, the language of the Tuaregs, slaves are called *iklan* and freed slaves *ilellan*. Arabic-speaking pastoralists use the terms *`abīd* for slaves and *ḥarāṭīn* for freed slaves. Arabic legal documents concerning issues of slavery are more precise, using the term *`atīq* to refer to a manumitted slave.
9. This was a recurrent story in interviews carried out in Songhay-speaking villages along the Niger River. One person told me, for example, that the Bellah were bandits, and that if one was caught by Songhay-speaking people, he would be tied up and delivered to the French authorities rather than to his Tuareg master because the master would release the Bellah without pun-

ishment, and may even have been a party to the banditry. Interview with Yacouba al-Mouhali, Moyadji Koïra, Cercle de Gourma-Rharous, Mali, 17 October 2002.

10. Martin Klein discusses this in "Slavery and French Rule in the Sahara," *Slavery and Abolition* 19 (1998), 80–82.
11. Cited in Baz Lecocq, "'That Desert is Our Country': Tuareg Rebellions and Competing Nationalisms in Contemporary Mali (1946–1996)," Ph.D. dissertation, University of Amsterdam, 2002, 51.
12. A. S. Kanya-Forstner, *The Conquest of the Western Sudan, A Study in French Military Imperialism* (Cambridge, 1969), 217–22.
13. Jean Clauzel, "L'administration coloniale française et les sociétés nomades dans l'ancienne Afrique occidentale française," *Politique Africaine* 46 (1992), 100.
14. Ordre de Mission No. 241, 1957, Archives, Cercle de Goundam, Mali,
15. See Pierre Boilley, *Les Touaregs Kel Adagh. Dépendances et révoltes: du Soudan français au Mali contemporain* (Paris, 1999), 99–153.
16. This respect was dependent on the continued cooperation of the nomadic group with the colonial administration. Those nomads who did not cooperate, or who rebelled, had some of their Bellah removed from their control by the colonial administration as punishment. On this, see Georg Klute, "Herren und Sklaven: Zur Frage der kolonialen Sklavenpolitik in Französisch-Westafrika," in *Macht der identität: identitäder macht. Politische prozesse und kultureller wandel in Afrika*, eds. Heidi Willer, Till Förster, and Claudia Ortner-Buchberger (Münster, 1995), 241–53.
17. "Rapport politique," Cercle de Tombouctou, December 1915, 1E–78–81, Archives Nationales du Mali, Bamako [hereafter ANMB].
18. "Rapport politique," Région de Tombouctou, 2ème trimestre, 1918, 1E–78–81, ANMB.
19. "Rapport de L'inspecteur Général Demaret," 1919, 1E 2361, Numérique, Sér.III, ANMB.
20. "Rapport du Sous-lieutenant Jacobi sur la région du Kissou parcourue pendant la reconnaissance," 20 August 1895, 1E–78–81, ANMB.
21. "Rapport du Lieutenant Cauvan sur la tournée de recensement faite dans le Bingha, le Gourma et le Kissou du 3 février au 3 mars, 1898," 15 March 1898, 1E–78–81, ANMB.
22. "Rapport politique," July 1914, 1E–78–81, Cercle de Tombouctou, ANMB. The sedentary population along the river to the east of Timbuktu suffered terribly from the famine. In 1914, as the colonial administration in Timbuktu began to offer emergency food supplies to the destitute, an estimated fifty percent of the sedentary population had already perished.
23. Capitaine Maziller,"Etude sur les populations de la Région de Tombouctou: Situation économique et agricole, sécurité et éléments de troubles intérieurs;

Rezzous venus de l'extérieur, organisation de la lutte contre eux, sûreté à organiser," 10 June 1906, 1D–59–11, ANMB.

24. Jean Gallais, *Pasteurs et paysans du Gourma: La condition sahélienne* (Paris, 1975), 93–94.
25. On the life of Ahmad Baba, see Mahmoud Zouber, *Ahmad Baba de Tombouctou (1556–1627): sa vie et son curve* (Paris, 1977).
26. In more recent local texts Ahmad Baba is referred to by the nisba given to him during his stay in North Africa: al-sudani. This refers to the place of his origin, but also carries the racial identifier of "black." His full name is Ahmad Baba bin Ahmad bin Ahmad bin `Umar bin Muhammad Aqit.
27. Ahmad Baba, "Mirāj al-ṣu`ūd ilā nayl ḥukm majlūb al-sūdān," ms. 6409, Institut des Hautes Etudes et de la Recherche Islamique – Ahmed Baba, Timbuktu, Mali (hereafter IHERIAB). This text has been published and translated by John Hunwick and Fatima Harrick in *Mi`rāj al-ṣu`ūd ajwibāt Aḥmad Bābā hawla al-istirqāq* (Rabat, 2000). There is a similar text written in the late nineteenth-century by an otherwise obscure scholar, probably from Timbuktu, Muḥammad al-Sanūsī b Ibrāhīm al-Jārimī: "Tanbīh ahl al-tughyān `alā ḥurriyyat al-sūdān" (Drawing the Attention of Tyrannical Folk to the Free Status of the Blacks), ms. 1575, IHERIAB. See Hunwick's discussion of these texts in "Islamic Law and Polemics over Race and Slavery in North and West Africa (16th–19th century)," *Princeton Papers* 7 (1997), 3–10.
28. For a recent discussion of the Haratin in the Maghrib, see El Hamel, "'Race', Slavery and Islam in Maghribi Mediterranean Thought." On the larger issue of the influence and possible spread of Arab North African ideas about race, see Amir Hasan Idris, *Sudan's Civil War: Slavery, Race and Formational Identities* (Lewiston, 2001).
29. On the development of the more familiar racial ideas about Arabs and Berbers by the French in North Africa, see Patricia Lorcin, *Imperial Identities: Stereotyping, Prejudice and Race in Colonial Algeria* (New York, 1995).
30. Here is not the place to go into a detailed discussion of how the French applied racial ideas in their early attempts to describe the Niger Bend, except to say that they managed to apply their racial ideas widely, so that, for example, they expended considerable energy identifying so-called "Arma" nobles to invest in the office of village chiefdom. As people who claimed descent from the soldiers sent by Morocco to invade the Songhay Empire in 1591, the "Arma" claimed and were accorded the status as "non-blacks" at the beginning of the colonial period.
31. "Tā'rīkh Azawād fī-'l-akhbār al-Barābīsh wa-ḥurūbihim ma` al-rakībāt wa-ḥajār afūghās w'-adnān wa-dhikr ba`ḍ akābirihim mithl Sīdī b. Muḥammad b. Amḥammad wa-Muḥammad b. Amḥammad wa-Maḥmūd b. Dahmān wa-dakhūl al-nisārī fī Tinbuktū wa-ghayr dhālak," ms. 279, fl.17, IHERIAB.
32. S. Feierman, *Peasant Intellectuals: Anthropology and History in Tanzania* (Madison, 1990), 33. I think it is useful to follow Steven Feierman's suggestive

work on peasant intellectuals in Tanzania and look at what elements of older discursive structures were sustained and what were dropped in the changing social context of the colonial period, and how local discourses mediated the relationship between local people and the larger field of colonial power.

33. "Maktūb fī sha'n aṣl imāra Iglād li-Kalansīd al-daib kānū qātinīn bi-arḍ Binba [Bamba]," ms. 1503, fl.4, IHERIAB.
34. In this context, the jizya was seen by the French as an Islamically-sanctioned tax on conquered people. It was paid in livestock by the pastoralists of the Niger Bend.
35. Ibid., fl.12.
36. Charles Stewart, "A Comparison of the Exercise of Colonial and Precolonial Justice in Mauritania," in *Nomades et commandants: Administration et sociétés nomades dans l'ancienne A.O.F.*, eds. Edmund Bernus, Pierre Boilley, Jean Clauzel, and Jean-Louis Triaud (Paris, 1993), 81–86.
37. On the development of Kunta authority in the nineteenth century, see Aziz A. Batran, *The Qadiryya Brotherhood in West Africa and the Western Sahara: The Life and Times of Shaykh al-Mukhtar al-Kunti (1729–1811)* (Rabat, 2001).
38. Nawā'zil al-Shaykh Bāy, #173, fl.218; #179, fl.229, ms 118, v.1, IHERIAB,
39. On Mauritania, see McDougall, "Topsy-Turvy World," 362–88.
40. Nawā'zil al-Shaykh Bāy, #551, fl.597; and #619, fl.655, ms 121, v.4. IHERIAB.
41. Nawā'zil al-Shaykh Bāy, #381, fl.425. ms 119, v.2, IHERIAB.
42. Nawā'zil al-Shaykh Bāy, #579, fl.630, ms 121, v.4, IHERIAB.
43. For example, Nawā'zil al-Shaykh Bāy, #241, fl.261; and #242, fl.262, ms 118, v.1, IHERIAB.
44. Nawā'zil al-Shaykh Bāy, #553, fl.598; and #554, fl.599, ms 121, v.4, IHERIAB.
45. Nawā'zil al-Shaykh Bāy, #529, fl.584, ms 121, v.4; and #335, fl.379, ms 119, v.2, IHERIAB.
46. Nawā'zil al-Shaykh Bāy, #597, fl.640, ms 121, v.4, IHERIAB.
47. Georges de Caunes, "Il y a encore des marchands d'esclaves," *Paris Match*, 25 June 1955. The case of Awad El Djoud, a Bellah from Goundam, sold in Mecca after accompanying his master Muhammad Ali ag Attaher on pilgrimage, is one of several examples of published denunciations of the continuing existence of slavery in French Africa. This particular article includes a critique of French administrators for knowingly supporting slavery.
48. This is only an approximation based on my reading of the colonial justice registers that are extant; however, this estimate is roughly corroborated by some contemporary observers. For example, see Horace Miner, *The Primitive City of Timbuctoo* (New York, 1965), 267–71.

49. "Etats des jugements et extraits des Registres d'Ecrou, Tombouctou," 20 April 1909, 2M–149 FA, ANMB.
50. "Procès-verbal d'enquête, Goundam," 27 October 1939, 2D–18 FR, ANMB.
51. A large Tuareg confederation.
52. "Etats des jugements et extraits des Registres d'Ecrou, Tombouctou," 29 October 1909, 2M–149 FA, ANMB.
53. For example, "États des jugements et extraits des Registres d'Ecrou, Tombouctou," 10 June 1910, 2M–149 FA, ANMB.
54. "États des jugements et extraits des Registres d'Ecrou, Tombouctou," 5 June 1920, 2M–149 FA, ANMB.
55. "Procès-verbal," Cercle de Tombouctou, 9 July 1945, 1M–16, Archives, Région de Tombouctou.
56. For an overview of OCRS politics, see Pierre Boilley, "L'Organisation commune des régions sahariennes (OCRS): une tentative avortée" in *Nomades et commandants*, eds. Bernus et. al., 215–39.

Chapter 13

LITERACY AMONG MUSLIMS IN NINETEENTH-CENTURY TRINIDAD AND BRAZIL

Nikolay Dobronravin

ARABIC SCRIPT LITERACY IN THE CARIBBEAN AND BRAZIL

West African written traditions and Arabic script literacy spread into the New World in the course of the trans-Atlantic slave trade and forced migration. Some African Muslims were able to take with them manuscripts and written amulets produced in Africa, including a copy of the Qur'an, which was brought to Trinidad between 1840 and 1867.[1] Others retained their literacy skills or learned Arabic script in their new homeland.

According to European sources, the use of Arabic and African languages (in Arabic script) was not uncommon in the Caribbean during the time of slavery and after its abolition in the nineteenth century, especially in Jamaica and Trinidad. There is even some evidence that some representatives of the diaspora were in correspondence with West African Muslims; however, the real dimensions and specific features of Arabic-script literacy in the Caribbean remain understudied, and it is not clear when and how it disappeared.[2] Very few documents written in Arabic script have been studied, such as the Arabic manuscript of Muḥammad Kaba Saghanughu of Jamaica (c. 1820) published by Yacine Daddi Addoun and Paul

Lovejoy.[3] It is hard to say how many forgotten Islamic manuscripts have survived in local and European archives. There is no doubt that some of the relocated African Muslims were able to use Arabic script for writing in an African language such as Mandingo (Mandinka, Malinke, or Bambara), but the existing evidence is scanty. According to the account of Captain John Washington, one example is Mohammedu Sisei from Gambia, who served in the Third West India Regiment between 1811 and 1825, and wrote Mandingo "indifferently in Arabic character."[4]

Scholars have been aware of Brazil's Arabic-script tradition since the early nineteenth century. Sometime between 1819 and 1826, José Bonifácio d'Andrada, a famous Brazilian politician and scholar, interviewed a few Hausa people in Brazil about the geography of central Africa. In his letter to Menèzes de Drumond, he described an informant, one Francisco from Kano: "Il a été prêtre mahométan et maītre d'école dans sa patrie, il connaīt fort bien l'arabe, il sait compter et écrire, comme vous vous en convaincrez par une traduction du *pater noster* en langue haussah, écrite par lui en caractères arabes, que je vous envoie ainsi qu'un petit vocabulaire…"[5]. This Hausa translation of the Paternoster in Arabic script has not been found, but it was certainly produced at the request of the Brazilian scholar. It is not clear whether Francisco used Hausa in writing for his own purposes.

It was the French traveler and diplomat Francis de Castelnau who first stated that non-Portuguese and multilingual literacy was a visible phenomenon in Bahia. His book on central Africa as remembered by Africans brought to this part of Brazil begins with the following words: "Le petit travail que je soumets en ce moment au public se compose de renseignements que j'ai pu obtenir des nègres esclaves de Bahia. Peu après mon arrivée dans cette résidence, je ne tardai pas à remarquer que plusieurs d'entre eux savaient lire et écrire l'arabe et le libyque."[6] There is no doubt that Castelnau referred here to Arabic-script literacy. According to his remark, Arabic was not the only written language used by African Muslims in Bahia. The language referred to as "libyque" (Libyan) could be any African language, but it is reasonable to suggest that the language mentioned by the French observer was Hausa.

After the Muslim insurrection of 1835 in Bahia, the criminalization of Arabic script may have contributed to the decline of the Arabic written tradition. In the early twentieth century several specimens of Islamic writings from Bahia were collected and published by Raymundo Nina Rodrigues.[7] By this time the tradition was dying out, so the next generations of researchers had to concentrate on the manuscripts, which were kept in the Bahia archives. Other surviving manuscripts were then found in Rio de Janeiro and Havre, and there is hope that more documents of the African Muslim diaspora might still be extant in Brazil or elsewhere.

The writing practices of African Muslims included the use of African languages in Arabic script, although Arabic was the main written language. The manuscripts examined in this chapter demonstrate that this tradition spread into the New World. African languages as well as European and creole languages were used in certain texts. Besides the languages written in Roman script (English, French, Spanish, Portuguese), Arabic remained the dominant language of literates in the Muslim African diaspora. The manuscripts described here are not new to scholars. Those in the library collections of Trinity College, Dublin and Bibliothèque Municipale du Havre have already been mentioned in some reference works, although they have not been thoroughly studied.[8]

THE DUBLIN MANUSCRIPT FROM TRINIDAD

The Dublin manuscript has been briefly mentioned in the *World Survey of Islamic Manuscripts*.[9] Jan Knappert and David James describe it as:

> a very interesting document written in West African Arabic characters. It consists of a prayer, partly in Arabic and partly in an unidentified African language. According to a note in English it was written by a Muslim "priest" (i.e. an *imām*), who was a freed slave in a British Regiment in Jamaica in 1817, for the colonel of the regiment. It is thus one of the earliest examples of written Arabic in the New World.[10]

As a matter of fact, the main language of this interesting and possibly unique document is not Arabic, but Hausa written in Arabic script. The manuscript also includes several words and phrases in Arabic, eastern Fula, Mandinka, and English or English-based Caribbean Creole, all in Arabic script. From the linguistic point of view, the text can be described as mostly Hausa with a sort of written code switching to eastern Fula and Arabic. The use of Fula seems to indicate that it was the author's mother tongue, although he preferred to write in Hausa. The text of the manuscript is fully vocalized, with the exception of a few Arabic sentences and personal names. The scribe was apparently used to writing in Arabic, but not in African languages. Even his Arabic sentences show that he was not always familiar with the orthography and resorted to a kind of phoneticized spelling.

The document is not just a prayer, but also a kind of African Islamic compendium. Section A includes an opening formula (Arabic); a list of infidel peoples (*Alyayyahūda – Annāsārā – Yājūjaⁿ ʻi-Mājūjaⁿ*) followed by an authorship note or a reference to the Qur'an (legible, but difficult to understand); an admonition (mainly Hausa, with some Arabic), and another obscure passage; the same list of peoples plus *baqara* "the whites" ("Buckra" or a similar variant in Caribbean creole), probably with a reference to the Qur'an; an authorship note (Fula); "explicit" (phoneticized Arabic).

The structure of Section B is no less complex: an admonition (Hausa); praise to God and the Prophet (Hausa); an authorship note in Hausa ("*M[u]ḥ[a]m[ma]d 'Ā'ishatu yay-yī taqardā qā mu-tāru mu-yyī niwūra,*" which translates as "Muhammadu A'ishatu wrote this letter, let us gather and pay attention [to it]);" another admonition and a prayer for protection in both worlds (mainly Hausa, with some Arabic, Fula, and Creole); five series of numerals (Hausa, Mandinka, Fula, English or Creole, and Arabic); a list of peoples different from the first one (*'Ārābī—Baqara—Alyāhūda—Ḥausa—Hulā—Mādigā* ["Arabs, "Buckra" ("whites"), Jews, Hausa, Fula, Mandinga]);" a list of holy books and religious communities (*Alyāhūdā—Taurita—[Al]linjīli [A]ly[a]hūd[a], Taurita—Alyāhūda, Linjīli—Anāsārā*); "explicit," (phoneticized Arabic) and colophon.

The unusual form of this document may be explained by the fact that it was commissioned by a European, as stated briefly on the outside of the bifolium: "Written by Private Philip Finlay—Grenadier Company 3d WI Regiment—(an Arabian Priest) Trinidad. Nov[ember] 21st 1817 for James B [Lenon], Assist[ant] Surgeon, 3rd W[est] I[ndian] Reg[iment]." Thus, the manuscript was written by a soldier from the Third West India Regiment for a military surgeon in Trinidad, and not in Jamaica.

Section A of the manuscript includes an authorship note that may be of interest for the study of Islam in the Caribbean: "*Fifirḥu M[u]ḥ[a]m[ma]d almājirī 'Usumānu bī-Hōduwā almajirī bī Muḥmaⁿ Tuqur almajirī-Mika'ilu M[u]ḥ[a]m[ma]d 'Ā'ishatu Ḥausaⁿ Gōbir*" (Philip (?) Muhammad, a student of Usumanu bi Hoduwa, student of the son of Muhamman Tukur [or: a student, a son of Muhamman Tukur], student of Mika'ilu, Muhammadu A'ishatu Hausa [from] Gobir"). The reference to Mika'ilu is of interest, as this was one of the names of Abdussalami ('Abd al-Salām), an Islamic scholar who preached in Gimbana. The Gimbanawa were crushed by a punitive expedition sent by Yunfa, the ruler of Gobir. According to the local tradition, the Gobir force was then stopped by the supporters of Shehu Usman who ordered the Muslim prisoners from Gimbana to be set free. This marked the beginning of the jihad in the region. If Muhammadu

A'ishatu referred to Abdussalami, he might belong to the Gimbana community. It is interesting that Muhammadu does not mention Sokoto, but only Hausa and Gobir in the document. At least one person with a similar name served in the Third West India Regiment, Muhammad Sisei, also a son of Aisha, a Mandingo from the Gambia, but his origin and Christian name (Felix Ditt) were different.[11]

Section A of the document begins with an Arabic phrase "*wa-bihī nasta'īnu*" (and we ask Him [Allah] for help). This initial formula is often used in West African texts, especially in written amulets, instead of the basmalah. The page ends with a sentence written in phoneticized Arabic "*tamat kisawatu*" (that is, "*tammat qiṣṣatu*ⁿ" [the story is finished]). Section B of the bifolium does not have any initial formula. It ends with the word written as *gishatu*ⁿ, probably the same as *kisawatu* in Section A (*qiṣṣa*), marking the end of the text. The names of Muhammad A'ishatu and "*Jim Burum Linām*" (John B. Lenon) are given on the last two lines. The word written as *wātamō* between the names may be part of the name of the scribe, possibly an English surname or a place-name.

The manuscript includes several words and phrases with uncertain interpretation, such as "*būqu tirī miqālatū būqu min lafawa*", after a reference to Jewish and Christian holy books and religious communities (section B). The beginning of the phrase "*būqu tirī*", may refer to the Qur'an, but no adequate interpretation of the whole passage has been found. Another reference to the Qur'an is seemingly used in the phrase "*fāsi*ⁿ *būqu 'ā 'l-rabī 'akin halbi M[u]ḥ[a]m[ma]d 'Ā'ashatu,*" probably written in creole. The tentative interpretation could be something like "first book of the Lord (*al-Rabb*); it can help Muhammadu A'ishatu."

The text of the document is undoubtedly Islamic; however, it does not include some very common words such as Allah, Qur'an, or Islam, even though the Muslims are mentioned as *jama'a* or *j[a]m[a]'[a] 'l-m[u]sl[i]min[a]* ([Muslim] community) and *Musulmīna* (Muslims). Allah is referred to as *'Ūba*ⁿ*qiẓi*, or *'Ūbāqīẓī*, and *'ā 'l-rabī*, while Islam is mentioned several times as *ad[d]ini* (religion, with various spellings) as well as *'adīnī mū* (our religion) and *'adinī-sa*ⁿ (his religion, Muhammad's). This omission of the significant words is certainly not occasional. The Muslim "priest" who wrote the text was certainly knowledgeable enough to be able to write these words. Instead he preferred to use euphemisms, maybe because the text was written for a Christian who could do harm even touching the paper with such words. The absence of any Qur'anic quotation in the manuscript may be explained by the same considerations. It cannot be derived from any attempt to conceal the religion of the scribe, as his Muslim identity was known to the addressee.

The lists that are found in the document were probably written down in answer to the questions of the European for whom the manuscript was produced. The lists of numerals in Hausa, Fula, Mandinka, Arabic, and English or English-based creole demonstrate the scribe's ability to count in several languages:

> *qili^{n}—ḥulā—ṣaba^{n}—nanī—lōlo—wōro—wōro galo—sayyī—qon[ō]tō—tā //ẓyybīyū —'ugu—hu'—biyā—shidā—bakou—taqos—tarra—qōmā // gogo—ẓẓ'—tātī—nayyī—jiwō gogo—jiwī tātī—jiwō nayyī—ṣafa^{n}// wā—tū—tiri—hō—fa^{n}—siqis—ṣabi^{n}—'it—nayyī—ta^{n} //—ḥam si^{n}—sitamīyya—ṣabamīyya—ṣaba'lafu—tamāniyya*
>
> 1, 2, 3, 4, 5, 6, 7, 8, 9, 10 (Mandinka); 1, 2, 3, 4, 5, 6, 7, 8, 9, 10 (Hausa); 1, 2, 3, 4, 6, 8, 9, 10 (eastern Fula); 1, 2, 3, 4, 5, 6, 7, 8, 9, 10 (English or creole); and 50, 600, 700, 7000, 8000 (phoneticized Arabic).

Unlike the lists, the admonitions and prayers seem to be addressed to a Muslim or even a Muslim community rather than an unbeliever: *tō jama'a mu-līṣafta maganar-ga* (Well, people (the community), let us consider these words). They mostly consist of simple sentences in plain Hausa, although the peculiarities of spelling sometimes hinder the interpretation, e.g. *bāwā kan bi-sharī'ā bi-ṣūna—ṣālā—ẓaqā—aẓumi—'adīnī—īmanji* (O slave [of God], follow the shari'a, follow the Sunna, [that is] daily prayers, the zakat, the fast [of Ramadan], religion and faith [in Islam]); *bi-sūna bi-sharia bi-qaskiyyā* (Follow the Sunna, follow the shari'a, follow the truth) (section A); *tō qa-dubā qay-yī karātu ka-samu albarqā qa-dubā qay-yī jīm[ma] qa-'inganta albarqā qa-dubā qay-yī 'aikin ka-samu albarqā* (Well, look, read, and may you obtain the blessing; look, perform your Friday prayers, reinforce the blessing; look, work, and may you obtain the blessing) (section B). The style of the Hausa text leaves an impression that at least part of it was translated from Arabic. As the scribe could hardly address a British military surgeon as a good Muslim at that time, not to mention his reference to the Muslim community, the possibility cannot be excluded that Philip Finlay translated or adapted an earlier manuscript written in Arabic by himself or somebody else in the *jama'a.*

It is not known whether Muhammadu A'ishatu was used to writing in Hausa or any other African language, especially on Islamic issues. There is some evidence that English or English-based creole was sometimes adapted to writing in Arabic script in the Caribbean and North America for the scribe's own purposes.[12] It is not clear, however, whether Hausa, creole, or any other language would be used in correspondence in the

African Muslim diaspora in the region. Even if there existed some hierarchy of languages written in Arabic script in the Caribbean, it remains unknown.

A BAHIAN INSURGENT'S BOOK IN HAVRE

Unlike the document brought to Dublin from Trinidad, the Brazilian manuscript in Havre was not intended for an outsider. According to the French note on f.2a, this manuscript was found in the pocket of an African who died during the rebellion of 25 January 1835 in Bahia[13] The work has forty-five folios. Written in Arabic script, in the beginning of the text (f.45) there are a few Qur'anic verses (94:1–4), reproduced as if it were a poem (seven lines, all ending in "*kāf*" except one line in the third verse of the sūra) and supplemented with the phrase *yā Muḥammad* (O Muḥammad). The last word in verse 94:4, *dhikraka*, is omitted. Indeed, it is quite possible that the whole text was intended for a *dhikr* recitation. The second section of the manuscript (f.44a–43b), similar to the first one, was probably used for the same purpose:

> *Hadhā ifkun qadīm. Wa-innahu la-qasamun law ta'lamūna 'aẓīm. Innahu la-qur'ānun karīm[.] Fī kitābin maknūn[.] Lā yamassuhu illā 'l-muṭahharūn[.] Tanzīlun min Rabbi 'l-'ālamīn. Fī samūmin wa-ḥamīm.*
> This is an ancient lie (Qur'anic quotation, part of 46:11). And lo! that verily is a tremendous oath, if ye but knew (56:76)—That (this) is indeed a noble Qur'an (56:77) In a Book kept hidden (56:78) Which none toucheth save the purified (56:79), A revelation from the Lord of the Worlds (56:80). In scorching wind and scalding water (56:42).[14]

Two talismans with the same quotation from 46:11 are kept in the Bahia archives, which have been published by Rolf Reichert, but he did not recognize the Qur'anic source of these words, because their Arabic was phoneticized.[15]

The third and largest section of the Havre manuscript (f.44a–19b) includes several Qur'anic sūras, 87–102, 104–114 (all vocalized), and al-Fātiḥa. The fourth section (f.19a–15b, vocalized) consists of four prayers, including several verses of the Qur'an (2:255, 9:128–129), and one more prayer based on a Qur'anic verse (28:16): *Allāhumma innī ẓalamtu nafsī ẓulman kathīran wa-la yaghfiru 'l-dhunūba illā anta, Fa-ghfir lī maghfiratan min ' indika wa-rḥamnī, innaka anta Ghafūr Raḥīm.* (O Lord! Verily I have wronged my soul with much wrong, and nobody forgives the sins apart from Thee. So forgive me with pardon from Thee and have Mercy on me! Verily Thou art the Forgiving, the Merciful). Unlike the preceding prayers, this one was phoneticized by the same scribe and altered almost beyond recognition: *Allāhumma innī aṣallamutu na f sī* (sic*) yuḍmā kathīra(n) wa-la yanfirhu anta sulmi wa-'l-'ami maghfirata(n) bani'nidaka maka anata Ghafūru Raḥīmu.* This spelling of the Arabic words appears to reflect some features of the African language spoken by the scribe. The absence of any kind of "z" may indicate that his main language was Yoruba which lacks the phoneme /z/. The reading of the Arabic letter "ḍāḍ" as /l/ was common in western and central Sudanic Africa, and that is why we can see *yuḍmā* instead of *ẓulman* in the text.

All four prayers in this section start with the word *'albarika* (blessing) before the basmalah. As suggested by João José Reis, the regular occurrence of this word as an initial formula—unusual for West African Islamic manuscripts—might be a reflection of the Brazilian use of the word *benēão*(Portuguese: blessing [used as a greeting]). The other possibility is a connection with the Yoruba Muslim tradition of *alubarika* found in invocations and described by Patrick Ryan.[16] The prayers end with a fā'ida (f.15b). After f.15a, which was left blank, there follows another series of vocalized prayers and possible incantations (f.14b–12b), including Qur'anic verses (38:54 and a quotation from 61:13) and two different phonetic variants of the taṣliya. Most of them start with a term for "blessing" (non-vocalized *'lbrk* on f.14a and f.13a, *albariqa* with an "alif" on f.12b).

The text on f.14b between the basmalah and taṣliya combines Arabic phrases with two obscure passages: *Fasanakaku yā rabi 'l-'alamīna* (vocalized).*T[a]m[ma]t. Fasalakaku yā rabi 'l-'ālā* (with a final "yā") *mīna. T[a]m[ma]t* "[...] (O Lord of the Worlds. Finished. [...]. O Lord of the Worlds. Finished). The obscure phrases are certainly not Hausa, Fula, Kanuri, or Manden. According to a personal communication from Isaac Ogunbiyi, the obscure passages do not seem to be Yoruba either. One possible interpretation of both passages is phoneticized Arabic (for example, *fa-ṣalli rak'atayn* "and pray in two rak'ahs,") or a kind of *abracadabra* used as an incantation. The quotation from the Qur'an (61:13) on f.13b, *naṣrun min Allāhi wa-fatḥun qarībun wa-bashshiri 'l-mu'minīn* (help from Allah and present victory. Give good tidings (O Muḥammad) to believers) is often found in Islamic amulets. A shorter quotation from the same sūra was described by Reichert.[17] Below this quotation there is a frame with three lines inside: *māk.*(or *ṣāk.*) *Māsalidhu* (vocalized) *Muḥammad*. It seems that this could be the personal name (maybe including a Portuguese Christian name) of the person seeking God's protection. On f.13a, the prayer is written as *allahum*, with a sukūn above the "mīm," *ahadinā nabiyu jā jujuluw*[18] (O God, show us the prophet [?] ...). followed by a taṣliya. The obscure passage *jā jujuluw* may be non-Arabic, although this interpretation is doubtful. Either phoneticized Arabic or a kind of incantation is more plausible.

The third series of prayers (f.11) is separated from the preceding text by one more blank page. On f.11b the whole text following after the basmalah is vocalized and generally legible, but hard to understand: *'uwa Allāhu lla rabū* (with a final "yā"), followed by a nonvocalized "alif"), *ghān* (?) *rubū* (with a final "yā"), *al-mūfun* (or *al-mūqun*, no dot above or below the line), *Allāhi khanidu takhanu.* The beginning of this passage may be a rendering of *huwa Allāhu rabbī* (He is Allah, my Lord) as in the Qur'an (18:38), but the rest cannot be easily explained as a phonetic transformation of this verse.

On f.11a, between the basmalah and *t[a]m[ma]t* [finished], the scribe invoked shaykh 'Abd al-Qādir together with Allah and Muḥammad: *yā-Allāh yā Muḥammad yā shayḥ 'abd k[a]d[i]r* (sic). This invocation seems to indicate that the scribe (and maybe the owner of the book) was a Qadiri. Below *t[a]m[ma]t*, there is a non-Arabic sentence, *'-l th-b-mā gh-f-rā*, probably written in Hausa*: Allah shi ba mu gafara* [God forgive us].[19] The spelling *'Ala,* instead of *Allāh,* is not rare in nineteenth century Hausa manuscripts, especially outside Hausa territories, but also crossreference f.12b where the Arabic preposition *'alā* was written as *ala* with an "alif."

The next pages are blank, except a basmalah on f.10a, which is the last passage written in Arabic-script in the book. The last folios of the manuscript (f.4a–3b) are covered with a few rough lines (almost illegible) and single words in French as well as a date (1840). There follows a page with the French note on the origin of the manuscript and a line below, which is partly written with Greek letters (f.2a in European foliation). Next to this page on f.1b there are a few more lines written in a peculiar manner and a "key" in the Roman alphabet (in the same hand as the note on f.2a) with the corresponding signs under each letter. These lines seem to include an obscene phrase in French and a few French names as well as one Brazilian name, Raymundo José (with the accent mark added to the word) de Mattos. As a matter of fact, the same name is written in Greek on f.2a. This person could have been the Brazilian owner of the manuscript after the rebellion.

There is little evidence that the encoded and Greek lines were written by the previous African owner of the book, although Arabic-Roman digraphia was not totally unknown in Bahia. As mentioned by João Reis, who described this digraphia as "scriptural syncretism," the French consul Marcescheau reported having seen one document written half in Arabic and half in Latin, with the Latin section being a transcription of a passage from the "Song of Songs." This talisman may have been used in a lover's conquest rather than a military maneuver.[20] Almost certainly the book in question was brought to Havre by a Frenchman, but it does not conform to the image of a half-Arabic and half-Latin talisman described by Marc-escheau.

BILINGUAL MANUSCRIPTS IN BAHIA'S PUBLIC ARCHIVES (SALVADOR)

The manuscripts kept in Bahia's public archives, Arquivo Público do Estado da Bahia, have been studied in detail by Reichert and Monteil.[21] A more theoretical approach to the written-oral interface in Bahia was taken by Jack Goody, although he did not make a systematic analysis of the manuscripts.[22]

Some Islamic writings in Bahia were apparently based on the oral transmission of the surviving tradition. The scribes who produced them were more or less familiar with Arabic script, but their knowledge of Arabic was rudimentary. The prayers and personal names (including the name of Allah) were written as they were pronounced, which makes such texts very interesting from the linguistic point of view. On the other hand, the style and orthography of some manuscripts studied by Reichert and Monteil indicate that their authors or scribes had deeper knowledge of Arabic. They had memorized many sūras, if not the whole Qur'an, and wrote them down with very few or no mistakes. A few of these people, who could be rightfully described as Islamic scholars, seemed to possess full copies of the Qur'an made in Brazil or brought from Africa.

In 1999 João Reis kindly sent me a compact disk (CD) containing reproductions of the Islamic manuscripts from the Bahian archives. One of the manuscripts turned out to be bilingual, written mainly in Hausa with some phrases in Arabic.[23] This is a private letter to Malam Sani written by a certain Abdul Qādiri. The author informs his correspondent that his wife Rakiyatu gave birth to Fatsumata and then asks for condolences or for a charm. The document was confiscated from Francisco Lisboa in 1844, a few years after the Malê uprising. The preliminary interpretation of the letter and a Portuguese translation based on my reading of the CD were published with due reference by João Reis.[24] This is the first manuscript with a significant non-Arabic text and also the first nonreligious text so far identified among the Bahian Muslim papers. There is no evidence that the letter was the only one of its kind or written on request, so it may be assumed that other similar documents were produced in Bahia in the nineteenth century. The corrected transliteration and suggested reading of the document are as follows:

> *'Alubarka bismillāhi 'l-raḥmāni 'l-raḥīmi. Ṣṣalā 'llāhu 'alā man lā 'l-nabiyyu ba'dahū. Mma llī Thānnī innī almājirī 'Abdu 'l-Qādiri. In na-'a-gīsha-ku. Mma llī Thānī inī almājirī 'Abdu 'l-Qādiri. In na-rokō gāfara domin 'Alla h domin Annabi Mmuḥamudun Rasūlu 'llāhi ṣṣalā 'llāhu 'alayhi salāmma. Ka-jī* (with a final "alif") *Mali Thānī, Mal* (with a sukūn above the "lām") *matanā Rakiyyatu in na-'a-gīsha-ku. Kā jī* (with a final "alif") *Mali Thānī matanā ta-khaifu sūnā diyā nata Faṭṭumāta. Mali Thānnī 'a-sharī nā dommin 'Alla domin Annabi yō ta-mūtu si di y[ē]rō* (or: *si di y[ā]rō*). *In na-rokō 'a-sharī nā. Wa 'l-ḥamdu lillāhi Rabbi 'l-'alamīn* (nonvocalized). *In na-ro[kō] Llāhammu Barubaru. In na-'a-gīsha-ku 'Abdu' llāhi Barubē ru. Wa man kataba ismuhū 'ā 'Abdu 'l-Qādirri. T[a]m[ma]t[.] Yā ḥa[...]* (crossed) *Nā 'aiko dē wanī 'abī shanā 'a-[b]ā mma llī minā.*

> *Albarka. Bismillahi 'l-raḥmani 'l-raḥim. Ṣalla 'llahu 'ala man la nabiyya ba'dahu. Malam Sani, inni (?) almajiri Abdul* Qādiri, *ina gaishe ku. Malam Sani, inni(?) almajiri Abdul* Qādiri, *ina roko[n] gafara domin Allah domin Annabi Muhammadu Rasūlu 'llāh ṣallā 'llāhu 'alayhi wa-sallim. Ka ji, Malam Sani, Mal[am], matana Rakiyyatu na gaishe ku. Ka ji, Malam Sani, matanā ta haifu; suna[n] iyā nata Fatsumata. Malam Sani, a share na* (or: *asirina*) *domin Allah domin Annabi. Yau ta mutu shi iya* (or: *shi dai yaro*). *Ina roko a share na* (or *asirina*). *Wa-'l-hamdu li-llahi Rabbi 'l-'alamin. Ina ro[ko] Llahammu. Barubaru (Barbeiro?) na gaishe ku, Abdullahi Baruberu(Barbeiro?). Wa man kataba ismuhu a Abdul Qādiri. Tammat. Na aiko da wani abi[n]shana a [b]a malamina.*

Even though some passages remain obscure, the Hausa/Arabic text is generally understandable, so this translates into English as:

> Blessing. In the name of Allah, the Beneficent, the Merciful. May God bless [Muḥammad] after whom there is no other prophet. Malam Sani, I am (?) *Abdul Qādiri*, a student, I am greeting you. Malam Sani, I am (?) *Abdul Qādiri*, a student, I am asking pardon for God's sake, for the sake of the Prophet Muḥammad, the Messenger of God, may God bless and greet him. Hear, Malam Sani, Malam, my wife Rakiyyatu is greeting you. Hear, Malam Sani, my wife gave birth. Her daughter's

> name [was] Fatsumata. Malam Sani, I am asking for condolences (or, I am asking for my charm) for God's sake, for the Prophet's sake. She died today, the child (or, the daughter). I am asking for condolences (or, I am asking for my charm). And praise be to God, Lord of the worlds. I am praying to God, Barubaru is greeting you, Abdullahi Baruberu (or, I am asking for Abdullahi Baruberu). I am greeting you, o man (God's slave), [I am asking for] (Baruberu). The name of the person who wrote [this letter] is *Abdul Qādiri.* Finished. I sent some drinks to[give] my teacher (or, my Malam)."[25]

The author of the letter wrote in a western dialect of Hausa. Some grammatical features show that he was not a native speaker. It is not surprising, as the document was confiscated from Franscisco Lisboa who was a Nupe. It is not clear whether he was the author of the letter. João Reis suggested that Malam Sani could be identified with Luís Sanim, also a Nupe.[26]

Not unlike the prayers in the Havre manuscript, the letter starts with an initial blessing (*albarka*). In modern Hausa this word would not normally be found at the beginning of a letter. In his message to me João Reis suggested that it might be a local influence, connected with the use of Portuguese *benēão* (blessing) as a greeting. Not excluding the possible influence of Portuguese, I am inclined to think that the new use of *albarka* (or: *alibarika*, *alubarika*) in Bahia was mainly inspired by the Muslim Yoruba tradition mentioned before.

As concerns the Hausa word(s) written as *'a–sharī na*, it may be a form of the verb *share* (to sweep), but in a particular context, Abraham gives it as *dangi sun share makoki* (relations called to offer condolences).[27] The greeting in this context is in fact *gaisuwar mutuwa* (condolence on a death). At the same time the presence of *na* (my), commonly used as a possessive marker with a noun, may indicate that *'asharī* should be interpreted as a single word, most probably *asiri* (secret; magic charm, or remedy),[28] This may be a reference to a written amulet known in both West Africa and Bahia and possibly mentioned as "(Allahumma) barubaru" in the same letter.

Two more documents from Bahia are undoubtedly bilingual and may be connected with the uprising of 1835. Unfortunately, the original of one of them is missing, so only the photo published by Reichert is examined here. Reichert tried to interpret this nonvocalized text as Arabic, but could not translate some of the words:

> In the name of Allah, the Beneficent, the Merciful. Blessings of Allah be upon [Muḥammad] after whom there is no

> other prophet. In the name of Allah. Praise be to Allah... The door...the door and the key (?)...The Beneficent (seven times). If Allah wills, Exalted is He.[29]

Vincent Monteil, who took an interest in this document before Reichert, also tried to interpret it as the Arabic *bāb sirri-k* (porte du ton secret), but could not decipher the whole text.[30]

Reichert was the first to suggest that the central part of the document could be a message. Indeed, if the document is interpreted as bilingual, the obscure section becomes more understandable: *M.dhā d.bū m.rī d.bū bāb. s.r.kī s.y. 'l bāb. w.d. m.f (?)t.j. s.y.w.d. n.fād.*, which may be read as *Maza dubu mari dubu. Babu sarki sai Allah. Babu wada [...] sai wada na fadi* (One thousand men, one thousand slaps. There is no god except Allah. There is no way of...only as I say.).[31] The phoneticized spelling *'ala* for Allah has already been mentioned. It is worth mentioning that in the book published by Nina Rodrigues there is a photo of an entrance in Salvador with the Yoruba inscription "KOSI OBÁ KAN AFI OLORUN." This phrase has the same meaning as *babu sarki sai Allah* in Hausa. Speaking about the Yoruba text on the photo, Haidar Abu Talib has already indicated that it was a translation of the standard Islamic formula *lā ilāha illā Allāh* (there is no god except Allah).[32] As concerns the passage written as *m.f (?)t.j.*, it is almost surely non-Arabic as well. One of the letters has no diacritical dots and may be read differently. The first syllable could be interpreted as Hausa *mu* (we) with a verb, so would translate as "there is no way we [...], only [to do] what I said."

The second Bahian manuscript with a similar Hausa text was not mentioned by Reichert.[33] In this manuscript, the Hausa section reads as follows: *M.dhā d.bū m.ri d.bū bāb. s.r.kī s.y. '.lā bā. [b.] w.t. m.gh. [n.] s.y.w.d. (?) n.f.d.*, that is, *Maza dubu mari dubu. Babu sarki sai Allah. Ba[bu] wata maga[na] sai wada (?) na fadi.* The last sentence could mean "there is nothing to say (or: to do) besides what I said." Most probably, the Hausa sections of both amulets were identical, but the exact text and meaning of the last sentence remains obscure.

Several other manuscripts from the Bahia archives probably contain non-Arabic passages as well. One of the documents includes the first sūra of the Qur'an and several frames with one or more words inside them. One of them includes a Portuguese personal name, Francisco (*faranthīthiku*), written twice.[34] No African language except Hausa has been identified. One of the texts seems to include a short passage in Fula. According to Francis Castelnau, the Fulani in Bahia were all literate and exerted much influence on local Blacks.[35]

Besides the documents mentioned above, Reichert found one more undeciphered text written in Arabic script in the Bahia archives.[36] Another slightly different copy of the same work was reproduced by Rodrigues, who had the manuscript in his private collection.[37] It is not clear where the manuscript is today. The text was identified as non-Arabic by the experts addressed by both scholars. As a matter of fact, this document represents a series of conjurings, a kind of *abracadabra,* with a few Arabic words. In the Falke collection in the Melville J. Herskovits Africana Library, Northwestern University, there is an identical text as well as a West African treatise on the possible application of these magic phrases. So this text may be described as neither Arabic nor non-Arabic.

ARABIC-SCRIPT BOOKS OF THE AFRICAN MUSLIM DIASPORA IN RIO DE JANEIRO

Besides the papers related to the 1835 rebellion in Bahia, there are a small number of Arabic-script Brazilian documents at the Instituto Histórico e Geográfico Brasileiro (Historical and Geographical Institute) in Rio de Janeiro. These include a small prayer book from Bahia[38] containing 102 pages (7.4 x 5 cm, so it could be also used as an amulet), and a larger book confiscated by the police in Rio Grande do Sul several years after the uprising of 1835.[39] The composition of both documents is similar to that of the book in the Havre collection.

On the last pages of the prayer book (marked 1 to 4) there is a note in Portuguese concerning the origin of this manuscript and some remarks on the writings used by the insurgents in Bahia. According to the note, this small book, described as *patiguá* or *patuá*, was found on the neck of an African killed during the uprising on 25 January 1835 and then presented to the collector who donated it to the Institute in 1839. The text written in Arabic script starts with an incomplete copy of the famous sūra "Yā Sīn" (36:1–60). The European pagination (61/74 followed by 42/73) may indicate that the whole sūra was initially copied by the scribe. The second part of the book (five pages) includes several verses from the sūra "al-Baqara" (2:127–129, 200–201), probably used as prayers.

The main third part (fifty-six pages) represents another series of quotations from the Qur'an. The beginning of this section is practically identical to the second part of the book (part of 2:127, 2:128–129, part of 2:200, 2:201, all vocalized). There follow more quotations from different sūras (2–7, 10, 14, 16, 18, 20–21, 23, 25, 28, 32–35, 38, 40–41, 44, 50, 59–60, and 66). Almost all these quotations start with, or include, the Arabic *rabbanā* (our Lord) and were apparently selected to be used as invocations. The main section of the manuscript ends with the colophon where a famous personal name is mentioned (f.15a): *katabahu Sulayman* (sic) *ibn Dawūd* (Sulaymān ibn Dā'ūd wrote it). In this case it is most probably the name of the presumed author of the sentences above, rather than the name of the scribe.

The last part of the book (eight pages, numbered from 5 to 12) includes several short texts (prayers or incantations). The main text on page 12, vocalized and written in the same hand as the main part of the manuscript, may be non-Arabic, phoneticized Arabic or an *abracadabra*-like incantation: *Bismi 'llāhi 'l-raḥmāni 'l-raḥīmi./ Fā sidhi kara kīki* (with an isolated vertical stroke or the letter "alif" after the words / *bābu tagar* (or: *taqar*) *makīki / dhaki qqaⁿmā makīki*, and with an isolated vertical stroke or the letter "alif" after the words / *dhaki in shā'a 'llāhu / ya-Rabbi t[a]m[ma]t).* The obscure passage might be a phoneticized quotation from the Qur'an (2:200); however, this interpretation is only tentative, even if we assume that the scribe did not possess a written copy of the verse and nearly forgot it. If the text was written in an African language, it remains unrecognizable.

The same doubts arise when one tries to interpret the text on the next page (11): *Bismi 'llāhi 'l-raḥmāni 'l-raḥīmi. / Bismi 'llāhi kaw lakawi/ masadaⁿ kau baytū* (with a final "alif" and a vertical stroke after it) / *sasulu fakulu saṣulu / 'inasaṣulu batakusihum / lam wadam bidayka.* On the next pages (10–7) there are some more prayers written in phoneticized Arabic, followed by an exact Qur'anic quotation (9:128) on page 6, and possibly some Arabic poetry on page 5. The last four pages were initially left blank and then used by the collector for a note in Portuguese about the origin of the manuscript.

The second book at the Instituto Histórico e Geográfico Brasileiro was donated to the institute in 1855 and described in the note as "a manuscript in strange letters found in a club of the Mina negroes in the capital of Rio Grande do Sul." The first pages of the book are legible, but heavily damaged; they were being prepared for restoration when I consulted the manuscript. The main section of the book includes more than two parts (*juz'*) of the Qur'an (sūras 62–65 and 67–114). This section ends with a colophon with the name of the scribe (nonvocalized): *wa-mā* (sic) *kataba ibn Ismay'īl ibn A'bd lillahi* (and [the person] who wrote [it] was ibn Ismā'īl ibn 'Abd Allāh). Then follow three series of prayers with Qur'anic quotations and "Yā Sīn" (sūra 36). At the end of the text of "Yā Sīn" there is a non-Arabic marginal gloss which is easily recognizable as Hausa: *Wanā duwā muna-rokō domī-'Ala*, that is, *wannan du'a muna roqo domin*

Allah ([With] this [invocatory] prayer we are praying for God's sake). No glosses in other African languages have been found in the book.

WRITTEN LANGUAGES OF AFRICAN ISLAM IN BRAZIL

Today there are few surviving books of the African Muslim diaspora in Brazil, but their study may shed some light on the peculiarities of the African Muslim book culture in Brazil. All of them have a similar structure: the beginning of the text is Arabic, usually consisting of a few prayers or Qur'anic quotations; then follows a large Qur'anic section, containing several short sūras or, as in the small prayer book, selected verses; the third section is made of prayers with extensive Qur'anic quotations; and followed by another set of prayers, usually combining Arabic and an African language or some kind of magic incantation. It is noteworthy that there were some specific elements in the local written tradition that are still to be explored. According to the wordlists collected by Castelnau, the word "book" was translated by his Bahian informants as *alcoran* into both Hausa and Fula (in both precolonial and modern Fula, *deftere*; in Hausa *littafi*), while "small book" was translated as *cundi* (Hausa) or *cunde* (Fula).[40] In modern Hausa, *kundi* is in fact a scholar's "book of recipes," a bundle of small sheets of paper with notes of the components of various charms, potions, and so forth. The *kundi* can be easily transported from one place to another, so it is not impossible that some of them could have been brought to Brazil from the African coast.

What is even more interesting, such "recipes" in West Africa are mostly written in Arabic, but the explanations are sometimes given in one or more African languages. Even the texts written in Arabic would often include local names of plants, animals, or illnesses in Hausa, Fula, and other languages. As the tradition apparently continued in Bahia, the *kundi* could include both African and Brazilian references in more than one language.

After the insurrection in Bahia the Malê writings were criminalized. The person who donated the small prayer book to the Historical and Geographical Institute in Rio de Janeiro wrote in his note (f.1a) about these manuscripts that, "Many similar, and bigger, books were found, as well as separate papers that we attributed to be their proclamations.... I do not know what was the end of the rest of the books."

All three books, which survived the 1835 rebellion and subsequent persecutions in Brazil, are difficult to classify as "*alcoran*" (in Castelnau's terms) or *kundi*. On the one hand, all of them include quite a few Qur'anic sūras and contain no charms with explanations similar to those found in West Africa. On the other hand, their dimensions and the presence of non-Arabic passages may indicate that they would be described as *kundi* by their scribes and owners. If this assumption is correct, larger books are still to be sought out, at least those that could have been used by Bahian Muslims in the early twentieth century.

While it was apparently difficult, if not impossible, to produce new books in Arabic script after 1835, less visible texts were still being written. One of them was the bilingual letter confiscated in 1844. Some written practices managed to survive until the early twentieth century, although they were mainly confined to the making of talismans like those collected by Rodrigues. The oral transmission of the most important Qur'anic verses also continued for almost a century after the Muslim uprising of 1835, as illustrated by the songs published by Querino.[41] These songs, beginning with the words *Ali-ramudo lilāi*[42] and *Cula-ús Bira binance*, are in fact two sūras from the Qur'an (1 and 114).

Querino described an Islamic ritual, *sala* (prayer), where the participants still used some Hausa words, mostly borrowed from Arabic and common in the life of Hausa Muslims today: *barica-da subá* or *barka da asuba* (good morning), *amuré* or *amre* (marriage in western Hausa), *maēalasi or masallaci* (mosque), and *sadáca do Alamabi or sadaka don Annabi* (a gift for the Prophet's sake).[43] It is not clear whether any of the African Muslims met by Querino could still write or read Arabic script. There is no doubt that they mainly wrote in Roman script if they were literate, and soon became practically monolingual, speaking Portuguese and some Nagō (Yoruba) rather than Hausa.

The extensive use of Hausa in the Islamic ritual and Arabic-script writing in Bahia (besides Arabic) cannot be explained by the number of first-language speakers, as they were apparently not comparable to the number of those who spoke various Nagō (Yoruba) dialects; however, the prestige of the Hausa as true Muslims was certainly higher than that of the Nagō. Castelnau made the following remark on the Bahian Hausa, including some Africans who were brought from Borno and Adamawa: "En général, ces noirs sont bien supérieurs, sous le rapport du développement intellectuel, aux nègres de la cōte."[44] This "comparative assessment of intellectual development" might be connected with the fact that many Hausa in Bahia were literate.

Multilingual literacy did not completely disappear with the decay of African Islam in Brazil. The use of Yoruba (in Roman script and in modern Nigerian orthography) is visible in Bahia now, while Arabic has resurfaced in the small Muslim community of Salvador and even decorates a Catholic church, but the new pattern of multilingual literacy and visual signs is totally different from that of the nineteenth century. Arabic, the main written language besides Portuguese, seemed to be used largely for magic and religious purposes. It was not a spoken language, although practically all Brazilian Muslims of African descent must have learned a few Arabic prayers and Qur'anic verses. As concerns other languages written in Arabic script, Hausa was second to Arabic (undoubtedly with a great lag). Even though Yoruba was the main spoken language of West African Muslims in Brazil, the role of this language in written texts was insignificant, except the peculiar use of the word *albarika* (blessing). The use of any other African languages or Portuguese in Arabic script was minimal or nonexistent.[45] The hierarchy of written languages as well as "restricted literacy," as described by Jack Goody in his studies of literacy in traditional societies, are strikingly similar to what is found in Wala, Gonja, and Dagomba in what is today's northern Ghana during the nineteenth and early twentieth centuries.

Notes

1. Maureen Warner-Lewis, *Trinidad Yoruba: From Mother Tongue to Memory* (Tuscaloosa, 1996), 27.
2. Yacine Daddi Addoun and Paul E. Lovejoy, "Muhammad Kaba Saghanughu and the Muslim Community of Jamaica," in *Slavery on the Frontiers of Islam*, ed. Paul E. Lovejoy (Princeton, 2004), 199–218.
3. Ibid.
4. C. Campbell, "Mohammedu Sisei of Gambia and Trinidad, c. 1788–1838," *African Studies Association of the West Indies Bulletin* 7 (1974), 34.
5. M. de Drumond, "Lettres sur l'Afrique ancienne et moderne adressées a M. le Rédacteur du Journal des Voyages," *Journal des Voyages* 32 (1826), 305.
6. Francis de Castelnau, *Renseignements sur l'Afrique Centrale et sur une nation d'hommes à queue qui s'y trouverait, d'après le rapport des nègres du Soudan, esclaves à Bahia* (Paris, 1851), 5.
7. R. N. Rodrigues, *Os Africanos no Brasil* (São Paulo, 1932).
8. The scholars and institutions that helped me to find and understand the sources mentioned below are too many to cite individually, but I am grateful to all of them. I owe special gratitude to Sonia Colpart, Stuart Ó Seanóir, and João José Reis, as no sources could have been studied without their support. I am indebted to the Trinity College Library, Dublin; Bibliothèque Municipale du Havre; Arquivo do Estado da Bahia, Salvador; and the Instituto Histórico e Geográfico Brasileiro, Rio de Janeiro, for providing microfilms or permission to consult their manuscripts. I am particularly thankful to John

Hunwick who has encouraged my work since 1997. A shorter Portuguese version of this paper has already been published: "Escritos multilíngües em caracteres árabes: novas fontes de Trinidad e Brasil no século XIX," *Afro-Ásia* 31 (2004), 297–326.

9. "Arabic MS written by Private Philip Finlay, 1817," TCD MS 2683, Trinity College Library, Dublin.
10. G. Roper, ed., *World Survey of Islamic Manuscripts* (London, 1993), 2:62–63.
11. Campbell, "Mohammedu Sisei," 29–38.
12. A. D. Austin, *African Muslims in Antebellum America: Transatlantic Stories and Spiritual Struggles* (New York and London, 1997), 24, 39.
13. "Livre trouvé dans la poche d'un noir Africain mort lors de l'insurrection qui éclata dans la nuit du 25 Janvier 1835 à Bahia," MS 556, Bibliothèque Municipale du Havre.
14. The English translation quoted here was made by Pickthal.
15. Nos. 20 and 26. Maēo 2848, Lúcio Nagō, both documents in Rolf Reichert, *Os Documentos Árabes do Arquivo do Estado da Bahia* (Salvador, 1970).
16. P. J. Ryan, *Imale: Yoruba Participation in the Muslim Tradition: A Study of Clerical Piety* (Missoula, 1977), 188.
17. No. 29, in Reichert, *Os Documentos Árabes.*
18. Or, *jā jujulū*, with a sukūn above the final "wāw."
19. An "alif" was used to mark the vowel-length in the pronoun *mū* (us).
20. J. J. Reis, *Slave Rebellion in Brazil* (Baltimore and London, 1993), 103.
21. V. Monteil, "Analyse de 25 documents arabes des Malés de Bahia (1835)," *Bulletin de l'Institut Fondamental d'Afrique Noire,* série B, 29 (1967), 88–98; and Reichert, *Os Documentos Árabes.*
22. J. Goody, "Writing, Religion, and Revolt in Bahia," *Visible Language* 20 (1986), 318–43.
23. Francisco Lisbōa, Maēo 2850, Arquivo Público do Estado da Bahia [hereafter APEB].
24. J. J. Reis, *Rebelião Escrava no Brasil. A História do Levante dos Malês em 1835* (São Paulo, 2003), 222–24.
25. Ibid.
26. Reis, *Rebelião Escrava no Brasil*, 223.
27. R. C. Abraham, *Dictionary of the Hausa Language* (London, 1962), 647.
28. Cf. also the Yoruba form *aṣiri* (secret), which is pronounced as /ashiri/.
29. No. 13, in Reichert, *Os Documentos Árabes.*
30. Monteil, Analyse de 25 documents arabes, 94.
31. Ibid.
32. H. Abu Talib, "Exame das circunstãncias que motivaram as revoltas dos Malês," http://www.islamemlinha.com/index.php?option=com_content&task=view&id=390 [accessed April 16, 2008].

33. Maēo 2848, Lubê, APEB.
34. No. 8, in Reichert, *Os Documentos Árabes*.
35. Castelnau, *Renseignements*, 9: "Ils exercent, même en captivité, beaucoup d'influence sur les nègres...Tous savent lire et écrire: ce sont des musulmans intolérants et vindicatifs."
36. No. 30, in Reichert, *Os Documentos Árabes;* and Francisco Lisbōa, Maēo 2850, APEB.
37. Rodrigues, *Os Africanos no Brasil*, 99.
38. "Livrinho male." For more information on this book, see Reis, *Rebelião Escrava no Brasil*, 197–205.
39. "Livro manuscrito c/caracteres arábicos," Instituto Histórico e Geográfico Brasileiro, Rio de Janeiro.
40. Castelnau, *Renseignements*, 52.
41. Manuel Querino and Raul Giovanni da Motta Lody, *Costumes africanos no Brasil* (Recife, 1988), 68.
42. Described as "corresponding to the Paternoster."
43. Querino, *Costumes Africanos*, 67.
44. Castelnau, *Renseignements*, 8–9.
45. After this chapter was prepared for publication, more marginal glosses in Hausa and a yet unknown West African language (Soninke?) have been found in Brazilian Muslim manuscripts. The latter, now in a private Brazilian collection, are especially worth further research.

Chapter 14

RELIGIOUS CONSTANCY AND COMPROMISE AMONG NINETEENTH CENTURY CARIBBEAN-BASED AFRICAN MUSLIMS

Maureen Warner–Lewis

BACKGROUND TO THE ISLAMIC PRESENCE IN THE CARIBBEAN

Islam came to the Caribbean largely by way of Africans who were adherents of that religion and who were transported as slaves or ex-slaves to the plantations and mines of the Americas. Such Africans generally came directly from West Africa, where Islam had penetrated the sub-Saharan Futa Jallon plateau during the late eleventh century by way of Berber merchants from the Maghrib dynasties on the Mediterranean shores south of Gibraltar. From the Futa Jallon, it gradually spread eastward with the Berbers who plied several trans-Saharan trade routes transferring horses, salt, silks, brocades, and beads from North Africa in exchange for gold, slaves, ivory, kola, gum, and ostrich feathers from the sub-Saharan Niger River kingdoms such as Ghana, Mali, and Songhay (or Songhai) after the thirteenth century.

Africans drawn from the coasts of Upper Guinea, the westernmost bulge of northwest Africa, as well as from the Congo, were among those brought into Iberia in the initial phase of the African-European slave trade. From the close of the fifteenth century they formed a noticeable segment of the urban populations in Lisbon and Seville, for instance, where their manual services in the domestic, monastic, and public sectors were significant.[1] It was from this cohort, as well as from among the Moors and Moriscos (Christianized Moors) reduced to slavery in Iberia after the final "re-conquest" of the southern half of the peninsula in early 1492, that a minority of blacks came to figure in the Portuguese and Spanish penetration of the Americas.[2] Some of these Africans would have been familiar with Islam either from their Upper Guinea homeland or from their contact with Moors in Iberia; however, intensive settlement of Africans in the Caribbean did not take place in the initial centuries of Spanish colonization. Spanish attention mainly focused on mineral extraction, and this proved profitable on the American mainland rather than on the Caribbean islands, which were either left abandoned or, as in the case of the Greater Antillean territories of Cuba, Puerto Rico, Hispaniola, and Jamaica, given over to livestock farming.

Once the Portuguese in the late sixteenth century, followed by the Dutch, British, and French as from the early seventeenth century, began to turn their colonization ventures toward plantation monoculture, their need for large manpower supplies soared. Since the majority of enslaved persons brought to the Caribbean derived from areas of Africa that were not contacted by Arabic and Islamized merchants and missionaries, the Muslim presence in the Caribbean was not particularly high. Among the more significant sources of Caribbean slaves was West Central Africa, particularly Angola and the Congo River basin and its hinterland. Another important source was the Niger River delta on the Bight of Biafra and its interior. Further west was Dahomey or the Slave Coast and its hinterland; further westward were the Gold and Ivory Coasts; and even further west was the Upper Guinea Coast, around the regions of the Gambia, Sierra Leone, Senegal, and Mali. This coastal hinterland lay in the area where Islam had long penetrated. Although much of the peasantry there still followed traditional ethnic religions based on ancestor veneration and animistic beliefs, Islam had filtered down from the political and trade leaders to have become the religion of urban settlements between the sixteenth and nineteenth centuries when the slave trade was at its height.[3] During the late eighteenth and nineteenth centuries militant jihadist movements had also brought Islam across the east-west savanna belt of West Africa. Thus, apart from the Mandingo (or Mande or Mali) peoples of the Upper Guinea Coast, the Muslim religion had also been embraced by ethnic groups such as the Dyula, the Fula (or Fulani or Peul), and the Hausa to the east of the Mandingo.

In both Caribbean oral and scribal sources, Muslims are referenced by several terms: Mandingo, Fula or Fulaman, Mussulman, Mahometan, and even Turk! Of these, the association of the Mandingo with Islam was so pronounced that, in several parts of the Caribbean, the nomenclature "Mandingo" came to designate, not an ethnic group, but rather Muslim religious affiliation. A good example of this broad-spectrum usage of the term is to be read in a nineteenth-century novel written by an Englishman resident in Trinidad: "Sayeb was a Mandingo of the tribe called *Foulahs*; he had been captured in war, and hurried down to the mouth of the Senegal, and then embarked on board of a slaver."[4] Another instance occurs in the thumbnail sketch of Mass [Master] Campbell, an old African member of the New Carmel congregation in Westmoreland, Jamaica, written around 1855 by Joseph Kummer, a Moravian minister. Campbell claimed to have been "a Mandingo negro," whose "African name was Abubuckar. His father's name was Malanta. He was a Prince. His mother's name was Aishutta." In fact, Aishutta is a version of the Arabic name, 'Ā'ishat, while Malanta is a Hausa term meaning "learned."[5] Campbell "spoke, wrote and read the Arabic language, and also the language of his own country, and was acquainted with the Mohomedan religion." He had been captured and enslaved when, as a boy "in the bushes killing birds, in his own country, [he] was taken up and stolen by a Papaw Negro, and carried thro' the Papaw country and the Eboe country to the sea."[6] If Abubukar was correct about the nationalities with whom he came in contact after being ambushed, then he was not in reality a Mandingo, since that ethnic group lived far to the west and north of Popo and Igbo countries in the savanna and sahel, whereas the Popo and Igbo were coastal peoples. Furthermore, the Popo of the Slave Coast lived quite far from the Igbo, whose homeland lies mainly to the east of the Niger River estuary. If he came from the Islamized savanna lands and did come into contact with either Popo or Igbo, then he was likely to have been Fula or Hausa or Mossi or Nupe, among several possible ethnic groups.[7] The recognizably Hausa form of his father's name suggests that he was in fact Hausa, rather than Mandingo

Further blurring of labels occurs in Guyana, where the somewhat derogatory term for "Muslim," even if an Asian descendant, was, and still is, "Fula-man."[8] This forging of a supra-ethnic identity through the transnational religious ideology of Islam was also evident in the twentieth century assertion by a Hausa descendant in Trinidad that Fula and Hausa were the same nation,[9] the term "nation" having been coterminous with the term "ethnicity" in the parlance of nineteenth-century Africans in the

Caribbean. "Papa" appears as another term, at least in Jamaica, which embraced some West African savanna peoples, as evidenced in the portrait of a servant initially identified as a Papau (Papa/Popo), but who, it emerges, was from Hausaland.[10]

PRAYER RITUAL AND LITERACY AS INDICATORS OF ISLAMIC IDENTITY

By the eighteenth and nineteenth centuries Europeans began to be alert to the religious life and practices of slaves. As such, occasional references to Islamic devotion are recorded in Caribbean literature. In 1777 Christian Oldendorp, a German Moravian missionary stationed in the Danish Antilles (today's Virgin Islands), mentions having encountered "Mandinga, Kanga, and Mangree from the Senegambia region," and although he did not refer to their religion or religions, he had received ample oral testimony from these sources that these neighboring peoples "conduct[ed] almost constant warfare among themselves. One nation attacks another for the sole purpose of capturing people and selling them as slaves to the Whites."[11] The Kanga merchants traded slaves, tiger skins, and elephant tusks to the English and French along the Gambia and Senegal Rivers in exchange for guns, powder, lead, iron beads, and rum. These men were "able to do arithmetic and to write."[12] Since the technology of writing had been introduced in West Africa through the medium of Islam, it is reasonable to conclude that these traders were Muslim.

At the other end of the Caribbean Basin, John Stedman, writing of Suriname, noted that he had heard "the Alcoran" recited by a black "from recollection only."[13] In 1793 Bryan Edwards in Jamaica also mentioned a short acquaintance with a "Mandingo servant, who could write with great beauty and exactness, the Arabic alphabet, and some passages from the Alcoran." Edwards, however, was deprived of the opportunity to interact further with this Muslim and more properly gauge his learning as he died soon after he came into Edwards' possession. The planter however still owned "[a]n old and faithful Mandingo servant, who stands at my elbow while I write this." He had been enslaved at a young age and was therefore not as conversant with the Muslim religion as the man who had died. As a boy, the former "had been sent by his father to visit a distant relation in a country wherein the Portuguese had a settlement, a fray happened in the village in which he resided." Many villagers had been killed and others taken prisoner. He himself had been put aboard a river canoe and sold to the captain of the ship that brought him to Jamaica. With respect to his native customs, he knew that circumcision was practiced, as he himself had undergone the operation.[14] He recalled that Friday was a day of "strict fasting," and remembered "the morning and evening prayer which his father taught him" to proclaim in an "audible and shrill tone."[15] Among the prayers was a sentence from the Qu'ran, *Lā 'illāha, 'illalāh*, which forms the "first pillar" of Islam, the affirmation "Nothing deserves to be worshipped but Allah/God." He also associated this prayer with "the first appearance of the new moon," either himself or Edwards conflating the regulation daily prayers with the beginning of *Eīd*, which was announced at the sighting of the new moon in the month of *Muḥaram.*

Edwards took the opportunity to comment on the superior air of "a few" of the Muslims among the slave cohorts, due to the advantage derived from their "being able to read and write." Edwards further elaborated that the Muslims displayed "such gentleness of disposition and demeanour, as would seem the result of early education and discipline." On the other hand, they seemed to him to be more disposed to theft than any of the other African ethnic groups. Another negative opinion of "the Mandingo nation" came from the narrative voice of a mid-nineteenth century novel by an Irish woman, Mrs. William Noy Wilkins, who had grown up in Trinidad. In that work the Mandingo were characterized as "a sly, cowardly, treacherous race, made ten times worse by being reduced to slavery."[16]

An approving portrayal of a Muslim is, however, presented by a minor fictional character, Sayeb(e), in E. L. Joseph's early nineteenth century novel *Walter Arundell.* Like several of the other Muslims in Caribbean literature, his literacy is fore grounded as part of that positive picture: he "could himself read a little Arabic, and was, therefore, not unacquainted with the advantage of letters," so much so that, perhaps rather fancifully, his young British ward's "good education" was attributed to Sayeb's formal training.[17] He was also devout in saying his "copious prayers." With "mellow voice," he "chanted his evening prayer to the God of Mahomet," beginning with "Allahoo". This was the *maghrib*, the sunset prayer. "The tones of his devotion had a solemn effect even on those who knew not one word of that most magnificent language, Arabic." But it is really his moral stature, which is made the lynchpin of his character, and by several noble actions he wins a "handsome gratuity for his services" from the commander of a British man-o'-war that he helped pilot, as also "a liberal subscription…for his benefit, in which most of the seamen joined…"[18]

If the narrator in this novel was impressed by an African savant, such praise is also to be detected in the presentation of a Jamaica-based African by Richard Madden, an Anglo-Irish surgeon who had been appointed a stipendiary magistrate in Jamaica in 1833.[19] Anna Moosa, whose father had been "one of the lords in the Carsoe nation" had come to be called Benjamin Cochrane in Jamaica.[20] Evidently coastal villagers had plundered his inland village and he had been among those taken prisoner and sold into slavery.[21] By the time Madden got to know him, he was "a free negro who practised with no little success as a doctor in Kingston." He was in the habit of visiting Madden on Sundays to give him "information about the medical plants and popular medicine of the country; and a more intelligent and respectable person, in every sense of the word, I do not know." He would come to visit, driven "in his own gig attended by his servant." In his native Mandingo country, he had preferred observation of botany to Qu'ranic scholarship; over a long period he had noticed what plants did harm to the cattle, and how they did them harm. He noticed what herbs they were fond of when they were sick, and he tried a great many of the good herbs for a long time, till he found which did most good to sick people. In Jamaica, his skill was acknowledged by European physicians, so much so that Cochrane himself "wished to become a member of the College of Physicians" in London, and Madden, "knowing no reason why a negro should not be admitted, if duly qualified...undertook to speak to one of the officers, and ascertain if there would be any opposition to his presentation as a candidate for examination..."[22] It seems, however, that Madden did not accomplish this mission during his short stay in England.

MUSLIM-CHRISTIAN ENCOUNTERS

Muslim religious attitudes and beliefs presented real challenges to Christian evangelists who were concerned with the spiritual life of the enslaved. The missionaries were glad for opportunities to engage with another monotheistic creed, although it differed from the practices and ideas the Christians espoused. By the mid-nineteenth century, John Buchner, a Moravian in Jamaica, commented that some of the slaves "were Mahomedans, who had learned to say their prayers in Arabic, but these were not numerous; by far the greater part adhered to their heathenish practices, such as the sacrifice of fowls, and other offerings at the grave of departed friends..."[23] The Baptist pastor James Phillippo also mentioned that some of Jamaica's blacks were Mohammedans.[24]

On 12 December 1815 the senior Moravian missionary in Jamaica, John Lang, reported in his diary that he had been visited by "a very extraordinary Negroe...the Mahometan Toby." Toby's intention was apparently to enter into disputation with Lang over the merits and demerits of their respective religions. For Toby "continue[d] a determined Turck," as summarized when he asserted: "Mahomet I cannot leave, there is God and his Mahomet from this I cannot part and if it cost my life." Lang's internal consolation was to put Toby's conversion in God's hands: "No man cometh unto me Except the Father draw him!" But outwardly he cautioned the Muslim: "Toby *you* are an honest man and if Mahomet is right you will be right but he was a cruel man and if he goes to Hell you must go with him." The threat of hell resulting from religious choice in this life surfaces in the novel *Warner Arundell* where the ship's surgeon mourns: "What a pity so good and sensible a man should be doomed to perdition on account of his being a Mahomedan!" To which the novel's narrator mentally remarked:

> I was at that time little of a theologian...but I then thought, and have since continued to think, that the man who conscientiously follows the religion of his fathers, and fulfils his duties to his God and to his fellow-men to the best of his abilities and limited knowledge, will never be doomed by his merciful Creator to eternal perdition.[25]

The theme of religious bigotry recurs in the real-life encounter on 20 July 1815 by the Moravians, Brothers Lang and Ward, with a Muslim in Black River, southwestern Jamaica. The African was obviously moved when he saw the missionaries defend two persons from being beaten: a boy by a fish-and-cake vendor whose plate he had broken, and whose reprisal was to strip the boy naked; and an old black man set upon by two mulatto men. The African claimed that his religious mentor (apparently in Jamaica) was a Mandingo who taught him to pray. "He said God and Mahomet were all his hope Jesus Christ was not for him. Then Br. Ward most earnestly recommended our Savior to him. The whole scene was very moving and the Negroe promised Br. Ward with tears that he would pray to our Savior."[26] Two decades later, on 15 September 1835, Jacob Zorn, superintendent of the Moravian Mission in Jamaica, wrote his stepfather in Pennsylvania, reporting that he had recently "had rather an interesting conversation with an old African negro, who had been a Mahometan in his country. In speaking with him concerning Baptism, for which he was anxious, he admitted that he had hitherto considered Jesus Christ, and the false Prophet, as the same person."[27] For Zorn, Muhammad was "the false Prophet."

A more thorough-going debate took place by mail between some Kingston-based Muslims and magistrate Madden. On 15 October 1835 Madden responded in an analytic and rather disproving manner to the lengthy religious positions put forward by the group, in particular by William Rainsford, the main author of a letter addressed to Madden dated 2 October 1834. Rainsford's letter speaks of the transitory nature of the world, and the longing of the souls of the dead for release from their graves and eventual attainment of eternal rest. On the other hand, he depicts the fear of the final judgment felt by the "bad souls [who] cry out, we beg you [God] not to do away with the world, we lay in torment but much greater pains are to come, so we beg thee to keep up the world, and not to do away with it." Rainsford attributes social status to divine destiny, and ascribes moral responsibility to the higher classes:

> All those that are in authority the Almighty made them to be so from the formation of the world...He gave a great charge to those who from the creation he so appointed in high places, not to oppress the poor class; and all those that do justice to them, and suffer no advantage to be taken of them, the Almighty will shower down blessings on them and their offsprings for ever, but those that will oppress the poor, at the great day they will go through a long and severe punishment...

His judgmental religious emphasis emerges where he waxes into vivid physical detail regarding the punishments to be inflicted on the unrighteous: "seven times a day he is set on fire, and from the crown of his head, as a torch is burnt down to the soles of his feet until he dissolves into ashes."[28]

Madden dissected the sources of Rainsford's beliefs, attributing them mainly to popular religious sources: "The condemnation of the wicked, after the manner of Pharaoh's punishment, is an alteration of a Jewish legend of the Talmud, which has no place in the Torah, or any other book of the Hebrew Scriptures;" however, "the mode of conducting the final judgment of the world is partly taken from the Qu'ran, though the greater part of your description is merely a Mussulman tradition." On the whole, Madden dismissed Rainsford's preoccupations with damnation as misplaced, in the light of larger ethical issues posed by religion. Rainsford's relish of the "trivial...minutiae" of punishment belonged in the realm of superstition, for, queried the Irishman, "what does it signify...how the trial is conducted?" Madden then confronted what he interpreted as the main thrust of the African's letter, which was a defense of Islam as against Christianity. He therefore began the final section of his letter by asserting: "It may be collected from your letter, that you profess the faith of Islam." He then proceeded to admit that it was a religion that had "effected good" and that he had known "a great many good men belonging to it," but he quite erroneously critiqued it as a religion "intended but for one people, and that people a very small portion of the human race" whereas Christianity "was intended, by its founder, to apply to the whole human race." He further accused Islam of sanctioning injustice, "one of the worst forms of which is slavery," while "oppression of every kind" was "hateful" to the tenets of Christianity, which did not authorize the injustice of slavery. He also belittled Islam's depiction of paradise as "a place of sensual pleasures" in contrast to "the spiritual idea of the Supreme Being" contained in the Christian concept of heaven. Islam, he felt, was guilty of inculcating intolerance and "the persecution of those who could not bring themselves to believe in it," whereas Christianity inculcated "forbearance to its enemies, and not extermination." For these reasons, he upheld that "the purity" of the "character" of Christianity was "superior to that of Islamism."[29] In addition, he faulted Islam's founder on account of what he considered "fanaticism," but he failed to acknowledge that aggressive solutions to resistance were outgrowths of the vigorous warrior traditions in which Muhammad, like several of the Old Testament figures, was socialized. It is instructive that the impassioned Rainsford himself was socialized in a similar manner: he identified himself as a native of Sancran,[30] a place—probably in Mali—renowned for its "refinement of learning," but he himself "was brought up as a warrior from a little boy, and was carried away before [he] had the opportunity of finishing [his] education."[31]

In 1840 another debate engaged three Quaker missionaries and the Trinidad Muslim, Samba Makumba. Makumba was highly critical of Christianity because of its toleration of certain practices that provided for him "sufficient evidence that the religion of Muhammad was superior to the religion of *Anna Bissa* [*al-nabī' 'Īsā* 'the prophet Jesus']." Among such practices was the consumption of alcohol, which was forbidden by the Qu'ran, and the enslavement by Christians of members of their own faith. In fact, the Qu'ran forbade the enslavement of Muslims by Muslims. The infringement of this edict was, according to Makumba, one of the complex of causes for the wars in Africa, since some Islamized groups had succumbed to the economic temptation of enslaving other Islamic peoples. This breach had itself provoked righteous Muslims to attempt to subdue groups who had broken the Prophet's law. In addition, Makumba "thought that the Christians degraded themselves by selling the Bible": "You ought not to sell your religion…or take pay for expounding it." On receiving the assurance of the Quakers that they conformed to his prohibitions, Makumba pronounced this benediction, "Then…you are men of God, and I hope the Lord will bless your labors, and make you useful in spreading his truth in the world."[32] This argument, in the account given by the Christian party, appears to end with both sides condescending toward each other. It is also noteworthy that another Trinidad-based Muslim had linked Muslims and Christians in the worship of the same deity: "the one and only true God of Christians and Mahommedans..."[33]

There was, however, the threat of physical confrontation in a situation that emerged in Belmont on the outskirts of Port of Spain, Trinidad's capital. The incidents occurred in the latter half of the 1830s when the Canadian Rev. Alexander Kennedy established his Presbyterian mission to Trinidad. In this mission, he encountered resistance from Muslims, one of whom was described as "a Mandingo African doctor (one who practised obeah, or the black art)." This suggests that he was a diviner, and/or, like Benjamin Cochrane of Jamaica, a homeopathic healer. He owned a "trash house" (thatched building) "at the back of the burial ground" at the northwest corner of Clifford and Pelham Streets, which Kennedy proposed leasing to accommodate a Sunday school. The owner himself lived in part of the building, and the other part had been "used as an African dance-house, where drum-dances with their corresponding orgies were held, and where animals were offered in sacrifice at their annual feast." This was an apparent allusion to the *saraka*, a feast of annual thanksgiving put on by Hausa and Yoruba, also adopted by Congo and other African ethnic groups and their descendants, and merging with the dance-event known as *bele.* But a month before the Sunday school began, Kennedy held a service there, which "rouse[d] the wrathful ire of the doctor," who apparently had not understood the purpose for which the Canadian wished to rent the premises. It was only through the intervention of the grandmother of Thomas St. Hill, whose memoirs constitute part of the account of Kennedy's stewardship in Trinidad, that the "Mandingo" was persuaded to let the Presbyterians continue to use the building as they desired. As a result, till mid-1844 Kennedy was able to hold in that location "a day-school, Sunday school and service on Sundays." He baptized "a large number" of the Eboe[Igbo], Kramanti, Congo, and Kru settled in what was then known as Freetown Valley; but the exceptions were "Yarraba [Yoruba] who became largely Roman Catholic, and the Mandingo who remained to a large extent Mahometan."[34]

MUSLIMS IN COMMUNITY

The literature on the early Islamic presence in the Caribbean occasionally indicates that there existed Muslim communities. These were sometimes physical enclaves but, where physically separated, coreligionists communicated through visits, intermediaries, and verbal as well as handwritten messages. The communal context becomes foregrounded in the postemancipation period when there tended to be an increasingly open reversion to the religious beliefs and practices of early socialization on the part of Africans once they were free of the restrictions of slavery. This was so for some 900 African soldiers who, after demobilization from their regiments between 1818 and 1825, had been settled in northeastern Trinidad.[35] They occupied seven villages east of the town of Arima, among them La Seiva, Turure, Quare, and Manzanilla. By the mid-1800s, Quare was described as "predominantly Muslim."[36] Also, the few inhabitants of Manzanilla who had been exposed to Christian instruction for several years after 1838 "had reverted to Mahommedanism." Of their number, "only one…was literate, and he had copied out portions of the Koran for the religious guidance of his colleagues."[37]

There is also evidence of Muslim communities elsewhere in Trinidad. In fact, the secular role of African Muslims in Trinidad came to public attention, attracting written documentation, precisely because they formed communities. One such commentary records an urbane disputation between some American Quakers with a level of religious tolerance, and the "Mahometan priest," Emir Samba Makumba. The Quakers advanced a rather sympathetic and fulsome representation of this personage who was "about sixty-six years old, his hair and beard, which he [had] allowed to grow long, [were] white. He wore the habit of his order, a flowing white tunic. Samba could speak several languages; he addressed us in Arabic, pronouncing the benediction of the Mahometans on those they esteem as people of God." He appears to have been a Fula, and declared himself to have been a Muslim priest in the Futa Toro empire, which lay on the south bank of the Senegal River. But he had been captured in one of the wars among neighboring peoples fostered by the demands of the trans-oceanic slave trade. After purchasing his freedom, Makumba had built up a community of "Mandingo" whose secular aims were first to secure their personal manumission, followed by the purchase of "small tracts of land, upon which they erected habitations, and were thus enabled by the produce of their gardens, etc., to support themselves respectably." They had become known for their distinct religious practices, and also "for their habits of temperance and exemplary deportment." From this base of communal consciousness, they combined to accumulate financial contributions toward the manumission of other Muslims, not only in Trinidad but also in other eastern Caribbean islands. Another approach was that "when a slave ship arrived at the colony, Samba and his friends were the first on board to inquire for Mandingoes, and if there were any among the captives, they ransomed them immediately." All told, by 1838, when slavery was effectively abolished in the British colonies, the group "had released from bondage upward of five hundred in Trinidad alone." The Quakers were high in their commendation of Makumba, whom they considered "one of the brightest philanthropists of the age."[38]

But Makumba may not have been the Muslim community's "headman" or spokesperson, but may rather have been one of its priests. By 1843, when the meeting with Makumba took place, the individual credited as the Mandingo community's leader was Mohammado Maguina, also known by the French name Auguste Bernard. He had been enslaved in the latter part of the eighteenth century and had been "taken to San Domingo where he had lived through the revolution and the downfall of the whites." Thereafter he served with a black grenadier company of the British Army in its 1797 Saint Domingue campaign and had come to Trinidad in 1816. He died in 1852, already a centenarian.[39] He had been the successor to Jonas Mahomed Bath, generally identified in the literature as the leader of the Trinidad "Mandingo" community until his passing in 1838 after fifty years in Trinidad. Bath was described by a writer to the editor of the *Glasgow Courier* as "a venerable, princely-looking old man, about 70 years of age." He had been taken prisoner when "sent by the Sultan, his father, with an army to attack a pagan nation, in order to make them become Mohammedans, but was in the expedition defeated…and sold for one hundred dollars as a slave…"

Bath was the chief signatory to an 1833 petition to King William IV of Britain, requesting repatriation for himself and others to "Senegal or Gambia, from which we can easily reach our country." At the close of the petition Bath identified himself as chief and almamb (*imām* [priest]) of "the Mandingoe and Fallah Nation," and at the beginning as "Sultan of Yullyallhad" and "Chief of the free negroes of the Mohametan Religion in the Island of Trinidad."[40] Bath had served in the First West India Regiment during the reign of King George III and, like a number of ex-West India Regiment soldiers, was, after demobilization, restless to return home. He himself had landed in Trinidad around 1804, and had later helped to constitute a fund from which enslaved contributors could purchase their freedom from slavery. This coterie numbered about 140 in 1838, a fraction in a slave population of upward of 22,000.[41] The *Glasgow Courier* writer commended Bath for commanding the "greatest respect" of the "whole Mandingo nation in Trinidad," but Bath's welfare association was perhaps the largest and best advertised of a number of coteries comprising free and enslaved African Muslims in the island. Certainly, it was considered that Bath's people "readily obey his directions, and he keeps them steady and industrious. He has a good deal of property himself…" The free Muslim community was further praised as "all sober, and the only free Africans in Trinidad who labour in the lighter kinds of tropical agriculture, such as cotton, coffee, cocoa, etc."

By the late 1960s a Carriacou-born resident of East Port of Spain, whose own great-grandmother had been Mandingo, indicated that there had been families of African Muslims who lived around Rose Hill, Scheuler Street, and Laventille Road in Laventille and the East Dry River area of Port of Spain.[42] That there may have been a link between such families and the earlier Muslim communities headed by Mahomed Bath and Samba Makumba is suggested by some of the family names that emerged in the data: Harragin, Harbin, and Kane.[43] Certainly, the name Mahommed Habin, otherwise Mahomed Littledale, is among those who signed an 1838 petition for repatriation to Africa.[44]

Given the dearth of details in the scribal sources regarding Islamic communities, oral commentary regarding the Hausa and Fula community in central Trinidad was fairly substantial, since the persons interviewed were themselves either the children, grandchildren, or great-grandchildren of Muslim Africans. The same obtains for the descendants of Manding, Kanga, and Hausa in the district of Moruga on the south coast of the island.[45] In these rural communities there had existed persons regarded as priests who, as late as the early twentieth century, came to say the opening prayers in Arabic at *saraka* hosted by descendants of this community in towns such as Tabaquite, Brasso, and Siparia.[46] These priests wore knee-length white shirts and pants that were loose but narrowed at the ankles, and while the women wore colorful headties and blouses and skirts, the men wore shirts of solid cream or blue along with khaki pants.[47] The use of these solid and pastel shades was very much in keeping with the Muslim aesthetic. Among rituals they observed was bathing before saying prayers at sunrise, which was also the time for killing any animal to be used for food.[48] And before meat could be eaten, these men said a *bisimillāh* [*bismillāhī al-Raḥmānī al-Raḥīm* "in the name of Allah, the Most Gracious, Most Merciful"].[49]

MULTIPLE RELIGIOUS AFFILIATIONS

Shifting religious allegiances were born among juniors of incomplete enculturation in their home environments. Among adults, it came from exposure to new ideas, the desire to link with power-bases in the immediate environment, and from spiritual questioning and questing, both of which involved interpersonal contestations and internalized debate.

The urge to shift allegiances that produced such internal religious conflict may be read into the dreams of a Muslim convert to Christianity who received extensive attention in the literature produced by the nineteenth-century Moravian establishment in Jamaica. This was Robert Peart whose original name was Muhammad Kaba.[50] Given the fact that a sprinkling of "Mandingo" turn up in the Moravian baptismal records, it is significant that Robert Peart made such an impression on several Moravians. This must speak to his articulateness and self-confidence, his leadership qualities, the fervor and persistence of his religious commitment, and the keenness of his pursuit of sacred knowledge. His life story and his conduct in religious matters evoked contemporary comment from John Lang, as well as Jacob Zorn, both of whom knew him personally.

Peart's slave name was Dick, but he took the name Robert Peart when he was baptized as a Moravian in 1813. He was admitted to Holy Communion on 30 July 1815, confirmed on 30 June 1816, and was elevated to the rank of helper, a deacon-like role, on 3 November 1816.[51] This significant position in the church no doubt appealed to Peart's sense of authority in spiritual matters. Peart was also, in a manner typical of both African and Islamic spirituality, given to comprehending dreams as guides to future events, and open to religious interpretation of their narratives and symbolism. The sketch given by Zorn contains two dream-events that Peart experienced and that pointed him toward Christian commitment. The first was of a voice that challenged him to pray, but since he was unacquainted with Christian prayers, all he could utter for the rest of the waking night was "Lord, have mercy upon me!" This midnight prayer session falls into the category of the Islamic voluntary prayer vigil called the *tahajjud* or *nāfilat*.[52] In addition, Peart's cultural conditioning within Islam had made him familiar with Islamic prayers, which he now felt were either or both inadequate/inappropriate for the new cultural ambience within which he now found himself.

In my interpretation, another of Peart's dreams was a foreshadowing or anticipation of Christian baptism, which he undertook on 17 October 1813 at the hands of John Lang of Old Carmel Moravian church.[53] Significantly this dream occurred on a Friday night, Friday being the Muslim holy day:

> he was in a dark house, when a man came in, and it became light. The person approached him, and kissed him three times. He enquired, 'Who are you?' and received in answer "I am Jesus of Nazareth, come to pardon all your sins,' "and immediately…I fell at His feet, and kissed them." Two days after, Sunday, he was sent for, and baptized by Br. [Brother] Lang.[54]

His movement from ignorance to enlightenment is indicated by the dark/light imagery of the setting. His receipt of three kisses is Christ's welcome to him, according to Arabic traditions, yet by Biblical allusion, it incorporates a motif of betrayal, whereby Christ is the prescient, compassionate prophet, and himself the Judas. Peart was indeed betraying his former faith. His incomplete fidelity to the religion of his forebears seems emblematized in the house: it is the setting of both his earlier and later dreams. In the first, he locates himself in the half-built house he was actually constructing at the time: its "door was not yet hung." In the later dream he envisioned himself "in a dark house," into which a man entered. The house became lit. The Friday to Sunday passage of time parallels the crucifixion and resurrection; just as the kissing of Jesus' feet echoes the devotion of the sinful woman who anointed Jesus' feet with balm, wiped them with her hair, and kissed them, but the removal of the spotlight from Friday to Sunday is a reenactment of his replacement of the Islamic holy day by the Christian Sabbath.[55]

It is informative that both on 23 July and 24 September 1815, after his incorporation into the Moravian church, Lang in his diary refers to Peart as "Robert the Mahometan." It suggests that Lang was continually aware of certain Islamic behaviors or ideas that were synonymous with Peart. Interestingly, however, these were not sufficient deterrents to Peart's reception into the church, nor did they prevent him from taking up a leadership position in the Fairfield congregation. On the contrary, Lang treasured Peart as "the first fruit of Mayday" since he was the first from the region of the Mayday hills to become a Christian convert. And Peart continued to call upon his skills that had been acquired through Islam, for we note that in 1817 Peart reported to his church that he had made a report to estate attorneys about the manner in which the Moravians delivered religious instruction to the slaves, winning their approval. This account had been written in Arabic, and Peart had promised to explain the document and its orthography to Lang at a later date.[56] Despite Peart's Muslim association, Lang, as seen in his 1816 diary entries, grew to refer to his church member as "Dick/Robert of Spicegrove" and "Br. Robert our Helper from Spicegrove," Spice Grove being the estate to which he belonged. Certainly the fact that Peart figures in officially sanctioned histories of the early Moravian Church indicate that Peart maintained himself in the good graces of the Church establishment till his death in 1845.[57]

Whether or not the Moravian hierarchy knew of it, we now have evidence that even after his involvement with the Moravian church Peart devoted himself to writing a treatise on Muslim prayer in the early 1820s. The Jakhanke caste[58] from whom he sprang was "much concerned with prayer, and prayer itself, in different forms, covers the entire spectrum of clerical work."[59] Thus it is, that by 1824 a book written by Kaba came into the hands of a Baptist minister in Spanish Town. It was entitled *Kitāb al-Ṣalāt* (The Book on Prayer) and drew upon his historical knowledge of Muslim holy men, prophets, and sacred writings. He discourses on prayer and its associated rituals of ablution, the fear of hell and desire for Paradise, and invocations sanctifying the act of marriage.[60] No doubt this treatise was written for his own spiritual edification, but it also suggests that he was fulfilling a teaching role vis-à-vis other Muslims as well. Certainly there were other Mandingo in his environs, at least four at Ryde estate, but to judge from their numbers in the Moravian records, they were in the minority; all the same, others may have refused to become part of the fledgling Christian community in the Spur Tree and St. Elizabeth lowlands vicinities.[61] Yet given the porous borders of plantations, and the multiple opportunities for cross-plantation social intermingling of slaves at Sunday markets, wakes, jobbing work, conveyance of goods, and messages between estates, it is likely that Peart was aware of Muslims both in his environs and in other parishes of the island. His book eventually reached Kingston, and then Spanish Town, perhaps travelling from Manchester by way of George Lewis, an enslaved but itinerant trader and preacher, who appears to have been Peart's main Baptist contact.

There is further evidence that Peart continued to practice his original faith after his arrival in Jamaica. He laid much emphasis on fasting, *ṣawm*, the third "pillar" of Islam, and resorted to subterfuge to achieve his objective: "whenever he wished to observe one of the Mahometan fasts, he pretended to be sick."[62] Indeed, the cross-fertilization of Christian and Islamic rituals worked out between Lewis and Peart showed itself in the practices observed at Spice Grove whenever Lewis visited the estate: in images echoic of Christ's Last Supper, Lewis' followers each contributed three pence with which "they made a supper, and sat up all night listening to his [Lewis'] instructions." Apart from this, they fasted three times a week, from sunrise to sunset. Whether this was exclusively during Ramadan or also observed at other times of the year was not stated. This practice of fasting irritated the Spice Grove overseer who felt that a weakened workforce was inimical to the goals of the plantation. For this reason, the overseer had "the names of three of the praying men[63] mentioned to him" and one day he observed them:

> When breakfast-time came, they took none, and as they told him, that they had eaten enough before it was day, he directed them to continue to break stones with sledge hammers, which they readily continued to do till evening without intermission,

> and so successfully, that he could not refrain from expressing his surprise.[64]

Peart's dreams, his writings, and his amalgam of religious practices and concerns were therefore iconic projections of an anguished religious sensibility, torn as he was between the cultural, economic, and religious pressures of bondage in an alien and distant land, and loyalty to his Muslim faith and his Jakhanke family traditions. He had been born in the mid-1700s in Bouka, near Timbo, the main urban center in the Futa Jallon plateau. The headwaters of the Senegal River rise in this plateau, which lies in the hinterland of present-day Guinea. His father ʻAbd al-Qādir had been "a substantial yeoman, possessing 140 slaves, several cows and horses, and grounds producing quantities of cotton, rice, and provisions, which he exchanged for European and other commodities brought from the coast by the Higglers."[65] Kaba had been educated by both his father and his uncle, an important Islamic lawyer, Muhammad Batul. In the 1770s Kaba was seized by robbers and carried to the coast where he was sold.[66] In 1834, shortly after general emancipation for British slaves was announced but not yet enacted, and after having endured some fifty-six years in slavery, he resumed his Muslim name when put in touch with another literate Muslim, Abu Bakr al-Siddīq. Al-Siddīq was known in Jamaica as Edward Donlan or Doulan.[67] Kaba commenced a letter to him in Arabic: "In the name of God, Merciful omniscient, the blessing of God, the peace of his prophet Mahomet. This is from the hand of Mahomed Caba, unto Bekir Sadiki Scheriffe."[68]

Yet a few lines on he calls Abu Bakr by his European name Edward Doulan and tells him to "send me a satisfactory answer for yourself this time by your real name, don't you see I give you my name, Robert Tuffit," which is the name he signs at the end of his letter. Doulan's reply is duly signed "Edward Doulan," and he gives both his Arabic name and his Christian name in the opening sentence of his correspondence. Within the body of his text, he addresses Tuffit/Peart as Mahomed Caba, and ends "Whenever you wish to send me a letter, write it in Arabic language; then I will understand it properly."[69]

The continued habits of belief and practice that had been ingrained from youth were commented upon by Magistrate Madden when he doubted the protestations of fidelity to Christianity made by a Jamaican "Mandingo" who, one Sunday in about 1835, showed him "a Koran written from memory by himself—but written, he assured me, before he became a Christian. I had my doubts on this point."[70] Madden also pointed up the contradictions between Peart's stated purpose in corresponding with

Donlan and the terminology used in the letter. Peart had told Benjamin Angell, a Manchester planter, that he had been writing to Donlan "inviting him to abjure Mahometanism and embrace the true religion." Indeed Peart had gone so far as to say that he did not "regret his captivity, as it was the means of bringing him to the knowledge of Christ."[71] In view of this intent, Madden expressed surprise when Peart's letter opened with the words: "In the name of God, merciful and omnipotent, the blessing of God, the peace of his prophet Mahomet!" "So much," remarked Madden, "for the old African's renunciation of Islamism." So was this double-speak a sign of willful deception on Peart's part, a means of ingratiating himself with Christian whites whose assistance he courted and to whom he therefore said what they would have wanted to hear?[72] Or was it the result of accommodations contained in a psyche that had been deeply conditioned not simply by one (Islam), but by two or more powerful religio-cultural regimens (Islam, Moravianism, Baptist)? We need to recall that Peart had been a young man when he left Africa, but that he had, by 1834, already spent *fifty-six* years in European-dominated Jamaica. Furthermore, we must also be sensitive to the fact that religious beliefs are embedded in cultural forms, so that just as the Arabic language and writing system comes with Islam, so also the salutation at the start of an Arabic letter must accord with certain formulae associated with the religion and its language.

Perhaps because Madden was an Irish Briton, he understood the psychological complexities of dual or multiple cultural loyalties, and therefore possessed a conscious or intuited sensitivity that allowed him to notice similar dualities in European-ruled Muslim societies. He observed, for instance, "that all the proselytes I have seen in Mahometan countries, have rather engrafted the doctrines of Christianity on the stem of Mahometanism, than plucked up the latter, root and branch, to make way for the former."[73] Thus, the magistrate was in a position to transfer his earlier observations from the Middle East to the attitudes of African Muslims in the slave societies of the Caribbean. In this vein, he commented with fine insight that "Few, very few, indeed, of the native Africans who have been instructed in their creed or their superstition, which[ever] you please, have given up their early rites and observances for those of the religion of the country they were brought to. But this they do not acknowledge, because they are afraid to do so."[74] Madden cited further proof of what he saw as conflicting religious loyalties and inclinations when Edward Donlan wrote two Christian clergymen thanking them "for the great boon" of their gift to him of "the Testament, both of the old and new law of our Lord and Saviour" printed in Arabic. He then made further request for "a prayer-book, the psalms, and an Arabic grammar—also a copy of the Alcoran."[75]

Dual religious affiliation can also be detected among the Hausa and Fula who, during the nineteenth century, lived at the villages of Guaracarite, Mayo, Mamoral, and Tortuga in central Trinidad. Several of them appear to have arrived in Trinidad as indentured laborers, some of them subsequent to the British abolition of the slave trade in 1807, others after the emancipation of slaves in 1838. They either worked on cacao estates or grew cacao on plots of land they had bought, and were already dead by the early years of the twentieth century. One Hausa Muslim who owned a Qu'ran and spoke Arabic was also a Catholic, the dominant Christian religion of the island. Another Hausa from Zaria became an Anglican, having first worked in Tobago where the state religion, the Church of England, was dominant; he also ate pork and drank rum; however, he could recite the Qu'ran and hosted thanksgiving prayers and sacrificial feasts called *saraka*.[76] These feasts were held annually by various families either on Emancipation Day (1 August) or on New Year's Day. He sacrificed goats at sunrise for this festival; sunrise was also a time when he said prayers—the *fajr*—but, in another Muslim custom, he bathed, cleansing himself physically before offering up his praise and petitions. It is unclear whether this was a full bath, or the partial ablution (*wudhū'*), the washing of face, hands up to the elbow, wiping of the head, and washing of the feet. Another Hausa hailed from Tumbu. He spoke and wrote Arabic, but had brought from Africa "a Hebrew Bible." This may have been on account of the fact that some of these indentured workers may have been recruited in Sierra Leone where freed slaves were settled in villages after being taken off slave ships breaking the ban on the slave trade. Christian catechization and English language training took place in these villages. Or he may have been introduced to Christianity in the British army if he had been a West India Regiment recruit. Then there was a Hausa in Guaracarite named Biabia, who was considered a priest and was already an old man in 1909. He had a Qu'ran that he placed in front of him as he sat on a sheep-skin to hear the petitions of those who came to consult him and request that he say prayers on their behalf. It is not certain that he could write, but he "had all his prayers in his head." He prayed with a long rosary that had black beads.[77] This was the *sibḥa* or *tasbīḥ* (Arabic meaning "glorification;" in Hausa *tasbaha* or *cazbi*); however, syncretically, it carried a cross attached to it, a design influenced no doubt by the example of the Roman Catholic chaplet that would have been common in a predominantly Roman Catholic country.

REPATRIATION AS SELF-RESTORATION AND RELIGIOUS AFFIRMATION

Some Africans resolved their anxieties over physical and psychological displacement by engineering repatriation to their native homelands. As Trinidad-based Mahomed Bath's 1833 petition had declared: "[W]e cannot forget our country. Death alone can make us to do." The determination to return home led some to act individually, out of frustration with the failure of collective bargaining. "In 1837 Mohammed Hausa (Philip Findlay) and Jackson Harvey returned [from Trinidad] to Benin with the help of the Royal Geographical Society in London and the Colonial Office."[78] Both men had been recruited from the liberated slave/indentured laborer ranks into the Third West India Regiment in 1809, were discharged in 1818, and had issued a petition for repatriation in the 1830s.[79] Yet another document written by Finlay survives, a manuscript written purportedly for a military assistant surgeon in the regiment, and consisting of a varia of prayers, numerals, exhortations, lists of non-Islamic peoples, a list of holy books, and notes on the identity of the author—"a compendium of what the author remembered about Islam and the African languages he might speak." The languages used included Fula, Mandinka, Arabic, and English Creole, but Hausa predominated, indicating something of the multilingual community of African soldiers who comprised the bulk of the regiment. The document uses Arabic script throughout, a script referred to as *ajami*. Finlay gave his Muslim name as Mohammed Hausa[80] in the joint petition he made with Harvey, but in the manuscript he identified himself as Muhammad 'Ā'ishatu (the latter his mother's name) from Gobir in Hausaland, a former student of Mīka'ilu 'Abd al-Salām, an Islamic scholar, and of Usman Dan Fodio, the Fulani jihadist in Hausaland at the turn of the nineteenth century, and also former student of Muhammad Tukur of Sokoto, a Muslim saint.[81]

Another co-regimentalist, and later another Trinidad repatriate, was Mohammedu Sisei [Cisse], called by the European name Felix Ditt. The Royal Geographical Society in England became interested in the geographical information which Sisei could give them in their attempt to map and commercially exploit the Senegambia. Sisei's key advantage in this connection was his having been an eyewitness to the 1805 visit of Mungo Park, the Scottish explorer, to his natal village of Nyani-Maru, some one hundred miles upstream of the River Gambia. At this time Sisei would have been in his late teens. His father 'Abu Bakr and mother 'Ā'ishah were both Muslim Mandingo. For eight years, between eight and sixteen, Sisei attended Qu'ranic school in Dār Salāmī or Dasilami in the upper Gambia, after which he was circumcised. His religious and academic training made him "a strict follower of Islam; he knew the Koran very well, and certain parts of it he always carried with him," even during his later exile. Apparently in an attempt to amass money for his marriage dowry, Sisei undertook a period of trading, which involved traveling by land, sea, and river to Gorée and Bundu. Such travels were later to enable him "to substantiate the existence of some places marked on the map of West Africa that the Royal Geographical Society possessed. Bondu was a very strategic area. It was south of the French trading area on the upper Senegal, and it was on the regular route from Gambia to the gold fields of Bambuk."

Between 1805 and 1810 Sisei became a teacher, but when in 1810 war erupted over the control of the banks of the Gambia in his vicinity, he was captured and "marched as a prisoner-of-war to Kansala where he spent five months, and then to the port town of Sikka. There he was sold to a French slaver which immediately sailed away." The boat was, however, intercepted by a British naval patrol five days out of port, and Sisei was recruited as a soldier in the Third West India Regiment, a corps of African and West Indian blacks formed to fight in Britain's colonial wars. He arrived in Trinidad in 1816, but his regiment was demobilized in 1825 and the soldiers settled on Trinidad's northeast coast. Whether or not Sisei received the promised land grant or pension, he did not choose to stay in Manzanilla but moved to Port of Spain, the island's capital, where "he became a member of the Muslim Mandingo group led by Jonas Mohammed Bath." Not content to wait on the results of the several petitions between 1833 and 1838 made by Bath and his followers, Sisei borrowed money and took his creole wife and child to England in 1838. There "he fell under the friendly protection of John Washington, secretary of the Royal Geographical Society." Apart from being debriefed for information on the Senegambian interior, Sisei assisted in supplying lexical items in Mandingo and assessing the accuracy of previous word-lists recorded by other European explorers. He also identified animals and plants stored at Kew Gardens that were endemic to his region. Eventually he was sent to the governor of the British settlement at Bathurst, at the mouth of the river Gambia, where it was expected that he would reach his home village even as his services could be tendered as an interpreter for British interests in the Gambia. After all, he spoke "Negro English" and wrote Mandingo "indifferently in Arabic character."[82]

'Abū Bakr al Ṣiddīq was another Senegambian who was repatriated, though less through his own agency than that demonstrated in the case of Sisei. Ṣiddīq's correspondence with Robert Peart or Muḥamad Kaba has already been discussed. Al Ṣiddīq had been born in Timbuktu around

1790, but at two years of age had moved to Jenne. He belonged to a long line of scholars and jurists, "men of learning, in whose hands the conduct of public affairs largely rested."[83] His father Kara Musa was a gold trader as well as a scholar learned in Qu'ranic exegesis. 'Abū Bakr's upbringing included trading journeys as well as study of the Qu'ran at Jenne and later at Bouna on the northern frontier of the Ashanti Empire. The young man was captured during the wars that broke out during the early years of the nineteenth century in a power struggle between new Islamic elements and traditional power-elites in the Asante kingdom. He and others were force-marched hundreds of miles down to Lago on the Gold Coast where he was put aboard an English ship and taken to the West Indies. Between 1805 and 1834 he slaved for various owners in Jamaica, until Magistrate Madden, impressed by his learning and family pedigree, persuaded Alexander Anderson, his owner as from 1823, to free him. 'Abū Bakr had been a valued slave, in that he kept Anderson's storeroom accounts in Arabic as well as "the accounts of the whole of his vast business" and Anderson testified that Donlan had been "a good servant to him—a faithful and good negro."[84] It was "by the mere accident of seeing the man sign his name in very well written Arabic," while he was being sworn in by Madden as a constable on his master's property, that Madden began to take note of him. The magistrate commented with enthusiasm that "his attainments as an Arabic scholar, were the least of his merits. I found him a person of excellent conduct, of great discernment and discretion."[85] Indeed Madden went on to compare him to an educated English nobleman. Through the agency of another stipendiary magistrate, Abu Bakr joined a British expedition to Timbuktu in 1835, since he, like Sisei, had useful language skills: he spoke English "well and correctly for a negro" though he did not read or write it. He appears to have reached Jenne sometime before 1841, although the expedition ran into disaster when its English leader was killed in late 1836.

ISLAMIC CULTURAL LEGACY IN THE CARIBBEAN

It appears that public adherence to Islam on the part of African Caribbean peoples did not survive the first generation of eighteenth and nineteenth century African Muslims. In some measure this may be due to the fact that the gender ratios for Senegambian migrants were heavily weighted in favor of males, traceably so in Trinidad, but perhaps following a similar pattern elsewhere. This meant that religious outsiders figured heavily among their mates,[86] and the maternal cultural influence, as a general rule, was likely to have been more effective than the paternal. The choice of exogamous mate was only one of the domains in which some African Muslim males, as we have seen, had begun to make their compromises with the dominant cultural and religious trends in the host society. Such compromises were normative, given the psychological imperative for migrants to conform in some degree to their host communities. These adjustments between customary behavior and new institutions resulted in syncretic worldviews and cultural forms. This pattern of adjustment is evident in the behavior of subjects from both Jamaica and Trinidad treated in this study.

Islam in the Caribbean today accounts for about 172,250 adherents out of a population of about 33 million. The religion is strongest in Suriname, 25 percent of the population, bolstered as it was by the advent since 1902 of Javanese, adding to the arrival of Muslims from Hindustan since 1873. As of 2002 the Muslim population of Jamaica stood at less than 1 percent, while that of Trinidad and Tobago accounted for 8 percent, and that of Guyana 13 percent.[87] In both these territories Muslim Indians from the eastern subcontinent began to arrive in large numbers between 1845 and 1917, giving rise to local perceptions that Islam was a religion confined to an ethnic group. Economic competition between Africans and Indians beginning in the colonial era has contributed to ethnic tensions in these societies, and these tensions have given rise to notions of religious separateness. In this scenario, the conversion of Africans to Islam in the first half of the twentieth century was a rare, sometimes, highly publicized event;[88] and it was only after the Black Power uprising of the 1970s that the stream of Islam coming out of the Black Muslim phenomenon of the United States began to account for a new religious community of African Muslims in Trinidad.[89] This influence has been supplemented across the ethnically-based divide by the impact of worldwide Islamic fundamentalism and its missionary expansion out of Saudi Arabia and Libya as of the 1980s, somewhat upstaging the traditional overseas links with Pakistan, Bangladesh, and India.

This late twentieth century trans-ethnic extension has marked a distinct innovation, unrelated to the earlier African cultural presence. This is so even though resistance to the adoption of Christianity was manifest among several of the earlier African Muslims. This resistance was underpinned in some instances by their physical distance from Christian/European control, a situation paralleled by regimental demobilization and emancipation from slavery or indenture, but the dominant society's pressure toward conformity with its own norms eroded the surface evidence of Islam's presence among the African-descended communities of the Caribbean. Residual behaviors stemming from Islamic practice continued past the first generation, particularly where such customs were reinforced by their adherence among other ethnic groups. In Trinidad there was the observance of the *saraka* (Hausa from Arabic *zakāt*, "alms") and its attendant foods.[90] Then the limited participation of Africans in the drumming for Hosay festivals during the nineteenth and twentieth centuries may also in part have been stimulated by knowledge, among some of the drummers, that Islam was part of their family or community heritage.[91] But it may be posited that residual influences stemming from the historical presence of African Muslims among the populations of the Caribbean[92] may be detected in several practices of Afro-Christian religions, such as Revival, Zion, and Pukkumina in Jamaica, and the analogous Shakers, Shouters, and Spiritual Baptists of the eastern Caribbean. Among these customs and rituals are the wearing of copious solid-color head ties—rather than patterned and multicolored ones as typical of general African dress; the significance attached to fasts[93] and retreats within these same Caribbean religions; and their weekly practice of distributing food to streetside homeless persons and beggars, to orphanages, and to the hospitalized sick—all reminiscent of practices associated with the Islamic *zakat* and West African *saraka* or *saraa*. Another instance of possible influence is the important role played by pilgrimages in their cycle of congregational activities. Pilgrimages are made to water locations, such as riversides, the seaside, and waterfalls—no doubt linked to the sacredness of such sites in African traditional religions, but reciprocal pilgrimages are also made between and among congregations, with some church sites acquiring the status of shrines requiring annual visitations.

There is also oral evidence that certain Muslim practices characterized the culture of ex-slaves from the United States who had been coopted into the British army in the American Revolutionary War, and who had been relocated to Trinidad after the defeat of the British. Some of these ex-soldiers had been settled on the eastern outskirts of Princes Town in south Trinidad, in the Third, Fourth, Fifth, and Sixth Company villages, so named after the regiments in which they had served. By 1824 the population of these villages was around 900 and included some liberated African women settled there after 1809 by officials to reduce the uneven sex ratio.[94] Even as these ex-militia men carried English names such as Braxton, Langley, and Dingwell, some sang songs in Arabic, it is said, and buried their dead on the same day of death, a custom upheld in the instance of descendants who died in Trinidad as late as the 1970s and 1991.[95]

While there is no necessary familial link between the new Afro-Caribbean Muslim converts and the eighteenth- and nineteenth-century African Muslims, the rise in Africa-centered research since the 1970s has revealed the early Muslim presence in the Caribbean and has made African descendants more favorable toward the religion than they might otherwise have been. Furthermore, the recognition that Islam is a universalistic religion rather than an ethnically specific faith has worked to break down the psychological barriers that had obtained in the early twentieth century.

Notes

1. See Ruth Pike, *Aristocrats and Traders: Sevillian Society in the Sixteenth Century* (Ithaca, 1972); and A. C. Saunders, *A Social History of Black Slaves and Freedmen in Portugal, 1441–1555* (Cambridge, 1982).
2. See for example, Ricardo Alegría, *Juan Garrido: El Conquistador Negro en las Antillas, Florida, México y California, c.1502–1540* (San Juan, 1990).
3. See Peter Clarke, *West Africa and Islam: A Study of Religious Development from the 8th to the 20th Century* (London, 1982), 28–86.
4. Edward L. Joseph, *Warner Arundell: The Adventures of a Creole,* ed. Lise Winer (Mona, 2001), 48.
5. Thanks to Mohammed Bashir Salau of York University for information as to the identification of these names and their meanings.
6. Joseph Kummer, "Biography of Mask Campbell," ms., in file denominated "Antigua, West Indies. Varia, incl. Monteith matieral (c.1855)," Moravian Archives, Bethlehem, PA.
7. It is not unusual that Africans have erroneously identified the ethnicity of the people who captured them and of the other ethnic groups they encountered on their way to the coast or river embarkation point leading to the sea because they had no prior knowledge of many of the other African peoples who neighbored them and did not know their languages. Compare the case of an Angolan who claimed to have been captured by the Yoruba and sold to the Portuguese. See Maureen Warner-Lewis, *Central Africa in the Caribbean: Transcending Time, Transforming Cultures* (Mona, 2003), 73. The Yoruba live in West Africa, thousands of miles distant from Angola in southwest Central Africa.
8. See Richard Allsopp, ed., *Dictionary of Caribbean English Usage* (Oxford, 1996), 247. Thanks to Professor Hubert Devonish for bringing this term to my attention.
9. Author's interview with Ann Simon, Whitelands, Trinidad, 1970.
10. Cynric Williams, *A Tour through the Island of Jamaica, from the Western to the Eastern End, in the Year 1823* (London, 1827), 32, 81.
11. Christian Oldendorp, *A Caribbean Mission: C. G. A. Oldendorp's History of the Mission of the Evengelical Brethren on the Islands of St. Thomas, St. Croix, and St. John,* ed. Arnold Highfield and Vladmir Barac (Ann Arbor, 1987), 161.

12. Ibid., 162.
13. John Stedman, *Narrative of a Five Years' Expedition against the Revolted Negroes of Surinam, in Guiana, on the Wild Coast of South America; from the Year 1772 to 1777* (London, 1796), 2:261.
14. See Ivor Wilks, "'Abū Bakr Al-Ṣiddīq of Timbuktu," in *Africa Remembered: Narratives by West Africans from the Era of the Slave Trade*, ed. Philip Curtin (Madison, 1967), 162n.38. Circumcision is practiced by some African ethnic groups all over the continent. In addition, the *Risāla* of Ibn Abī Zayd, well known in West Africa, enjoined it, even though it was not commanded in the Qu'ran.
15. Bryan Edwards, *The History, Civil and Commercial, of the British Colonies in the West Indies* (London, 1819), 2:71–72.
16. *The Slave Son*, ed. Lise Winer (Kingston, [1854] 2003), 200.
17. One wonders how Sayeb's literacy in Arabic could have impacted his ward's education, which was no doubt in English.
18. Joseph, *Warner Arundell*, 44, 49, 50.
19. Richard Madden, *The Memoirs (Chiefly Autobiographical) of Richard Robert Madden*, ed. Thomas More Madden (London, 1891), 29. The specific job of stipendiary magistrates was to police the measures introduced by the British Government as of the 1820s to improve the condition of the slaves. Madden had traveled to Constantinople in 1824 where he "succeeded in acquiring some little smattering of the ordinary phrases and medical terms in most common use, in Turkish as well as in Arabic." He also lived in Egypt between 1825 and 1827.
20. Kassonke from Mali, according to Allan D. Austin, *African Muslims in Antebellum America: Transatlantic Stories and Spiritual Struggles* (New York, 1997), 41, 44.
21. Richard R. Madden, *A Twelvemonth's Residence in the West Indies, During the Transition from Slavery to Apprenticeship* (Westport, CT, [1835] 1970), 1:129–30.
22. Madden, *Twelvemonth's Residence*, 1:131.
23. John H. Buchner, *The Moravians in Jamaica: History of the Mission of the United Brethren's Church to the Negroes in the Island of Jamaica, from the Year 1754 to 1854* (London, 1854), 30.
24. James M. Phillippo, *Jamaica: Its Past and Present State* (London, 1843), 269.
25. Joseph, *Warner Arundell,* 49–50.
26. John Lang, 20 July 1815, in "Diary of the Mission at the Bogue, 1813–18," Q–7 Fairfield, Moravian Church Documents, Jamaica Archives.
27. Letters from Jacob Zorn to J. G. Kummer, 1827–36, in B 3, Kummer Collection, Moravian Archives, Bethlehem, PA.
28. Madden, *Twelve Month's Residence*, 1:140–41.
29. Ibid., 1:146, 147.

30. Austin, *African Muslims,* 41. Austin characterizes Rainsford as "a forceful preacher from Kankan" in present-day Guinea.
31. Madden, *Twelvemonth's Residence,* 1:141
32. George Truman, John Jackson, and Thomas B. Longstreth, *Narrative of a Visit to the West Indies in 1840 and 1841* (Philadelphia, 1844), 110, 111.
33. In Carlton Ottley, *Slavery Days in Trinidad* (Port of Spain, 1974), 58.
34. C. B. Franklin, *After Many Days: A Memoir being a Sketch of the Life and Labours of Rev. Alexander Kennedy—First Presbyterian Missionary to Trinidad, Founder of Greyfriar's Church, and its Pastor for Fourteen Years, January 1836–December 1849* (Port of Spain, 1910), 76–77.
35. See Keith O. Laurence, "The Settlement of Free Negroes in Trinidad before Emancipation," *Caribbean Quarterly* 9 (1963), 26–52.
36. Bridget Brereton, *A History of Modern Trinidad, 1783–1962* (London, 1981), 69.
37. Letter from C. Wood to the bishop of Barbados, Port of Spain, Trinidad, 19 May 1847, Trinidad, 1835–1854, Society for the Propagation of the Gospel Archives, London.
38. George Truman, John Jackson, and Thomas B. Longstreth, *Narrative of a Visit to the West Indies, in 1840–1841* (Coconut Grove, FL, 1844), 108–11.
39. Details from the *Trinidad Free Press,* 9 July 1852, reproduced in Donald Wood, *Trinidad in Transition: the Years after Slavery* (London, 1968), 39– 40.
40. Reprinted in the *Port of Spain Gazette*, 10 September 1833, enc. in CO 300/3, National Archives of the United Kingdom, Kew [hereafter NAUK], quoted in Ottley, *Slavery Days*, 58.
41. Brereton, *History of Modern Trinidad*, 67; and Wood, *Trinidad in Transition*, 39.
42. Author's interview with Elizabeth Beddoe, Rose Hill, Port of Spain, Trinidad, 1968.
43. I had presumed that this latter was "Khan," a typical Muslim name among Asians in Trinidad. Since the informant referred to African Muslims, I interpreted this either as a discrepancy or as an instance of the residential mingling of Africans and Asians of the Muslim faith. Subsequent awareness of the Mande name "Kane" made the African context clearer.
44. CO 295/106, NAUK.
45. Interviews by the author in Trinidad with Reynold Benjamin, Pargassingh Trace, Moruga, 1971; Benjamin Brazle, Petit Café, Moruga, 1968; Queen Caesar, Basse Terre, Moruga, 1968; Gomes Jones, Minna London and Francis Noel, St. Mary's, Moruga, 1968; and Anderson Pierre, Cachipe, Moruga, 1968.
46. Interviews by the author in Trinidad with Simon Jude Alexander, Caratal, 1972; Jane-Ann Joseph, Bonaventure, Caratal, 1968; Mary Poposite Simon, Whitelands, Mayo, 1970.

47. Author's interview with Albertina Yearwood, Fyzabad, Trinidad, 1991.
48. Author's interview with Jane Ann Joseph, Caratal, Trinidad, 1968.
49. Author's interview with Minna Moses London, St. Mary's, Moruga, 1968.
50. Yacine Daddi-Addoun and Paul Lovejoy, "Muhammad Kaba Saghanughu and the Muslim Community of Jamaica," in *Slavery on the Frontiers of Islam*, ed. Paul E. Lovejoy (Princeton, 2004), 199–218. In one of his letters, Peart gives his name as Robert Tuffit, a name that Daddi Addoun and Lovejoy suggest may have resulted from a misinterpretation caused by Peart's Arabic script; however, I note that Benjamin Angell used both Peart and Tuffit when introducing Peart to Madden. Angell is not likely to have understood Arabic script. On the other hand, he too might have been an orientalist like Madden, given that one of his estates was named "Tombuctoo."
51. F-1 Fairfield, entry 27, Moravian Church documents, Jamaica Archives.
52. Muhammad 'Ali, *The Religion of Islam: A Comprehensive Discussion of the Sources, Principles and Practices of Islam* (Lahore, 1936), 408.
53. F.-1. Fairfield, entry 27, Moravian Church documents, Jamaica Archives.
54. Letter from Jacob Zorn, Fairfield, Jamaica, 26 September 1837, *Periodical Accounts Relating to the Missions of the Church of the United Brethren* (London), 14:296.
55. *The Holy Bible.* Luke 7: 38–39.
56. Entry for 27 August 1817, Lang's diary.
57. See Walter Hark and Augustus Westphal, *The Breaking of the Dawn, or, Moravian Work in Jamaica, 1754–1904* (London, c.1904); and S. U. Hastings and B. L. MacLeavy, *Seedtime and Harvest: A Brief History of the Moravian Church in Jamaica, 1754–1979* (Kingston, 1979).
58. Lamin Sanneh, *The Jakhanke: The History of an Islamic Clerical People of the Senegambia* (London, 1979), 1. The Jakhanke are a specialized caste of Muslim clerics and educators, originating c1200 among the Serakhulle or Soninke people, and dispersing throughout Senegambia from the town of Dia or Diakha in Masina in modern-day Mali.
59. Ibid., 185.
60. See Daddi Addoun and Lovejoy, "Muhammad Kaba Saghanughu."
61. Examination of the baptismal records in the Carmel Church book during 1825 and 1828, when ethnic identification was supplied, indicates only twelve Mandingo among slightly more than 800 persons. The majority of persons receiving baptism were Eboe [Igbo], Congo, Creole or Jamaican, and Guinea. There was one Mongola (from Angola), and a smattering of Chamba, Papa, Coromantee, and Banda, apart from the few Mandingo.
62. Buchner, *Moravians in Jamaica*, 51.
63. Phillippo, *Jamaica,* 337. Phillippo indicates that "praying people" was a term applied to "professing Christians, especially those attached to missionary churches."

64. Zorn, 26 September 1837, *Periodical Accounts,* 296.
65. Benjamin Angell, 7 October 1834, in Madden, *Twelvemonth's Residence,* 2:135.
66. Wilks, "'Abū Bakr Al-Ṣiddiq of Timbuktu," 164. Daddi Addoun and Lovejoy, "Muhammad Kaba Saghanughu," have suggested that Kaba was a native of Bouaké in modern Ivory Coast, whose family was involved in the kola nut trade, and a nephew of a significant Muslim cleric named Muḥammad al-Mustafā ben al-'Abbās.
67. The difference between Donlan and Doulan is probably the result of handwriting. The letters "n" and "u" would not be easily distinguished in some scripts.
68. In *Twelvemonth's Residence,* v.1, Madden reproduced some of the correspondence in Arabic between Peart and Donlan.
69. Letter dated 18 October 1834, in Madden, *Twelvemonth's Residence,* 2:136–37.
70. Madden, *Twelvemonth's Residence,* 2:127.
71. Angell to Madden, 7 October 1834, in ibid., 2:135. One needs to be extremely guarded in accepting at face value the expressions of contentment over their enslavement put forward by Caribbean slaves. For a classic instance of hypocrisy and subterfuge, see A.C. Carmichael, *Domestic Manners and Social Conditions of the White, Coloured, and Negro Populations of the West Indies* (London, 1833), 229–33. In Carmichael's interviews with fourteen slaves on St. Vincent, not one wished to return to Africa. They considered it a cruel, heathen place, and endorsed the benefaction of their removal to the Caribbean, while attesting to their well-being as slaves. When read against evidence of the desire for repatriation, suicides, expressions of disillusionment with life made to missionaries, and sundry acts of resistance, it becomes clear that slaves were very canny about who they said what to.
72. Abd ar-Rahman, a Fula slave in America, gave the impression that he wrote the Lord's prayer in Arabic and that he was interested in converting Muslims in his homeland to Christianity, when in fact this was not the case. See Austin, *African Muslims,* 73–76.
73. Letter from Madden to Beattie, 20 October 1834, in Madden, *Twelvemonth's Residence,* 2:134.
74. Madden, *Twelvemonth's Residence,* 2:131–32.
75. Ibid., 2:133–34.
76. Author's interview with Jane Ann Joseph, Caratal, Trinidad, 1970.
77. The prayer beads may consist of 33, 99, or even 1,000 counters. Thanks to Mohammed Bashir Salau of York University and Sule Aliyu for information on this item of Muslim prayer practice.
78. Brereton, *History of Modern Trinidad,* 68. Perhaps they were those instanced in David Trotman and Paul Lovejoy, "Community of Believers: Trinidad Muslims and the Return to Africa, 1810–1850," *Slavery on the Frontiers*

of Islam, ed. Paul E. Lovejoy (Princeton, NJ, 2004), 219–32. On the basis of CO 267/159 and 267/175, Christopher Fyfe wrote: "In 1837 two Hausa, emancipated in Trinidad, arrived in Freetown on their way to Badagry, a slave-trading centre in the Bight of Benin, whence they meant to return to their homeland. Their inspiring story stirred many recaptives. Three combined in 1839, bought a condemned slave-ship at auction, and sailed to Badagry themselves with sixty-seven passengers." See "Four Sierra Leone Recaptives," *Journal of African History* 2 (1961), 82,

79. The Humble Memorial of Philip Finlay and Jackson Harvey Natives of Africa, CO 295/119, NAUK; referenced in Trotman and Lovejoy, "Community of Believers."
80. The use of an African ethnonym, here Hausa, as the second element of a personal name was common in the plantation era in British, Spanish, and French territories. It served as a means of differentiating enslaved persons with the same first name.
81. For an analysis of the language and content of this document, see Nikolai Dobronravine, "A West Indian Arabic-script Document in Hausa, Fula, Mandinka, Arabic, and English-based Creole," typescript, 2002, ms. 2683, Trinity College, University of Dublin.
82. Carl Campbell, "Mohammedu Sisei of Gambia and Trinidad, c.1788–1838, *African Studies Association of the West Indies Bulletin* 7 (1974), 29–38.
83. Wilks, "'Abū Bakr Al-Ṣiddīq of Timbuktu," 152.
84. Unless otherwise indicated, quotations and biographical information relating to Abū Bakr in this paragraph derive from the letter to J. Buckingham, 29 September 1834, in Madden, *Twelvemonth's Residence*, 2:109, 121–123, 130.
85. Letter to J. Buckingham, 15 September 1834, in Madden, *Twelvemonth's Residence*, 2:108.
86. See Laurence, "The Settlement of Free Negroes," 35–36; and Barry Higman, "African and Slave Family Patterns in Trinidad," *Africa and the Caribbean: The Legacies of a Link*, eds. Margaret Crahan and Franklin Knight (Baltimore, 1979), 44, 57, 59.
87. See http://www.factbook.net/muslim_pop.php [19 March 2008].
88. In the late 1950s, one Trinidad newspaper gave front page coverage to the conversion to Islam of an Afro-Trinidadian, Adolphus Walker, from El Dorado, Tunapuna.
89. See Selwyn Ryan, *The Muslimeen Grab for Power: Race, Religion and Revolution in Trinidad and Tobago* (Port of Spain, 1991); Bishnu Ragoonath, "Religion and Insurrection: 'Abū Bakr and the Muslimeen Failure in the 1990 Attempted Coup in Trinidad and Tobago," in *Identity, Ethnicity and Culture in the Caribbean,* ed. Ralph Premdas (St. Augustine, 1999), 409–46.

90. See Maureen Warner-Lewis, *Guinea's Other Suns: The African Dynamic in Trinidad Culture* (Dover, MA, 1991), 115–16. On Muslim communities on the Gullah islands, see Lydia Parrish, *Slave Songs of the Georgia Sea Islands* (Athens, GA, [1942] 1992), 27; and Austin, *African Muslims*, 98, 109.
91. See Judith Bettelheim and John Nunley, "The Hosay Festival," *Caribbean Festival Arts,* eds. J. Nunley and J. Bettelheim (Seattle, 1988), 119–35. Hosay is a street procession taking place over three days in the Muslim month of Muharram, in which crowds including singers, drummers, and stickfight players follow several elaborately decorated tombs (*tadjahs*) made of *papier maché*. The tombs represent those of Hassan and Hussein, the grandsons of the Prophet Mohammed, who were martyrs of the Faith.
92. In the United States, the incidence of melisma in the vocal style of African American gospel and secular music is highly likely an Arabic/Islamic continuity.
93. Patrick Ryan, "African Muslim Spirituality: The Symbiotic Tradition in West Africa," *African Spirituality: Forms, Meanings and Expressions*, ed. Jacob K. Olupona (New York, 2000), 297. In Trinidad, Spiritual Baptist fasting is known as "mourning." The following comment may help account for the use of this word: "In much of West Africa, fasting implies mourning."
94. Wood, *Trinidad in Transition*, 38.
95. Author's interview with Albertina Collins, Fyzabad, Trinidad, 1991.

GLOSSARY

Abd	(pl. *abid*): slave
Ahardan	(pl. *ihardanen*): a Berber term is an equivalent of *Haratin* (q.v.)
Ashardan	a Berber racial designation for mulattos or "*izzegayen*" ("reds") or "copper" colored people in Algeria
Asiri	Hausa (Arabic, *sirr*, pl. *asrar*): secret or secrecy
Barnus	a woolen garment common in North Africa
Bellah	An *Amazhighi* (Tuareg) term denoting black slaves and freed slaves
Bidan	a term used to designate the inhabitants of the western Sahara of mixed Arab, Berber and African descent
Bikeç	concubine of a Crimean khan
Birni	Hausa, walled town
Biyim	legal wife of a Crimean khan
Dhikr	literally remembrance, a Sufi practice wherein the name of Allah is invoked
Dhimma	contract of hospitality and protection for non-Muslims (see also *Dhimmi* and *Jizya*)
Dhimmi	a non Muslim living under the protection of Muslim rule
Eyalet	Ottoman province
Fakku raqaba	freeing a bond, a slave
Fityan	(sing. *fata*). Literally young men, denoted pages as well as eunuchs in parts of the Muslim world
Gambari	Yoruba designation for Hausa

Hachachna	a term used to denote free blacks who claimed Ethiopian descent in the Oed R'hir area in Algeria
Hadith	the traditions of the Prophet Mohammad
Haratin	(sing. *Hartani*): Blacks of servile status, descended from slaves
Harem	secluded portion of a compound Muslim household reserved for women, including concubines
Humusi	Hausa term, the portion of booty (one-fifth) given to the Muslim ruler for distribution
Ibn al abd	son of a slave, a derogatory term
Ijtihad	personal or self-exertion for good cause. It is also to struggle to exercise judgment in legal matter by analogy, free from prior opinion in order to interpret Islamic law
Jama`a	the Islamic community.
Jizya	the poll-tax payable by non-Muslims, mainly Jews and Christian, as a tribute to the Muslim ruler (see *jizya*)
Khammas	sharecroppers
Khadim	literally, servant, but often a eunuch
Kitab as-Salat	Book of Prayers
Kul	slaves of European origin in the Ottoman Empire.
Legmi	palm sap
Lu'lu	pearls
Maghreb	the sunset prayer. The Maghreb also designates the Muslim territories in northwest Africa. It is also the name of Morocco in Arabic
Malama	Muslim scholar (*malanta*, female).
Murgu	Hausa term referring to practice of allowing slaves to work on their account; not involving manumission
Nafilat	(pl. *nawafil*): voluntary act of worship
Ousfan	mixed free and freed black population in Algeria
Shari'a	Islamic law
Sancak	Ottoman sub-province
Sadaka	Hausa, alms

Sawm Arabic, pl. *siyam,* fasting, abstension from sexual intercourse, particularly during Ramadan

Shurfa Arabic, sing. *sharif*, descendants of the Prophet Mohammad's lineage

Sudani a person from the "land of blacks," *Bilad as-Sudan*

Tahajjud voluntary prayers performed at night between *Isha* (the night prayer) and *Fajr* (the prayer before daybreak)

Tanzimat reorganization, a term used for reforms in the Ottoman Empire

Ulama or ulema Arabic, sing. *Alim*, the learned class and religious scholars in Islamic civilization

Taqlid imitation; following the opinion of an established *mujtahid* without considering the evidence. It is an established doctrines of the Muslim schools of law and it is an opposite of *ijtihad* (q.v.)

Umma people or community; the brotherhood of Islam

Usul al-Fiqh Islamic legal theory, jurisprudence

Waqf also *habous*: endowment set aside in perpetuity for a religious or charitable purpose

Zakat the religious tithe on property, livestock, and harvests.

Zawiya a Sufi lodge, sometimes with the tomb of the shaikh whose name it bears

BIBLIOGRAPHY

Abd-El-Kader-ben-Abou Bekr et Touaty. "Le Sahara et le Soudan, Documents historiques et géographiques," trans. Abbé Bargès. *Revue de l'Orient* (février 1853).

Abdelkafi, Jellal. *La Médina de Tunis: Espace Historique* (Tunis, 1989).

'Abduh, Muhammad. *Tafsīr juz' 'Ammā* (Cairo, 1967).

Abimbola, Wande. "The Ruins of Oyo Division." *African Notes* 2 (1964), 16–19.

Abraham, R. C. *Dictionary of the Hausa Language* (London, 1962).

Abu-Lughod, Janet L. "The Islamic City-Historic Myth, Islamic Essence and Contemporary Relevance." *Journal of Middle East Studies* 19 (1987), 155–76.

Abun-Nasr, Jamil M. *A History of the Maghrib in the Islamic Period* (Cambridge, 1987).

______. "The Tunisian State in the Eighteenth Century." *Revue de l'Occident Musulman et de la Méditerrannée* 33 (1982), 33–66.

Academia das Ciências de Lisboa, and Bulhão Pato. *Documentos remettidos da India, ou Livros das monções* (Lisboa, 1880-1935).

Acloque, Benjamin. "Embarras de l'administration coloniale: la question de l'esclavage au début du XXème siècle en Mauritanie." In *Groupes serviles au Sahara. Approche comparative à partir du cas des arabophones de Mauritanie*, ed. Mariella Villasante-de Beauvais (Paris, 2000).

Adamu, Mahdi. "The Aftermath of the Jihad in the Central Sudan as a Major Factor in the Volume of the Trans-Saharan Slave Trade in the Nineteenth Century." In *The Human Commodity: Perspectives on the Trans-Saharan Slave Trade*, ed. Elizabeth Savage, 111–28.

______. "The Delivery of Slaves from the Central Sudan to the Bight of Benin in the Eighteenth and Nineteenth Centuries." In *The Uncommon Market: Essays in the Economic History of the Atlantic Slave Trade*, ed. Henry A. Gemery and Jan S. Hogendorn, 163–80.

Aḥmad Shafīq. *L'esclavage au point de vue musulman* (Le Caire, 1891).

Ajayi, J. F. A., and Michael Crowder, eds. *History of West Africa* (London, 1985).

Ajisafe, Ajayi K. *History of Abeokuta* (Abeokuta, 1924).

Akinjogbin, Idowu A. "The Prelude to the Yoruba Civil Wars of the Nineteenth Century." *Odu*, 2nd series 1 (1965), 24–46.

Akinjogbin, Idowu A., and G. O. Ekemode, eds. *Yoruba Civilization* (Ile-Ife, 1976).

Akinyele, Isaac B. *Iwe Itan Ibadan ati die ninu awon ilu agbegbe re bi Iwo, Osogbo, Ikirun* (Ibadan, [1911] 1980).

Alegría, Ricardo. *Juan Garrido: El Conquistador Negro en las Antillas, Florida, México y California, c.1502–1540* (San Juan, 1990).

'Ali, Muhammad. *The Religion of Islam: A Comprehensive Discussion of the Sources, Principles and Practices of Islam* (Lahore, 1936).

al-Jundī, Khalīl ibn Isḥāq, *Mâliki Law; Being a Summary from the French Translations of the Mukhtasār of Sīdī Khalīl, with Notes and Bibliography*, ed. and trans. F. H. Ruxton, Perron, Napoléon Seignette, and Ernest Zeys (London, 1916).

al-Kairawani, Ibn Abi Dinar. *Al-Mu'nis fi Akhbar Ifriqiya wa-Tunis* (Tunis, 1968).

al-Maghīlī, Muḥamad. *Taj al-din yajib 'ala-mulūk*, trans. T. H Baldwin (Beyrouth-Liban, 1932).

al-Mamālik, Dust ʿAlī Khān Muʿayyir. *Rijāl-i 'Ahd-i Nāṣirī* (Tihrān, 1361).

______. *Yāddāshthāī az Zindigānī-yi Khuṣuṣī-yi Nāṣir al-Dīn Shāh* (Tihrān, 1362).

al-Nabhānī, Yūsuf. *Sa'ādat al-anām fi ittibā' dīn al-islām wa tawḍīḥ al-farq baynahu wa bayna dīn al-naṣara fī al-'aqā'id wa al-aḥkām* (*Happiness in Following the Religion of Islam and Clarifying the Difference between Islam and Christianity in Terms of Beliefs and Rules*) (n.p., 1908).

al-Salṭana, Muḥammad Ḥasan Khān Iʿtimād. *al-Ma'āṣir va al-a'ṣār* (Kitābkhāna-yi Sanā'ī, 1307).

al-Salṭana, Tāj. *Khāṭirāt-i Tāj al- Salṭana*, ed. Manṣura Ettiḥādīa and Sīrus Saʿdvandīān (Tihrān, 1361).

al-Saltanah, Itimad. *Yaddashth-yi Itimad al-Saltanah Marbut bi Sal-i 1300 H.Q.* (Tihran, 1350).

al-Ṭahhān, Muhammad Jamal, ed. *Al-a'māl al-kāmila lil-Kawākibī* (Beirut, 1995).

al-Timbuktawi, Ahmad b. al-Qadi Abi Bakr b. Yusuf b. Ibrahim. "Hatk al-Sitr Amma Alayhi Sudani Tunis min al-Kufr" (Piercing the Veil Being an Account of the Infidel Religion of the Blacks of Tunis). MS., Bibliothèque nationale de Tunisie, Tunis.

Allen, James de Vere. "Swahili Culture Reconsidered: Some Historical Implications of the Material Culture of the Northern Kenya Coast in the Eighteenth and Nineteenth Centuries." *Azania* 9 (1974), 105–38.

Allibert, C. "Une description turque de l'océan Indien au XVIe siècle, l'océan Indien occidental dans le *kitab-i Bahrije* de Piri Reis (1521)." *Études Océan Indien* 10 (1988), 9–51.

______, ed. *Textes anciens sur la côte est de l'Afrique et l'océan Indien occidental* (Paris, 1990).

Allsopp, Richard, ed. *Dictionary of Caribbean English Usage* (Oxford, 1996).

Allworth, Edward, ed. *The Tatars of Crimea: Return to the Homeland: Studies and Documents*, 2nd ed. (Durham, 1998).

Alonso, C. *Los Agustinos en la costa Suahili (1598–1698)* (Valladolid, 1988).

Alpers, Edward A. "Africans in India and the Wider Context of the Indian Ocean." In *Sidis and Scholars*, ed. Amy Catlin-Jairazbhoy and E. A. Alpers, 27–41.

______. *The East African Slave Trade* (Nairobi, 1967).

______. "The French Slave Trade in East Africa (1721–1810)." *Cahiers d'études Africaines* 37 (1970), 80–124.

______. *Ivory and Slaves in East Central Africa: Changing Patterns of International Trade to the Later Nineteenth Century* (London, 1975).

Amanat, Abbas. *Pivot of the Universe: Nasir al-Din Shah Qajar and the Iranian Monarchy, 1831–1896* (Berkeley, 1997).

Ambrose, W. Gerald. "Annual Report on Northeast District." In *Lagos Annual Report 1901–1902* (Lagos, 1902).

Andrade, António Alberto Banha de. *Relações de Moçambique setecentista* ([Lisboa], 1955).

Anonymous and Mrs. William Noy Wilkins. *Adolphus, a Tale and The Slave Son,* ed. Lise Winer (Mona, Kingston, [1854] 2003).

Ansari, Sarah, and Vanessa Martin, eds. *Women, Religion and Culture in Iran* (Surry, 2002).

Arafat, W. "The Attitude of Islam to Slavery," *Islamic Quarterly* 10: 1-2 (1966).

Armstrong, James C. "Madagascar and the Slave Trade in the Seventeenth Century." *Omaly sy Anio* 17–20 (1984), 211–33.

Atanda, Joseph A. "Comments on 'A Little New Light on the Collapse of the Alafinate of Yoruba'." In *Yoruba Historiography,* ed. Toyin Falola, 105–21.

______. "The Fall of the Old Oyo Empire: A Reconsideration of Its Causes." *Journal of the Historical Society of Nigeria* 5 (1971), 477–90.

Austen, Ralph A. *African Economic History, Internal Development and External Dependency* (London, 1987).

______. "The Mediterranean Islamic Slave Trade out of Africa: A Tentative Census," in Elizabeth Savage, ed., *The Human Commodity: Perspectives on the Trans-Saharan Slave Trade* (London, 1992)

______. "Social Bandits and Other Heroic Criminals: Western Models of Resistance and Their Relevance for Africa." In *Banditry, Rebellion and Social Protest in Africa*, ed. D. Crummey, 89–108.

Austin, Allan D. *African Muslims in Antebellum America: Transatlantic Stories and Spiritual Struggles* (New York, 1997).

Axelson, E. *Portuguese in South-East Africa 1488–1600* (Johannesburg, 1973).

______. *Portuguese in South-East Africa 1600–1700* (Johannesburg, 1960).

______. "Viagem que fez o Padre Ant. Gomez, da Comp.[a] de Jesus, ao Imperio de de [sic] Manomotapa, e assistencia que fez nas ditas terras d.[e]. Alg'us annos." *Studia* 3 (1959).

Ayalon, David. *Eunuchs, Caliphs and Sultans: A Study in Power Relationships* (Jerusalem, 1999).

______. "The Eunuchs in the Mamluk Sultanate." In *Studies in Memory of Gaston Wiet*, ed. Myriam Rosen-Ayalon, 282–95.

______. "On the Eunuchs in Islam." *Jerusalem Studies in Arabic and Islam* 1 (1979), 67–124.

Baba of Karo and Mary F. Smith, *Baba of Karo, a Woman of the Muslim Hausa* (New Haven, 1981).

Bābā, Aḥmad ibn Aḥmad. *Mi`rāj al-ṣu`ūd ajwibāt Aḥmad Bābā hawla al-istirqāq, ed.* John O. Hunwick, and Fatima Harrak (Rabat, 2000).

Backwell, H. F. *The Occupation of Hausaland 1900–1904; Being a Translation of Arabic Letters Found in the House of the Wazir of Sokoto, Bohari, in 1903* (London, 1969).

Baikie, William B. *Narrative of an Exploring Voyage Up the Rivers Kwora and Binue Commonly Known as the Niger and Tsadda in 1854* (London, [1856] 1966).

"Bakhchisaraiskiia arabskiia i turetskiia nadpisi." *Zapiski Imperatorskago Odesskago Obshchestva Istorii i Drevnostei* 2 (1850), section 2–3, 489–528.

Baltimore, Frederick Calvert. *A Tour to the East, in the Years 1763 and 1764: With Remarks on the City of Constantinople and the Turks; Also Select Pieces of Oriental Wit, Poetry and Wisdom* (London, 1767).

Barendse, R. J. *The Indian Ocean World of the Seventeenth Century* (Armonk and London, 2002).

Barreto, Manuel. "Informação do estado e conquista dos Rios de Cuama, em 11 de dezembro de 1667." *Boletim da Sociedade de Geographia de Lisboa* 4 (1883).

Barth, Heinreich. *Travels and Discoveries in North and Central Africa Being a Journal of an Exhibition Undertaken under the Auspices of H. B. M.'s Government in the Years 1849–1855* (London, 1965).

Bassett, James. *Persia, the Land of the Imams: a Narrative of Travel and Residence, 1871–1885* (London, 1887).

Bataillon, Claude, ed. *Nomades et nomadisme au Sahara.* Recherches sur la zone aride, no.19 (Paris, 1963).

______. "Les Rebaia, semi-nomades du Souf." In *Nomades et nomadisme au Sahara*, ed. C. Bataillon, 113–22.

Bathurst, R. D. "Maritime Trade and Imamate Government: Two Principal Themes in the History of Oman to 1728." In *The Arabian Peninsula, Society and Politics*, ed. Derek Hopwood, chapter 5.

Batran, Aziz A. *The Qadiryya Brotherhood in West Africa and the Western Sahara: The Life and Times of Shaykh al-Mukhtar al-Kunti (1729–1811)* (Rabat, 2001).

Beachey, R. W. *The Slave Trade of Eastern Africa* (London, 1976).

Beaulieu, Augustin de, and Denys Lombard. *Mémoires d'un voyage aux Indes orientales, 1619-1622: un marchand normand à Sumatra.* Collection «Pérégrinations asiatiques» ([Paris], 1996).

Beccari, C., ed. *Rerum Aethiopicarum scriptores occidentales inediti a saeculo XVI ad XIX,* 12v. (Rome, 1912).

Bellil, Rachid. *Les oasis du Gourara (Sahara algérien).* V.1: *Le temps des saints* (Paris and Louvain, 1999).

Benjamin, S. G. W. *Persia and the Persians* (London, 1887).

Bennigsen, Alexandre and Chantal Lemercier-Quelquejay. "Le khanat de Crimée au début du XVIe siècle de la tradution mongole a la suzeraineté ottomane d'après un document inédit des Archives ottomans." *Cahiers du monde russe et soviétique* 13 (1972), 321–37.

Berezhkov, M. N. "Russkie plienniki i nevol'niki v Krymu." In *Trudy VI Arkheologicheskago s"iezda v Odessie, 1884 g.,* 2v. (Odessa, 1886–1889), 2:342-72.

Bernus, Edmond, Pierre Boilley, Jean Clauzel, and Jean-Louis Triaud, eds. *Nomades et commandants: administration et sociétés* (Paris, 1993).

Bettelheim, Judith, and John Nunley. "The Hosay Festival." In *Caribbean Festival Arts,* ed. J. Nunley and J. Bettelheim, 119–35.

Bin Nasir, Abdallah bin Ali. *Al-Inkishafi, Catechism of a Soul* (Nairobi, 1977).

Biobaku, Saburi O. *Egba and its Neighbours 1830–1874* (Oxford, 1957).

Bishop, Isabella [Isabella L. Bird]. *Journeys in Persia and Kurdistan,* 2v. (London, 1891).

Blunt, Wilfrid Scawen. *Secret History of the English Occupation of Egypt; Being a Personal Narrative of Events* (London, 1924).

Boahen, A. Adu. "The Caravan Trade in the Nineteenth Century." *Journal of African History* 3 (1962), 349–59.

Bocarro, Antonio. *Década 13 da história da Índia* (Lisbon, 1876).

______, and A. B. de Bragança Pereira. *História de Damão. Notas ao livro das plantas de tôdas as fortalezas do estado da India Oriental* (Bastorà, 1939).

______, and Pedro Barreto de Resende. *O livro das plantas de todas as fortalezas, cidades e povoações do estado da India Oriental* ([Lisbon], 1992).

Boilley, Pierre. "L'Organisation commune des régions sahariennes (OCRS): une tentative avortée." In *Nomades et commandants: administration et sociétés nomades dans l'ancienne A.O.F.*, ed. Edmond Bernus et al, 215–39.

______. *Les Touaregs Kel Adagh. Dépendances et révoltes: du Soudan français au Mali contemporain* (Paris, 1999).

Bouderba, Ismaël. "Voyage a Rhat." *Revue algérienne et Coloniale* 1 (décembre, 1859), 241–305.

Bovill, Edward. *The Golden Trade of the Moors* (Oxford, 1958).

Bowen, Thomas. *Adventures and Missionary Labours in Several Countries in the Interior of Africa from 1849–1856* (London, [1857] 1968).

Brenner, R."Renseignements obtenus relativement au sort du Baron de Decken et informations géographiques sur le pays de Brava." *Annales des voyages, de la géographie, de l'histoire et de l'archéologie* (1868).

Brereton, Bridget. *A History of Modern Trinidad, 1783–1962* (London, 1981).

Brower, Benjamin Claude. "A Desert Named Peace: Violence and Empire in the Algerian Sahara, 1844–1902." Ph.D. dissertation, Cornell University, 2005.

______. "Niger Bend—Algerian Slave Trade and Abolition, 1848–1905." Paper presented at the conference on "Africa's Intellectual Caravans: *Bilad as-Sudan* and *al Maharani*," Vassar College, 7–9 October 2002.

Brown, W. Howard. "History of Siyu: The Development and Decline of a Swahili Town on the Northern Kenya Coast." Ph.D. dissertation, Indiana University, 1985.

Brunschvig, Robert. "Abd,"[Slavery]. In *The Encyclopaedia of Islam* (Leiden, 1960), 24–40.

Buchner, John H. *The Moravians in Jamaica: History of the Mission of the United Brethren's Church to the Negroes in the Island of Jamaica, from the Year 1754 to 1854* (London, 1854).

Buckeridge, Nicholas, and John R. Jenson. *Journal and Letter Book of Nicholas Buckeridge 1651–1654* (Minneapolis, 1973).

Buckley, Roger Norman, ed. *Slaves in Red Coats: The British West India Regiments, 1795–1815* (New Haven, CT, 1979).

Bull, Mary, and Margery Perham, eds. *The Diaries of Lord Lugard. Vol. 4, Nigeria, 1894-5 and 1898* (London, 1963).

Burnham, Philip "Raiders and Traders in Adamawa: Slavery as a Regional System," in *Asian and African Systems of Slavery,* ed. James L. Watson (Berkeley, CA, 1980), 43–72.

Burton, Richard. *Abeokuta and the Camaroons Mountains: An Exploration,* 2v. (London, 1863).

Campbell, Carl. "Mohammedu Sisei of Gambia and Trinidad, c.1788–1838. *African Studies Association of the West Indies Bulletin* 7 (1974), 29–38.

Campbell, Gwyn, ed., *The Structure of Slavery in the Indian Africa and Asia* (London, 2004).

______. *Abolition and Its Aftermath in the Indian Ocean Africa and Asia* (London, 2004).

Capot-Rey, Robert. *Le Sahara français* (Paris, 1953).

Carette, E. *Du commerce de l'Algérie avec l'Afrique centrale et les états barbaresques* (Paris, 1844).

Carmichael, A. C. *Domestic Manners and Social Conditions of the White, Coloured, and Negro Populations of the West Indies* (London, 1833).

Castelnau, Francis de. *Renseignements sur l'Afrique Centrale et sur une nation d'hommes à queue qui s'y trouverait, d'aprés le rapport des négres du Soudan, esclaves à Bahia* (Paris, 1851).

Catlin-Jairazbhoy, Amy, and E. A. Alpers, eds. *Sidis and Scholars: Essays on African Indians* (Noida and Trenton, 2004).

Cauneille, Auguste. *Les Chaanba leur nomadisme: Évolution de la tribu durant l'administration française* (Paris, 1968).

Caunes, Georges de. "Il y a encore des marchands d'esclaves." *Paris Match*, 25 June 1955.

Centro de Estudos Históricos Ultramarinos. *Documentos sobre os Portugueses em Moçambique e na África Central, 1497–1840,* 7v. (Lisbon, 1962–1975).

Chamberlain, John Weir. "The Development of Islamic Education in Kano City, Nigeria, with Emphasis on Legal Education in the Nineteenth and Twentieth Centuries." Ph.D. dissertation, Columbia University, 1975.

Chérif, Mohamed-Hédi. *Pouvoir et société dans la Tunisie du Husayn bin Ali: 1705–1740* (Tunis, 1984).

Chittick, H. N. "The East Coast, Madagascar and the Indian Ocean." In *The Cambridge History of Africa*, ed. R. Oliver, 3:183–231.

Christelow, Allan. *Muslim Law Courts and the French Colonial State in Algeria* (Princeton, 1985).

______, ed. *Thus Ruled Emir Abbas: Selected Cases from the Records of the Emir of Kano's Judicial Council* (East Lansing, 1994).

Clapperton, Hugh. *Hugh Clapperton into the Interior of Africa: Records of the Second Expedition, 1825-1827*, ed. Jamie Bruce-Lockhart, and Paul E. Lovejoy, 2v. (Leiden, 2005).

______. *Journal of a Second Expedition into the Interior of Africa* (London, 1829).

Clarence-Smith, William Gervase. *Islam and the Abolition of Slavery* (Oxford, 2006).

Clarke, Peter. *West Africa and Islam: A Study of Religious Development from the 8th to the 20th Century* (London, 1982).

Claudot-Hawad, Hélène. "Bandits, rebelles et partisans: vision plurielle des événements touaregs, 1990–1992." *Politique Africaine* 46 (1992), 143–49.

______. "Captif sauvage, esclave enfant, affranchi cousin. La mobilité statutaire chez les Touaregs." In *Groupes serviles au Sahara: approche comparative à partir du cas des arabophones de Mauritanie*, ed. M. Villasante-de-Beauvais.

______. "Identité et altérité d'un point de vue touareg. Eléments pour un débat." In *Touaregs et autres Sahariens entre plusieurs mondes. Définitions et redéfinitions de soi et des autres*, ed. H. Claudot-Hawad, 7–16.

______, ed. *Touaregs et autres Sahariens entre plusieurs mondes. Définitions et redéfinitions de soi et des autres* (Aix-en-Provence, 1996).

Clauzel, Jean. "L'administration coloniale française et les sociétés nomades dans l'ancienne Afrique occidentale française." *Politique Africaine* 46 (1992).

Cohen, Abner. *Custom and Politics in Urban Africa: A Study of Hausa Migrants in Yoruba Towns* (Manchester, 1969).

Colin, G. S. "Hartani." *Encyclopedia of Islam* (Leiden, 1960), 230–31.

Collins, Leslie. "On the Alleged 'Destruction' of the Great Horde in 1502." *Byzantinische Forschungen* 16 (1991), 361–99.

Commins, David Dean. *Islamic Reform: Politics and Social Change in Late Ottoman Syria* (Oxford, 1990).

Conant, F. P. "Peoples of Kontagora and Zuru: Kambari." In *Peoples of the Middle Niger Region Northern Nigeria*, Ethnographic survey of Africa, part 15 (London, 1960), 21–29.

Cooper, Frederick. *Plantation Slavery on the East Coast of Africa* (New Haven, 1977).

Coquery-Vidrovitch, Catherine, and Paul E Lovejoy, eds. *The Workers of African Trade* (Beverley Hills, CA, 1985).

Cordell, Dennis D. "No Liberty, Not Much Equality, and Very Little Fraternity: The Mirage of Manumission in the Algerian Sahara in the Second Half of the Nineteenth Century." In *Slavery and Colonial Rule in Africa*, ed. Suzanne Miers and Martin Klein, 38–56.

Coupland, Reginald. *East Africa and Its Invaders, from the Earliest Times to the Death of Seyyid Said in 1856* (Oxford, 1938).

Couto, Diogo do. *Da Ásia de Diogo de Couto; dos feitos, que os Portuguezes fizeram na conquista, e descubrimento das terras, e mares do Oriente. Decada quarta. Parte primeira* (Lisboa, 1778).

Crahan, Margaret, and Franklin Knight, eds. *Africa and the Caribbean: The Legacies of a Link* (Baltimore, 1979).

Crowther, Samuel and John C. Taylor. *The Gospel on the Banks of the Niger: Journals and Notices of the Native Missionaries Accompanying the Niger Expedition of 1857–1859* (London, [1859] 1968).

Crummey, Donald, ed. *Banditry, Rebellion and Social Protest in Africa* (London, 1986).

______. "Introduction: 'The Great Beast'." In *Banditry, Rebellion and Social Protest in Africa*, ed. D. Crummey, 1–29.

Curtin, Phillip C., ed. *Africa Remembered: Narratives by West African from the Era of the Slave Trade* (Madison, 1976).

Curto, Jose C. and Paul E. Lovejoy, eds. *Enslaving Connections: Changing Cultures of Africa and Brazil during the Era of Slavery* (Amherst, NY, 2004).

Daddi Addoun, Yacine, and Paul Lovejoy. "Muhammad Kaba Saghanughu and the Muslim Community of Jamaica." In *Slavery on the Frontiers of Islam*, ed. Paul E. Lovejoy, 199–218.

Dashkevych, Ia. R. "Iasyr z Ukraïny (XV–persha polovyna XVII st.) iak istoryko-demohrafichna problema." *Ukraïns'kyi arkheohrafichnyi shchorichnyk*, n.s. 2 (1993), 40–47.

Declaration of the Conference on Arab-led Slavery of Africans, Sunnyside Park Hotel, Johannesburg, 22 February 2003.

DeJong, Garrett E. "Slavery in Arabia," *The Muslim World* 24 (1934): 126-44.

Delheure, Jean. "Le travail de la laine à Ghardaïa." *Revue de l'occident musulman et de la Méditerranée* 27 (1979), 5–74.

Denham, Dixon. *Narrative of Travels and Discoveries in Northern and Central Africa in the Years 1822, 1823 and 1824 by Major Denham, Captain Clapperton and the Late Doctor Oudney, Extending across the Great Desert to the Tenth Degree of Northern Latitude, and from Kouka in Bornou, to Sackatoo, the Capital of the Fellatah Empire* (London, 1826).

Deporter, Victor Benjamin. *A propos du Transsaharien. L'extrême sud de l'Algérie. Le Gourara, le Touat, In-Salah, le Tidikelt, le pays des Touareg Hoggar, l'Adrar, Tin bouctou, Agadès, 1888–1889* (Alger, 1890).

Dermenghem, Émile. *Le pays d'Abel: Le Sahara des Ouled-Naïl, des Larbaa et des amour* (Paris, 1960).

DeWeese, Devin. *Islamization and Native Religion in the Golden Horde: Baba Tükles and Conversion to Islam in Historical and Epic Tradition* (University Park, PA, 1994).

"Diário da viagem da caravela Nossa Senhora da Esperança [1613–1614]." In *Os dois descobrimentos da Ilha de São Lourenço mandados fazer pelo vice-rel D. Jerónimo de Azevedo nos anos de 1613 a 1616,* ed. Humberto Leitão and Jerónimo de Azevedo.

Diouf, Sylviane A. *Servants of Allah: African Muslims Enslaved in the Americas* (New York, 1999).

Dobronravin, Nikolay. "Escritos multilíngües em caracteres árabes: novas fontes de Trinidad e Brasil no século XIX." *Afro-Ásia* 31 (2004), 297–326.

______. "A West Indian Arabic-script Document in Hausa, Fula, Mandinka, Arabic, and English-based Creole." Typescript, 2002, MS.2683, Trinity College, University of Dublin.

Drumond, M. de. "Lettres sur l'Afrique ancienne et moderne adressées a M. le Rédacteur du Journal des Voyages." *Journal des Voyages* 32 (1826).

Du Champ, E. *Le pays du Mouton. Des conditions d'existence des troupeaux sur les hauts-plateaux et dans le sud de l'Algérie* (Alger, 1893).

Duffill, M. B. and Paul E Lovejoy. "Merchants, Porters, and Teamsters in the Nineteenth-Century Central Sudan." In *The Workers of African Trade,* ed. Catherine Coquery-Vidrovitch and Paul E Lovejoy, 137-167.

Dumett, R., and B. K. Schwartz, eds. *West African Culture Dynamics: Archaeological and Historical Perspectives* (New York, 1980).

Dunn, Ross E. *The Adventures of Ibn Battuta: A Muslim Traveler of the 14th Century* (Berkeley, 1986).

Edwards, Bryan. *History, Civil and Commercial, of the British Colonies in the West Indies* (London, 1819).

el Hamel, Chouki. "'Race', Slavery and Islam in Maghribi Mediterranean Thought: The Question of the Haratin in Morocco." *Journal of North African Studies* 7 (2002), 29–52,

el-Eghwaati, Abd ed-Din. *Notes of a Journey into the Interior of Northern Africa*, trans. William Brown Hodgson (Washington, DC, 1830).

Ellis, Stephen. "Un texte du XVIIème siècle sur Madagascar." *Omaly sy Anio* 9 (1979), 151–66.

Eltis, David and David Richardson, eds. *Routes to Slavery: Direction, Ethnicity and Mortality in the Transatlantic Slave Trade* (London, 1997).

Emerit, Marcel, ed. *La révolution de 1848 en Algéria* (Paris, 1949).

Ennaji, Mohammed. *Serving the Master: Slavery and Society in Nineteenth-Century Morocco*, trans. Seth Graebner (New York, 1998).

Erdem, Y. Hakan. *Slavery in the Ottoman Empire and its Demise, 1800–1909* (London, 1996).

Ėrnst, N. L. "Bakhchisaraiskii Khanskii dvorets i arkhitektor vel. kn. Ivana III friazin Aleviz Novyi." *Izvestiia Tavricheskogo obshchestva istorii, arkheologii i ėtnografii* 2 (1928), 39-54.

Espìrito Santo, Domingos do, Ambrósio dos Anjos, and António Àlvares. *Breve relaçam das christandades que os religiosos de N. Padre Sancto Agostinho tem a sua conta nas partes do Oriente & do fruyto que nellas se faz, tirada... das cartas que nestes annos de lâ se escrevem, em que se contem cousas muy notaveis* (Lisbon, 1630).

Evliyâ Çelebi b. Derviş Mehemmed Zillî. *Evliyâ Çelebi Seyahatnāmesi*, 10 vols. ed. M. Sabri Koz (Istanbul, 1996-2007).

Falola, Toyin. "From Hospitality to Hostility: Ibadan and Strangers, 1830–1904." *Journal of African History* 26 (1985), 51–68.

______, ed. *Ghana in Africa and the World: Essays in Honor of Adu Boahen* (Trenton, NJ, 2003).

______, ed. *Yoruba Historiography* (Madison, 1991).

Fanon, Frantz. *The Wretched of the Earth*, trans. Constance Farrington (New York, 1963).

Fareed, Muneer Goolan. *Legal Reform in the Muslim World: The Anatomy of a Scholarly Dispute in the 19th and the Early 20th Centuries on the Usage of Ijtihād as a Legal Tool* (San Francisco, 1996).

Fedorov-Davydov, G. A. *Obshchestvennyi stroi Zolotoi Ordy* (Moscow, 1973).

______. *Zolotoordynskie goroda Povolzh'ia* (Moscow, 1994).

Feierman, Steven. *Peasant Intellectuals: Anthropology and History in Tanzania* (Madison, 1990).

Ferguson, Douglas E. "Nineteenth Century Hausaland: Being a Description by Imam Imoru of the Land, Economy and Society of his People." Ph.D. dissertation, University of California at Los Angeles, 1973.

Ferrier, J. P. *Caravan Journeys and Wanderings in Persia, Afghanistan, Turkistan, and Beloochistan* (London, 1857).

Feuvrier, Jean Baptiste. *Trois ans a la cour de Perse* (Paris, 1900).

Filliot, J. M. *La traite des esclaves vers les Mascareignes au XVIII*[e] *siècle* (Paris, 1974).

Fisher, A. G. B. and Humphrey Fisher. *Slavery and Muslim Society in Africa: The Institution in Saharan and Sudanic Africa and the Trans-Saharan Trade* (London, 1970).

Fisher, Alan. "Chattel Slavery in the Ottoman Empire." *Slavery and Abolition* 1 (1980), 25–45.

______. "Studies in Ottoman Slavery and Slave Trade," *Journal of Turkish Studies* 4 (1980): 49-56.

______. *The Crimean Tatars* (Stanford, 1978).

______. "Muscovy and the Black Sea Slave Trade." *Canadian-American Slavic Review* 6 (1972), 575–94.

Fisher, Humphrey. *Slavery in the History of Muslim Black Africa* (London, 2001).

Fontenay, Michel. "Chiourmes turques au XVIIe siècle." In *Le Genti del mare Mediterraneo,* ed. Rosalba Ragosta, 2:889–97.

Frank, Louis. *Tunis, description de cette régence* (Paris, 1850).

Franklin, C. B. *After Many Days: A Memoir being a Sketch of the Life and Labours of Rev. Alexander Kennedy—First Presbyterian Missionary to Trinidad, Founder of Greyfriar's Church, and its Pastor for Fourteen Years, January 1836–December 1849* (Port of Spain, 1910).

Fraser, James Baillie. *A Winter's Journey from Constantinople to Tehran,* 2v. (New York, [1838] 1973).

Freeman-Grenville, G. S. P. "The Coast 1498–1840." In *History of East Africa,* ed. G. Mathew and R. Oliver, 1:129–68.

______, ed. *The East African Coast, Select Documents from the First to the Earlier Nineteenth Century* (Oxford, 1962).

______. *The French at Kilwa Island: An Episode in Eighteenth-Century East African History* (Oxford, 1965).

Fryer, John, and William Crooke. *A New Account of East India and Persia: Being Nine Years' Travels, 1672–1681* (London, 1915).

Fyfe, Christopher. "Four Sierra Leone Recaptives." *Journal of African History* 2 (1961), 77–85.

Galand, Lionel, ed. *Lettres au Marabout: Messages Touaregs au Père de Foucauld* (Paris, 1999).

Gallais, Jean. *Pasteurs et paysans du Gourma: La condition sahélienne* (Paris, 1975).

Gaspar de São Bernardino, *Itinerário da Índia por terra até à Ilha de Chipre* (Lisbon, 1953).

Gautier, E. F. *La conquête du Sahara: Essai de psychologie politique* (Paris, 1910).

______. *Sahara algérien* (Paris, 1908).

Gbadamosi, Tajudeen G. O. *The Growth of Islam among the Yoruba 1841–1908* (London, 1978).

Geggus, David. "Sex Ratio, Age and Ethnicity in the Atlantic Slave Trade: Data from French Shipping and Plantation Records." *Journal of African History* 30 (1989), 23–44.

Gemery, Henry A., and Jan S. Hogendorn, eds. *The Uncommon Market: Essays in the Economic History of the Atlantic Slave Trade* (New York, 1979).

Ghazal, Amal. "Sufism, Ijtihād and Modernity: Yūsuf al-Nabhānī in the Age of 'Abd al-Hamīd II." *Archivum Ottomanicum* 19 (2001), 239–71.

Glassman, Jonathon. *Feasts and Riot: Revelry, Rebellion, and Popular Consciousness on the Swahili Coast, 1856–1888* (Portsmouth, NH, 1995).

Glover, Elizabeth Rosetta Scott, and Richard Temple. *Life of Sir John Hawley Glover R.N., G.C.M.G.* (London, 1897).

Gomez, Michael A. *Exchanging Our Country Marks: The Transformation of African Identities in the Colonial and Antebellum South* (Chapel Hill, NC, 1998).

_______. *Reversing Sail: A History of the African Diaspora* (Cambridge, 2005).

_______. *Black Cresent: The Experience and Legacy of African Muslims in the Americas* (Cambridge, 2005).

Goody, Jack. "Writing, Religion, and Revolt in Bahia." *Visible Languge* 20 (1986), 318–43.

Gordon, Murray. *Slavery in the Arab World* (New York, 1989).

Ghoraba, Hammouda. "Islam and Slavery," *Islamic Quarterly* 2 (1955): 153-59.

Grandguillaume, Gilbert. "Régime économique et structure du pouvoir: Le système des foggara du Touat." *Revue de l'occident musulman et de la Méditerranée* 13–14 (1973), 437–57.

Grandidier, Alfred and Guillaume Grandidier. *Ouvrages ou Extraits d'ouvrages français [jusqu'à 1630], portugais, hollandais, anglais, allemands, italiens, espagnols et latins relatifs à Madagascar: 1613 à 1640* (Paris, 1904).

Gray, J. "Zanzibar Local Histories (Part II)." *Swahili* 31 (1960), 111–39.

Guillain, C., ed. *Documents sur l'histoire, la géographie et le commerce de l'Afrique Orientale* (Paris, 1856).

______. *Documents sur l'histoire, la géographie et le commerce de la partie occidentale de Madagascar* (Paris, 1845).

Haafkens, J. *Chants Musulmans en Peul: Textes de l'héritage religieux de la communauté musulmane de Maroua, Cameroun* (Leiden, 1983).

Haivorns'kyi, Oleksa. "Khanskii dvorets v Bakhchisarae: Vozniknovenie Krymskogo Khanstva...," <http://www.hansaray.iatp.org.ua/r_ist_devlet.html> [accessed 1 March 2004].

Hallaq, Wael "Was the Gate of Ijtihad Closed?" *International Journal of Middle Eastern Studies* 16 (1984), 3–41.

Hamilton, Alexander. *A New Account of the East Indies, Being the Observations and Remarks of Capt. Alexander Hamilton, Who Spent His Time There from the Year 1688. to 1723. Trading and Travelling, by Sea and Land, to Most of the Countries and Islands of Commerce and Navigation, between the Cape of Goodhope, and the Island of Japon* (Edinburgh, 1727).

Hammer-Purgstall, Joseph von. *Geschichte der Goldenen Horde in Kiptschak, das ist: Der Mongolen in Russland* (Amsterdam, [1840] 1979).

Hansen, M. H., ed. *A Comparative Study of Thirty City-State Cultures* (Copenhagen, 2000).

Hark, Walter, and Augustus Westphal. *The Breaking of the Dawn, or, Moravian Work in Jamaica, 1754–1904* (London, c.1904).

Harrak, Fatima, and Mohammad El-Mansur, *A Fulani Jihadist in the Maghreb: Admonition of Ahmad Ibn al-Qadi al-Timbukti* (Rabat, 2000).

Harris, J. E. *The African Presence in Asia, Consequences of the East African Slave Trade* (Evanston, 1971).

______. ed. *Global Dimensions of the African Diaspora* (Washington, D.C., 1993).

Ḥashāishī, Muḥammad ibn Uthmān. *Al-Ādāt wa-al-taqālīd al-Tūnisīyah: al-hadīyah aw al-fawāid al-ilmīyah fī al-ādāt al-Tūnisīyah* (Tūnis, 1994).

______. *al-Riḥlah al-sāḥrāwīyah abra arādòī Ṭarābulus wa-bilād al-Tawrāq* (*Voyage au pays des Senoussia à travers la Tripolitaine et les pays Touareg*) (Tunis, 1988).

Hassen, Mohammed. *The Oromo of Ethiopia: A History, 1570–1860* (Cambridge, 1990).

Hastings, A. C. G. *The Voyage of the Dayspring: Being the Journal of the Late Sir John Hawley Glover* (London, 1926).

Hastings, S. U., and B. L. MacLeavy, *Seedtime and Harvest: A Brief History of the Moravian Church in Jamaica, 1754–1979* (Kingston, 1979).

Haywood, A., and F. A. S. Clarke. *The History of the Royal West African Frontier Force* (London, 1964).

Heers, Jacques. *Esclaves et domestiques au moyen âge dans le monde mediterranéen* (Paris, 1981).

Heywood, Linda, ed. *Central Africans and Cultural Transformations in the American Diaspora* (Cambridge, 2001).

Hezarfen Hüseyin Efendi. *Telhîsü'l-beyan fî kavânîn-i Âl-i Osmân*, ed. Sevim İlgürel (Ankara, 1998).

Higman, Barry. "African and Slave Family Patterns in Trinidad." In *Africa and the Caribbean: The Legacies of a Link*, ed. Margaret Crahan and Franklin Knight (Baltimore, 1979).

Hinderer, Anna Martin. *Seventeen Years in the Yoruba Country: Memorials of Anna Hinderer, Wife of the Rev. David Hinderer, C.M.S. Missionary in*

Western Africa, comp. and ed. Richard Brindley Hone, C. A. Hone, and D. Hone (Piccadilly, London, 1872).

Hiskett, Mervyn. "*Kitab-al-farq*: A Work on the Habe Kingdoms Attributed to 'Uthman dan Fodio." *Bulletin of the School of Oriental and African Studies* 23 (1960), 558–579.

______. *The Sword of Truth* (New York, 1973).

Hobsbawm, Eric. *Primitive Rebels. Studies in Archaic Forms of Social Movement in the 19th and 20th Centuries* (New York, 1963).

Hoca, Remmal. *Tāriẖ-i Ṣāḥib Giray H̱ān Histoire de Sahib Giray, Khan de Crimée de 1532 à 1551* [with French translation by M. Le Roux], ed. Özalp Gökbilgin (Ankara, 1973).

Hodgson, Marshall G. S. *The Venture of Islam*. v.2: *The Expansion of Islam in the Middle Period* (Chicago, 1974).

Hogendorn, Jan S. "The Location of the 'Manufacture' of Eunuchs." In *Slave Elites in the Middle East and Africa: A Comparative Study,* ed. Miura Toru and John Edward Philips, 41–68.

______. "Slave Acquisition and Delivery in Precolonial Hausaland." In *West African Culture Dynamics: Archaeological and Historical Perspectives*, ed. R. Dumett and B. K. Schwartz, 477–93.

Holsinger, Donald Charles. "Migration, Commerce and Community: The Mizabis in Nineteenth-Century Algeria." Ph.D. dissertation, Northwestern University, 1979.

Hopkins, N. S. "Traditional Tunis and Its Transformations." *Annals of New York Academy of Social Science* 220 (1974), 427–32.

Hopwood, Derek, ed. *The Arabian Peninsula, Society and Politics* (London, 1972).

Horn, Maurycy. "Chronologia i zasięg najazdów tatarskich na ziemie Rzechypospolitej polskiej w latach 1600–1647." *Studia i materialy do istorii wojskowości* 8 (1963), 3–71.

Horton, Mark and John Middleton. *The Swahili: The Social Landscape of a Mercantile Society* (Oxford, 2000).

Houdas, Octave Victor, and Edmond Benoist. *Tedzkiret en-nisīan fī akhbār molouk es-Soudān.* Documents arabes relatifs à l'histoire du Soudan (Paris, 1966).

Hourani, Albert, and S. M. Stern, eds. *The Islamic City* (Philadelphia, 1970).

Hunwick, John O. "Black Africans in the Islamic World: An Understudied Dimension of the Black Diaspora." *Tarikh* 5 (1978), 20–40.

______. "Black Africans in the Mediterranean Islamic World." In *The Human Commodity: Perspectives on the Trans-Saharan Trade*, ed. Elizabeth Savage, 5-36.

______. "Islamic Law and Polemics over Race and Slavery in North and West Africa (16th–19th Century)." *Princeton Papers* 7 (1997), 3–10.

______. "The Religious Practice of Black Slaves in the Mediterranean Islamic Lands." In *Slavery on the Frontiers of Islam,* ed. P. E. Lovejoy, 149-171.

______. *West Africa and the Arab World: Historical and Contemporary Perspectives. The J. B. Danquah Memorial Lectures. Twenty-third Series–February 1990* (Accra, 1991).

______, and Eve Troutt Powell, eds. *The African Diaspora in the Mediterranean Lands of Islam* (Princeton, 2002).

Iakobson, A. L. *Srednevekovyi Krym: Ocherki istorii i istorii material'noi kul'tury* (Leningrad, 1964).

ibn Abī Zayd al-Qayrawānī. *Risalah,* trans. Leon Bercher, 3rd edition (Algiers, 1949).

Ibn Baṭṭūṭa. *The Travels of Ibn Baṭṭūṭa, A.D. 1325–1354,* ed. H. A. R. Gibb, 4v. (London, 1958–2000).

______. *Voyages d'Ibn Batoutah: Text arabe, accompagné d'une traduction,* ed. and trans. C. Defrémery and B. R. Sanguinetti, 3v. (Paris, 1874–1879).

______. *Voyages,* ed. C. Defremery and B. R. Sanguinetti (Paris, 1982).

Idris, Amir Hasan. *Sudan's Civil War: Slavery, Race and Formational Identities* (Lewiston, 2001).

Inalcik, Halil. "The Khan and the Tribal Aristocracy: The Crimean Khanate under Sahib Giray I." *Harvard Ukrainian Studies* 3/4 (1979–1980), 445–66.

______. "Kırım—Kırım hanlığı." In *İslâm ansiklopedisi* (Ankara, 1940–1988), 6:746–56.

Ingrams, William H. *Zanzibar, Its History and Its People* (London, 1931).

İslām ansiklopedisi (Ankara, 1940–1988).

Johnson, Samuel. *The History of the Yorubas from the Earliest to the Beginning of the British Protectorate* (Lagos, [1921] 1976).

Joseph, Edward L. *Warner Arundell: The Adventures of a Creole*, ed. Lise Winer (Mona, 2001).

Kanya-Forstner, A. S. *The Conquest of the Western Sudan, a Study in French Military Imperialism* (Cambridge, 1969).

Karpov, Gennadii Fedorovich, and G. F. Shtendman. *Pamiatniki diplomaticheskikh snoshenii Moskovskago gosudarstva s Krymom, nagaiami i Turtsieiu*, v.2: *1508–1521*, Sbornik Imperatorskago Russkago Istoricheskago Obshchestva, 95 (St. Petersburg, 1895).

______. *Pamiatniki diplomaticheskikh snoshenii Moskovskago gosudarstva s Krymskoiu i Nagaiskoiu ordami i s Turtsiei*, v.1: *S 1474 po 1505 god, ėpokha sverzheniia mongol'skago iga v Rossii*, Sbornik Imperatorskago Russkago Istoricheskago Obshchestva, 41 (St. Petersburg, 1884).

Keeling, William. "A Journall of the Third Voyage to the East India…Written by William Keeling [1608]." In *Hakluytus Posthumus or Purchas his Pilgrimes,* comp. S. Purchas, v.2.

Keenan, Edward Louis, Jr. "Muscovy and Kazan, 1445–1552: A Study in Steppe Politics." Ph.D. dissertation., Harvard University, 1965.

Kent, Raymond K. *Early Kingdoms in Madagascar, 1500–1700* (New York, 1970).

Khenzel' [Hensel], V. "Problema iasyria v pol'sko-turetskikh otnosheniiakh XVI–XVII vv." In *Rossia, Pol'sha i Prichernomor'e v XV–XVIII vv*, ed. B. A. Rybakov, 147–58.

Khudiakov, Mikhail. *Ocherki po istorii Kazanskogo khanstva* (Kazan, [1923] 2004).

Kleeman, Nikolaus Ernst. *Nikolaus Ernst Kleemanns Reisen von Wien über Belgrad bis Kilianova, durch die Butschiack-Tartarey über Kavschan, Bender, durch die Nogew-Tartarey in die Crimm, dann von Kaffa nach Konstantinopel, nach Smirna und durch den Archipelagum nach Triest und Wien, in den Jahren 1768, 1769 und 1770 nebst einem Anhange von den besondern Merkwürdigkeiten der crimmischen Tartarey, in Briefen an einen Freund* (Vienna, 1771).

Klein, Martin A. *Slavery and Colonial Rule in French West Africa* (Cambridge, 1998).

______. "Slavery and French Rule in the Sahara." *Slavery and Abolition* 19 (1998), 73–90.

Klute, Georg. "Herren und Sklaven: Zur Frage der kolonialen Sklavenpolitik in Französisch-Westafrika." In *Macht der identität: identitäder macht. Politische prozesse und kultureller wandel in Afrika*, ed. Heidi Willer et al, 241–53.

Kopytoff, Igor, ed. *The African Frontier* (Bloomington, IN, 1987).

Kummer, Joseph. "Biography of Mask Campbell." MS., Moravian Archives, Bethlehem, PA.

Kurat, A. N. *IV–XVIII yüzyıllarda Karadeniz kuzeyindeki Türk kavimleri ve devletleri* (Ankara, 1972).

Kusimba, Chapurukha M. *The Rise and Fall of Swahili States* (Walnut Creek, CA, 1999).

______, S. B. Kusimba, and D. K. Wright. "The Development and Collapse of Precolonial Ethnic Mosaics in Tsavo, Kenya." *Journal of African Archaeology* 3 (2005), 243–66.

La Roque, Jean de. *Voyage de l'Arabie heureuse, par l'Ocean oriental, & le dé troit de la mer Rouge. Fait par les françois pour la premiere fois, dans les années 1708, 1709 & 1710. Avec la relation particuliere d'un voyage du port de Moka à la cour du roi d'Yemen, dans la seconde expedition des années 1711, 1712 & 1713. Un memoire concernant l'arbre & le fruit du café, dressé sur les observations de ceux qui ont fait ce dernier voyage. Et un traité historique de l'origine & du progrés du café, tant dans l'Asie que dans l'Europe; de son introduction en France, & de l'établissement de son usage à Paris* (Amsterdam, 1716).

LaCapra, Dominick. *History and Criticism* (Ithaca, 1985).

Lacroix, N., and H.-M. P. de La Martinière. *Documents pour servir a l'étude du Nord-ouest Africain. Réunis et rédigés par ordre de Jules Cambon.* Tome III: *Les Oasis de l'Extrême sud Algérien* (Alger, 1897).

Lambton, A. K. S. "Al-Mar'a—in Persia—before 1900." *The Encyclopaedia of Islam*, 2nd ed. (Leiden, 1960–2002), 6:481–85.

Lander, Richard and John Lander. *Journal of an Expedition to Explore the Course and Termination of the Niger* (New York, 1832).

______. *Journal of an Expedition to Explore the Course and Termination of the Niger, with a Narrative of a Voyage down that River to Its Termination,* 2v. (New York, 1858).

Lapidus, Ira. *Muslim Cities in the Later Middle Ages* (Cambridge, 1967).

Lashkov, F. F., ed. *Pamiatniki diplomaticheskikh snoshenii Krymskago khanstva s Moskovskim gosudarstvom v XVI i XVII v.v., khraniashchiesia v Moskovskom Glavnom Arkhive Ministerstva Inostrannykh Diel* (Simferopol', 1891).

Last, Murray. "Reform in West Africa: The Jihad Movements of the Nineteenth Century." In *History of West Africa,* ed. J. F. A. Ajayi and M. Crowder, 2:15–35.

______. *The Sokoto Caliphate* (London, 1967).

Laurence, Keith O. "The Settlement of Free Negroes in Trinidad before Emancipation." *Caribbean Quarterly* 9 (1963), 26–52.

Law, Robin. "The Constitutional Troubles of Oyo in the Eighteenth Century." *Journal of African History* 12 (1971), 25–44.

______. "Legal and Illegal Enslavement in West Africa in the Context of the Trans-Atlantic Slave Trade." In *Ghana in Africa and the World: Essays in Honor of Adu Boahen,* ed. Toyin Falola, 513–533.

______. "The Northern Factor in Yoruba History." In *Yoruba Civilization*, ed. I. A. Akinjogbin and G. O. Ekemode, 103–32.

______. *The Oyo Empire c.1600–c.1836: A West African Imperialism in the Era of the Atlantic Slave Trade* (Oxford, 1977).

______, and Paul E Lovejoy, eds. *The Biography of Mahommah Gardo Baquaqua* (Princeton, 2001).

Lecocq, Baz. "'That Desert is Our Country': Tuareg Rebellions and Competing Nationalisms in Contemporary Mali (1946–1996)." Ph.D. dissertation, University of Amsterdam, 2002.

Leitão, Humberto, and Jerónimo de Azevedo, eds. *Os dois descobrimentos da Ilha de São Lourenço mandados fazer pelo vice-rel D. Jerónimo de Azevedo nos anos de 1613 a 1616* (Lisbon, 1970).

Levtzion, Nehemia, and J. F. P. Hopkins, eds. *Corpus of Early Arabic Sources for West African History* (Princeton, 2000).

______, and Randall Lee Pouwels, eds. *The History of Islam in Africa* (Athens, OH, 2000).

Lewis, Bernard. *Race and Slavery in the Middle East: An Historical Enquiry* (New York, 1990).

Limam, Rachad. *Siyassat Hammouda Pacha fi Tunis* (Tunis, 1980).

______. "Some Documents Concerning Slavery in Tunisia at the End of the 18th Century." *Revue d'Histoire Maghrebine* 8 (1981), 349–57.

Linschoten, Jan Huygen van, Arie Pos, and Rui Loureiro. *Itineràrio, viagem ou navegação para as Indias orientais ou portuguesas* (Lisboa, 1997).

Lô, Capitaine. "Les foggaras du Tidikelt." *Travaux de l'Institut de recherches sahariennes* 10 (1953), 139–81; and 11 (1954), 49–79.

Lobo, Jerónimo, Donald M. Lockhart, and M. Gonçalves da Costa. *The Itineràrio of Jerónimo Lobo*. Works issued by the Hakluyt Society, 2nd ser., no. 162 (London, 1984).

Lofkrantz, Jennifer. "Ransoming Policies and Practices in the Western and Central Bilād al-Sūdān c1800–1910." Ph.D. dissertation, York University, 2008.

Lorcin, Patricia. *Imperial Identities: Stereotyping, Prejudice and Race in Colonial Algeria* (New York, 1995).

Lovejoy, Paul E. "Slavery, Bilad al-Sudan and the Frontiers of African Diaspora," in Paul E. Lovejoy, ed., *Slavery on the Frontiers of Islam* (Trenton NJ, 2004).

______. "Background to Rebellion: The Origins of the Muslim Slaves in Bahia." *Slavery and Abolition* 15 (1994), 151–80.

______. "The Bello-Clapperton Exchange: The Sokoto Jihad and the Trans-Atlantic Slave Trade, 1804–1837." In *The Desert Shore: Literatures of the African Sahel,* ed. Christopher Wise, 201–27.

______. *Caravans of Kola: The Hausa Kola Trade 1700–1900* (Zaria, 1980).

______. "The Characteristics of Plantations in the Nineteenth-Century Sokoto Caliphate (Islamic West Africa)." *American Historical Review* 84 (1979), 1267-92.

______. "Concubinage in the Sokoto Caliphate." *Slavery and Abolition* 21 (1990), 159–89.

______, ed. *The Ideology of Slavery in Africa* (Beverly Hills, 1981).

______. "Plantations in the Economy of the Sokoto Caliphate." *Journal of African History* 19 (1978), 341–68.

______. "The Role of the Wangara in the Economic Transformation of the Central Sudan in the Fifteenth and Sixteenth Centuries." *Journal of African History* 19 (1978), 173–93.

______. *Transformations in Slavery: A History of Slavery in Africa* (Cambridge, 1983; 2nd ed. 2000).

______. "Slavery in the Sokoto Caliphate." In *The Ideology of Slavery in Africa,* ed. P. E. Lovejoy, 200–43.

______, ed. *Slavery on the Frontiers of Islam* (Princeton, 2004).

______, and David V. Trotman, eds. *Trans-Atlantic Dimensions of Ethnicity in the African Diaspora* (London, 2003).

______, and Jan Hogendorn. *Slow Death for Slavery. The Course of Abolition in Northern Nigeria, 1897–1936* (Cambridge, 1993).

______, Abdullahi Mahadi, and Mansur Ibrahim Mukhtar. "C. L. Temples, "Notes on the History of Kano." *Sudanic Africa: A Journal of Historical Sources* 4 (1993), 7–76.

Lydon, Ghislaine. "On Trans-Saharan Trails: Trading Networks and Cross-Cultural Exchange in Western Africa 1840s–1930s." Ph.D. dissertation, Michigan State University, 2000.

Madden, Richard R. *A Twelvemonth's Residence in the West Indies, during the Transition from Slavery to Apprenticeship,* 2v. (Westport, CT, [1835] 1970).

______, and Thomas More Madden. *The Memoirs (Chiefly Autobiographical) of Richard Robert Madden* (London, 1891).

Mahadi, Abdullahi. "The State and the Economy: The Sarauta System and its Roles in Shaping the Society and Economy of Kano with Particular Reference to the Eighteenth and the Nineteenth Centuries." Ph.D. dissertation, Ahmadu Bello University, Zaria, 1982.

Mahdavi, Shireen. "Women, Shi'ism and Cuisine in Iran." In *Women, Religion and Culture in Iran,* ed. Sarah Ansari and Vanessa Martin, 10–26.

Malcolm, Sir John. *Sketches of Persia* (London, 1827).

Malikzāda, Mahdī. *Tārīkh-i Inqilāb-i Mashruṭīyyat-i Īrān* (Tihrān, 1335).

Mann, Kristin and Edna Bay, eds. *Rethinking the African Diaspora: The Making of a Black Atlantic World in the* Bight of Benin and Brazil (Portland, OR, 2001).

Manstein, Cristof Hermann. *Zapiski Manshteina o Rossii, 1727–1744* (St. Petersburg, 1875).

Manz, Beatrice Forbes. "The Clans of the Crimean Khanate, 1466–1532." *Harvard Ukrainian Studies* 2 (1978), 282–309.

Marcel, J. J. Review of Louis Frank, *Tunis, description de cette régence.* In *l'Univers pittoresque: histoire et description de tous les peuples de leurs religions, moeurs, coutumes, etc...*(Paris, 1850).

Marey Monge, Guillaume Stanislas. *Expédition de Laghouat, dirigée aux mois de mai et juin 1844* (Alger, 1845).

Marmon, Shaun. *Eunuchs and Sacred Boundaries in Islamic Societies* (New York, 1995).

______, ed. *Slavery in the Islamic Middle East* (Princeton, 1999).

Martin, A.-G.-P. *À la frontière du Maroc: Les oasis sahariennes* (Paris,1908).

Martin, Bradford G. "Arab Migrations to East Africa in Medieval Times." *International Journal of African Historical Studies* 7 (1974), 377–89.

Martin, E. B., and T. C. Y. Ryan. "A Quantitative Assessment of the Arab Slave Trade of East Africa, 1770–1896." *Kenya Historical Review* 5 (1977), 71–91.

Mathew, G., and R. Oliver, eds. *History of East Africa* (Oxford, 1962).

Matuz, Joseph. "Eine Beschreibung des Khanats der Krim aus dem Jahre 1669." *Acta Orientalia ediderunt Societates Orientales Danica, Norvegica, Svecica* 28 (1964) 129–51.

McCall, D. F., and N. R. Bennet, eds. *Aspect of West African Islam* (Boston, 1971).

McDougall, E. Ann. "Camel Caravans of the Saharan Salt Trade." In *The Workers of African Trade,* ed. Catherine Coquery-Vidrovitch and Paul E Lovejoy, 99–121.

______. "A Topsy-Turvy World: Slaves and Freed Slaves in the Mauritanian Adrar, 1910–1950." In *The End of Slavery in Africa*, ed. Suzanne Miers and Richard Roberts, 362–88.

McIntyre, W. D. "Commander Glover and the Colony of Lagos, 1861–1873." *Journal of African History*, 4 (1963), 57–79.

Meillassoux, C. *Anthropologie de l'esclavage: le ventre de fer et d'argent* (Paris, 1986).

Mercadier, F. J. G. *L'esclave de Timimoun* (Paris, 1971).

Meyers, Allan R. "Class, Ethnicity, and Slavery: The Origin of the Moroccan '*Abid*." *International Journal of African Historical Studies* 10 (1977), 427–42.

______. "Slavery in the Hausa-Fulani Emirates." In *Aspects of West African Islam*, ed. D. F. McCall and N. R. Bennett, 177–81.

Middleton, John. *The World of the Swahili: An African Mercantile Civilization* (New Haven, 1992).

Middleton, Sir H. "The Sixth Voyage, Set Forth by the East Indian Company." In *Hakluytus Posthumus or Purchas his Pilgrimes,* comp. S. Purchas, v.3.

Miers, Suzanne, and Martin Klein, eds. *Slavery and Colonial Rule in Africa* (London, 1999).

Miers, Suzanne, and Richard Roberts, eds. *The End of Slavery in Africa* (Madison, 1988).

Miller, Joseph. "Muslim Slavery and Slaving, A Bibliography," in Elizabeth Savage, ed., *The Human Commodity:Perspectives on the Trans-Saharan Slave Trade* (London, 1992), 249-71.

Milum, John."Notes of a Journey from Lagos up the River Niger to Bida, the Capital of Nupe and Ilorin in the Yoruba Country, 1879–80." *Proceedings of the Royal Geographical Society* 3 (1881), 26–37.

Miner, Horace. *The Primitive City of Timbuctoo* (New York, 1965).

Montana, Ismael Musah. "Ahmad Ibn al-Qadi al-Timbuktawi on the *Bori* Ceremonies of Sudan-Tunis." In *Slavery on the Frontiers of Islam*, ed. Paul E. Lovejoy, 173–79.

______. "The Trans-Saharan Slave Trade, Abolition of Slavery and Transformation in the North African Regency of Tunis, 1759–1846." Ph. D dissertation, York University, 2007.

Monteil, Vincent. "Analyse de 25 documents arabes des Malés de Bahia (1835)." *Bulletin de l'Institut Fondamental d'Afrique Noire,* série B, 29 (1967), 88–98.

Morton-Williams, Peter. "The Oyo Yoruba and the Atlantic Slave Trade, 1670–1830." *Journal of the Historical Society of Nigeria* 3 (1964), 25–45.

Mosca, L. "Slaving in Madagascar: English and Colonial Voyages in the Second Half of the XVII Century." Paper presented at the Conference on the Siddis of India and the African Diasporas in Asia, Goa, January 2006.

Muḥammad al-Amīn ibn Muḥammad, and E. J. Arnett. *The Rise of the Sokoto Fulani, Being a Paraphrase and in Some Parts a Translation of the Infaku'l Maisuri of Sultan Mohammed Bello* (1922).

Muhammad, Dalhatu. "The Tabuka Epic in Hausa: An Exercise in Narratology," in *Studies in Hausa Language, Literature and Culture: Proceedings of the Second Hausa International Conference*, eds., Ibrahim Yaro Yahaya, Abba Rufa'i, and Al-Amin Abu-Manga (Kano, 1982), 397-416.

Muḥammad Ḥasan Khan, Iʿtimād al-Salṭanah. *Khalsa* (Tihrān, 1348).

Nachtigal, Gustav. *Sahara and Sudan,* trans. Allan B Fisher and Humphrey J Fisher, 2v. (London, 1980).

Nast, Heidi J. *Concubines and Power: Five Hundred Years in a Northern Nigerian Palace* (Minneapolis: London, 2005).

______. "The Impact of British Imperialism on the Landscape of Female Slavery in the Kano Palace, Northern Nigeria," Africa 64 (1994), 34–73.

Necipoğlu, Gülru. *Architecture, Ceremonial, and Power: The Topkapı Palace in the Fifteenth and Sixteenth Centuries* (New York, 1991).

Newitt, M. "The Comoro Islands in Indian Ocean Trade before the Nineteenth Century." *Cahiers d'études Africaines* 89–90 (1983), 139–65.

Niebuhr, C. *Travels through Arabia, and Other Countries in the East,* 2v. (Edinburgh, 1792).

Nogueira, João, and Manuel Barreto. *Socorro que de Moçambique foi a S. Lourenço contra o rei, arrenegado de Mombaça fortificado na Ilha Massalagem, sendo capitão-mor Roque Borges e vitória que do rei se alcançou este ano de 1635; poema épico* (Lourenço Marques, 1971).

Norris, H. T. *Shinqiti Folk Literature and Song* (London, 1968).

Novosel'skii, A. A. *Bor'ba Moskovskogo gosudarstva s tatarami v pervoi polovine XVII veka* (Moscow and Leningrad, 1948).

Nunley, John., and Judith Bettelehim, eds. *Caribbean Festival Arts* (Seattle, 1988).

O'Hear, Ann. *Power Relations in Nigeria, Ilorin Slaves and Their Successors* (Rochester, 1997).

Ogot, B. A. "Les mouvements de population entre l'Afrique de l'Est, la corne de l'Afrique et les pays voisins." In *La Traite negriére du XVe au XIXe siècle: documents de travail et compte de la reunion d'experts organisée,* ed. *UNESCO*, 1:183–91.

Ojo, Olatunji. "Warfare, Slavery and the Transformation of Eastern Yorubaland c.1820–1900." Ph.D. dissertation, York University, Toronto, 2003.

Oldendorp, C. G. A. *Oldendorp's History of the Mission of the Evangelical Brethren on the Caribbean Islands of St. Thomas, St. Croix, and St. John*, ed. Johann Jakob Bossart, Arnold R. Highfield, and Vladimir Barac (Ann Arbor, MI, 1987).

Oliver, Roland, ed. *The Cambridge History of Africa* (Cambridge, 1977).

Olivier de Sardan, Jean-Pierre. *Quand nos péres étaient captifs: récits paysans du Niger* (Paris and Nubia, 1976).

Olupona, Jacob K., ed. *African Spirituality: Forms, Meanings and Expressions* (New York, 2000).

Olusanya, G., ed. *Studies in Yoruba History and Culture: Essays in Honour of Professor S. O. Biobaku* (Ibadan, 1983)

Orhonlu, Cengiz. "Khāṣī—In Turkey." *The Encyclopaedia of Islam*, 2nd ed. (Leiden, 1960–2002), 4:1092–93.

Oroge, E. Adeniyi. "The Fugitive Slave Question in Anglo-Egba Relations 1861–1886." *Journal of the Historical Society of Nigeria* 8 (1975), 61–80.

______. "The Institution of Slavery in Yorubaland with Particular Reference to the Nineteenth Century." Ph.D. dissertation, University of Birmingham, 1971.

Orta Rebelo, Nicolau de, and Joaquim Verissimo Serrao. *Un voyageur portugais en Perse au debut du XVIIe sècle* (Lisbon, 1972).

Ostapchuk, Victor. "The Publication of the Documents on the Crimean Khanate in the Topkapı Sarayı: The Documentary Legacy of Crimean-Ottoman Relations." *Turcica* 19 (1987), 247–76.

Ottley, Carlton. *Slavery Days in Trinidad* (Port of Spain, 1974).

Oyerinde, Nathaniel D. *Iwe Itan Ogbomoso* (Jos, 1934).

Palmer, H. R. "An Early Fulani Conception of Islam (Continued)." *Journal of the Royal African Society* 53 (1914), 53–59.

______. "The Kano Chronicle." *Journal of the Royal Anthropological Institute of Great Britain and Ireland* 38 (1908), 58–98.

Parrish, Lydia. *Slave Songs of the Georgia Sea Islands* (Athens, GA, [1942] 1992).

Patton, Adell, Jr. "An Islamic Frontier Polity: The Ningi Mountains of Northern Nigeria, 1846–1902." In *The African Frontier*, ed. Igor Kopytoff, I95–2I3.

Pearson, M. N. *Port Cities and Intruders: The Swahili Coast, India, and Portugal in the Early Modern Era* (Baltimore, 1998).

Peel, John D. Y. *Religious Encounter and the Making of the Yoruba* (Bloomington, IN, 2000).

Pein, Théodore. *Lettres familières sur l'Algérie, un petit royaume arabe* (Alger, 1893).

Peirce, Leslie. *The Imperial Harem: Women and Sovereignty in the Ottoman Empire* (New York and Oxford, 1993).

Pelligrin, Arthur. *Le vieux Tunis: Les noms de ruès de la villes arabe* (Tunis, n.d.).

Penzer, Norman. *The Harem* (London, [1936] 1965).

Pereira, A. B. de Bragança. *Arquivo português oriental. Nova edição* (Bastorá-Goa, 1940).

Pérennes, Jean-Jacques. *Structures agraires et décolonisation, les oasis de l'Oued R'hir (Algérie)* (Alger, 1979).

Peters, Rudolph. "Ijtihād and Taqlīd in the 18th and 19th Century Islam." *Die Welt des Islams* 20(1980), 131–45.

Pétré-Grenouilleau, Olivier. *Les traites négrières, essai d'histoire globale* (Paris, 2004).

Peyssonel, [Louis Charles] de. *Traite sur le commerce de la Mer Noire* (Paris, 1787).

Peyton, Walter. "The Second Voyage of Captaine Walter Peyton into the East-Indies…in January 1614." In *Hakluytus Posthumus or Purchas his Pilgrimes*, comp. S. Purchas, v.4.

Phillippo, James M. *Jamaica: Its Past and Present State* (London, 1843).

Pickering, C. *The Races of Man and their Geographical Distribution* (Philadelphia, 1848).

Pike, Ruth. *Aristocrats and Traders: Sevillian Society in the Sixteenth Century* (Ithaca, 1972).

Pipes, Daniel. *Slave Soldiers and Islam* (New Haven, 1981).

Polak, Jakob Eduard. *Persien, das Land und seine Bewohner* (Leipzig, 1865).

Pouwels, Randall Lee."The Battle of Shela: The Climax of an Era and a Point of Departure in the Modern History of the Kenya Coast." *Cahiers d'études Africaines* 123 (1991), 363-89.

______. "The East African Coast, c.780 to 1900 C.E." In *The History of Islam in Africa*, ed. N. Levtzion and R. L. Pouwels, 251–71.

______. "Eastern Africa and the Indian Ocean to 1800: Reviewing Relations in Historical Perspective." *International Journal of African Historical Studies* 35 (2002), 385–425.

______. *Horn and Crescent: Cultural Change and Traditional Islam on the East African Coast, 800–1900* (Cambridge, 1987).

Powell, Eve Troutt. "The Silence of the Slaves." In *The African Diaspora in the Mediterranean Lands of Islam,* ed. John Hunwick and Eve Troutt Powell, xxv–xxxvii.

Prasad, Kiran Kamal and Jean-Pierre Angenot, eds. *TADIA - The African Diaspora in Asia: Explorations on a Less Known Fact* (Bangalore, 2008).

Premdas, Ralph, ed. *Identity, Ethnicity and Culture in the Caribbean* (St. Augustine, 1999).

Prestholdt, Jeremy G. "As Artistry Permits and Custom May Ordain. The Social Fabric of Material Consumption in the Swahili World, circa 1450 to 1600."

Working Papers #3, Program of African Studies, Northwestern University, 1998.

Purchas, S., comp., *Hakluytus Posthumus or Purchas his Pilgrimes* (London, [1625–1626] 1965).

Querino, Manuel, and Raul Giovanni da Motta Lody. *Costumes africanos no Brasil* (Recife, 1988).

Ragoonath, Bishnu. "Religion and Insurrection: 'Abū Bakr and the Muslimeen Failure in the 1990 Attempted Coup in Trinidad and Tobago." In *Identity, Ethnicity and Culture in the Caribbean,* ed. Ralph Premdas (St. Augustine, 1999), 409–46.

Ragosta, Rosalba, ed. *Le Genti del mare Mediterraneo* (Naples, 1981).

Rahal, Ahmed. *La communauté noire De Tunis: thérapie initiatique et rite de possession* (Paris, 2000).

Rantoandro, G. "Une communauté mercantile du nord-ouest: les Antalaotra." *Omaly sy Anio* 17–20 (1984), 195–210.

Reichert, Rolf. *Os documentos àrabes do Arquivo do Estado da Bahia* ([Salvador], 1970).

Reis, João José. *Rebelião escrava no Brasil: a história do levante dos malês em 1835* (São Paulo, 2003).

______. *Slave Rebellion in Brazil: The Muslim Uprising of 1835 in Bahia* (Baltimore, 1993).

Renault, F., and S. Daget. *Les traites négrières en Afrique* (Paris, 1985).

Richardson, James. *Narrative of a Mission to Central Africa, Performed in the Years 1850–51, under the Orders and at the Expense of Her Majesty's Government,* 2v. (London, 1853).

Risso, P. *Oman and Muscat, an Early Modern History* (London, 1986).

Robinson, Charles H. *Hausaland; or Fifteen Hundred Miles through the Central Soudan* (London, 1896).

Rodrigues, Raymundo Nina. *Os Africanos no Brasil* (São Paulo, 1932).

Roe, Thomas. "Observations Collected Out of the Journall of Sir Thomas Roe [1615]." In *Hakluytus Posthumus or Purchas his Pilgrimes,* comp. S. Purchas, v.4.

Roper, Geoffrey, ed. *World Survey of Islamic Manuscripts,* 4v. (London, 1993).

Rosen-Ayalon, Myriam, ed. *Studies in Memory of Gaston Wiet* (Jerusalem, 1977).

Ross, R. "The Dutch on the Swahili Coast, 1776–1778: Two Slaving Journals." *International Journal of African Historical Studies* 19 (1986), 305–60.

Ruf, Urs Peter. *Ending Slavery: Hierarchy, Dependency and Gender in Central Mauritania* (Bielefeld, 1999).

Ryan, Patrick J. "African Muslim Spirituality: The Symbiotic Tradition in West Africa." In *African Spirituality: Forms, Meanings and Expressions,* ed. Jacob K. Olupona, 284–304.

______. *Imale: Yoruba Participation in the Muslim Tradition: A Study of Clerical Piety* (Missoula, 1977).

Ryan, Selwyn. *The Muslimeen Grab for Power: Race, Religion and Revolution in Trinidad and Tobago* (Port of Spain, 1991).

Rybakov, B. A. et al, eds. *Rossia, Pol'sha i Prichernomor'e v XV–XVIII vv* (Moscow, 1979).

Sabatier, Camille. *Touat, Sahara et Sudan* (Paris, 1891).

Sa'id (Hadj). "Histoire de Sokoto." In *Tedzkiret en Nissian fi akhbar moulouk es Soudan*, ed. O. Houdas, 303–61.

Salīl ibn Ruzīk, and George Percy Badger. *History of the Imâms and Seyyids of Omân, from A.D. 661–1856*. Works issued by the Hakluyt Society, no. 44 (London, [1871] 1967).

Salur, Mas'ud and Iraj Afshar. *Ruznamah-i Khatirat-i 'Ayn al-Saltanah (Qahraman Mirza Salur)*, Ganjinah-i Khatirat va Safarnamah-ha-yi Irani, 8-17 (Tehran, 1374).

Samb, Amar. "L'Islam et l'esclavage," *Notes Africaines* 168 (1980): 93-97.

Sanneh, Lamin. *The Jakhanke: The History of an Islamic Clerical People of the Senegambia* (London, 1979).

Santini, P. "Contribution d'un médecin à l'étude de *bayoudh* maladie du palmier-dattier." *Archives de l'institut Pasteur d'Algérie* XV (1937), 51–57.

Santos, Joao dos, Manuel Lobato, Eduardo Medeiros, and Maria do Carmo Vieira. *Etiópia Oriental e vària história de cousas notàveis do Oriente* (Lisbon, 1999).

Saunders, A. C. *A Social History of Black Slaves and Freedmen in Portugal, 1441–1555* (Cambridge, 1982).

Sauvaget, A. "La relation de Melet du voyage de la Haye aux Indes Orientales." *Études Océan Indien* 25–26 (1999), 94–289.

Savage, Elizabeth, ed. *The Human Commodity: Perspectives on the Trans-Saharan Trade* (London, 1992).

Schön, Frederick and Samuel Crowther, *Journals of the Rev. Frederick Schön and Mr. Samuel Crowther: Expedition Up the Niger in 1841* (London, [1842] 1970).

Schön, J. F. *Magana Hausa. Native Literature or Proverbs, Tales, Fables and Historical Fragments in the Hausa Language* (London, 1885).

Segal, Ronald. *Islam's Black Slaves: The Other Black Diaspora* (New York, 2001).

Sheil, Lady Mary. *Glimpses of Life and Manners in Persia* (New York, [1856] 1973).

Sheriff, Abdul. *Slaves, Spices and Ivory in Zanzibar: Integration of an East African Commercial Empire into the World Economy, 1770–1873* (London, 1987).

Shmidt, S. O. "Russkie polonianiki v Krymu i sistema ikh vykupa v seredine XVI v." In N. V. Usiugov et al., eds., *Voprosy sotsial'no-ėkonomicheskoi istorii i istochnikovedeniia perioda feodalizma v Rossii: Sbornik statei k 70–letiiu A. A. Novosel'skogo* (Moscow, 1961).

Sinclair, P. J. J., and T. Håkansson. "The Swahili City-State Culture." In *A Comparative Study of Thirty City-State Cultures,* ed. M. H. Hansen, 461–82.

Sipihr, Mirza Muhammad-Taqi Lisan al-Mulk. *Nasikh al-Tawarikh: Dawra-yi Kamil-i Tarikh-i Qajariya,* ed. Jahangir Qa'im-Maqami, 4v. (Tehran, 1344).

Smirnov, V. D. *Krymskoe khanstvo pod verkhovenstvom Otomanskoi Porty do nachala XVIII vieka* (St. Petersburg, 1887).

______. *Krymskoe khanstvo pod verkhovenstvom Otomanskoi Porty v XVIII stolietii* (Odessa, 1889).

Smith, Abdullahi [H. F. C. Smith]. "A Little New Light on the Collapse of the Alafinate of Yoruba." In *Studies in Yoruba History and Culture: Essays in Honour of Professor S. O. Biobaku,* ed. G. Olusanya, 42–71.

Smith, H. F. C, D. M. Last, and Gambo Gubio. "Ali Eisami Gazirmabe of Bornu." In *Africa Remembered: Narratives by West African from the Era of the Slave Trade,* ed. Phillip C. Curtin, 199–216.

Smith, M. G. *Government in Kano 1350–1950*. (Boulder, CO, 1977).

______. *Government in Zazzau, 1800–1950* (Oxford, 1960).

Spear, T. "Early Swahili History Reconsidered." *International Journal of African Historical Studies* 33 (2000), 257–90.

Spuler, Berthold. "Ḳırım." *The Encyclopaedia of Islam*, 2nd ed. (Leiden, 1960–2002), 5:136–43.

______. *Die Goldene Horde: Die Mongolen in Russland, 1223–1502*, 2nd ed. (Wiesbaden, 1965).

Stedman, John Gabriel. *Narrative, of a Five Years' Expedition, against the Revolted Negroes of Surinam, in Guiana, on the Wild Coast of South America, from the Year 1772, to 1777: Elucidating the History of That Country, and Describing Its Productions, Viz. Quadrupedes, Birds, Fishes, Reptiles, Trees, Shrubs, Fruits, & Roots ; with an Account of the Indians of Guiana, & Negroes of Guinea,* ed. William Blake, Thomas Holloway, and Francesco Bartolozzi, 2v. (London, 1796).

Stewart, Charles C. "A Comparison of the Exercise of Colonial and Precolonial Justice in Mauritania." In *Nomades et commandants: Administration et sociétés nomades dans l'ancienne A.O.F.*, ed. Edmund Bernus et al, 81–86.

Stilwell, Sean. "Culture, Kinship, and Power: The Evolution of Royal Slavery in Nineteenth Century Kano." *African Economic History* 27 (1999), 137–75.

______. "The Kano Mamluks: Royal Slavery in the Sokoto Caliphate, 1807–1903." Ph.D. dissertation, York University, 1999.

______. "Power, Honour, and Shame: The Ideology of Royal Slavery in the Sokoto Caliphate." *Africa* 7 (2000), 394–421.

Strandes, J. *The Portuguese Period in East Africa* (Nairobi, 1961).

Syroechkovskii, V. E. "Mukhammed-Gerai i ego vassaly." *Uchenye zapiski Moskovskogo gosudarstvennogo universiteta* 61 (1940), 3–71.

Talhami, Ghada Hashem. "The Zanj Rebellion Reconsidered." *International Journal of African Historical Studies* 10 (1977), 443–61.

Talib, H. Abu. "Exame das circunstãncias que motivaram as revoltas dos Malês" http://www.islamemlinha.com/index.php?option=com_content&task=view&id=390 [accessed April 16, 2008].

Tambo, David C. "Sokoto Caliphate Slave Trade in the Nineteenth Century." *International Journal of African Historical Studies* 9 (1976), 187–217.

Tangi, Majda. "Les Fatawa d'al-Wansharisi et d'ibn Rushd." In *Contribution à l'étude de l'histoire des 'Sudan' au Maroc du début de l'islamisation jusqu'au début du XVIIIème siècle.* Thése de doctorat [nouveau] régime, Université de Panthéon-Sorbonne, Paris, 1994 (published Villeneuve d'Ascq, 1998).

Tardy, Lajos. *Sklavenhandel in der Tartarei: Die Frage der Mandscharen* [trans. Mátyás Esterházy] (Szeged, 1983).

Taylor, Raymond. "Of Disciples and Sultans: Power, Authority and Society in the Nineteenth-Century Mauritanian Gebla." Ph.D. dissertation, University of Illinois at Urbana-Champaign, 1996.

Terray, Emmanuel. "Long-distance Exchange and the Formation of the State: The Case of the Abron kingdom of Gyaman." *Economy and Society* 3 (1974), 315–45.

Tizengauzen [Tiesenhausen], V., ed. and trans. *Sbornik materialov, otnosiashchikhsia k istorii Zolotoi Ordy*, v.1: *Izvlecheniia iz sochinenii arabskikh* (St. Petersburg, 1884).

Toledano, Ehud R. *The Ottoman Slave Trade and Its Suppression, 1840–1890* (Princeton, 1982).

______. *Slavery and Abolition in the Ottoman Middle East* (Seattle and London, 1998).

______. "Will That Subaltern Ever Speak? Finding African Slaves in the Historiography of the Middle East." Paper presented at the conference on "Twentieth Century Historians and Historiography of the Middle East," Boğaziçi University, Istanbul, Turkey, 23–26 May 2002.

______. *As If Silent and Absent: Bonds of Enslavement in the Islamic Middle East* (New Haven, CN, 2007).

Tomiche, N. "Al-Mar'a—In the Arab World." *The Encyclopaedia of Islam*, 2nd ed. (Leiden, 1960–2002), 6:466–72.

Toru, Miura, and John Edward Philips, eds. *Slave Elites in the Middle East and Africa: A Comparative Study* (London and New York, 2000).

Tremearne, J. N. *The Ban of the Bori: Demons and Demon-Dancing in West Africa* (London, 1968).

______ "*Bori* Beliefs and Ceremonies." *Journal of the Royal Anthropological Institute of Great Britain and Ireland* 45 (1915), 23–68.

Trepavlov, V. V. *Istoriia Nogaiskoi Ordy* (Moscow, 2001).

Trotman, David, and Paul Lovejoy. "Community of Believers: Trinidad Muslims and the Return to Africa, 1810–1850." In *Slavery on the Frontiers of Islam,* ed. Paul E. Lovejoy, 219–32.

Trudy VI Arkheologicheskago s"iezda v Odessie, 1884 g., 2v. (Odessa, 1886–1889).

Truman, George, John Jackson, and Thomas B. Longstreth. *Narrative of a Visit to the West Indies in 1840 and 1841* (Philadelphia, 1844).

Tukur, Muhammad. "Busuraa'u." In J. Haafkens, *Chants Musulmans en Peul: Textes de l'héritage religieux de la communauté musulmane de Maroua, Cameroun* (Leiden, 1983).

United Nations Educational, Scientific, and Cultural Organization (UNESCO). *La Traite negriére du XVe au XIXe siécle: documents de travail et compte de la reunion d'experts organisée,* v.1 (Paris, 1979).

Université de Paris VII. *Le Mal de voir: ethnologie et orientalisme : politique et épistémologie, critique et autocritique ... : contributions aux colloques Orientalisme, africanisme, américanisme, 9–11 mai 1974, Ethnologie et politique au Maghreb, 5 juin 1975. Cahiers Jussieu* no. 2 (1976).

'Uthmān ibn Fūdī [Usuman dan Fodio]. *Bayān wujūb al-hijra 'ala '—'ibad*, ed. and trans. F. H. El Masri (Khartoum, 1978).

______. *Tanbīh al ikhwā alā ard al-sūdān.* In H. R. Palmer, "An Early Fulani Conception of Islam (Continued)." *Journal of the Royal African Society* 53 (1914), 53–59.

Vel'iaminov-Zernov, Vladimir Vladimirovich. *Izsliedovanie o Kasimovskikh tsariakh i tsarevichakh*, 4v. (St. Petersburg, 1863–1887).

______ [and Huseyn Feyzhanoğlı], eds. *Materialy dlia istorii Krymskago khanstva izvlechennyia, po rasporiazheniiu Imperatorskoi Akademii Nauk, iz Moskovskago Glavnago Arkhiva Ministerstva Inostrannykh Diel=Matériaux pour servir à l'histoire du khanat de Crimée: e par ordre de l'Académie Impériale des Sciences, des Archives Centrales du Ministère des affaires étrangères, à Moscou* (St. Petersburg, 1864).

Verger, Pierre. *Trade Relations between the Bight of Benin and Bahia Seventeenth to Nineteenth Century* (Ibadan, 1976).

Vérin, Pierre. *Les échelles anciennes du commerce sur les côtes nord de Madagascar* (Lille, 1975).

Verlinden, Charles. *L'esclavage dans l'Europe médiévale*, 2v (Brugge, 1955–1977).

Vernet, Thomas. "Les cités-États swahili de l'archipel de Lamu, 1585–1810. Dynamiques endogènes, dynamiques exogènes." Ph.D. dissertation, Centre de Recherches Africaines, Université Paris 1 Panthéon-Sorbonne, 2005.

______. "Les cités-États swahili et la puissance omanaise (1650–1720)." *Journal des Africanistes* 72 (2002), 89–110.

______. "Le commerce des esclaves sur la côte swahili, 1500–1750." *Azania* 38 (2003), 69–97.

______. "Le territoire hors les murs des cités-États swahili de l'archipel de Lamu, 1600–1800." *Journal des Africanistes* 74 (2004), 381–411.

Villasante-de Beauvais, Mariella, ed. *Groupes serviles au Sahara. Approche comparative à partir du cas des arabophones de Mauritanie* (Paris, 2000).

Ville, Ludovic. *Voyage d'exploration dans les bassins du Hodna et du Sahara* (Paris, 1868).

Warner-Lewis, Maureen. *Central Africa in the Caribbean: Transcending Time, Transforming Cultures* (Mona, 2003).

______. *Guinea's Other Suns: The African Dynamic in Trinidad Culture* (Dover, MA, 1991).

______. *Trinidad Yoruba: From Mother Tongue to Memory* (Tuscaloosa, 1996).

Washington, John. "Ethnic-Regional Origins of African-Born Recruits of the Fifth West India Regiment, 1798–1808." In Roger Norman Buckley, *Slaves in Red Coats: The British West India Regiments, 1795–1815.*

______. "Some Account of Mohammedu-Sisëi, a Mandingo, of Nyáni-Marú on the Gambia." *Journal of the Royal Geographical Society* 8 (1838), 448–54.

Watson, James L., ed. *Asian and African Systems of Slavery* (Berkeley, CA, 1980).

Watson, Ruth. "Murder and the Political Body in Early Colonial Ibadan." *Africa* 70 (2000), 25–48.

Webb, James L. A. *Desert Frontier: Ecological and Economic Change along the Western Sahel, 1600–1850* (Madison, 1995).

Werner, Alice. "The Bantu Coast Tribes of the East Africa Protectorate." *Journal of the Royal Anthropological Institute* 45 (1915), 326–54.

______. "Some Notes on the Wapokomo of the Tana Valley." *Journal of the African Society* 12 (1912), 359–84.

Wilkins, Mrs. William Noy. *The Slave Son,* ed. Lise Winer (Mona, Kingston, [1854] 2003).

Wilkinson, J. C. *The Imamate Tradition of Oman* (Cambridge, 1987).

Wilks, Ivor. "'Abū Bakr Al-Ṣiddīq of Timbuktu." In *Africa Remembered: Narratives by West Africans from the Era of the Slave Trade*, ed. Philip Curtin, 152–69.

Wills, Charles James. *In the Land of the Lion and Sun or Modern Persia* (London, New York, and Melbourne, 1891).

Willis, John Ralph, ed., *Slaves and Slavery in Muslim Africa* (London, 1985).

Willer, Heidi, Till Förster, and Claudia Ortner-Buchberger, eds. *Macht der Identität, Identität der Macht: politische Prozesse und kultureller Wandel in Afrika.* Beiträge zur Afrikaforschung (1995).

Williams, Cynric. *A Tour through the Island of Jamaica, from the Western to the Eastern End, in the Year 1823* (London, 1827).

Wise, Christopher, ed. *The Desert Shore: Literatures of the Sahel* (Boulder, 2001).

Wood, Donald. *Trinidad in Transition: The Years after Slavery* (London, 1968).

Woodford, J. S. *The City of Tunis: Evolution of an Urban System* (Outwell, Wisbewch, Cambridgeshire, England, 1990).

Wright, H. T., P. Vérin, Ramilisonina, D. Burney, L. P. Burney, and K. Matsumoto. "The Evolution of Settlement Systems in the Bay of Boeny and the Mahavavy River Valley, North-western Madagascar." *Azania* 31 (1996), 37–73.

Yeld, E. R. "Islam and Social Stratification in Northern Nigeria." *British Journal of Sociology* 2 (1960), 112–28.

Ylvisaker, M. *Lamu in the Nineteenth Century: Land, Trade, and Politics* (Boston, 1979).

Yunusa, Yusuf. "Slavery in the Nineteenth Century Kano." B. A. essay, Department of History, Ahmadu Bello University, Zaria, 1976.

Zaitsev, I. V. *Astrakhanskoe khanstvo* (Moscow, 2004).

Zawadoski, G. "Le role des Nègres parmi la population Tunisienne." In *En Terre d'Islam* (2e semester, 1942).

Zouber, Mahmoud. *Ahmad Baba de Tombouctou (1556–1627): sa vie et son curve* (Paris, 1977).

NOTES ON CONTRIBUTORS

Benjamin Claude Brower is Assistant Professor of History at the University of Texas, Austin and formerly taught at Texas A&M University. He has been a member of the School of Social Sciences, the Institute for Advanced Study, Princeton University, 2007-2008. He is the author of *A Desert Named Peace: The Violence of France's Empire in the Algerian Sahara, 1844-1902* (2009) and is currently working on a book-length project on the Algerians who performed the *hajj* during the colonial period.

Nikolay Dobronravin, Professor of the Department of World Politics in the School of International Relations, St. Petersburg State University, Russia, is a specialist on Hausa language studies and has written several papers on Hausa in Ajami script.

Amal Ghazal is Assistant Professor of History at Dalhousie University. She earned her B.A. in history from the American University of Beirut and her M.A. and Ph.D. from the University of Alberta. She has also held a postdoctoral fellowship at the University of Toronto. She is currently interested in the relationship between Salafi Islam and nationalism in the Arab world, intellectual networks between the Middle East, North and East Africa, the Omani rule in Zanzibar, and slavery in Islamic history.

Bruce S. Hall is an assistant professor in the Department of History at Duke University. He holds a Ph.D. in history from the University of Illinois at Urbana-Champaign (2005). His dissertation was entitled: "Mapping the River in Black and White: Trajectories of Race in the Niger Bend, Northern Mali." Much of his research has been based in Timbuktu, Mali and he is currently continuing research focused on circum-Saharan commercial and intellectual networks, circum-Saharan ideas of "racial difference", nineteenth-century Ghadames-Timbuktu trade, and literate slaves in the circum-Saharan world. Research for this chapter in this volume was supported by the Social Science Research Council and by the Social Science and Humanities Research Council of Canada.

Maryna Kravets is a Ph.D. candidate in the Department of Near and Middle Eastern Civilizations, University of Toronto. She specializes in the history of the Ottoman Empire, post-Mongol Muslim states, and East European steppe frontier. Her research focuses on slavery in the seventeenth-century Crimean Khanate, an Ottoman vassal state and, at the time, the main supplier of white slaves for the Empire.

Jennifer Lofkrantz, Visiting Assistant Professor in History at Franklin and Marshall College, received her Ph.D in African history from York University (2008). She has also taught at Furman University and the University of Southern Indiana. In 2007 she was involved in the British Library Endangered Archives Programme funded "Northern Nigeria: precolonial documents preservation scheme," a pilot project in association with Arewa House, Kaduna and the Harriet Tubman Institute for Research on the Global Migrations of African Peoples, York University. Her research interests include slavery, the trans-Atlantic and trans-Saharan slave trades, Maghrib and West African Muslim intellectuals, West African Islam, and the African Diaspora.

Paul E. Lovejoy FRSC, Distinguished Research Professor, Department of History, York University, holds the Canada Research Chair in African Diaspora History and is Director, Harriet Tubman Institute for Research on the Global Migrations of African Peoples. His recent publications include *Slavery, Commerce and Production in West Africa: Slave Society in the Sokoto Caliphate* (2005); *Ecology and Ethnography of Muslim Trade in West Africa* (2005); and *The Biography of Mahommah Gardo Baquaqua: His Passage from Slavery to Freedom in Africa and America* (2nd ed., 2006). He has also edited or co-edited various volumes on the African diaspora, including *Trans-Atlantic Dimensions of Ethnicity in the African Diaspora* (2004); *Enslaving Connections: Western Africa and Brazil during the Era of Slavery* (2004); and *Slavery on the Frontiers of Islam* (2004).

Behnaz A. Mirzai is Assistant Professor of Middle Eastern history at Brock University. Her areas of specialization include comparative and cross-cultural studies, ethnicity, slavery, gender, as well as social, economic and religious interactions in the Middle East. Her Ph.D. thesis, "Slavery, the Abolition of the Slave Trade and the Emancipation of Slaves in Iran 1828-1928" is being revised for publication. She also has written several papers, including "The Trade in Enslaved Africans in Nineteenth-Century Iran" in Kiran Kamal Prasad and Jean-Pierre Angenot (eds.), *TADIA - The African Diaspora in Asia: Explorations on a Less Known Fact* (2008); "African Presence in Iran: Identity and its Reconstruction," in O. Petre-Grenouilleau, (ed.), *Traites et Esclavages: Vieux Problemes, Nouvelles Perspectives?* (2002); "The 1848 Abolitionist *Farmān*: a Step Towards Ending the Slave Trade in Iran," in Gwyn Campbell, (ed.), *Abolition and its Aftermath in Indian ocean Africa and Asia* (2005); "The Slave Trade and the African Diaspora in Iran," in Abdul Sheriff (ed.), *Monsoon and Migration: Unleashing Dhow Synergies* (2005); and "Le commerce des esclaves africains dans l'Iran du XIXe siècle," *Les Cahiers des Anneaux de la Mémoire*, 9 (2006). In 2008, she produced a documentary, "Afro-Iranian Lives," which features the African diaspora in Iran.

Ismael Musah Montana is Assistant Professor of History at Northern Illinois University and a postdoctoral fellow at Wissenschaftskolleg zu Berlin in 2008-2009. He received his Ph.D in African history from York University (2007). Montana has been visiting assistant professor in the Department of History at Trent University (Canada). His research interests range from the social and economic history of slavery in Northwest Africa and the Islamic world in the 18th and 19th centuries to development cooperation between the European Union and African, Caribbean, and Pacific States in the post cold war era. He has published "Ahmad Ibn al-Qadi al-Timbuktawi on the Bori Ceremonies of Sudan-Tunis," in Paul E. Lovejoy (ed.), *Slavery on the Frontiers of Islam* (2003). He teaches African history, slavery and its abolition in the African continent, the African Diaspora, as well as the history of Islam in Africa.

Olatunji Ojo is Assistant Professor, Department of History, Brock University. He received his Ph.D. from York University and has taught at Ohio University and Syracuse University. His recent publications include "Slavery and Human Sacrifice in Yorubaland: Ondo c.1870-1894," *Journal of African History*, 46, 3 (2005); "The Organization of the Atlantic Slave Trade in Yorubaland, ca. 1777 to ca. 1856," *International Journal of African Historical Studies*, 48, 1 (2008); and "Beyond Diversity: Women, Scarification, and Yoruba Identity," *History in Africa: A Journal of Method*, 35 (2008).

Mohammed Bashir Salau, Assistant Professor, Department of History, the University of Mississippi, received a Ph.D. in African diaspora history at York University, in 2005. His research on the history of Northern

Nigeria includes his study, "The Gbagyi Engagement with Early Colonialism," in Femi J. Kolapo and Kwabena O. Akurang-Parry (eds.), *Latitudes of Negotiations and Containment: African Agency and European Colonialism* (2007), and "Ribats and the Development of Plantations in the Sokoto Caliphate: A Case Study of Fanisau," *Africa Economic History*, 34 (2006).

Ehud R. Toledano holds the Chair in Ottoman Studies and is Director of the Graduate School of Historical Studies at Tel-Aviv University, Israel. He received his Ph.D. from Princeton University (1979), and subsequently taught at Oxford University, the University of Pennsylvania, and UCLA. He has conducted research in Istanbul, Cairo, London, and Paris. Among his books are *The Ottoman Slave Trade and Its Suppression, 1840-1890* (1982), which has also been published in Turkish; *State and Society in Nineteenth Century Egypt* (1990), *Slavery and Abolition in the Ottoman Middle East* (1998); and *As If Silence and Absent: Bonds of Enslavement in the Islamic Middle East* (2007). He also published two introductory textbooks in Hebrew and numerous articles.

Thomas Vernet received his Ph.D. from the Sorbonne in 2005 and holds a *maître de conférences* in early modern African history at Université Paris I Panthéon-Sorbonne. He is a member of the Centre d'Etudes des Mondes Africains (CEMAf), a combined research group of the Centre National de la Recherche Scientifique (CNRS) and Université Paris 1. His area of research is the East African coast and the western Indian Ocean ca. 1500-1820, and particularly focusing on the Swahili world. He is interested in the connections between Swahili city-states and Indian Ocean networks and also coast-interior relations. He has published several articles on power and social change in Swahili society, spatial organization of the Swahili polities, and Portuguese and Omani expansion. Currently he is working on French and Omani slave trading in East Africa between 1750 and 1810 as well as on agricultural slavery of Swahili society before the 1810s.

Maureen Warner-Lewis is Emeritus Professor of African-Caribbean Language and Orature in the Department of Literatures in English, University of the West Indies, Jamaica, where she has taught Anglo-Saxon, West Indian, African, and Oral Literatures. Her research on African cultural and linguistic retentions in the Caribbean resulted in the publication of *Guinea's Other Suns: the African Dynamic in Trinidad Culture* (1991), *Yoruba Songs of Trinidad* (1994), *Trinidad Yoruba: from Mother Tongue to Memory* (1996, 1997), *Central Africa in the Caribbean: Transcend-*

ing Time, Transforming Cultures (2003), awarded the Gordon and Sybil Lewis Prize of the Caribbean Studies Association for 2004, and *Archibald Monteath: Igbo, Jamaican, Moravian* (2007), which again won the Lewis Prize in 2008.

INDEX